Slavery and South Asian History

Slavery & South Asian History

Edited by
Indrani Chatterjee and
Richard M. Eaton

INDIANA UNIVERSITY PRESS
Bloomington & Indianapolis

This book is a publication of

Indiana University Press
601 North Morton Street
Bloomington, Indiana 47404-3797 USA

http://iupress.indiana.edu

Telephone orders   800-842-6796
Fax orders   812-855-7931
Orders by email   iuporder@indiana.edu

The paper used in this publication meets the minimum
requirements of American National Standard for Information
Sciences—Permanence of Paper for Printed Library
Materials, ANSI Z39.48-1984.

Manufactured in the United States of America

Library of Congress Cataloging-in-Publication Data

Slavery and South Asian history / edited by Indrani Chatterjee
and Richard M. Eaton.
     p. cm.
  Includes bibliographical references and index.
  ISBN 0-253-34810-2 (cloth : alk. paper) — ISBN 0-253-21873-X
(pbk.)
  1. Slaves—India—History. 2. Slavery—India—History. 3.
Slaves—South Asia—History. 4. Slavery—South Asia—History.
I. Chatterjee, Indrani. II. Eaton, Richard Maxwell.
  HT1246.S495 2007
  306.3'620954—dc22
                                        2006008098

1 2 3 4 5 11 10 09 08 07 06

To all present and future historians of slavery

CONTENTS

MAPS

PREFACE AND ACKNOWLEDGMENTS

Despite its pervasive presence in the South Asian past, slavery has been marginal to the historiography of South Asia. This marginality is itself the product of political, cultural, and intellectual currents of the last fifty years. From the late 1950s and until the '70s, the development of the civil rights movements in the United States paralleled the burgeoning of the historiography of slavery in the plantation economies of the eighteenth and nineteenth centuries. The same decades witnessed the development of historical research initiatives in postcolonial universities in South Asia focused on the formation and nature of various states.

In both hemispheres at the same time, identity politics within the confines of the nation thus came to play very significant roles in rewarding particular kinds of investigations. In the U.S., identifying slaves and their descendants had considerable meaning in the context of racial desegregation and the "affirmative action" policies of federal and local governments. In India, and in South Asia generally, the identification of slaves and of the descendants of slaves was pegged to the removal of "untouchability," and therefore to *jati*-based (caste-based) affirmative action promised by the central government. Such a transposition of the concepts of "race" and "caste" was not entirely novel in the late twentieth century. Itself a product of colonial interactions from the sixteenth century, it became critical when the anti-imperialist intelligentsia in South Asia appropriated the term "slavery" to describe the condition of colonized peoples in general, and of specific groups like women and imported laborers in colonially owned tea plantations of Assam in particular. The ready assimilation of all categories of impressed, indentured, coerced, and exploited laborers into the category of "slaves" enhanced the emotional and political resonances of equivalent words in various vernacular languages but also firmly wedded "ethnicity" to "class," "race" to "caste."

By the middle of the twentieth century, when history writing became increasingly professionalized within postcolonial universities, the capaciousness of the term "slavery" appears to have precluded fresh excavations of its forms and meanings for older pasts. Additionally, since most historical studies became implicitly tied to nation-building exercises, postcolonial South Asian scholars in turn were expected to make their work "useful" and "relevant" by identifying rightless, marginalized groups for the developmentalist projects of the new states. Demands of such kinds further stayed the scholar's hand, while lay notions of slavery as a permanent and timeless condition removed it dramatically from the sphere of historical investigation and rethinking as a whole.

Those who might yet have resisted were hobbled in their turn. The attrition of classical and contemporary languages deprived many postcolonial students of the means to access older expressive traditions within the subcontinent. Besides, the archives were fragmented over multiple territorial units along the Indian Ocean and in the Mediterranean and Atlantic worlds, as well as within the landmasses of South, Southeast, and Central Asia. International political and financial barriers prevented easy access to the early or modern European-language archives necessary to studying South Asia between the fifteenth and nineteenth centuries. As for local-language archives, uneven local governance and variable investments of local literati in each knowledge-power project assured motley archiving practices across the subcontinent. Some local-language archives survived better than others. As late as the end of the twentieth century, a basic printed collection of early nineteenth-century English-language records authorized by the House of Commons (known as the *Report on Slavery in India,* 1841) was absent from all of independent India's archives and libraries. Such material hurdles in the development of a historiography of slavery within South Asia thus reinforced an isolationist tendency already inherent within the specialized subdivisions of the professional historians. It became impossible for a single scholar to amass materials from a wide enough range of sources to arrive at a complete and full understanding of slavery without sacrificing complexity and nuance.

As nationalist boundaries ossified around trade and legal barriers, the North American academe also carved up Asian histories into bite-sized "area studies" units. Here, greater prestige and funds were reserved for the study of the problematic present, while a methodological "multidisciplinarity" legitimated the denial of temporal depth and changing perceptions of temporality to these multiregional histories. Paradoxically, such changes occurred just as the historical research on slavery in the Atlantic world began to deconstruct older histories of slavery both in the United States and in medieval European pasts. While these developments reconfirmed the equation of "race"-based and "caste"-based coercive labor forms for Euro-American scholars of South Asian pasts in one hemisphere, news of these revisions traveled exceedingly slowly to the South Asian scholars in the other. Cut off from each other by regional, disciplinary, and chronological specializations, scholars in South Asia nevertheless produced a collaborative volume on slavery in 1985.[1] Although dominated by studies of laboring groups in postcolonial society, and containing only three historical essays, this volume came to define South Asian slavery for the rest of academe.

It was with great trepidation two decades later that we initiated conversations about the historicity of slavery among scholars of South Asia at the annual Asian Studies Conference in 2001. The enthusiastic reception given us there inspired Rebecca Tolen of Indiana University Press to urge us to seek audiences for our work beyond nationalist frames. The editors of this volume jointly thank Rebecca, Lois Kain, our cartographer, and each of the contributors for their patience with us. This volume would not have seen the light of day without all of them. Revising and putting together the essays in this volume has been a painfully slow and protracted labor of love. We thank each of them for their diligence and patience, and apologize to those who could not be included here despite our best efforts.

In addition to this, Indrani Chatterjee takes this opportunity to thank her own colleagues in the history department at Rutgers University for their enormous support through the last four years, especially Deborah White, Nancy Hewitt, Temma Kaplan, Ziva Galili, and Barry Qualls, Dean of Humanities, Faculty of Arts and Sciences, all of whose encouragement made a critical difference to this project. She also thanks her undergraduate students Samir Ali, Subah Dayal, Anupama Mehta, Asad Rizvi, and Alex Sheick for their persistent criticism of the absence of such a volume from their reading lists—and apologizes that it is coming too late for them. Indrani also acknowledges the following colleagues and friends for their major contributions to the completion of this project: Engin Akarli, Tuna Akarli, Edward Alpers, Anjali Arondekar, participants in the international conferences on slavery held at Avignon in 2001 and 2003, Gautam Bhadra and friends at the Center of Social Science Studies at Kolkata, Gwyn Campbell, Carolyn Dean, Angela Davis, Gina Dent and the Feminist Studies Seminar at UC Santa Cruz, Geraldine Forbes, Lina Fruzzetti, Rosemary George and the participants in the seminar on South Asian Feminisms at UC San Diego, Nancy Jacobs, Nayanjot Lahiri and friends in the department of history at Delhi University, Joseph C. Miller, Michael Salman, Sudipta Sen, Sirpa Tenhunen and participants in the seminar on family at the University of Helsinki, and Susan Wadley, and participants in the South Asia seminar at Syracuse.

Richard Eaton would like to thank the staff at the Harlan Hatcher Graduate Library, University of Michigan; Barbara D. Metcalf, Director of the Center for South Asian Studies, University of Michigan; and the staff of the Manistee County Library, Wellston, Michigan. He also wishes to thank

Brian Newbould for his inspired realization of the Tenth Symphony of Franz Schubert.

Both editors remain grateful to their families for their forbearance.

Note

1. Utsa Patnaik and Manjari Dingwaney, eds., *Chains of Servitude: Bondage and Slavery in India* (Madras: Sangam and Oxford University Press, 1985).

NOTE ON TRANSLATION
AND TRANSLITERATION

Unless otherwise indicated in the notes, all translations into English are those of the individual authors. The transliteration of non-English words follows standard conventions, except that all diacritical marks other than the medial hamza have been omitted. Punctuation and capitalization follow the *Chicago Manual of Style*.

Slavery and South Asian History

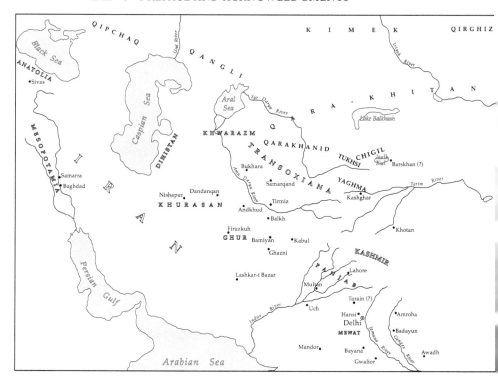

Map 1. Central Asia, Iran, and north India (12th and 13th centuries)

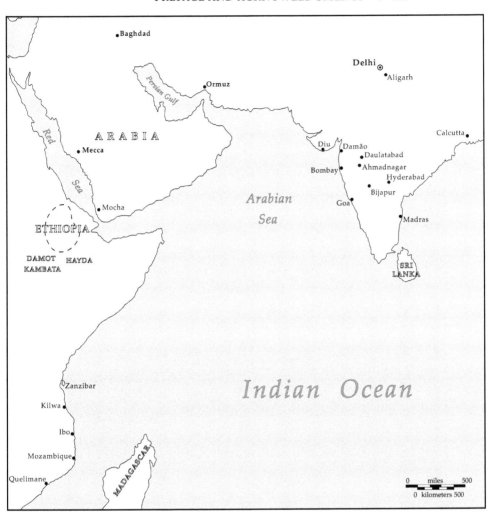

Map 2. The Arabian Sea rim

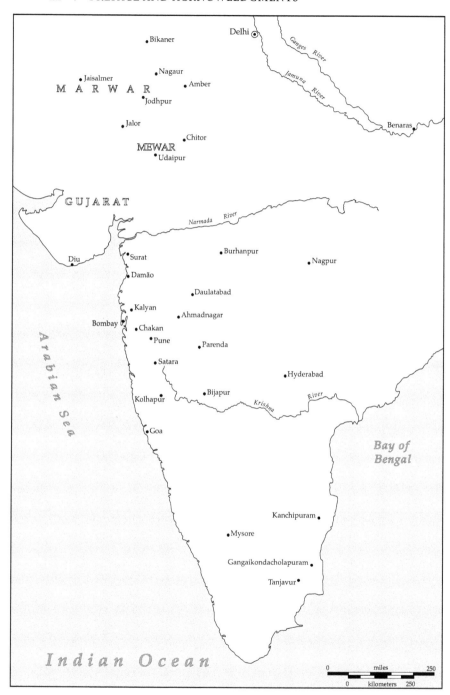

Map 3. Western and southern India

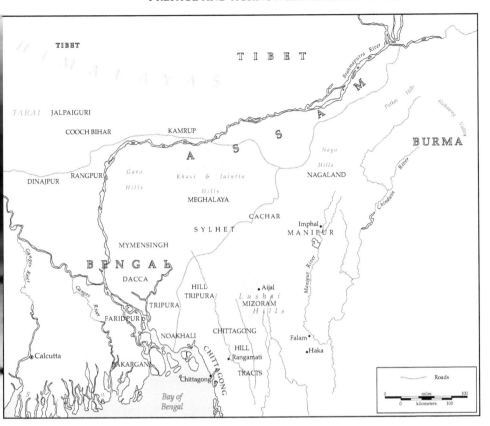

Map 4. Eastern India

Introduction

RICHARD M. EATON

One of the aims of this volume is to document the remarkable range of types of slavery that appeared across a thousand years of South Asian history. Some of these types appeared at isolated moments, some spanned large swaths of time and space, some occurred simultaneously with others. Thus in the seventeenth century, enslaved female performers circulated among elite Rajput houses even while Arab merchants delivered slave-soldiers from Africa to buyers on the Deccan plateau. A century later, the Maratha state was deploying for menial labor in its hill forts women who had been enslaved for their household's failure to pay revenue. On the far eastern side of the subcontinent, meanwhile, endemic warfare between states in Manipur, Tripura, Cachar, and Assam produced enslaved captives whom those states then deployed to clear forests for cultivation.

There is, then, no single story of slavery in South Asian history. There is no overarching master narrative, no tidy sequence of evolutionary "stages" of the sort that theorists like Condorcet, Marx, or Toynbee envisioned for other historical phenomena. Each instance of slavery in South Asia was shaped by a unique conjunction of contingent factors; hence each, in order to be properly understood, must be placed in its own unique context, which is what these essays endeavor to do.

There are sound reasons for documenting the varieties of slavery found in South Asia's history. For one thing, such an exercise can broaden our understanding of an institution that is commonly but mistakenly understood as a monolithic, one-size-fits-all phenomenon, characterized by features such as natal alienation, persons-as-property, coercion, or "social death." Data from South Asia can also serve to correct the widespread tendency to view histories of slavery in teleological terms, that is, as a triumphant march from bondage to "freedom." A prominent academic unit at Yale University, for example, is named the "Gilder Lehrman Center for the Study of Slavery,

Resistance, and Abolition," as though resistance were a natural corollary to slavery, and abolition its inevitable destiny. Postulating "freedom" as slavery's universal antithesis is especially problematic, if only because it subtly encourages the idea that the burden of "free" peoples is to complete a Euro-American project of liberating the post-1789 world from "unfreedom."[1] After all, in the late nineteenth century Europeans conquered a good part of Africa precisely in the name of "liberating" Africans from a form of capitalist slavery that Europeans themselves had introduced.[2]

The study of slavery thus carries an immense load of ideological baggage. What is more, scholars must contend with the overwhelming, even hegemonic, influence exerted on slavery studies by the Atlantic plantation model, instances of which appeared in the Caribbean, Brazil, and the American South. While this volume does not question the validity of that model so far as it describes one well-known form of slavery, it would reject efforts to project the Atlantic model, or any model, onto all other instances of the phenomenon, most certainly those found in the history of South Asia. Rather, we hope that the variety of forms described in this volume will contribute to expanding the conceptual range of slavery as a category of historical study. Eventually, scholars may be able to place *all* varieties of slavery, including the Atlantic plantation model, in broader frameworks of comparative history and even world history.[3]

Definitions

The appearance in this volume of indigenous terms like *ghulam, banda, laundi, boi,* and *dasa* demonstrates that each of the societies herein examined identified certain of their members as occupying a position clearly distinct from those of other members. But what did such indigenous terms actually mean? What was it that persons so designated shared in common that warrants our calling them all "slaves?" And what do we mean by that term? Notably, few of the contributors to this volume cite any of the myriad definitions of slavery that exist in the literature, or venture to offer definitions of their own. This might reflect an implicit assumption that "everyone knows" what slavery is. Or perhaps it stems from a certain diffidence among South Asianists to venture onto terrain so long trod by, among others, classicists, Africanists, and historians of the antebellum United States.

It nonetheless seems appropriate to consider how our contributors understand and deploy the term. Speaking very broadly, the cases examined in this volume suggest an understanding of slavery as *the condition of uprooted outsiders, impoverished insiders—or the descendants of either—serving persons or institutions on which they are wholly dependent.* This is not intended to be a universal definition, but merely a characterization of the people that the contributors to the present volume write about when they speak of "slaves," and the condition they write about when they speak of "slavery." Formulating it was therefore an inductive exercise; it may or may not describe slaves or slavery in other historical contexts. It is offered, however, in the interest of initiating a conversation on what might be unique about cases of slavery in South Asia, and what those cases might have shared in common with other instances of what is a practically universal historical phenomenon.

Omitting features typically associated with industrial slavery—e.g., chattel status, violence, coercion, race, kinlessness, and dishonor—the characterization offered above stresses the slaves' state of total dependency, however that dependency might have been manifested.[4] This is because the varieties of slavery described in this volume all involved reciprocal, virtually contractual, relations between slaves and masters: the slave owed obedience and loyalty as well as service and labor to the master, while the latter owed protection and support to the slave. In South Asia where nearly all members of society were embedded in webs of hierarchically structured groups, classes, or castes, it would therefore seem that the antithesis of slavery was not "freedom" in the European Enlightenment sense of autonomous, self-directed, individual agency, but rather a state of complete detachment from such culturally specific webs. In other words, the slaves considered in this volume were in every instance relatively more dependent on the will and the power of someone else than were non-slaves.

This is not to suggest that slavery in South Asia should be thought of as unique, or as an "Oriental" exception to some imagined ideal type. Indeed, the cases examined in this volume exhibit many features associated with well-known historical instances of slavery. In five essays we find slave markets where human chattel were bought and sold at known and specified prices. One essay (Ali) reports instances of slaves being branded to indicate the identity of their owners. In all but three we find life-long alienation from natal kin, village, even country. Five essays refer to masters endowing their slaves with new names and hence with new identities. And one (Vatuk) documents humiliation and beating, even unto death, by oppressive masters or mistresses. Yet none of these features was common to all the cases herein examined. The only common denominator was the slaves' condition of total dependency on some powerful person or institution. That said, there is considerable variation in the ways that slaves were recruited, the uses to which they were put, the manner of their manumission, the processes by which they became assimilated into dominant cultures, and the fate of their offspring.

Recruitment and Usages

By far the largest number of both male and female slaves described in this volume were former war captives. In our earliest case study, Daud Ali documents the mechanisms by which the imperial Cholas captured and enslaved women who then served as "reproductive pools" for the development of a cadre of military men, the *kaikkolars*, loyal to the imperial dynasty. In view of its basically martial purpose, the Chola pattern presents a variation on better-known instances of military slavery found in twelfth- and thirteenth-century north India, or in the fifteenth- and sixteenth-century Deccan. In these latter cases, men captured in distant Central Asia or Ethiopia were recruited, trained, and deployed as soldiers in the service of sultanates in Delhi, Ahmadnagar, or Bijapur. Although the Chola state enslaved female and not male captives, the outcome was the same as in those sultanates—i.e., the creation of a cadre of fighting men whose loyalty focused solely on the state. The Chola evidence thus documents an early and indigenously Indian case of military slavery, refuting claims that such an institution was imported from the Middle East, or that it represents a peculiarly "Islamic" form of slavery.[5]

Not all war captives, however, were put to military uses. At various times between the fifteenth and seventeenth centuries, females captured in war served Rajput ruling houses as concubines, domestic slaves, or dancers. In the eighteenth century, war captives supplied the bulk of the Maratha kingdom's slaves, many of whom were placed in state-controlled forts where they provided agricultural labor, worked in horse or elephant stables, or prepared gunpowder. Medieval and early modern states in the Indo-Burmese borderlands also enslaved war captives, a process that intensified when the English East India Company began introducing firearms in the region. As in the case of the Marathas, such enslaved captives served courts typically in menial capacities.

A singular use of female slaves was as tokens of exchange in political negotiations between elite households. Among Rajput chiefly houses, the circulation of slave-performers served to articulate political hierarchies both amongst those houses and with dynasties beyond Rajasthan.[6] In eighteenth-century Maharashtra, too, women passed through powerful households, as subordinate chiefs sent the peshva female slaves as a form of tribute, or as the Maratha ruling house distributed slaves to its favored subordinates. In both the Rajput and Maratha cases, the circulation of slave-performers and other domestic slaves served not only to establish relations between ruling elites, but also to reproduce those same elite classes over time.

Slaves were also recruited by outright purchase, a mechanism that presupposed the growth of commercial markets and monetized economies, together with conceptions of humans as saleable commodities. We first hear of such transactions as India's commercial integration with Central Asia intensified in the late twelfth and thirteenth centuries. Sultan Iltutmish, who himself had been sold into slavery, as ruler of Delhi sent agents into Central Asia to purchase military slaves in that region's great slave markets. The trend continued in the wake of the conquest of Central Asia by Mongol invaders, who sold off surplus supplies of captured men for cash. In the sixteenth century, war captives in India's eastern hills were sold for coined silver. And in the cash-flush eighteenth century, Rajput chiefs purchased slaves whom they then gave as dowries in interstate marriages. At the same time, Maratha households bought female slaves with cash.

Although slaves in South Asia changed hands in a variety of ways—through tributary payments, gifting, or cash purchase—their original enslavement arose from one of two conditions: capture in war, discussed above, and impoverishment.[7] In eighteenth-century Maharashtra, famine-induced poverty forced many peasants to sell their own children, presumably to more prosperous households. About the same time, notes Sylvia Vatuk, the nawabs of the Karnataka acquired most of their domestic slaves from local markets in which impoverished parents sold their children, destitute adults sold themselves, and husbands sold their wives to avoid starvation. Sometimes politics, not the market, led to the enslavement of impoverished villagers. In the hills of eastern India, ambitious chiefs gained leverage over famine-stricken families by supplying them with grain. When such families subsequently attempted to repay the chiefs, the latter would refuse repayment on the grounds that the families had become their slaves.

New paths leading from poverty to enslavement emerged with the rise of British power in India. Michael Fisher writes that in the 1760s the British government forced the East India Company to bond Indian servants to their English masters. Although the government's intent was to extend a measure of security to indigent Indian servants residing in England, the action effectively granted English masters proprietary rights over those same servants. And in eastern India, the colonial regime's introduction of commercial crops and its demand that taxes be paid in cash opened the door to unscrupulous moneylenders, who advanced cash to impoverished farmers while taking the latter's children as security. Similarly, when adults defaulted on their revenue payments, they themselves became bonded to petty revenue farmers.

These two primary mechanisms of enslavement in South Asia, capture in war and impoverishment, had different implications for the slaves' cultural position in their host societies. Those entering slavery from impoverishment were usually cultural "insiders," since their masters tended to be nearby patrons, chiefs, moneylenders, or tax farmers. Powerful local elites like these typically held impoverished subjects in a condition of debt bondage that was theoretically terminable upon paying off the loan. But in practice, as is seen most clearly in Indrani Chatterjee's concluding chapter, people held in debt bondage often slipped into a state of permanent, even inheritable, dependency, and hence slavery.

War captives, by contrast, were normally outsiders to the culture of their host societies, at least originally. It was their uprooted and alien status that had made these outsiders vulnerable, and hence dependent on their masters, which in principle ensured their loyalty to them. This is why Chola kings enslaved women captured from their Chalukya enemies, why the early Delhi Sultanate recruited slaves from Central Asia, and why the sultanates of Bijapur and Ahmadnagar recruited slaves from East Africa. It also explains why Rajput chiefs obtained their slaves from lineages other than their own and from places as distant as Afghanistan, and why Portuguese officials in Goa, apprehensive about the loyalty of their own Indian sepoys in the midst of north India's "sepoy mutiny" of 1857, sought military "recruits" from distant Mozambique.

Manumission and Assimilation

Although uprooted slaves like those just cited began their careers as cultural outsiders, they—and especially their offspring—did not usually remain such. One of this volume's more important contributions is its collective picture of slavery as a historical process and not, as it is so often depicted, a static "institution." One repeatedly encounters slaves who, though introduced from alien and often distant environments, became by various means assimilated into their host societies. The several instances of military slavery encountered in this volume (Jackson, Kumar, Eaton, Walker) suggest that such slavery was understood not as a fixed status, but as a particular origin, a particular career, and a particular relationship to a ruler or politically important master. One's origins could be forgotten over time or submerged by new regional identities; one's career could evolve as one moved from cadet to commander, or even became an employer of other military slaves; and one's relationship to a ruler could, over time, mutate from a master-slave connection to a patron-client one. All these categories were fluid, as historical processes pushed slaves toward ever greater cultural and social assimilation with their host societies.

Such a process is seen in naming patterns. In South Asia as elsewhere, naming or renaming individuals was one means by which masters asserted their control over the identity of their slaves. Whereas high-status women in the Chola court bore names identifying them with their fathers or husbands, female slaves were named simply "daughters of god," indicating their kinless status. And in early modern Rajasthan, Rajput wives retained their birth names after marriage, whereas female slaves were given new names by their masters, effectively erasing former identities. Thus Jaswant Singh, while on Mughal assignment in Afghanistan between 1668 and 1672, renamed ten female singers he had obtained there before dispatching them to his harem in Jodhpur. But new names, while erasing former identities, could also create new ones. In the nineteenth century Karnataka, child slaves bought by Muslim nobles were given, and hence grew up with, Arabo-Persian names. And as Michael Fisher's essay shows, most bonded servants in England either were given a "Christian" name by their master, or adopted one themselves if they converted to Christianity. Others simply Anglicized their original Indian names, as happened when "Munnoo," upon marrying an English woman and raising a British family, emerged fully assimilated in English society as "Munnew."

In one notable instance explored by Sunil Kumar, however, masters resisted their slaves' assimilation into the host culture. By giving slaves recruited from Central Asia new, Turkish names, officials of the early Delhi Sultanate endeavored to perpetuate the alien status of those men, forestalling their assimilation into Persian, Islamic, or north Indian socio-cultural worlds. Inasmuch as both the slaves and the rulers were ethnic Turks, the enterprise suggests an attempt to maintain an ethnic division not between slave and master—as was usual in cases of military slavery—but between the *entire* ruling class and the subject population. For a while, the policy apparently succeeded, since contemporary Sufis referred to Delhi's rulers as anonymous "Turks," while Persian literati identified the language of power and wealth in the sultanate as Turkish, which "everybody" had to learn. But ultimately, as Delhi's rulers strategically recruited ever more free Afghans and other non-elite elements into their power structure, the descendants of Turkish slaves merged with north Indian society, and the Turkish language vanished from north India.

In the sixteenth- and seventeenth-century Deccan, on the other hand, slaves imported from Ethiopia were rapidly integrated into the households of their masters, who themselves were often assimilated ex-slaves from East Africa. Their Ethiopian names having been replaced by new Arabo-Persian secular names, these men embraced Deccani culture, identified with the

Deccani political faction as opposed to that of Iranian immigrants, and intermarried with Deccani women. Their assimilation into Deccani culture and society, moreover, seems to have occurred even before their formal manumission, which generally took place on the death of their masters.

And what of caste? Since caste identity presupposed belonging to a community defined in part by kinship, it may seem paradoxical that kinless and hence supposedly "socially dead" slaves could have had any caste at all. Yet data from eighteenth-century Maharashtra suggest that Hindus did not lose their caste identity upon being enslaved. To the contrary, high-caste masters, anxious about suffering social degradation from contact with their own slaves, appear to have been careful to identify and publicize those slaves' precise caste identity. If caste identity tended to remain stable across time, however, slave status did not. Indeed, the experience of many peoples discussed in this volume suggests that barriers between slave and non-slave status were often quite permeable. Some slaves actually managed to obtain manumission on their own initiative. In the Maratha kingdom, notes Sumit Guha, slaves closely tied to powerful households inherited land from their masters, evidently with a view to using such property to emancipate themselves. Others obtained their manumission by simply presenting their master with a substitute slave, whom they often acquired by purchase.

One gets the sense, then, of slavery as very much a process—of vast numbers of people in South Asian history moving through various kinds of slavery, with a range of different outcomes. Consider the fates of slaves' offspring. In the case of the Cholas, daughters of slave-women remained in their mothers' *velam* (a palace institution) and inherited their mothers' slave status, thereby perpetuating a breeding pool for elite Chola soldiers. But their sons joined military units and thus disappeared from slave society. The sultanates in Delhi and the Deccan, having no such mechanism for on-site reproduction, continually recruited slaves from great distances. But because the careers of these men seldom outlasted the lives of their masters, military slavery tended to be "one-generational." Remnants of that generation nonetheless survived, as children of freed slaves in both Delhi and Ahmadnagar married one another and created de facto endogamous communities—what Kumar calls the "debris of past dispensations"—that struggled to retain some sort of patronage in the sultanates' evolving ruling structure.

Something of the same sort happened in Rajput households, where children of slaves, though remaining in those households, inherited a "debt of food" and fell to a lower status, especially in the eighteenth century when preoccupations with lineage "purity" barred children of kinless mothers from attaining real power. With the Marathas, too, children of enslaved war captives inherited their parents' slave status. But even they could and did gain manumission by marriage, since doing so created a set of affinal kin. In the eastern hills under British colonial rule, on the other hand, debt bondsmen who inherited their status from their parents failed to extricate themselves from the grip of their chiefs. When Christian missionaries began ransoming bondsmen who had deserted those chiefs and flocked to the missions for succor, the colonial regime intervened by returning the ransom money to the missionaries and the bondsmen to their former owners, thereby restoring slavery while denying that slavery existed.

In one way or another, then, the descendants of slaves endeavored to claw their way into mainstream society or, failing that, to carve out new identities for themselves, though with only varying degrees of success in either endeavor.

Slavery, Chroniclers, and Historians

Past instances of slavery in South Asia never present themselves through crystal-clear glass. What images we have must be painstakingly reconstructed from records that—when we have any at all—are typically fragmentary, opaque, and tainted by the politics of the day. Both contemporary and subsequent observers often resorted to a number of rhetorical strategies when writing of slavery. Many simply ignored the phenomenon; when it could not be ignored, they disguised it; and when it could not be disguised, they rationalized it.

Avril Powell thus shows that even William Muir, one of the most rabidly anti-slavery English officers in colonial India, ignored instances of slavery practiced in particular Indian courts or households for fear of offending elites who were collaborating with the Raj. Such self-censorship was not confined to Europeans. The social reformer Chiragh 'Ali refrained from commenting on the practice of concubinage in Hyderabad for fear of offending the Nizam, whose government had conferred a prestigious title on him when he resided for several years at that ruler's capital. And nineteenth-century Rajput chroniclers, influenced by British colonial preoccupations with genealogical "purity," left no room for kinless slaves in their remembered past. As a result, they were quite unable to recognize how the circulation of female slaves among ruling houses, which necessarily distinguished donors from recipients, served to define hierarchies among Rajput lineages.

When slavery could not be ignored, rhetorical ruses were deployed to disguise it. In 1857, when a nervous Portuguese colonial government in Goa wished to import military slaves from Mozambique at a time when the transport of slaves on the Indian Ocean was prohibited, it was decided to offer Africans a bounty of five or six *patacas* for agreeing to be recruited. The reasoning, as Timothy Walker explains, was that paying these men a nominal remuneration would nullify their status as slaves and magically transform them into wage-laborers. Another ruse was to disguise their transfer to Goa as a routine "exchange" of labor between two Portuguese colonies.[8] Indrani Chatterjee's concluding essay illustrates still another way of masking slavery: by adapting for their own purposes indigenous ideas of debt bondage, British colonial officials in India's remote eastern hills connived at preserving what they were publicly committed to ending.

When slavery could be neither ignored nor disguised, however, it was rationalized. Peter Jackson draws our attention to the dilemmas of the Delhi Sultanate's early court chroniclers who had to explain, for example, the anomaly of a slave inheriting property from his master—even an entire kingdom!—when Islamic law sanctioned only the reverse. Likewise, Sunil Kumar considers how chroniclers steeped in Persian conceptions of "civilized" society and hereditary aristocracy wrote about their patrons when the latter were uncultured and kinless Turkish slaves. Such writers were especially challenged when they had to confront flagrant breaches of legal and customary norms, as when those same slave-patrons usurped power for themselves. Such dilemmas prompted an array of elaborations, fabrications, or simply erasures, some of which persisted into successive generations, or even survive today as received "history." Paramount, however, was the need to rationalize. Kumar notes the creative sleight of hand performed by contemporary Persian chroniclers who referred to the Turkish slave as "a paradigmatic hero of the Delhi sultans and servitor of Islam."

Another mode of rationalizing slavery in one's own society was to contrast it with slavery elsewhere. Addressing English audiences in the 1870s, a young Amir ʿAli defended "Islamic" slavery on the grounds that whereas neither Moses nor Jesus had abolished slavery, the Prophet Muhammad "almost" abolished it; and that, in any event, slavery was worse in ancient Rome than it was in the Muslim world. For their part British colonial officers, always mindful of the horrors of Atlantic plantation slavery, felt that slavery in the India they governed was relatively "mild."[9] Some even persuaded themselves that for people facing the prospects of starvation, slavery actually represented a form of social welfare.

Slavery and the World

The case studies included in this volume open doors to a number of academic fields: the history of South Asia and its neighbors, slavery studies, and world history.

It is no coincidence that the volume's maps, departing from traditional perspectives, link the Indian subcontinent to Central Asia, East Africa, and the Indo-Burmese borderlands. Like long-distance trade, to which it is closely related, the interregional movement of slaves helped integrate peoples, economies, and cultures of South Asia with those of Central Asia and the Indian Ocean rim. A focus on slavery as a unit of study, then, not only expands our notion of India's historical space. It can also help release South Asian scholarship from the grip of "area studies," which, by walling off South Asia from the rest of the world, has proven quite inadequate for understanding an array of global processes, of which the history of slavery is one.

For example, if one looks at Mughal history through the lens of slavery, noting the sorts of slavery-related policies that Mughal rulers did or did not adopt, one may reach a deeper understanding of their strategic priorities as well as of India's ties with adjacent territories in the early modern period. In the first place, the Mughals did not conquer or govern north India with the help of military slaves, as did the founders of the Delhi Sultanate. Rather, in 1526 Babur arrived in Delhi with kinsmen and allies comprising free Turks, Iranians, and Mughals who settled down as permanent immigrants. Moreover, the Mughals very early on endeavored to limit the scope of slavery within their frontiers. In 1562 Akbar abolished the practice of enslaving the families of war captives (though not war captives themselves),[10] and twenty years later he freed his own enslaved war captives.[11] In 1608 his son and successor Jahangir banned the sending of eunuch slaves from Bengal to the imperial capital as tribute in lieu of cash revenue, which had been the custom since the fourteenth century.[12]

These measures notwithstanding, the Mughals actively participated in an ancient trade with Central Asia in which slaves figured prominently. Throughout the sixteenth and seventeenth centuries, they deported to Central Asia state "rebels" or subjects who had defaulted on revenue payments,[13] in this respect following precedents inherited from the days of the Delhi Sultanate. Balban (1266–87) had ordered the enslavement of those who resisted his authority, suggesting defaulters, and Sultan ʿAla al-Din Khalaji (1296–1316) reportedly legalized the enslaving of revenue defaulters.[14] In Akbar's reign (1556–1605), the Ghakkar community of the Panjab served as middlemen in the export of Indian slaves to Central Asian markets, where they were exchanged mainly for war horses, on which the Mughal military system was strategically dependent.[15] In Jahangir's reign (1605–28), this pattern continued, as men annually captured in the Agra region were enslaved and sent to Kabul, where they too were bartered for horses.[16]

Although the rhetoric of slavery survived as a metaphor for political loyalty—imperial officers routinely styled themselves "slaves of the emperor"[17]

—as just noted, the Mughals did not maintain enslaved soldiers or commanders. Nor did they recruit and manage slaves for economic purposes within their borders. That is, the state did not take over the domain of private merchants by running vast plantations to produce labor-intensive cash crops, as occurred, for example, in the East Indies under Dutch imperial rule. Indeed, apart from domestic slavery, which flourished in elite Mughal households just as it did among their Rajput and Maratha contemporaries, the Mughals prohibited all uses of slaves within their frontiers. Although some have dismissed such prohibitions as merely "pious wishes,"[18] it is not difficult to discern here a political motive—that is, the desire to prevent Mughal officers from building up independent power bases by transforming captured slaves into personal retainers, or by selling them for their own enrichment. Equally important were fiscal considerations. When tax-paying peasants were for any reason enslaved, they were effectively removed from imperial tax registers, thereby depriving the central government of potential revenue.

Conversely, the Mughals consistently authorized the capturing and enslaving of rebels and of men who had defaulted on revenue payments (these were often the same people). Inasmuch as enslaved captives were then transformed into commodities for India's commerce with Central Asia, it is evident that such a policy met several state goals at once: pacifying "rebel" lands within the empire, enhancing revenue collection by intimidating potential defaulters, and acquiring horses for the imperial cavalry.

The Mughals' policies on slavery yield other insights into India's ties to the early modern world. Unlike in contemporary Brazil, where neither the native population nor the Portuguese crown could prevent merchant capital from transforming the land into vast sugar plantations worked by alien slave labor, in India the Mughals endeavored to keep European venture capital out of their realm whenever such capital threatened to enslave their subjects. We witness this in their dealings with the neighboring kingdom of Arakan, the coastal strip along the Bay of Bengal that straddles an amphibious zone between agrarian South Asia and maritime Southeast Asia. In the 1630s and 1640s, Dutch merchants imported textiles, iron, Chinese porcelain, and firearms to the Arakanese capital of Mrauk-U in exchange for rice, and especially for slaves. The Dutch East India Company then shipped the latter to Java to work as domestic servants or to islands in the Moluccas to work as agricultural laborers.[19] The Arakanese, often in concert with renegade Portuguese, had acquired these slaves by launching maritime raids on Mughal Bengal and seizing communities of coastal villagers. At the height of the slave trade in the early 1640s, the Dutch bought from the Arakanese at least a thousand Bengali slaves annually.

Mughal authorities, however, took vigorous steps to suppress this traffic, which had been depopulating the lower delta by removing whole villages. In 1632 Mughal arms expelled the Portuguese from the Bengali port of Hugli, owing to Portuguese association with the slave trade.[20] The Mughal conquest of the port of Chittagong in 1666 was similarly aimed mainly at driving Arakanese slave raiders out of Bengal. Standing behind these raids, of course, was the specter of European merchant capital which, through Portuguese-Arakanese intermediaries, indirectly threatened to remove productive Bengali cultivators from the empire's tax base.

One may situate Mughal India's dealings with Bengal and Arakan in the theoretical framework of historian Joseph Miller, who has studied slavery from a world history perspective. Miller proposes that around 1600, as the Indian Ocean and Atlantic economies became ever more commercialized and mutually integrated, slaving emerged as a principal strategy by which transregional merchants replaced local interests in commanding economic activity.[21] In Europe, where powerful monarchs taxed peasant communities, merchants were constrained from introducing untaxable labor in the form of slaves; so they focused instead on controlling wage-earning populations financially, through their access to gold and silver. In Africa, transregional merchants extended financial credit in the form of manufactured commodities—many of Indian origin—to intermediaries who covered their debts by exporting slaves. In much of the Americas, by contrast, merchants were unhindered either by local powers or by distant European monarchs from introducing untaxable labor for industrial agriculture. In such a *tabula rasa,* merchants underwrote investments in land, equipment, and labor for sugar cultivation, which led to the emergence of entire plantation societies based on slave labor.

But in the Indian Ocean region, Miller notes, transregional merchants encountered no such *tabula rasa,* and hence were compelled to adapt to slaving strategies inherited from centuries of power struggles over labor, which included corvée, debt bondage, and enslaved outsiders. Significantly, the rise to prominence of Dutch and English trading companies in the seventeenth century coincided with the height of the Mughals, who were able to prevent European capital from transforming India into a plantation society on the Atlantic model. The only Indian Ocean regions that proved susceptible to such a transformation were some islands in the Moluccas in the Indonesian archipelago. As it happens, many of the slaves that worked the clove and nutmeg plantations of those islands had been shipped by the Dutch East India Company from Arakan. These would have been the same Bengalis who had been seized by Arakanese raiders and then bartered to the Dutch for firearms and Chinese porcelain. Owing, however, to successful interventions by emperors Shah Jahan and Aurangzeb, the combined forces of Dutch capital and Arakanese sea power were unable to do any more than nibble around the Mughal periphery, and at that only briefly.

That is one way that histories of slavery in South Asia can lead one to world history. Data in this volume may also be used to test theories of slavery formulated by scholars of Southeast Asia—a region that not only shares much in common with South Asia ecologically, culturally, and historically, but in respect to which more scholarship on slavery has been devoted than is the case for South Asia. As long ago as 1900, H. J. Nieboer proposed a correlation between land use and agrestic slavery, arguing that when there is a shortage of labor and an abundance of accessible land, coercion—hence, "industrial" slavery—becomes necessary to keep cultivators on the land.[22] More recently another historian of Southeast Asia, Peter Boomgaard, has suggested a correlation between the extent of monetization and debt bondage, arguing that since cash is at a premium in undermonetized states, those who have it hoard it, which in turn drives up interest rates, preventing peasants from repaying loans and forcing them into debt bondage. Boomgaard has also proposed that slaves are more likely found in weak than in strong states, since weak rulers are less able to constrain their nobles from punishing their own underlings by enslavement. And he suggests looking at possible correlations between slavery and natural or man-made disasters, since people at such times can be expected to be more vulnerable and hence more likely than otherwise to sell themselves into debt bondage.[23] Such are some of the lines of inquiry that both scholars of slavery and historians of South Asia might profitably take up.

This volume is in no way an exhaustive inventory. As its essays are but a first stroke on an enormous canvas, we see the volume as an intermediate stage in the historiography of South Asian slavery. On the one hand, it seeks to bring to light fresh data on a subject that has suffered neglect for far too long. But at the same time, it calls on other scholars to take up leads suggested on these pages and to push them further—to test them, and confirm or reject them in light of new data. It is an immense topic; much more needs to be done.

Notes

1. Such a notion was satirized in a Steve Bell cartoon that depicts George W. Bush gazing wistfully upon an image of the Statue of Liberty and musing, "One day Mars will be free." See *Guardian Weekly* 173, no. 8 (Aug. 12–18, 2005), 3.

2. As Indrani Chatterjee notes in her second chapter in this volume, between 1872 and 1894 British imperialists annexed parts of eastern India using the rhetoric of freeing captives enslaved by local chiefs.

3. For previous attempts to place the study of slavery in such broader frameworks, see Orlando Patterson, *Slavery and Social Death: A Comparative Study* (Cambridge, Mass.: Harvard University Press, 1982); Claude Meillassoux, *The Anthropology of Slavery: The Womb of Iron and Gold,* trans. Alide Dasnois (London: Athlone, 1991); and Alain Testart, *L'esclave, le dette et le pouvoir: Études de sociologie comparative* (Paris: Editions Errance, 2001).

4. In a recent volume surveying the history of slavery in the Indian Ocean world, Gwyn Campbell suggests that to understand slavery in that region, we need to replace the free/slave dichotomy and the idea of persons-as-property with "a vision of society as a hierarchy of dependency, in which 'slaves' constituted one of a number of unfree groups from which menial labour was drawn to perform services both productive and nominally unproductive." See Gwyn Campbell, "Introduction: Slavery and Other Forms of Unfree Labour in the Indian Ocean World," in Gwyn Campbell, ed., *The Structure of Slavery in Indian Ocean Africa and Asia* (London: Frank Cass, 2004), xxii.

5. For a discussion of the tenacity of the idea of an "Islamic" form of slavery, and the problems of such a formulation, see Sean Stillwell, *Paradoxes of Power: The Kano "Mamluks" and Male Royal Slavery in the Sokoto Caliphate, 1804–1903* (Portsmouth, N.H.: Heinemann, 2004), 8–9; see also Matthew Gordon, *The Breaking of a Thousand Swords: A History of the Turkish Military of Samarra* (Albany: State University of New York Press, 2001), 6–7.

6. As Ramya Sreenivasan notes in this volume, Jaswant Singh's failure to send Aurangzeb ten singers he had acquired from Afghanistan could have symbolized the Rajput chieftain's relative autonomy in the Mughals' political galaxy.

7. In the broader field of slavery studies, the topic of original enslavement has been much neglected. For a useful discussion of various forms of original enslavement and its impact on slave-producing societies, with a special focus on Africa, see Pier M. Larson, *History and Memory in the Age of Enslavement: Becoming Merina in Highland Madagascar, 1770–1822* (Portsmouth, N.H.: Heinemann, 2000), especially 6–23.

8. Such verbal machinations recall the French colonial policy of exporting African workers to the Indian Ocean islands of Reunion and Mayotte under the guise of a "free-labor emigration" scheme, after the metropolitan government had abolished the slave trade in 1848. Similarly, up to the 1840s the Dutch East Indies government continued to buy slaves from Nias and to put them to work in mining, port labor, or domestic service in western Sumatra. This, too, was slavery under a different name. A contemporary observer wryly noted how "the Dutch gravely talk of 'debtors'" and of "sending to Nias for debtors." See Anthony Reid, "The Decline of Slavery in Nineteenth-Century Indonesia," in Martin A. Klein, ed., *Breaking the Chains: Slavery, Bondage, and Emancipation in Modern Africa and Asia* (Madison: University of Wisconsin Press, 1993), 71.

9. For reviews of the clash between abolitionists and the East India Company in the early nineteenth century, and the emergence of official views on slavery in India, see Nancy Gardner Cassels, "Social Legislation under the Company Raj: The Abolition of Slavery Act V 1843," *South Asia* 11 (1988), 59–87; see also Mark Naidis, "The Abolitionists and Indian Slavery," *Journal of Asian History* 15 (1981), 146–58.

10. Abu'l-fazl 'Allami, *Akbar-nama,* trans. H. Beveridge (Delhi: Ess Ess Publications, 1977), 2:246.

11. Shireen Moosvi, trans. and ed., *Episodes in the Life of Akbar* (Delhi: National Book Trust, 1994), 88.

12. Gavin Hambly, "A Note on the Trade in Eunuchs in Mughal Bengal," *Journal of the American Oriental Society* 94, no. 1 (Jan.–Mar. 1974), 128–29.

13. This policy was reported by observers such as Badauni, Pelsaert, Manrique, Bernier, and Manucci. See Scott C. Levi, "Hindus beyond the Hindu Kush: Indians in the Central Asian Slave Trade," *Journal of the Royal Asiatic Society* 12, no. 3 (Nov. 2002), 282; see also Hambly, "A Note on the Trade in Eunuchs," 130.

14. Levi, "Hindus beyond the Hindu Kush," 282.

15. In 1581 a European witness reported that it was on account of this traffic that the Ghakkars had become associated with the proverb "slaves from India, horses from Parthia." Ibid., 280.

16. Dirk H. A. Kolff, *Naukar, Rajput, and Sepoy: The Ethnohistory of the Military Labour Market in Hindustan, 1450–1850* (Cambridge: Cambridge University Press, 1990), 11.

17. One of Akbar's poet laureates, Abu'l Faiz, or Faizi, referred to Mughal subjects as "slaves of the emperor," *bandagan-i hazrat zill-i Allah,* or *ghulaman-i 'alampanah.* See A. D. Arshad, *Insha-yi Fayzi* (Lahore: Majilis-i Taraqqi-i Adab, 1973), 77–79, 153, cited in Muzaffar Alam and Sanjay Subrahmanyam, *Indo-Persian Travels in the Age of Discoveries* (Cambridge: Cambridge University Press, forthcoming).

18. Sanjay Subrahmanyam, "Slaves and Tyrants: Dutch Tribulations in Seventeenth-Century Mrauk-U," *Journal of Early Modern History* 1, no. 3 (Aug. 1997), 215.

19. See ibid., 213–53.

20. On this occasion, the Mughals reputedly liberated ten thousand slaves held in that city. See ibid., 209.

21. See Joseph C. Miller, "A Theme in Variations: A Historical Schema of Slaving in the Atlantic and Indian Ocean Regions," in Campbell, ed., *Structure of Slavery,* 170–71.

22. H. J. Nieboer, *Slavery as an Industrial System: Ethnological Researches* (The Hague: Nijhoff, 1900). Arguing in a similar vein, Anthony Reid has recently suggested that in areas of low population density control of people is more important than is control of land, which in turn leads to coercive forms of labor. Anthony Reid, "The Decline of Slavery in Nineteenth-Century Indonesia," in Klein, ed., *Breaking the Chains,* 65.

23. Peter Boomgaard, "Human Capital, Slavery, and Low Rates of Economic and Population Growth in Indonesia, 1600–1910," in Campbell, ed., *Structure of Slavery,* 89–91.

1

Renewed and Connected Histories: Slavery and the Historiography of South Asia

Indrani Chatterjee

This volume is conceived as an attempt to reconnect the histories of South Asian slavery with the new revisionist scholarship of slave holding that is appearing elsewhere. We hope to enable South Asianist scholars of all shades and disciplinary training to rethink some of their formulations about power, culture, identity, voice, and memory in temporally and spatially sensitized contexts. Consider, for instance, the new work on slavery in the eastern Mediterranean between the sixth and eleventh centuries by Youval Rotman,[1] alongside that of northern Africa during the same centuries.[2] Arguing that scholars had hitherto presumed upon Roman legal concepts like *res* and Marxist concepts of a discrete proletariat of labor, Rotman reveals how these categories prevented scholars from understanding the nature of slavery in the eastern Mediterranean world during the post-Roman centuries. These were the very centuries in which slavery was believed hitherto to have ended. Instead, Rotman argues, wars between Arab princes and Byzantine potentates led to new doctrines regarding the treatment, status, and ransoming of "captives." These shifted ideas of freedom and slavery in turn. Janet Ewald suggests that the Roman Catholic military orders allied with two religious orders, the Trinitarians and the Mercedarians, to collect alms with which to ransom "Christian" captives during the twelfth and thirteenth centuries.[3] During the fifteenth and sixteenth centuries, as Iberian and other sailors came increasingly into conflict with Arab sailors and traders in the waters off the northwestern coasts of Ifriqiya (current Africa), the ransoming of captives became even more organized and was supported by the newly reorganized states in the Iberian peninsula.[4] Thus, as Ewald notes, at the very historical moment when Iberians and other Europeans began to use African slaves on plantations in the Atlantic Ocean, an image of "Muslim slavery" as particularly brutal emerged in the western Mediterranean.

Such revisions of the historiography of slavery that tie together different theaters of warfare with the shifting discourses on slavery and freedom and ethico-spiritual epistemes can be productive for scholars of South Asian pasts. First, these new histories explain the transportation of ideas regarding "Muslim slavery" into early modern South Asia by Portuguese sailors and elites. They also invite a reappraisal of the discourses on captivity and redemption produced by Portuguese and Catholic friars in the Indian Ocean.[5] Second, these histories draw attention to the surprising gaps in the social history of warfare in early medieval and early modern South Asian histories as a whole. Notwithstanding the new scholarship on warfare and warriors,[6] and the studies of slave-soldiers and slave-commanders presented in this volume (Jackson, Kumar, Eaton, and Walker), till Daud Ali's essay herein, South Asian historiography had left unstudied the fates of combatant prisoners and hostages and their subsequent treatment by host societies.

Perhaps this neglect can only be explained by the hostility that professionals trained in post-Rankean methods feel for records characterized— also by those nineteenth-century conventions—as "literary," "hagiographic," "religious," or "eulogic." Notwithstanding the inroads of literary criticism and hermeneutic developments, few scholars of South Asia deploy such interpretative practices when faced with older literatures,[7] and hence they continue to discount the historical fidelity of "narrative" records. But as Ali's essay herein suggests, all records, even when writ on stone, are "literary" in specific ways that demand attention. Such sensitivity is even more necessary when narratives and poetry alike persist in their suggestion that warfare was just as fundamental to South Asian slave making as it had been in Greek or Roman antiquity. Consider the seventh-century tale by Banabhatta of a moon-god's love for an earthly girl, a character called Patralekha. She is described as a prepubescent "maiden" "brought here with the other captives taken by our great king" and "reared" in the house of her captors, by the mother of the hero. The mother fostered and raised the captive as "if she were my own daughter." Having judged that the captive maiden was "fit to be an attendant and betel-box bearer" for her son, she made a gift of her to him. Along with the gift came instructions on how to use her: "She is to be cherished like a child . . . to be looked upon as a pupil, and to be initiated into all your confidences like a friend . . . take pains by all means such that she long remains your fit attendant." We are told that Patralekha, zealously devoted to the recipient at first sight, "turned into his shadow."[8]

Historians of South Asia who acknowledge this constant change from material body to shadow, from young captive to daughter to personal attendant, as a fundamental aspect of slavery in history can better connect these records to emerging histories of alienation, intimacy, and gender in the medieval and early modern world. They are better situated to understand epigraphic records that speak of the collection of women in the hands of "gods" after particularly violent phases of the past, as well as their transfers between earthly lords and palaces and the invisible lords in temples of the medieval world. Philosophically speaking, it is this captive young shadow who constitutes the Other of both adult and non-slave male and female in these narrative landscapes. Patralekha's story suggests to the student of history that slavery in the Sanskritic *kavya* or poetic traditions may have been conceptualized as a dialectic of captivity and transfers along a socially integrated continuum, as a dialectic between alienation and intimacy, not as a static problem of "un-freedom," coerced labor, "commodity," or "property."

Rather than define slavery in absolutely dichotomous terms ("free" versus "slave," for instance), or in prefabricated and inadequately historicized units of legal theory (such as "property with voice"), or by occupational tests which cannot deal with the variety of positions and offices in which all slaves were put to work in preindustrialized rural, urban, and courtly contexts, this volume foregrounds locally specific usages, relationships, terms, institutions, and processes as they shifted in time. We thus hope to emphasize the changing gendered and generational shifts within the recruitment, acquisition, transfers, uses, and abuses of slaves and non-slaves alike within each social formation.

The contributors have paid special attention to the shifting boundaries between slave and non-slave as they have pondered the use of slaves or the nature of the reproduction of slave status. Cumulatively, then, they offer a picture of slaves and non-slave servants coexisting between the ninth and the nineteenth centuries, while they outline the subtle shifts between one and the other. Kumar portrays the simultaneous use of slave- and non-slave men as soldiers in thirteenth- and fourteenth-century north India. He also indicates the variety of fortunes that descendants of slaves could experience—from assimilation into government within a generation as "dependent" clients, to active erasure from memory. While Walker suggests a similar coexistence of slave and criminal conscripted into the Portuguese armies of the early modern period, Fisher refers to the coexistence of slave and bondsman in the early trade between South Asia and Britain. A similar coexistence of slave and indentured laborer or servant appears to have characterized the west coast of the eighteenth century in Guha's essay, while a profusion of indigenous terms within the Rajput histories studied by Sreenivasan suggests that similar trends characterized landlocked polities and societies as well. But by the late nineteenth century, as I suggest in the final chapter, not only were the distinctions between slaves and indentured laborers being eroded in practice by newly emergent colonial regimes, but, equally significantly, the descendants of slaves were not allowed to forget their slave pasts at all.

Our insistence on the shifting nature of slavery over time—shifts that, from the perspective of the human beings concerned, were experienced also as geographical, cultural, and political changes—accounts for the absence of numbers in this volume. Historians of slaves in South Asian pasts, attempting to engage comparativist scholarship, are unfairly confronted by demands for quantification that scholars of the seventeenth- to nineteenth-century trades in the Atlantic and Indian Ocean routes take as basic to their studies.[9] We, however, feel that the study of slavery in older South Asian pasts needs to discuss the changing nature of the entity itself, before reliable numbers can be produced for any century.

The absence of numbers in turn has some relevance to assessments of "markets," "transfers," and "routes of exchange" for the subcontinent. A bewildering variety of currencies and exchange mechanisms in the precolonial and colonial periods in South Asia has made it impossible to assess the monetary or currency values of transfers of human wealth in the most characteristic of such forms in the region—the "donations" given by the devout to Buddhist and Hindu temples from the third to the eighteenth centuries.[10] As Ali points out here, many such "donations" had already served in the households of the donors before being "gifted" to the temple. It is understandably difficult to compute the exact "additions of value" to these servants before they became "gifts" to overlords of different kinds.

As for later periods and other modes of acquisition of slaves, we can only infer the existence of markets from the price regulations of a fourteenth-century Khalaji sultan, or the memoirs of a Moroccan visitor to the Tughluq court at Delhi.[11] Even accounts by traveling European merchants of later centuries provide only scattered information on the buying and selling of slaves. However, taken together, these suggest that each "type" of slave could be sold for a standardized monetary price. But since slaves were acquired from far-away places in a widening arc during the early modern period, not every slave-dealing person may have used cash in a transaction involving such transfers. Eaton, for instance, suggests that Indian merchants buying slaves in eastern Africa during the sixteenth century paid for their purchases of Ethiopians with Indian textiles.

The absence of numbers is further explained, and magnified, by the attempts of some seventeenth-century regimes, like that of the Mughals, to prohibit the "seizures" of slaves from their dominions. These attempts were frustrated by the Portuguese and Dutch mercantilist presence in the Indian

Ocean. The latter facilitated the trade in slaves from the Mughal hinterlands to regimes either in the Mughal periphery or beyond.[12] So while seventeenth-century combinations of Arakan (Magh) and Portuguese sailors raided and sold their captives around the regions and ports of the Bay of Bengal,[13] their Dutch, French, and English successors in the eighteenth century transported such slaves to a much wider range of markets.[14] If European mercantile observers themselves are to be believed, these centuries saw provincial Mughal governors attempting to halt such transfers.[15]

Notwithstanding such evidence, most scholars of these centuries in South Asia exclude themselves from the debate about the role of European mercantilist commerce in deepening the markets in slaves, a debate which has been so vibrant a part of Africanist historiography. The evidence in this volume suggests that there is little warrant for such exclusion. Timothy Walker hints at the assimilation of the Portuguese to slave-using societies of the Indian Ocean as a whole. Michael Fisher and Sumit Guha touch upon English factors of the seventeenth and eighteenth centuries who carried small numbers of slaves to the metropolis. Similar connections can be suggested between the English East India Company's entrepôts in Fort St. George (modern Madras) and York Fort (modern Sumatra).[16]

The hesitation of South Asianist scholarship in this regard is attributable almost entirely to the absence of systematic analyses of Lusophone, French, and British mercantilisms as they inserted Asian slaves into metropolitan or other colonial societies, and the absence of studies thereof.[17] Unlike scholars of the Dutch in Southeast Asia and the Indian Ocean,[18] scholars of early British and French empires in South Asia remain indifferent to complicating their "nationalist" pasts with Asian slaves. In terms of global history, this results in erasing the polycentric connections between piracy on the Mediterranean and Atlantic oceans in the early modern period,[19] on the Pacific,[20] on the Indian Ocean, and within early American societies at the same time. The unwillingness of scholars of European mercantilism in Asia and those of eighteenth-century South, West, and Central Asian mercantilism to study slave markets as a significant component of the tussles for dominance over regional routes, markets, and trades redoubles the effect of elisions in the historiography of a later period as well.

Students who encounter European colonial histories in South Asia from the late eighteenth century onward can hardly "provincialize Europe" when all their ideas of "state," "culture" and "family" come to them shorn of European slaveholding and slave-trading histories. Nor can students of Asian societies between the fifteenth and twentieth centuries refine notions of "class" —especially categories like "elite" or "subaltern"—without knowing the work that slaves-as-elites did in developing Safavid and Ottoman "absolutisms," mercantilism, art, and architecture. Nor can they understand differences *within* Islamic slave systems without such histories.[21] We are reminded of these gaps again in encounters with Rajput-Mughal regimes in the late seventeenth century and Maratha regimes in the eighteenth, which tried to establish "monopolies" of sorts over slave holdings. In the latter instance, ruling groups ensured the displacements and relocations of specific human subjects in state-controlled forts, stables, and palaces. An ever-changing group of "criminals," unable to pay fines or taxes, were either auctioned by the state or kept to labor on one of its public buildings; they could go "free" only if they supplied substitutes for themselves, paid "ransoms" for themselves, or consented to the marriages arranged for them by their owners.

Readers must surely wonder what kind of connections might be found in the future between eighteenth-century regimes with coastal outlets such as the Marathas, the post-Mughal regimes at Hyderabad, Mysore, Awadh, Bengal, and the contemporary Kandyan regime in Sri Lanka, and the oceanic slave trades of all the European powers of these centuries. Only a synthesis of such articulations can demystify later colonial South Asian histories and situate them in terms of their larger global connections.[22] Most critically for a scholarship obsessed with nationalism, such a synthesis may yet explain certain nationalist enunciations to latter-day scholars—for instance, the distinction between the Indian housewife and the "truly unfree" domestic servant.[23] This was a distinction that thinking men in the nineteenth century never erased. It is one that we, the professional scholars of gender, class, and history, have ignored.

Slaves and Identities

Since it is not nationalism per se, but a peculiarly postcolonial and ethnographic presentism, that has led to this impasse in South Asianist historiography, it might be helpful to remind ourselves of the example of early medieval "English" nationalism as it worked itself out in language. David Pelteret traces the evolution of the word *wealh,* originally meaning both "foreigner" and "slave," into the notion of a "Welsh person" in medieval poetry.[24] Moreover, his research findings corroborate the global demographic profiles of such "foreigners/slaves" before oceanic trades changed the nature of slave holding and slave trading dramatically. For instance, in Pelteret's case, the *wealh* was female, and was apparently used as a dairymaid. A similar predominance of females among slaves in urbanized Mediterranean societies has been noticed by legal historians. Steven Epstein, for one, finds that in the Genoa of 1458, a city of around fifty thousand inhabitants, there were 2005 female and only 54 male slaves. Equally significantly, these female slaves had been brought from the Black Sea area, and came from groups identified as "Circassians, Tartars, Russians, Abkhazians" and others.[25] Indeed, the term "slave" comes to us from the general identity of these groups, "Slav," reflecting—as with *wealh* and "Welsh"—the fluidity of ethnic identities, geographical frontiers, and social categories.

Such scholarship situates the problems of "identifying" slaves, as they moved into and out of slavery, within a consistently shifting matrix of early modern European, African, and Asian pasts.[26] Since most first-generation slaves in antiquity and later were conceived of as, or were, "foreigners," historians can no longer base their studies of slave lives on retroactive limits of territorially defined nationalistic frontiers and immutable natal cultural identities. When "Genoese" slaves turn out to be "Russian," it follows that historical studies of slavery in South Asian societies, too, have to rethink boundary making itself as a historical social process. While wars and battles can make explicit the nature of a particular boundary between villages and jurisdictions, other social activities, such as lawmaking or justice, can reveal boundaries between humans within the same clan, worship group, village, or household. Matters of interiority or belonging and exteriority or alienation, determined by multiple kinds of boundaries, cannot be presumed upon at any point. This has particular relevance, of course, for those individuals and families dragged or pushed across multiple geographical, social, or cultural boundaries at different times and thus made "slaves" by virtue of being expelled or captured. But equally, since slave making and boundary transgressions went together, the nature of our scholarly and modern boundaries of knowledge also needs constant interrogation.

South Asianist historians are especially well poised to enter these conversations because of their considerable advances in deconstructing the presentist and nationalist cartographies which have hitherto undergirded studies of the region's past.[27] Calls for replacing the hyper-nationalist and hopelessly atemporal assumptions of the older scholarship with sophisticated time-space formulations that reveal connections between different parts of the world have characterized the new historiography of South (and Southeast) Asia for a while now.[28] Indeed, even the names "South Asia" and "India" have been historicized repeatedly. "South Asia" was a name given by the Allied powers after the Second World War to a newly decolonized region. Obviously, such a name cannot be found in a history written in the eleventh century, where a student might find terms like "Hindustan," "al-Hind," or other unidentifiable names. While "al-Hind," itself an Arabophone distortion of "Sind," referred to an ambiguous set of places in the early modern period, the term "India" came to mean a very specific set of territorial and cultural attributes from the eighteenth century onward. Like "South Asia," this usage too was a product of historical developments. Fisher's study of "Indians" bound for Britain in the seventeenth and eighteenth centuries, and Walker's essay on Portuguese India in the same period, suggest the nuanced and shaded aspects of the term "India" at different historical points. These studies both expand and inflect the apparent homogeneity, monolithicity, and timelessness that imperialist and nationalist historians alike had attributed to units like "India" or "Pakistan" or "Sri Lanka," especially in the nineteenth and twentieth centuries. Each of these states was conflated with particular "cultures," which were treated as shorthand for simplistic and abstract religions—so India was associated with Hinduism, Pakistan (and Bangladesh) with Islam, Sri Lanka and Burma (and Bhutan) with Buddhism, and so on.[29]

Studying these as separate and antagonistic cultures across time had then made it difficult to unpack terms such as "Buddhist," "Turushka/Turk," "Tajik," "Mongol," "Rajput," "Bengala," and "Feringhi" in the period between 1100 and 1900. Even if we could identify a "region" indicated by such a term—say, Central Asia for "Turk"—other histories (along with Jackson here) would instantly reveal that social groups in this region were enormously mobile, either as nomadic-pastoral or as transhumant groups trading with others located toward rivers and seas.[30] "Turk"-ishness referred to an ever-changing culture. Depending upon the particular linguistic, temporal, and political context of the production of the record, identical nomenclatures of social groups ("Hindu/Gentoo," "Turushka/Turk," "Uzbek," "Mongol," "Rajput") not only referred to different entities at different times, they also referred to cultures of mobility.

While it would be fascinating to investigate the institutions that enabled slaves to "become" Turk, or "Rajput" or "Feringhi" or any other cultural being—as the Africanists have done for the eighteenth and later centuries[31]—this volume currently limits itself to a simple statement on cultural change. It suggests that the institutions of the master's household, craft workshop, army, and worship group were critical to the shaping of slaves' identities across different generations. But it also emphasizes the impossibility of separating historical cultures; none can be treated by scholars as though it were hermetically sealed off from others, were bounded by physical space, or were changeless.[32] With each essay, this volume reveals that the study of slavery renders transparent the ideological investments made by scholars in the adoption of unchanging or monolithic categories. These categories of character (the "loyal slave" of the Persian chroniclers studied by Sunil Kumar) or ethnicity ("Turkish," "Habshi," "Rajput," and "English," as studied by Jackson, Eaton, Sreenivasan, and Fisher) or religion ("Hindu," "Muslim," and "Christian," as studied by Vatuk, Powell, and myself), each essay suggests, could in turn contain others that have escaped historical scrutiny. The study of slavery is here intended to put into motion the contingent categories of space (region), sect (religion), sex, and status in historical pasts, and to therefore render transparent the nature of ideological investments that insist upon their fixedness. Put bluntly, historians of South Asia should no longer be able to treat sex-gender, sectarian, or caste-class categories and collectives in the historical past without attending to the fault lines within each. At the same time, we hope that complicating these identities over time and space will refine the questions asked by historians of the "African diaspora" about cultures of performance and identity around the subcontinent in the twentieth century.[33]

Politics of Representation

Practices of representation and the politics of memory have been complicit in all historiographic contexts. Indeed, Peter Hunt has even suggested that the Greek scholars credited with the invention of history writing—Herodotus, Thucydides, and Xenophon—were silent about the contributions of helots and slaves to the successful waging of Greek wars between the fifth and fourth centuries BCE.[34] Nigel Worden refers to the absence of slavery from the Dutch historical consciousness, noting that debates about slavery in the formerly Dutch and slave-importing colonies in Mauritius and the Cape occurred after Mauritius was ceded to the French in the eighteenth century, and the Cape to the British in the early nineteenth. In both these places, the public memory of the slave past was obscured. Descendants of African slaves were classified alongside descendants of French masters and yet marked off from other categories of Mauritians, such as "Muslim," "Hindu," and "Sino-Mauritian." Anxieties about the electoral dominance of this or that category of the population during the 1960s drove the memory of slavery further underground.[35]

Scholars of Muslim societies ringing the Indian Ocean explain amnesia about slave pasts in more structuralist terms. Arguing that a pattern of "ascending miscegenation" characteristic of slave-keeping Muslim households led to generational integration of "foreign" slaves into a community of worship (in his case, of "Arabs"), Abdul Sheriff suggests that the absence of records of this assimilation should not be taken to indicate practices of deliberate oblivion.[36] John Hunwick adds that the Arabo-Berber Muslim reluctance to acknowledge a past in slavery is linked to a denial of history, since a past in slavery points implicitly to a past in "unbelief" (*kufr*), i.e., at one's ancestors having been at some earlier stage "pagans," which was a particularly heavy burden to bear.[37]

Clearly, the aftermath of slavery conditions both the remembering and the forgetting. However, no historian to date has studied the nature of commemoration in the absence of a finite emancipation of slaves—as in South Asia.[38] Nor, given the differences in valuation of memory-work, have scholars of South Asian slavery asked themselves how they might recover the history of "memory" as it worked in precolonial centuries. Kumar points out that thirteenth-century Muslim jurists' discomfiture about particular acts by slaves in the past was distilled as a "local memory," tamed, and then conveyed to the Moroccan Muslim visitor, Ibn Battuta, who then wrote it down as the "history" of the sultans. Court-based Persian chroniclers and historians, patronized by the very descendants of such slaves, responded to such jurists, critics, and "local memory" by generating symbolic frameworks—of the "loyalty" and "kinship/sonship" of the slave—to conjure away the threat of slave resistance and violence. Kumar thus suggests the intertwined existence of "history," "memory," and "communication" in all South Asian pasts. Thus he raises the possibility of reexamining both the modes of communication—the languages, for instance—and the various textual and extra-textual sites where such memory-work might have been performed.

Both systems of communication and signification are important to the history of slavery. Chroniclers of the fourteenth century, too, lived and wrote in societies with ethical and legal sanctions against the explicit addressing or naming of slaves. Such proscriptions are repeatedly suggested for major literary languages in the region. In keeping with the Buddhist injunction to monks to abstain from commerce of all sorts, including that in slaves, the editors of the *Tripitaka* literature systematically avoided all references to the trade. Instead, Pali terms like *manussa, purisa,* and *sevaka* referred to male slave-servants and men in general simultaneously. Explicit references to slave birth, as in the term *dasi-putta* ("son of a female slave"), were understood as abusive.[39] Such linguistic codes resonated with Arabophone *hadith* literature, in which we read that "one should not say 'my slave *('Abidī),'* or 'my girl-slave *(Amatī),'* but should say 'my lad *(Fatāī),'* 'my lass *(Fatātī),'* and 'my boy *(Ghulāmī).'"*[40]

Alongside the unwillingness to address a slave as "slave," repeated in other language groups in South Asian pasts, the ethico-legal limits of all speech reinforced diglossia where slaves were concerned. Those who were not slaves signaled their commitment to particular lords by appropriating to themselves the local equivalent of "slave"—as did the Tamil-speaking followers of the gods Siva and Vishnu between the sixth and tenth centuries in referring to themselves as "slaves" (*adiyar*) of the lord.[41] The Chola poets and inscriptions clearly inherited such linguistic practices, as outlined in Ali's essay. In the considerably sophisticated Sanskrit canon, poets could thus represent the incorporation of alien regions into princely domains by refer-ring to a long-established grammar of devotional "oblation" or "donation." An epic verse composed in the fourteenth century as a "history" of the pe-riod between the seventh and the twelfth centuries in regions identified with "Kashmir," the *Rajataringini* (The River of Kings), thus bestows blame and praise upon specific women of the interior (*avaruddhaa*) according to whether they followed their lords along "the path of fire" or failed to do so. A close scrutiny reveals that these "interior" ones were "oblates" to the gods, "acculturated" by temple authorities and by them "gifted" to an overlord—the king.[42] Indeed, the language of the "dedication" of slaves to overlords was so widespread by the sixteenth century that a Mughal emperor keen to pro-hibit the making and selling of eunuchs within his dominions nevertheless accepted them when provincial governors sent them as "offerings" (*nazr*) to the throne.[43] Similarly, a seventeenth-century Portuguese Catholic friar, eager to gather his scattered flock of Christians within a single parish, re-sorted to this grammar when he asked an Arakanese Buddhist ruler to dedi-cate local converts as slaves to the newly established Christian shrine at Di-anga—a "donation" readily made to the supplicant padre.[44]

Such symbolism obfuscated the "facts," Kumar suggests, in conversation with other, often invisible, interlocutions. Many of these interlocutions ap-pear to have been rooted in categories of thought which were simultane-ously religious and juridical. Though violence perpetrated by slaves (as mil-itary commanders or as household servants) was suppressed by medieval historians, and by a Muslim mistress in nineteenth-century Karnataka, the juridical-ethical imperatives working on both groups seem to have been shared. Recall the provisions in Islamic law that slaves should be given half the punishment imposed on a free person for the same crime. Similarly, nar-rations (by Rajasthani bards and chroniclers) of violence done to slaves and their children also recast such violence as either "self-sacrifice" or "self-de-struction" in order to address larger audiences of "followers" in hierarchi-cally organized polities. No serious scholar of precolonial pasts can afford to overlook the larger ethical landscapes within which all representations of slavery and violence occurred. Indeed, the transformations wrought by colonial law in eroding exemptions from punishments offered to slaves under older dispensations in South and Southeast Asia need to be studied in greater detail than has been attempted so far.[45]

The relation between slavery and violence in precolonial centuries in turn reflects upon the representation of slaves in South Asian historical pasts. Given many regimes' long traditions of "incorporating" slaves into ad-ministrative and military personnel, violence by slaves and ex-slaves against those who "spoke" of their slave pasts could also indicate the fullness of the "acculturation" of such ex-slaves in the ethical-juridical codes of locally dominant groups. The violence turned against truth-tellers in the past (by the descendants of slaves) thus is also a cautionary tale about the act of chronicling the past "realistically." For instance, an eighteenth-century Ahom diplomat's history of a sixteenth-century incident in another region refers to an official who had described a ruling monarch's step-brother as *bandir po* (son of a slave-woman).[46] When the man thus described heard of it, he is said to have killed the official. For a historian of slavery, such a description is double-edged. Even as it explains the absence of histories of slavery in earlier contexts, such stories gesture at eighteenth-century Ahom literati attitudes toward descent from slaves. These attitudes are confirmed in references to the physical destruction of chronicles that mentioned the "captive" ancestries of officers of Ahom kings (*Chakripheti Burunji*).[47] This suggests that it is not the "reliability" of descriptions that is at stake for a historian of memory, but the perceptible limits of speech and address generated within slave-using societies. It is these limits that conditioned the creation and transmission of both the memory and the history of slaves in the South Asian pasts.

The simultaneity of proscription, prescription, and description thus marks all the "histories" produced between the sixteenth and the nineteenth centuries. Such histories reveal a great deal about the ideologies of non-slaves (as literati) and their expectations of their own slaves. Valued behaviors were attributed to slaves in the past, when and if they wrote about them. It is in this way that we can read a late eighteenth-century historian's praise of a male slave of a Mughal emperor for the quiet fortitude with which he received "five hundred lashes for some offence."[48] Or a story of slave-eunuchs who embodied polite, noble speech, or stories of the valor of slave-guards-women.[49] While they constitute "sites" to be excavated for "memories" of slaves, they were also shaped by the ethico-juridical limits placed around "memory" itself.[50] Sreenivasan's study of the chroniclers of Rajput histories reveal them to be similarly trying to describe particular slaves and masters in ways that speak more to the chroniclers' ideologies and social relationships than to those of the slave-actors in the historical past.

Slave "Voices" and South Asian Pasts

If normative codes of conduct required deflection and indirection when slaves were described by non-slaves, and the latter appropriated to their own personas the servility, loyalty, and devotion that they valued in their slaves, it must surely be asked whether slaves themselves could have developed a distinct discursive "voice" within such cultures of representation. Since slaves could be found across the social spectrum, scholars can hardly persist with a one-size-fits-all notion of "slave life." Even less can they presume to know what "slave voices" in such a complex history might have sounded like. Yet such subtleties have merited little attention from the sophisticated critical scholarship of South Asianists. So we can only gesture here to paths not yet taken, to what we hope will be more fruitful and interconnected explorations of slavery around the Indian Ocean world.

Despite arguing that the voices of slaves were "contained" and "represented" by their master or other non-slaves in Ottoman pasts, Ehud Toledano has rued the unavailability of first-person and direct accounts by slaves in Ottoman and all other "Muslim" societies alike.[51] While a memoir does exist of an ex-slave named Tahmasp Khan Miskin from Mughal Hindustan of the later eighteenth century,[52] Toledano's characterization of "containment" appears to fit the literary sources from South Asia. There is some evidence that words and gestures produced by skilled slaves were incorporated into those of their masters and mistresses. Verses composed by a *khavasa-pasvan* (lit. "intimate servant") of the poet-prince of Krishengarh in the early eighteenth century were interwoven into the verses composed by her master.[53] Again, an early nineteenth-century British visitor to the *amir*s of Sindh witnessed one of the *amir*s appropriating the Persian lyrics composed by his male courtier, a Georgian slave purchased eighteen years before the Briton's visit but treated "like an adopted son."[54] This suggests that instead of dismissing all apparently "elitist" records as not carrying adequate traces of slave voices, we need to attend to these records even more assiduously to discern "slave voices" within them. Sreenivasan provides us with the example of the female slave-retainer who was the "voice" of her mistress in negotiations with the British, much as the Georgian slave mentioned above acted as his master's envoy to the British encampment. Such extended agency of owners thus left room for maneuvers by slaves and servants in particularly delicate tussles within particular households and communities—a situation that enabled British colonial regimes in the nineteenth century to refashion many of these polities.[55]

In order to hear "slave voices," whether on their own or in their containment or in dialogue with others surrounding them, scholars need to rethink the limits of a Habermasian "public culture" in the context of South Asia between the sixteenth and the twentieth centuries. While the Reformation in Europe evicted the Church from the "public" sphere, recent studies of north Indian monks and peasants and south Indian merchants and temples, as much as the elaboration of mosque- and shrine-based settlements through the period, reveal the extent to which religiosity and commerce have symbiotically constituted the Asian "modern" and "public."[56] Such co-constitution is being increasingly commented on for Islam in the African and early colonial American past as well.[57]

Scholars of slavery and discourse find these elaborations interesting precisely because of the persistence of "syncretic" versions of such discourses when authored by slaves. As work on the possession cults of the east African belt has shown, slaves inverted the orthodox traditions of religious discourse "through a continuous refashioning and reworking of three bundles of meaning: religion, descent and historical consciousness"—the three attributes that define humanity for masters in most places.[58] Thus historians of post-slave societies in Africa attend simultaneously to the embodied thought and communication of "ritual"[59] and those of "syncretic" Islam or "Sufism." In some place, the spirit of the Sufi shaikh was assimilated into *tumbura* (a cult of spirit possession); in others the veneration of a Sufi shaikh made the ground in which he was buried the carrier of *baraka*, or blessings, and therefore the center of a shrine-centered devotionalism complete with ecstatic dancing, singing, and weeping.[60] Abdelhamid Largueche has argued, for instance, that in the French colony of Tunisia annual festivals celebrating the lives of "black" Sufi saints (Sidi Saad and Sidi Frej) with song and dance brought together slaves from different "houses." These celebrations succeeded in getting manumission, rather than revolt or flight, accepted as the believers' path long before abolition occurred in the region.[61] In a similar vein, John Mason has suggested that Sufi Islam constituted the slaves' route to spiritual and social resurrection in colonial South Africa.[62]

The identification of each regional and temporal articulation of Sufi Islam by slaves appears to be the key with which to unlock slaves' own discourses on manumission and slavery. For South Asia, such attempts have been feeble precisely because historians have had no way of connecting captivity in childhood to courtly cultures or to spiritual kinship and community building. Yet as more individualized biographies of such figures emerge, we will be better placed to forge these studies into a distinctive whole. Muzaffar Alam has recently found a history of childhood captivity, spatial and social dislocation, service, and eventual "return" as a centerpiece of the story of one Sufi *silsilah* (literally "chain of transmission"; a brotherhood) in north India.[63] It appears to parallel the historical life of another well-known figure of seventeenth-century eastern India. Alaol, who began life as a young captive and rose to be a poet at the seventeenth-century court of Arakan, might be presented to us as a Bengali-language echo of a Persian Sufi poet of the fourteenth century.[64] But it is significant that Alaol's prohibitions on the buying and selling of slaves went further than is suggested by the original "moral" instruction.[65] In chapters on *saudagiri* (commerce), Alaol's poem urged its audiences not only to abstain from the "trade" in slaves but also to treat the male slave, once bought, "like a brother" (*bhratri-saman*) and the female slave in ways that allowed her to be sexually monogamous and "chaste."[66]

In early nineteenth-century Central Asia, the sound of slaves praying and weeping at the local Sufi shrine reached the ears of a Persian-knowing scribe in the entourage of a British military expedition. He also reported the words of a male Qizlbash (Shi'a) slave guarding a respectable Turkic household, who said that he hoped to be "liberated through the favour of God" (and whose patient demeanor irritated the scribe).[67] Such indirect communications should prompt historians of South Asian pasts to refine their own auditory skills if we are to open ourselves to the multiplicity of "slave voices" in the complex Asianist "public" culture.

For many objects and buildings associated with "sacred" pasts in the region similarly carried the ritual signatures of slaves and ex-slaves. Ali refers to donations to temples made by the *pentattis* and members of the *velams*. Sreenivasan and Guha refer to ponds, lakes, and dams built by slave-performers or slave-concubines. I have visited a circular building (Golkothi) in the heart of the city of Kolkata which was built by the eunuch of the nawab of Murshidabad. One must surely study these concrete gestures in brick and stone as part of the history of slavery that has shaped both physical and intellectual landscapes in the region. The mosques, mausolea, and other monuments to memory sponsored by slaves[68] were not simple expressions of wealth held by them but expressions of "value" that have been unappreciated as part of slave-authored commentary on their lords and masters.

Reinterpretations of the Nineteenth Century

Discursive, aesthetic, and ritual signatures associated with slaves can thus be found in a wide variety of "archives" and records of the South Asian past. A more rigorously historicized understanding of cultures of representation might help us to find more of these traces. But we also need to refashion cultures of interpretation to take us beyond the metaphysic of presence, accessed through either the visual or the mimetic faculties. Scholarly failures in this regard have burnished the status of the documents published as the *Parliamentary Papers on Slavery in India*, 1828–41. Rather than situate such records as part of triangulated conversations around slavery (and abolition) in global historical contexts, scholars have hitherto treated such records as repositories of "facts." They have thus overlooked the shifts in the meaning and politics of "slavery" from the very inception of colonial British governance. They have, as a result, lost the opportunity to hear the silences within contemporary indigenous as well as mid-century colonial records. Nothing has been published about the erasure from the *Parliamentary Papers* of slaves in early colonial European (including British) households in the eighteenth and nineteenth centuries. Even less has been written about these documents' erasure of the ascetic warriors and female rulers who began their careers as children sold during famines or captives in war.[69] These documents positioned their readers in an apparently universal mode of slave labor, whose contours were supposed to be the same everywhere. Thus there is little or no correspondence of data between these official papers on slavery in India and the precolonial and indigenous-language records.

Nor have these documents enabled scholars to contextualize the hide-and-seek nature of slavery in the nineteenth- and twentieth-century vernacular records either. As British colonial officers confronted many slave figures within regimes that they needed to control, Atlantic-style racialized notions of segregation and ancestry began to evolve within colonial jurisprudence. Tussles around slave birth in British-controlled courts of the region led to the dispossession of older slave-born lineage members in many parts of South Asia. Some of the dishonor and shame of this round of dispossession made it imperative for nineteenth-century historians of such households to resort to silence as a strategy of survival for "dependents" of such households. So, for instance, while the English-language records of the Nizamat of Dhaka by the 1840s include paylists and detailed notes on the slaves within, the Persian-language history of the same household written at the same time is completely silent on these people. This silence, a way to put off imperialist dispossessions, is the sort of silence that Powell refers to in this volume. It was critical to the ways in which nineteenth-century non-slave English-educated Muslim lawyers contended with the social reality of slave lives around them. Prohibited by older ethical norms from naming slaves and slave-using mistresses and masters, and united in a finely tuned resistance to colonial expansion after 1857, they turned to the source of moral authority and history itself—the Qur'an. Discussions about Islamic "principles" became oblique discussions about time, and therefore a "history" of slavery.

Powell's argument pushes us to rethink debates around "Islamization" in the subcontinent—the transformation of "popular" practices into "scholarly and juridically" authorized ones.[70] It also provides a framework for analyzing the relationship between the "writing" and the "memory" of slavery in South Asian literatures of the nineteenth and twentieth centuries. For instance, by locating silence at the center of "history," Powell's work allows us to see Act V of 1843—which prevented judges, owners, and slaves alike from calling a slave a slave—as continuous with older diglossic and ethical imperatives. Not naming slaves could in turn enable British officials, under attack in a transatlantic context and within metropolitan politics, to claim that slavery itself did not exist in the British Indian empire thereafter. The claim was especially strongly made for areas "under British law," such as the province of Bengal, which had been the first to be annexed. It was here in the 1870s that British officials and judges refused to accept that terms like *bandi* and *dasi,* used by females to describe their own conditions in legal suits, could be translated as references to slavery.[71] Increasingly, too, official correspondence in the late nineteenth century represented the institutions of raiding, captive selling, and tax gathering in forms of human wealth as part of "un-British rule" in parts of northwestern India, or in princely states[72] within the subcontinent where British rule was exercised only indirectly, or in lands that bordered Inner Asia.[73] Since slave keeping became the identifier of Otherness, it became important for almost all critically anti-imperialist "nationalist" intelligentsia to insist that slavery as a state of unfreedom continued *within* areas of British rule.

It was in this resistant, but mimic, mode that indigenous intellectuals deployed mid-nineteenth-century plantation-based meanings of slavery as unfree labor in pointing to the failures of imperial rule. One author represented all the non-Brahmans of the region as "classical Sudra" castes and all Sudra as slaves. Joti Govindrao Fule wrote a tract titled *Gulamgiri, or Slavery in This Civilized British Government under the Cloak of Brahmanism.* Incidentally, he dedicated it to the "good people of the US as a token of admiration for their sublime disinterested and self sacrificing devotion in the cause of the Negro slavery."[74] Politically significant as this was, the identification of low castes as slaves was itself a product of European concepts of liberty and "possessive individualism." Given that caste-formation and status was commonly believed to be suprahistorical anyway, and *jati* status was widely believed to be a matter of birth, the underlying effects of this stance were politically limiting for the nationalists. As slavery, caste, and race began to collapse into each other in nationalist Indian thought, nationalist groups required to portray themselves as people capable of self-rule actually drew away from alliances with African populations in England, as well as within the subcontinent. Naoroji, an eminent nationalist Indian standing for parliamentary election in 1886 and 1892 on a Liberal ticket, illustrates this veering away from populations with a past in Atlantic slavery.[75] Within Indian intellectual traditions, the merging of slavery with lower-caste status gathered momentum with the growth of various caste-ranking movements in the late nineteenth century. In narrative terms, representing someone as born of a "low-caste" mother became equivalent to implying "slave birth," and the terms were used interchangeably in historical prose from the late nineteenth century.

Even as colonial education and history books remained the channels through which European philosophies of "liberty" influenced the new literati, local intellectuals struggled to recast older genres and the narrative cultures of their childhood into these new categories and forms. Tensions within the epistemologies of such intellectuals abounded, and could be resolved only by familiar deflective strategies. A good example is the work done by Bankim Chandra Chattopadhyaya (1838–94). He had studied the newly institutionalized subject of history in the newly founded Calcutta University, from which he graduated in 1858. Some of the institutional history lessons on slavery in the Roman Empire, and on history, stayed with him and were articulated in his journalistic prose of 1879.[76] However, having read the colonial translations (by James Tod and Alexander Dow) of Rajput "histories" of various parts of India, he continued to believe that historical truth could best be told in genres of older provenance, like the romance. One of Bankim's last compositions was set in the period 1772–77, which was marked by a well-remembered famine as well as armed peasant rebellions. Bankim described a figure who was clearly immediately recognizable: a young female called Nishi, stolen from her parents as a child (*chhelebelai amai chheledhorai churi koriya*), sold to a landlord-raja, a fugitive from concubinage, sheltered and adopted as a daughter by the leader of the bandit-rebels, and finally "married" to a god, Sri Krishna. In this portrayal of a female with no memory of kin, "original" name, or home, only her own self-fashioned kinship and friendship with the female protagonist, Bankim outlined the critical social divide that separated some women from others. He thus clearly signaled that the single category of "Brahman women" was divided along the fault line of permanent natal alienation, rather than massed together in the rightlessness common to all women. Nishi's startling resemblance to the seventh-century creation Patralekha suggests that romance as the most favored form of truth-telling had encompassed the discipline of history as science. This familiar weaving of romance with history-as-moral-truth can be read in Michael Madhusudan Dutt's work as well. This eminent Francophile of nineteenth-century Bengal wrote two plays, *Sarmishtha* and *Ratnavali*, apparently set in "ancient" Indian pasts. The central themes of these plays were the problems of stratification among women in households populated by female slaves and their children. Finally, both the form and the content (as well as the older devotional metaphors) were deployed by Rabindranath Tagore in his drama *Notir Puja:* here the female slave-performer in a royal household, rather than the queen mother defined by the lineage, articulated the redemptive possibilities of Buddhist *dhamma* in India's ancient past.

If the nationalist intelligentsia embedded these discussions of slavery in forms that were unrecognizable to professional historians as "evidence," their aestheticized discourses on slavery can surely be contextualized within the same ethico-jural constraints that Jackson, Kumar, and Sreenivasan out-line here, and that I have outlined elsewhere. Just as in the fourteenth cen-tury, so in the late nineteenth and early twentieth centuries, the requirement to maintain normative discourse while addressing the presence of slaves in the past was at odds with the demand to bear accurate witness to the lives of slaves.[77] A famous social reformer could thus write the memory of slave holding in his family and his childhood in the 1830s and '40s, but simulta-neously distance himself from that past as a "reformer."[78] Intellectuals in the nineteenth century who recorded their great fear of "being given away for-ever" provided indirect testimony to the lives of slaves in genteel society in colonial India.[79] Others remembered that, as ignorant child brides, they had been instructed to behave "like female slaves" by the concubines and mis-tresses associated with their male affines.[80] Memoirs of others, such as a Muslim deputy magistrate and judge in the late nineteenth century, re-counted legal cases brought by masters and mistresses against their slaves, long years after the so-called de-legalization of slavery.[81] In 1896 Pandita Ramabai, the famous scholar of the Puranas, newly converted to Christian-ity, wrote of parents in famine-stricken central India taking girl-children around the country and selling them for a rupee or a bit of grain, and regret-ted that "the children who have been sheltered in Poor Houses and eaten food from the hands of people of other castes will not be taken back into their caste, but will be in lifelong slavery if they are 'adopted.'"[82] A veritable archive of memories of such slaves persisted into the late twentieth century. Some Iranians remembered African and Indian slaves among the pastoral Bakhtiari ilkhans.[83] Elite women told anthropologists who asked about mar-riage practices stories of family members' "bride-prices" that included a "grown woman slave."[84] Another anthropologist in eastern Indonesia found herself witnessing the gift of a nineteen-year-old slave-woman during a royal funeral in 1988.[85]

It is our hope that the essays that follow will spur others to recover some of these intertwined histories and memories for the South Asian academe. It is also our hope that such recoveries will enable another round of critically engaged interpretative exercises and scholarly exchanges about the past in the Indian Ocean world. Thus only in dialogue do we hope for a genuinely global history of slavery.

Notes

1. Youval Rotman, *Les esclaves et l'esclavage: De la Méditerranée antique à la Méditerranée médiévale, VIe–XIe siècles* (Paris: Belle Lettres, 2005). I thank Caroline

Bynum for bringing this book to my attention, and the author for providing me with an English-language summary.

2. For a survey, see Robert O. Collins, "Slavery in the Sudan in History," *Slavery and Abolition* 20, no. 3 (Dec. 1999), 69–95.

3. Janet Ewald, "Africa and the Mediterranean," paper presented as part of "Globalizing Africa: Roundtable II" at the annual conference of the African Studies Association, October 30–November 2, 2003.

4. For Muslim captives between the twelfth and fifteenth centuries in Christian Spain, see Manuela Marin and Rachid El Hour, "Captives, Children, and Conversion: A Case from Late Nasrid Granada," *Journal of the Economic and Social History of the Orient* (henceforth *JESHO*) 41, no. 4 (Nov. 1998), 453–73; and John Hunwick and Eve Troutt Powell, eds. *The African Diaspora in the Mediterranean Lands of Islam* (Princeton, N.J.: Markus Weiner Publishers, 2002). For Christian captives, see Robert C. Davis, *Christian Slaves, Muslim Masters: White Slavery in the Mediterranean, the Barbary Coast, and Italy, 1500–1800* (New York: Palgrave Macmillan, 2003).

5. See a sixteenth-century example in *The Peregrination of Fernao Mendes Pinto,* translated and abridged by Michael Lowery (Manchester: Carcanet in association with the Calouste Gubenkian Foundation and the Discoveries Commission, Lisbon, 1992), 14–15.

6. Jos J. L. Gommans and Dirk H. A. Kolff, eds., *Warfare and Weaponry in South Asia, 1000–1800* (New Delhi: Oxford University Press, 2001); and Vijay Pinch, "*Gosain Tawaif*: Slaves, Sex, and Ascetics in Rasdhan, ca. 1800–1857," *Modern Asian Studies* 38, no. 3 (July 2004), 559–97. For recent additions to the history of warfare in Southeast Asia, see articles in *JESHO* 46, no. 2 (June 2003); for South Asia, see Jos Gommans, ed., special issue of *JESHO* 47, no. 3 (Sept. 2004), in honor of Dirk Kolff.

7. This may explain its absence from scholarship of classical societies in the subcontinent, such as Ludo Rocher, "Dasadasi," *Journal of the American Oriental Society* 122, no. 2 (Apr.–June 2002), 374–80.

8. There are many editions and translations of this tale; the one quoted here is Gwendolyn Lane, trans., *Kadambari: A Classic Sanskrit Story of Magical Transformation* (New York: Garland Publishing, 1991). See Robert A. Hueckstedt, *The Style of Bana: An Introduction to Sanskrit Prose Poetry* (Lanham, Md.: University Press of America, 1985).

9. Scholars of slave trades in the Atlantic, as well as in the Persian Gulf, set the standards for enumeration from the nineteenth century onward. For a survey see Patrick Manning, ed., *Slave Trades, 1500–1800: Globalization of Forced Labour* (Brookfield, Vt.: Variorum, 1996).

10. For instances of such transfers, see D. C. Sircar, *Studies in the Religious Life of Ancient and Medieval India* (Delhi: Motilal Banarsidass, 1971), 202–205; and Leslie Orr, *Donors, Devotees, and Daughters of God: Temple Women in Medieval Tamil Nadu* (New York: Oxford University Press, 2000); for Sri Lanka during the same period, see Chandima Wickramasinghe, "A Comparative Study of Slavery in Ancient Greece and Ancient Sri Lanka" (Ph.D. diss., University of Nottingham, 2004).

11. Major A. R. Fuller, "Translation from the *Tarikh-i-Firuzshahi*," *Journal of the Asiatic Society of Bengal* 39, pt. 1, no. 1 (1870), 1–51, gives the standard value of the "working girl" as fixed between 5 and 12 *tanka*s, the price of a singing girl as between 20 and 40 *tanka*s, the price of a handsome young slave-boy as between 20 and 30 *tanka*s, and that of a working man as between 10 and 15, while "ill-favored boys"

were priced at 7 or 8 *tanka*s. Clearly such prices of the thirteenth century should be treated with caution, since these are "remembered" prices recounted by historians writing much later. A Moroccan visitor to the Tughlaq court in the mid-fourteenth century extolled the "cheapness" of the slaves, in comparison to those of his native country, when he described the purchase of a "pretty young slave boy" for two gold dinars and of a slave-girl of "outstanding beauty" for a single gold dinar. For this, see *The Travels of Ibn Battuta, A.D. 1325–1354*, translated with revisions and notes from the Arabic text edited by C. Defrémery and B. R. Sanguinetti, by H. A. R. Gibb (Cambridge: Published for the Hakluyt Society at the University Press, 1971), 4:867–68.

12. Sanjay Subrahmanyam, "Dutch Tribulations in Seventeenth-Century Mrauk-U," in *Explorations in Connected History: From the Tagus to the Ganges* (Delhi: Oxford University Press, 2005), 200–47.

13. Pipli, Tamluk, Balasore, and Chittagong are mentioned in J. J. A. Campos, *History of the Portuguese in Bengal* (Calcutta: Butterworth and Company, 1919), 96–97.

14. Richard B. Allen, "Carrying Away the Unfortunate: The Exportation of Slaves from India during the Late Eighteenth Century," in Jacques Weber, ed., *Le monde créole: Peuplement, sociétés et condition humaine, XVIIe–XXe siècles; Mélanges offerts à Hubert Gerbeau* (Paris: Les Indes savantes, 2005), 285–98.

15. For the execution of a female trader in male slaves in Kabul, see Niccolò Manucci, *Storia do Mogor, or Mogul India, 1653–1708,* trans. William Irvine (London, 1907; reprint, Calcutta, 1966), 1:193–94; for the interception of a Persian embassy taking away slaves from India in the eighteenth century, see François Bernier, *Travels in the Mogul Empire*, 2nd ed., revised by Vincent A. Smith (Milford: Oxford University Press, 1916), 151.

16. See reports of slaves sent by the merchant who served the East India Company as its governor at these forts in *The Private Letter Books of Joseph Collet,* ed. H. H. Dodwell (London: Longmans, Green and Co., 1933).

17. For instance, the absence of Asian slaves is considered part of the "colonial slavery" of the French powers in Marcel Dorigny, ed., *The Abolitions of Slavery: From Léger Félicité Sonthonax to Victor Schoelcher, 1793, 1794, 1848* (New York: Berghahn Books and UNESCO Publishing, 2003).

18. In addition to Anthony Reid, ed., *Slavery, Bondage, and Dependency in Southeast Asia* (New York: St. Martin's Press, 1983), see Gerrit J. Knaap, "Slavery and the Dutch in Southeast Asia," in Gert Oostindie, ed., *Fifty Years Later: Antislavery, Capitalism, and Modernity in the Dutch Orbit* (Leiden: KITLV [Royal Institute of Linguistics and Anthropology], 1995), 193–206; and Nigel Worden, "Indian Ocean Slavery and Its Demise in the Cape Colony," in Gwyn Campbell, ed., *Abolition and Its Aftermath in the Indian Ocean, Africa, and Asia* (London: Routledge, 2005), 29–49.

19. See Nabil Matar, "Introduction: England and Mediterranean Captivity, 1577–1704," in Daniel J. Vitkus, ed., *Piracy, Slavery, and Redemption: Barbary Captivity Narratives from Early Modern England* (New York: Columbia University Press, 2001), 1–54.

20. James F. Warren, *The Sulu Zone, 1768–1898: The Dynamics of External Trade, Slavery, and Ethnicity in the Transformation of a Southeast Asian Maritime State* (Singapore: Singapore University Press, 1981); also idem, "The Structure of Slavery in

the Sulu Zone in the Late Eighteenth and Nineteenth Centuries," in Gwyn Campbell, ed. *The Structure of Slavery in Indian Ocean Africa and Asia* (London: Frank Cass, 2004), 111–28; and Peter Boomgaard, "Human Capital, Slavery, and Low Rates of Economic and Population Growth in Indonesia, 1600–1910," in ibid., 83–96. The same issues on land are tracked for a later period in Andrew Turton, "Violent Capture of People for Exchange on Karen–Tai Borders in the 1830s," in ibid., 69–82.

21. For this, see Sussan Babaie, Kathryn Babayan, Ina Baghdiantz-McCabe, and Massumeh Farhad, *Slaves of the Shah: New Elites of Safavid Iran* (London: I. B. Taruis, 2004).

22. For recent additions, see Madhavi Kale, *Fragments of Empire: Capital, Slavery, and Indian Indentured Labor Migration in the British Caribbean* (Philadelphia: University of Pennsylvania Press, 1998); also Michael Anderson, "India, 1858–1930: The Illusion of Free Labor" and Prabhu P. Mohapatra, "Assam and the West Indies, 1860–1920: Immobilising Plantation Labor," in Paul Craven and Douglas Hay, eds., *Masters, Servants, and Magistrates in Britain and the Empire, 1562–1955* (Chapel Hill: University of North Carolina Press, 2004), 422–54, 455–80.

23. Dipesh Chakrabarty, "Postcoloniality and the Artifice of History: Who Speaks for 'Indian' Pasts?" in Ranajit Guha, ed., *A Subaltern Studies Reader, 1986–1995* (Minneapolis: University of Minnesota Press, 1997), 263–93. For the crucial connection between household slavery and nationalism, see Beth Baron, "The Making of the Egyptian Nation," in Ida Blom, Karen Hagemann, and Catherine Hall, eds., *Gendered Nations: Nationalisms and Gender Order in the Long Nineteenth Century* (Oxford: Berg, 2000), 137–58; and idem, *Egypt as a Woman: Nationalism, Gender, and Politics* (Berkeley: University of California Press, 2005).

24. David A. E. Pelteret, "The Image of the Slave in Some Anglo-Saxon and Norse Sources," *Slavery and Abolition* 23, no. 2 (Aug. 2003), 75–88, esp. 76. See also his *Slavery in Early Medieval England: From the Reign of Alfred until the Twelfth Century* (Woodbridge: Boydell Press, 1995).

25. Steven A. Epstein, "A Late Medieval Lawyer Confronts Slavery: The Cases of Bartolomeo de Bosco," in *Slavery and Abolition* 20, no. 3 (Dec. 1999), 49–68.

26. See Joseph C. Miller, "A Theme in Variations: A Historical Schema of Slaving in the Atlantic and Indian Ocean Regions," in Campbell, ed., *Structure of Slavery*, 169–94.

27. For the most recent articulation of these connections in the early modern period, see Subrahmanyam, *Explorations in Connected History*.

28. See, for instance, Richard M. Eaton, "Was There Ever a Northwest Frontier? Persia and India from Alexander the Great to Alexander Cunningham," paper presented at the annual conference of the Asian Studies Association, May 17, 2003; for another interpretation, see Manu Goswami, *Producing India: From Colonial Economy to National Space* (Chicago: University of Chicago Press, 2004); David Ludden, "Investing in Nature around Sylhet: An Excursion into Geographical History," *Economic and Political Weekly*, November 29, 2003, at http://www.sas.upenn.edu/~dludden/luddenEPW_files/showArticles.htm. For Southeast Asia, see Victor Lieberman, *Strange Parallels: Southeast Asia in Global Context, c. 800–1830*, vol. 1, *Integration on the Mainland* (Cambridge: Cambridge University Press, 2003).

29. See David Gilmartin and Bruce Lawrence, eds., *Beyond Turk and Hindu: Rethinking Religious Identities in Islamicate South Asia* (Miami: University of Florida Press, 2000), especially the introduction.

30. See examples of scholarship in Daniel Power and Naomi Standen, eds., *Frontiers in Question: Eurasian Borderlands, 700–1700* (New York: St. Martin's Press, 1999); also Nicola Di Cosmo and Don J. Wyatt, eds., *Political Frontiers, Ethnic Boundaries, and Human Geographies in Chinese History* (London: Routledge Curzon, 2003).

31. Pier M. Larson, *History and Memory in the Age of Enslavement: Becoming Merina in Highland Madagascar, 1770–1822* (Portsmouth, N.H.: Heinemann, 2000); Sandra E. Greene, *Gender, Ethnicity, and Social Change on the Upper Slave Coast: A History of the Anlo-Ewe* (Portsmouth, N.H.: Heinemann, 1996); and idem, *Sacred Sites and the Colonial Encounter: A History of Meaning and Memory in Ghana* (Bloomington: Indiana University Press, 2003).

32: For the case of a Chinese man becoming a "Naga" slave, see Gordon P. Means, "Human Sacrifice and Slavery in the 'Unadministered' Areas of Upper Burma during the Colonial Era," *Sojourn: Journal of Social Issues in Southeast Asia* 15, no. 3 (Oct. 2000): 184–221.

33. For a succinct analysis of the limitations of Black Atlantic models to societies around the Indian Ocean, see especially Edward A. Alpers, "The African Diaspora in the Indian Ocean: A Comparative Perspective," in Shihan De Silva Jayasuriya and Richard Pankhurst, eds., *The African Diaspora in the Indian Ocean* (Trenton, N.J.: Africa World Press, 2003), 19–52. For anthropological investigations of cultural histories of the western peninsula, see Amy Catlin-Jairazbhoy and Edward A. Alpers, eds., *Sidis and Scholars: Essays on African Indians* (Noida, U.P.: Rainbow Publishers, 2004).

34. Peter Hunt, *Slaves, Warfare, and Ideology in the Greek Historians* (Cambridge: Cambridge University Press, 1998), and review by Paul Cartridge in *Slavery and Abolition* 20, no. 3 (Dec. 1999), 136–38; see also Peter Garnsey, *Ideas of Slavery from Aristotle to Augustine* (Cambridge: Cambridge University Press, 1996).

35. Nigel Worden, "The Forgotten Region: Commemorations of Slavery in Mauritius and South Africa," in Gert Oostindie, ed., *Facing Up to the Past: Perspectives on the Commemoration of Slavery from Africa, the Americas, and Europe* (Kingston, Jamaica: Ian Randle Publishers, 2001), 48–55.

36. Abdul Sheriff, "The Slave Trade and Slavery in the Western Indian Ocean: Significant Contrasts," in Oostindie, ed., *Facing Up to the Past*, 43–47.

37. John Hunwick, "The Same but Different: Africans in Slavery in the Mediterranean Muslim World," in Hunwick and Powell, eds., *The African Diaspora*, xii.

38. Indrani Chatterjee, "Abolition by Denial: The South Asian Example," in Campbell, ed., *Abolition and Its Aftermath*, 150–68.

39. Devraj Chanana, *Slavery in Ancient India* (Delhi: People's Publishing House, 1960), 73.

40. Quoted in Mohammed Ennaji, *Serving the Master: Slavery and Society in Nineteenth-Century Morocco*, trans. Seth Graebner (New York: St. Martin's Press, 1998), 94. For an Urdu translation of this *hadith*, see Said Ahmad, *Islam mein ghulami ki haqiqat* (Deoband, 1357 AH, Ziul hajj), 99–101. This text reiterates that masters (*maliks*) will appear conceited if they use the word ʿ*abd* to describe their slaves; instead they should address and describe male and female slaves as "my child" (*bacchhe* or *bacchi,* according to gender). In response, the male or female slave (*ghulam* or *bandi,* respectively) should refer to the master or mistress as "my leader" (*sardar* or *sardarni*).

41. Vidya Dehejia, *Slaves of the Lord: The Path of the Tamil Saints* (Delhi: Munshiram Manoharlal, 1988).

42. *Kalhana's Rajatarangini: A Chronicle of the Kings of Kasmir,* 3 vols., trans. M. A. Stein (1896; reprint, Delhi: Motilal Banarsidass, 1961), 1:325–26, 335.

43. *The Jahangirnama: Memoirs of Jahangir, Emperor of India,* translated, edited, and annotated by Wheeler M. Thackston (Washington, D.C.: Freer Gallery of Art, Smithsonian Institution; New York: Oxford University Press, 1999), 98, 108 (prohibitions), 139, 148, 357, 361 (offerings of eunuchs).

44. *Travels of Fray Sebastien Manrique, 1629–1643,* trans. C. Eckford Luard (Oxford: Printed for the Hakluyt Society, 1927), 1:139–59, 181, 193–204; also see the summary in Maurice Collis, *The Land of the Great Image: Being Experiences of Friar Manrique in Arakan* (London, 1945; reprint, New Delhi: Asian Educational Services, 1995), 172–79.

45. Contrast the descriptions of slaves being brutalized by colonial Dutch law in eighteenth-century Batavia and on the Cape of Good Hope in John Splinter Stavorinus, *Voyages to the East-Indies,* 3 vols., trans. Samuel H. Wilcocke (London, 1798), 1:288–91, 571, with English travelers' silence on the similar brutality of British colonial laws of the same period.

46. *Tripura Burunji, or, A Chronicle of Tipperah written in 1724 A.D. by Ratna Kandali Sarma and Arjun Das Bairagi, Swargadeo Rudra Singha's Envoys to Raja Ratna Manikya of Tipperah,* ed. S. K. Bhuyan (Assam: Dept. of Historical and Antiquarian Studies, 1938), 42–43.

47. Lila Gogoi, *The Buranjis: Historical Literature of Assam* (New Delhi: Omsons Publications, 1986), 29, 126–28.

48. Nawwab Samsam-ud-Daula Shah Nawaz Khan and Abdul Hayy, *Maathir-ul-Umara, Being Biographies of the Muhammadan and Hindu Officers of the Timurid Sovereigns of India from 1500 to about 1780 A.D.,* 2 vols. in 3, trans. H. Beveridge, revised and annotated by Baini Prashad, 2nd ed. (Patna: Janaki Prakashan, 1979), 1:811. During Shah Jahan's reign as emperor, the slave who had received those lashes rose to be the chief of artillery (*mir-i atish*), and died in battle.

49. Ibid., 2, 682.

50. *The Tabaqat-i-Akbari of Khwajah Nizamuddin Ahmad,* 3 vols., trans. and ed. Brajendranath De, revised by Baini Prashad (Calcutta, 1936; reprint, Delhi: Low Publications, 1992), 2:141–73 (the demand, by a slave-girl of Hasan Khan Afghan, that her son be raised to power is interpreted as the origin of Sher Shah Afghan's disaffection), 2:230–31 (a slave-gatekeeper's failure to recognize a Mughal official is said to be the reason for his master's dismissal from high office).

51. Ehud R. Toledano, "Representing the Slave's Body in Ottoman Society," *Slavery and Abolition* 23, no. 2 (Aug. 2002), 57–73.

52. For discussion of Tahmasp Khan Miskin's narrative, see Indrani Chatterjee, "A Slave's Search for Selfhood in Eighteenth-Century Hindustan," *Indian Economic and Social History Review* 37, no. 1 (Jan.–Mar. 2000), 53–86.

53. Pandit Mohanlal Vishnulal Pandia (late prime minister of the Partabgarh state in Rajputana), "The Antiquity of Poet Nagari Das and His Concubine Rasik Bihari alias Bani Thani," *Journal of the Asiatic Society of Bengal* 66, pt. 1, no. 1 (1897), 63–75.

54. James Burnes, *A Narrative of a Visit to the Court of Sinde: A Sketch of the History of Cutch from Its First Connection with the British Government in India till the*

Conclusion of the Treaty of 1819 (Edinburgh: Printed for Robert Cadell, Whittaker, Treacher and Arnot, 1831), 110–11.

55. See Pamela Price, "Kin, Clan, and Power in Colonial South India," in Indrani Chatterjee, ed., *Unfamiliar Relations: Family and History in South Asia* (Delhi: Permanent Black; New Brunswick, N.J.: Rutgers University Press, 2004), 192–221.

56. See Joanne Punzo Waghorne, *Diaspora of the Gods: Modern Hindu Temples in an Urban Middle-Class World* (New York: Oxford University Press, 2004), 142–48; William R. Pinch, *Peasants and Monks in British India* (Delhi: Oxford University Press, 1996), 1–47; for similar arguments about how Islamic "public" space was shaped by court and masjid, see Faisal F. Devji, "Gender and the Politics of Space: The Movement for Women's Reform, 1857–1900," in Zoya Hasan, ed., *Forging Identities: Gender, Communities, and the State* (New Delhi: Kali for Women, 1994), 22–37.

57. See Paul E. Lovejoy, *Slavery on the Frontiers of Islam* (Princeton, N.J.: Markus Weiner, 2005); and David Robinson, *Muslim Societies in African History* (Cambridge: Cambridge University Press, 2004); also Sylviane A. Diouf, *Servants of Allah: African Muslims Enslaved in the Americas* (New York: New York University Press, 1998).

58. G. P. Makris, *Changing Masters: Spirit Possession and Identity Construction among Slave Descendants and Other Subordinates in the Sudan* (Evanston, Ill.: Northwestern University Press, 2000), 3–4.

59. Rosalind Shaw, *Memories of the Slave Trade: Ritual and the Historical Imagination in Sierra Leone* (London: University of Chicago Press, 2002).

60. For early modern Deccan, Bengal, and Panjab, see Richard Eaton, *The Rise of Islam and the Bengal Frontier, 1204–1760* (Berkeley: University of California Press, 1993); and idem, *Essays on Islam and Indian History* (New Delhi: Oxford University Press, 2000).

61. Abdelhamid Largueche, "The Abolition of Slavery in Tunisia: Towards a History of the Black Community," in Dorigny, ed., *Abolitions of Slavery*, 330–39.

62. John Edwin Mason, *Social Death and Resurrection: Slavery and Emancipation in South Africa* (Charlottesville: University of Virginia Press, 2003), 176–207. This is particularly significant for linking slaves from Indonesian and Malaysian archipelago to the growth of Sufism in South Africa.

63. Muzaffar Alam, *The Languages of Political Islam in India, c. 1200–1800* (Delhi: Permanent Black, 2004), 99–103.

64. Amritalal Bala, "Alaoler Sufi Chetana," *Bangla Akademi Patrika* 35, no. 1 (Dhaka, Baisakh-Asar 1398 BS/May–June 1991), 7–50; also Swapna Bhattacharya (Chakraborti), "Myth and History of Bengali Identity in Arakan," in Jos Gommans and Jacques Leider, eds., *The Maritime Frontier of Burma: Exploring Political, Cultural, and Commercial Interaction in the Indian Ocean World, 1200–1800* (Leiden: KITLV Press, 2002), 199–212; and Ramya Sreenivasan, *The Many Lives of a Rajput Queen* (Delhi: Permanent Black, forthcoming). I thank Ramya for sharing the unpublished manuscript with me.

65. For a summary of the original, see Simon Digby, "The Tuhfa i nasa'ih of Yusuf Gada: An Ethical Treatise in Verse from the Late Fourteenth-Century Delhi Sultanate," in Barbara Daly Metcalf, ed., *Moral Conduct and Authority: The Place of Adab in South Asian Islam* (Berkeley: University of California Press, 1984), 91–123.

66. *Kobi Alaol birochito Tohfa,* ed. Golam Samdani Qoraishi (Dhaka: Bangla Akademi, 1975), chapter 18, 68; chapter 20, 71; chapter 44, 108–109.

67. Mohan Lal, *Travels in the Panjab, Afghanistan, and Turkistan to Balkh, Bokhara and Herat; and a Visit to Great Britain and Germany* (London: W. M. Allen and Company, 1846; rev. ed., Delhi: ICHR, 1977), 97.

68. For patronage of Shiʿa religious complexes by slaves associated with the Bengal governors, see Catherine B. Asher, *Architecture of Mughal India* (Cambridge: Cambridge University Press, 1995), 330–31.

69. William Pinch, "Who Was Himmat Bahadur? Gosains, Rajputs, and the British in Bundelkhand, ca. 1800," *Indian Economic and Social History Review* 35, no. 3 (July–Sept. 1998), 293–335; and Indrani Chatterjee and Sumit Guha, "Slave-Queen, Waif-Prince: Slavery and Social Capital in Eighteenth-Century India," *Indian Economic and Social History Review* 36, no. 2 (Apr.–June 1999), 165–86.

70. Such transformations have been studied in the context of either "conversion" or "communalism" hitherto. For the most recent, see Pradip K. Datta, *Carving Blocs: Communal Ideologies in Early Twentieth-Century Bengal* (Delhi: Oxford University Press, 1999); Francis Robinson, *Islam and Muslim History in South Asia* (New York: Oxford University Press, 2000); and Gail Minault, *Secluded Scholars: Women's Education and Muslim Social Reform in Colonial India* (Delhi: Oxford University Press, 1998); for revisions of older themes, see Barbara D. Metcalf, *Islamic Contestations: Essays on Muslims in India and Pakistan* (New York: Oxford University Press, 2004).

71. See correspondence between the commissioner of Dacca Division and the deputy magistrate of Perozpur, September 1871, in Bengal Judicial (Judicial) Proceedings, December 1871, nos. 185–87 and enclosures, West Bengal State Archives, Kolkata.

72. For comments on slavery in the princely states, see George Lawrence, agent of the governor general (henceforth AGG) for the states of Rajputana to officiating secretary to the government of India (henceforth GOI), January 20, 1862, National Archives of India, New Delhi (henceforth NAI), Foreign Political A, February 1862, no. 51; Political Agent Alwar to AGG, January 8, 1862, NAI, Foreign Political A, February 1862, no. 52; Major R. J. Meade, AGG for Central India, Indore Residency, to Durand, Sec. GOI, October 30, 1862, NAI, Foreign Political A, November 1862, no. 111; and Political Agent for Bundelkhand to AGG for Central India, October 11, 1862, NAI, Foreign Political A, November 1862, no. 112.; for reports on the states of Gwalior, Bhopal, Nimar, Dhar, and Indore, see R. J. Meade to Henry Mortimer Durand, September 15, 1862, NAI, Foreign Political A, October 1862, nos. 7–8.; for Nimar also see inspector general of police, Central Provinces (henceforth C.P.), to secretary to the chief commissioner, C.P., January 24, 1871, NAI, Home Police Proceedings, April 1, 1871, no. 13.

73. Indrani Chatterjee, "Manumission and Imperialist Designs in Central Asia," *Asia Annual,* 2000, 7–26.

74. Joti Govindar Fule, *Gulamgiri: Brahmani adapadaghata, or Slavery in the Civilized British Government under the Cloak of Brahmanism* (1873; 2nd ed., Mumbai: Education Department, Government of Maharashtra, 1991), dedication.

75. See Antoinette Burton, "Tongues Untied: Lord Salisbury's 'Black Man' and the Boundaries of Imperial Democracy," *Comparative Study of Society and History* 42, no. 3 (2000), 632–61. For Gandhi's experience in South Africa, see his *The Story*

of My Experiments with Truth (Navjivan Trust, 1927; reprint, London: Penguin, 1982), 286–89.

76. Bankim Chandra Chatterjee, *Samya,* trans. in M. K. Haldar, *Renaissance and Reaction in Nineteenth Century Bengal: Bankim Chandra Chattopadhyay* (Calcutta: Minerva Press, 1977), 156.

77. See Indrani Chatterjee, "Gossip, Taboo, and Writing Family History," in Chatterjee, ed., *Unfamiliar Relations,* 222–60, for a discussion of Kailashchandra Singha, *Rajamala ba Tripurar Itihasa* (Agartala, 1896).

78. Gurucharan Mahalanobis, *Atmakatha,* in Nareshchandra and Manu Jana, eds., *Atmakatha* (Calcutta: Ananya, 1982), 12–14.

79. Rasasundari Debi, *Autobiography,* trans. Tanika Sarkar (Delhi: Kali for Women, 1999).

80. Haimabati Sen, *Autobiography,* trans. and ed. Tapan Raychaudhuri and Geraldine Forbes (Delhi: Roli Press, 1999), 84–85.

81. Abdul Ghaffur Nassakh, *Khudnawisht sawanih hayat-i-nassakh,* ed. Abdus Subhan (Calcutta: Asiatic Society, 1986), 100–103.

82. *Pandita Ramabai through Her Own Words: Selected Works,* compiled and edited with translations by Meera Kosambi (Delhi: Oxford University Press, 2000), 255, 271.

83: Thomas Ricks, "Slaves and Slave Trading in Shiʻi Iran, A.D. 1500–1900," *Journal of Asian and African Studies* 36, no. 4 (Nov. 2001): 416n4. For a general history of slavery in nineteenth-century Iran, see Behnaz A. Mirzai, "Slavery, the Abolition of the Slave Trade, and the Emancipation of Slaves in Iran (1828–1928)" (Ph.D. diss., York University, 2004). I am grateful to Behnaz for allowing me to read the thesis.

84. Lian H. Sakhong, *Religion and Politics among the Chin People in Burma (1896–1949)* (Uppsala, Sweden: Uppsala University Press, 2000), 112.

85. Janet Hoskins, "Slaves, Brides, and Other Gifts: Resistance, Marriage, and Rank in Eastern Indonesia," *Slavery and Abolition* 25, no. 2 (Aug. 2004), 90–107.

2

War, Servitude, and the Imperial Household: A Study of Palace Women in the Chola Empire

Daud Ali

Problems in Historiography

The nature and history of the forms of servitude and slavery in early medieval India are still not clearly understood. This lack of understanding is only partly due to the sources, which are fragmentary, episodic, and often obscure. More often, formulaic theories of society and colonial definitions of productive work have weighted down the interpretation of available sources. Perhaps unsurprisingly, the most important discussions have taken place around the question of agrestic labor. Some of the initial assessments in this field stretch back to the nineteenth century, when colonial officials sought to understand the land-holding and tenurial systems which they encountered across the subcontinent. In south India, the situation seemed inconsistent, though varieties of agrestic servitude which bore the characteristics of both serfdom and slavery were palpable and widespread.[1] Such debates formed the backdrop for the rise in south India of historical studies of the great lowland empires like the Cholas, though the results have been equally uncertain.

Though the corpus of some ten thousand inscriptions[2] so far recorded from the Chola period (c. 950–1250 CE) in south India (see map 3) constitute an undoubtedly rich bequest when compared with their north Indian counterparts, they by no means present us with an entirely clear picture of contemporary social dynamics. Like nearly all the lithic records from this period, Chola inscriptions are chiefly concerned with temple affairs. Most often they record various types of donations for the establishment and maintenance of services to gods in temples, and do not seek to portray social or economic relationships not directly relevant to such affairs in any systematic fashion. The names, titles, corporate bodies, and financial and revenue arrangements they record give us only an incidental and fragmentary picture of the wider dynamics of Chola society. The records also typically relate to elite groups of the social order, and information relating to the lower echelons of society is indirect at best.

Despite these difficulties, most historians now concur in characterizing the lowest ranks of cultivators, mostly *paraiyar*s and *pallar*s, as substantially "unfree" by the tenth century. Though the precise conditions of this unfreedom are unclear, some of these cultivators appear to have been "owned" by landholders and wealthier cultivators. Yet it has not been definitely resolved whether such ownership constituted "slavery" or "bondedness."[3] At stake in this debate, following Marx, has been the "feudal" or "Asiatic" character of the early medieval state. It appears that this debate has been conducted in a partial vacuum, since there is little evidence for the Chola period which can yield a sense of the scale of unfree labor—the degree to which productive processes as a whole relied on people of such status.[4] The evidence of "ownership" of cultivators leads us to infer that such cultivating serfs or slaves were probably found in areas of intensive irrigated agriculture.

However, the majority of references to slavery are not connected to the transfer of men and women between landowners. The majority refer to the dedication, sale, or gift, by men of various stations, of slaves to temples—the famous *tevaratiyar* (or *devadasi*s) who have been the subject of so much interest in modern times. In many cases, these men and women seem to have been the household or personal servants of the donors in question rather than agrestic laborers granted by landlords.[5] This points to an important lacuna in the historiography to date, a comparative indifference to the apparently widespread practice of domestic servitude and slavery in Chola times. Not only did many *tevaratiyar* probably come from domestic contexts, but they performed similar labors in the temple setting—service and attendance functions, and menial tasks. The temple was, after all, a palatial residence, the house of a god. Many temple servants mentioned in Chola period inscriptions, then, might be usefully considered a special and highly ranked subset of the larger category of domestic and personal servants whose prevalence must have been extensive. This wider world of social relations has yet to receive its due attention. Since nineteenth-century conceptions of productive work largely excluded domestic labor from the analytical field, historiography shaped by such notions has also been disinclined to study the complexity of domestic servitude in medieval south Indian society. In the case of *tevaratiyar*, this indifference has been compounded by the fact that such men and women in many cases seemed to enjoy certain economic and social privileges. Inscriptional references, for example, often record their donations to temples, implying the ability to own property. Their association with religious institutions has predictably created a historiography of "sacrality" and "auspiciousness," obscuring, as Leslie Orr has forcefully demonstrated, both the mundane and quotidian nature of their work as well as the considerable agency they exercised.[6] Orr's careful study of temple women, as well as recent scholarship on domestic slavery in other historical contexts, suggests that historians of medieval south India revisit their records with new questions and sensitivities.

One of the most intractable problems in assessing the status of servile men and women in medieval India is terminological. Though it might be easy to identify "slaves," or *atiyar*, a term derived from the word for "foot" (*ati*)—meaning literally those "at the feet" of another—in the inscriptional records, it is far from certain what such status actually meant.[7] This is in part because of the great importance placed on the language of servitude to represent the reciprocal bonds of affiliation between superiors and inferiors in medieval south India. Relations of hierarchy during Chola times were expressed and experienced through vocabularies of submission, devotion, and intimacy drawn from an existing terminology of servitude and slavery. In courtly and religious contexts the language of servitude was imbricated with power dynamics in particularly complex ways. To assume a posture of exaggerated deference, submission, or even self-deprecation often served to draw attention to the humility, devotion, and even eminence of a man or woman. Slave-status terminology, therefore, is often particularly difficult to understand, as it functioned both as a marker of subordination and as a language of distinction. Moreover, the widespread use of this and related terminologies of subordination to refer to people of varying constraints and privileges suggests a continuum of servitude and lordship rather than clearly opposed categories.

The Organization of Labor in the Imperial Household

This chapter seeks to explore a group of people, mostly women, and the establishments to which they belonged, which are both poorly understood and rarely treated in the historiography of the period—the lower echelons of imperial servants known as *pentattis* who were organized into palace establishments, or *velams*, attached to the Chola household. The working assumption of this chapter, which will be borne out and refined through an examination of the evidence, is that palace women, like their temple counterparts, despite possessing certain privileges, constituted a category of un-free labor. But once again, the treatment of these women in studies of medieval south India has been minimal. The eminent historian Nilakanta Sastri, who, to his credit, took more time than most to consider their status, concluded that "we have to look upon this crowd of personal servants as in the enjoyment of a fair competence in return for generally very light work; the status of the members of the *velam*s was perhaps that of a not unpleasant servitude to which the less sensitive among them might have reconciled themselves in a short time."[8] Such characterizations of domestic labor, perhaps comfortably familiar to historians of the nineteenth century, have remained unchallenged interpretive obstacles to coming to grips with the nature of both the royal household and the gendered labor relations which sustained it.

To convey a sense of the scale of this work force, we may turn to the Chinese traveler Chau Ju-Kua, who claims to have visited south India sometime in the late twelfth or early thirteenth century, and reports that the Chola king retained for his escort some ten thousand "dancing girls," three thousand of whom attended him at a time, in rotation.[9] Such observations are legion among travelers to other parts of India in medieval times, and would seem to be corroborated by a variety of indigenous sources. Architectural and sumptuary manuals rank the majesty of kings by the size of their palaces, the splendor of their regalia, and the number of women attached to their households. Indeed, like the gods who ruled in the heavens, the lordly personages who walked the earth were to be surrounded by a luminous female presence. The imperial king, according to the architectural treatise *Manasara,* was to have an entourage of millions of women.[10] Women like these, so close to imperial authority, yet devoid of the benefit of name or lineage, litter medieval sources. In medieval poetry they appear as voluptuous *nayika*s thronging the streets of the royal city and seeking the attention of the king as he moves in procession. Such representations certainly had pronounced symbolic dimensions relating to both kingship and religious experience, which have been effectively drawn out by scholars like David Shulman and Velcheru Narayana Rao.[11] Yet this scholarship has occasionally dismissed enquiries into the sociological world which formed the backdrop to these exquisite literary depictions.[12] As Cynthia Talbot points out, inscriptions too are literary artefacts, and deserve the same regard as other literary sources.[13] Noboru Karashima has even suggested that scholars deploy other faculties to decipher the "whisperings" of inscriptions on the walls of medieval temples.[14] Only then can we understand the scores of women who appear in inscriptions associated with the Chola household—a category of servants Leslie Orr has usefully called "palace women."[15]

From what we can glean from inscriptions, the Chola kings had complex extended households. In order to secure political alliances with powerful local lineages, they took numerous wives, many of whom probably lived in separate quarters within the royal palace complex.[16] Beyond members of the royal family, there were functionaries at the royal court, whose number and variety grew significantly in the eleventh century. The person of the king was also surrounded by bodyguards as well as hereditary military retainers who were attached to the royal household. Then there were special "intimates" (masc. *anukkan,* fem. *anukki*), "concubines" (*poki*), and "friends" (*saciva*) who enjoyed elevated status and sometimes lordly titles. These people often appear as members of the heterogeneously staffed retinues or entourages (*parivaram*s) of high-ranking family members as they toured the kingdom making religious donations and such. Such people may have been drawn from a wider cadre of domestic servants of lower rank, the men of which were known for a brief period in the eleventh century as "servants," literally "work-sons" (*pani makan*).[17]

Many of these lower-ranking men and women who served the royal household, mentioned in inscriptions, are said to be attached to institutions called *velam*s, a problematic and insufficiently understood term, rendered variously by scholars, but which most likely denoted a collection of palace servants.[18] The handful of references to *velam*s in Tamil inscriptions (and the term's single literary occurrence) all date to the Chola period and the term does not seem to have any prevalence in the literature and epigraphy of either previous or successive royal houses in south India. Chola inscriptions furnish the names of some twenty-seven different *velam*s between the reigns of Parantaka I (907–55) and Kulottunka I (1070–1120). The royal household was often served by many *velam*s at any given time, and some seem to have been quartered outside of the palace itself. The nomenclature of *velam*s gives us some clue as to their organization and function. The titles of many *velam*s clearly derived from the names of members of the royal family and the various titles which they bore, but the royal names in their titles do not seem to provide any certain indication of the persons to whom the services of their members were directed. The royal titles of *velam*s seem to have had a commemorative rather than functional sense. During the reign of Rajaraja I (985–1014), inscriptions at the Chola capital of Tanjavur and elsewhere record the names of no fewer than nine *velam*s bearing different royal titles (most of which were associated with Rajaraja himself), and at least one *velam* named after his queen Pancavanmateviyar.[19] Beyond such titulary names, some *velam*s were designated by terms suggesting more hierarchical and functional roles. Inscriptions of widely differing dates mention the "old" (*palaiya*) and "big" (*periya*) *velam*s, and a single record uses the term *alvar,* referring to junior member(s) of the household.[20] The titles of at least two *velam*s suggest they were named after a particular conquest by the king, and may have indicated the regional origin of their inhabitants—a significant fact in considering the personnel of these palace establishments, below.[21] Various other titles suggest particular functions in the daily routine of the king and royal family. Numerous records across the tenth and eleventh centuries, for example, mention *velam*s connected with the royal bath (*mancanam, tirumancanam*), and occasionally records also refer to *velam*s connected with the handling and supply of ceremonial vessels (*tiruparikalam*) and the performance of protective evening rites (*antikappu*).[22] Many of these more specialized *velam*s are referred to as composed of "select" (*terinta*) personnel, suggesting a hierarchy among the personnel who filled the *velam*s.

The individuals most typically associated with *velam*s were identified as *pentatti*s and, to a lesser extent, *kaikkolar*s. The term *kaikkolar,* literally "of strong arms," referred to a member of a class of apparently hereditary military retainers who often resided near the palace and who formed an integral part of the Chola armies. While a small number of *velam* references mention *kaikkolar*s, the incidence of *kaikkolar*s in Chola inscriptions is far larger, as they often appear as part of the elite military coteries of the Chola kings, being selected for staffing personal entourages (*parivaram*s) and perhaps acting as bodyguards, but at the very least constituting, on occasion (but not always), part of an inner core of permanent troops around the royal household.[23] It may be that these identifications were not mutually exclusive, and that all *kaikkolar*s were in fact associated with *velam*s, but the evidence is far from certain in this regard.[24] Even in early Chola inscriptions, these men possessed a strong corporate identity, which, like that of other hereditary military groups, was transformed into a caste status in post-Chola times.[25]

Female members of *velam*s are almost always described as *pentatti*s, a difficult word because of a long historical sedimentation and multiple usage. Though used in contemporary Tamil (in informal contexts) to mean "wife," in medieval times the term denoted more particularly a woman of generally servile status and most usually one connected with the royal palace in some capacity. It literally meant a woman "ruled" or a "slave/servile woman," but the generic nature of the vocabulary of servility mentioned above prevents any conclusions about the status of such women on the basis of terminology alone.[26] In at least one reference a *pentatti* seems to also be identified with a term which less ambiguously denoted a "slave" (*atiyal*), but for the same reasons this may mean very little.[27] Not all inscriptional references to *pentatti*s mention *velam*s. They are sometimes identified simply by the term or are designated as *pentatti*s of particular members of the royal family or their entourages (*parivaram*).[28] In two cases *pentatti*s are mentioned as cooks for the imperial household.[29] It may be the case that *pentatti* referred to a more generic category of female servant who took on a variety of roles at the Chola court, but the majority of records do place them within *velam*s, and I will assume that this was their typical affiliation.[30]

War and the Gendering of Imperial Households

The inscriptions are for the most part silent as to the origins and identities of *pentatti*s, but we are not entirely bereft of information bearing on this question. Exceptional evidence comes from the late twelfth century, when an inscriptional eulogy (*meykkirtti*) of the Chola king Kulottunka III (1178–1218), describing his protracted struggles with Vira Pandya of Madurai, boasts that, having beaten the Pandya king on the battlefield, he "caused the best of his women to enter his *velam*."[31] A later version of the same eulogy adds that the Chola king caused Vira Pandya's "young queen" to enter his *velam* (*matakkotiyai ve[lam] erri*).[32] Though we have no further record of who these women might have been or their subsequent fate, this record makes it clear that at least one source of women in the *velam* was warfare. To this extent, the status of *pentatti* was born from the violence of war and from an initial but decisive severance from natal kin.

Tamil literature patronized by the Chola court also provides some relevant, if indirect, information on *velam*s and the identities of the women within them. The *Kalinkattupparani,* a poem celebrating the victory of Kulottunka I over the Eastern Ganga king Anantavarman Codaganga, composed by the court poet Cayankontar at the beginning of the twelfth century, devotes its first substantive canto to a long entreaty to the women of the royal city to "open their doors" to the returning Chola army. A string of verses are specifically addressed to women of the *velam*:

> You gentle women of the Pandya country, the flag of which bears the fish, who have entered the *velam* after running through the wilderness in tears, open your doors! Women of Tulunatu, women of Malainatu, give tribute to Kulottunka, from the land of the splashing waters, open the doors to your houses . . . You Karnata women, approaching uttering a confusing mix of beautiful words in Tamil and Vaduku in your gentle speech, open your doors![33]

It is clear enough here that the women of the *velam* were captives of war, taken in the military campaigns of the Chola kings.[34] The practice of capturing or forcibly abducting women as part of annual military campaigns in rival kingdoms is well attested. "Seizing women" is a conventional boast in the royal eulogies that cover the walls of hundreds of Chola-period temples in south India. Medieval south Indian armies traveled with large trains of supporting personnel—children of the royal family, slaves, and various ranks of male and female servants—and if they were routed these people fell into the victor's hands. Chola *meykkirtti*s are often quite particular about the fate of the women captured from their rivals.[35] In some instances they were "defaced"—their noses cut off[36]—and in others they were simply added to the Chola household as war booty. Typical is a *meykkirtti* which boasts that, having defeated the Chalukya king Ahavamalla, the Chola king captured a number of famous elephants and well-bred horses and camels, the banner of the Chalukya army and other insignia of royalty, and in addition the illustrious queens Sattiyavai and Sangappai, as well as lesser wives, along with crowds of women left on the battlefield by the retreating king.[37] The forcible abduction of women of lesser rank from the countryside is also attested. A famous Chalukya inscription dated 1007, at the village of Hottur in contemporary Dharwar district, describes the campaign of a large Chola army from the perspective of the other side, as it "ravaged the whole country, murdering women, children and Brahmans, seizing women (*pendiram pididu*) and overthrowing the order of castes."[38] Though the claims of some *meykkirtti*s seem exaggerated, the repeated emphasis on capture, and the often very specific details given in the accounts, cannot be ignored.

Medieval *ula* (poetic descriptions of royal processions), which focus on the reactions of crowds of women of different ages to the king as he moves through the royal city, also have some significance for locating the origins of these women. One of these describes the crowds of women who lined the royal street during processions as women of diverse birth descended from women brought to the Chola country as war booty from various regions and settled by the king in areas assigned to them by royal order.[39] Though the word *velam* is not used in the poem, the passage clearly invokes these establishments. This arrangement is broadly corroborated by a contemporary Sanskrit text on architecture composed in south India, *Mayamata*, which recommends that the royal street (*rajavithi*) should be lined with mansions (*malika*), where the king's retinue was to reside—these may have been the residences of the *velam*s we hear about in the Tanjavur inscriptions, which extended into the suburbs around the palace, and past which royal processions would have been made, forming the immediate setting of the *ula* as a poetic genre.[40]

Closely related to capture through war was the receipt of women as tribute from subordinate kings, a practice which was not unknown elsewhere in early medieval India. The appearance of women in descriptions of battlefield loot suggests that lower-ranking servants were incorporated into the transactional economy of gifts and tributes between men of lordly rank. The *Kalinkattupparani,* which portrays the magnificence of the assembled Chola court, describes among the annual tribute gifts required of subordinate kings "the forehead bands [*pattam*] of women who are rightfully yours."[41] At least one *pentatti,* a woman who served one of Rajaraja's queens, Pancavan-mateviyar, is known to have been in the Kotantarama velam at Tanjavur, and her name, Vanakovaraiyan Porkali, identifies her with a lineage known to be subordinate to the Cholas. It is possible that this woman, who was clearly not a wife but a servant, was presented as a gift to the Chola family. It is quite likely that the women of the *velam*s entered the palace as a result of the military campaigns of Chola kings or as tribute received from subordinate lords. Indeed, the period when the greatest number of *velam*s are mentioned in the epigraphic record coincides with the successful military campaigns and territorial expansion of the Chola empire in the eleventh century under Rajaraja I and his son Rajendra I.

The extent to which *velam*s were filled with captive and tribute women remains an open question, however, as does whether there were other methods of recruitment into *velam*s. Though *pentatti*s shared a number of characteristics with temple women, there is no existing epigraphic evidence of the presentation, sale, or purchase of *pentatti*s to or by the royal court. It is likely that the mechanisms of war and tribute obviated the need to acquire personnel through purchase. It is also true that such transactions, being irrelevant to temple affairs, would not have appeared in the inscriptional record, and must be inferred indirectly. Important in this regard is an inscription dated to the reign of Kulottunka I, which records the transfer of a number of temple slaves found in the king's retinue back to the temple authorities. This "return" involved removing the king's mark from their bodies and rebranding them with a trident, sign of their proper master.[42] The practice of branding, encountered in a significant handful of temple inscriptions relating to the temple's own slaves, seems to have been a royal practice as well. Thus the confusion of the women in this case offers an extremely suggestive glimpse into such lives. While the lower-ranking women among palace servants clearly overlapped with their temple counterparts, such similarities might in turn have provided avenues for "escape" from one holder to another. However, the temple authorities' reclamation of "their" slaves from the royal entourage also suggests a degree of surveillance of servants, and the fact that marks on servile bodies pronounced the "names" and identities of holders first.

Obviously, such inscriptions disable overly simplistic attributions of gender and identity that assume that the personal names and affiliations of such servants are transparent. For instance, some *pentatti* names appear to be "male."[43] If body-marks spoke of the identities of holders, then there is no necessary identification between the bearer of a name and the persona of the bearer. The "male" named might be the holder of the *pentatti*. However, we could also infer that the bearer of the name, while embodied as a woman, performed tasks that were identified as masculine and might therefore have merited a "socially" male name. Or we could see such names as having been given to androgynous beings in those societies. At the very least, such names ask for a refinement of modern dimorphic perspectives when we engage in gendering the pasts of older societies. *Pentattis* often had compound names, like Katan Accatevi, Kallici Uttamata, or Kari Catti, which raises the question of the significance of each name segment. It is possible that in some cases, paternal names were prefixed to proper names, as has been common practice in south India during more recent times, and, some have argued, was equally so in Chola times.[44] The evidence, however, is far from conclusive. In some compound names, the first element is either clearly feminine or incorporates the name of a deity or place. There is, therefore, no consistent naming pattern among *pentattis*.

Nevertheless, the names of *pentattis* do reveal clear evidence of stratification among the women of the *velam*. Some women may have entered the *velam* with elevated rank—women of high standing given as tribute or captured from the chiefly and royal families of subordinate lineages. For instance, Vanakovaraiyan Porkali, a servant of the Chola queen Pancavanmateviyar in the Kotantarama velam, seems to have retained the title of an earlier affiliation with a feudatory family.[45] Others appeared to have acquired titles of distinction once within the *velam*, like the *pentatti* Tevayan Pulalakkan of the Kilai (Kilanatikal?) velam, who was also known as "Crest-Jewel of the Earth" (Avanisikhamani), and Cattan Ramadevi of the Rajendracola Periya velam, who had the title "Ruby of the Sacred Jambu Fruit" (Tirunnavalmanikkam).[46] The term *manikkam*, or "ruby," seems to have been a title incorporated into a number of personal names of *pentattis* in the eleventh century, and was even more widespread among temple women.[47] Its significance, however, is uncertain. Clearer in meaning are the titles *anukki* and *poki*, which referred to an intimate or concubine of a member of the royal family. In some cases such women appear as donors in inscriptions without any association with *velams*. So we have two records at different temples noting the gift of lamps by one Nankai Cattaparemanar, a "concubine" (*pokiyar*) of the king Aditya I (871–901), and very extensive gifts made by one Nakkan Paravai, identified as an "intimate" (*anukki*) of Rajendra I— neither of which mentions *pentatti* status or affiliation with a *velam*.[48] On the other hand, Cattan Ramadevi, the *pentatti* mentioned above, has the title of "intimate" (*anukki*), suggesting that women of the *velam* were eligible for such distinction.[49] We also have cases of the children of favorites appearing among the women of the *velam*.[50] What these host of titles suggests is that there was considerable scope for favor and advancement among the women of the *velam*.

Such advancement can be assessed along many grids at once. The most obvious is that of their provisioning. Like their temple counterparts, *velam pentattis* received maintenance and appear to have accumulated modest amounts of wealth. It was not unusual, either in northern parts of the subcontinent in this period or in Chola contexts, for slaves and others of servile status attached to powerful households to enjoy specific, albeit circumscribed, privileges and material support. In one record, for example, we have a slave (*atiyal*) donated to the temple with a maintenance grant (*jivanam*) for picking flowers in a temple garden.[51] Once again, while temple inscriptions have much to say about *tevaratiyar,* they provide little information about maintenance arrangements within the palace. The inscriptions relating to *pentattis* indicate only that they were able to donate wealth to temples. As is the case with *tevaratiyar,* most inscriptions relating to *pentattis* record gifts of money for the establishment of perpetual lamps in temples. How *pentattis* acquired this wealth is unclear—it may have been given to them as maintenance (clothes, jewelry, daily or yearly allowances for food or land) by the royal household, or as support from children or others, or it may have accompanied them into servitude.

Given this larger silence, we might gainfully interpret an unusual record (dating from the time of Rajaraja) of the intervention of the palace *kaikkolar*s on behalf of the royal household. The record outlines their attempt to collect payment on a loan that a powerful Brahman member of the local assembly (*sabha*) had taken from a *pentatti* belonging to the Mancanattar velam.[52] The debtor had died and his son had inherited his property, but neither he nor other relatives were willing to settle the debt. So the *sabha* took over the debtor's property and sold the land to the temple to repay the debt. Throughout the entirety of this process the *pentatti* seems to have been a passive conduit of wealth actually held by the royal palace.

Clearly great caution needs to be exercised in attributing control over the use and disposal of such wealth to the *pentattis*. Some inscriptions suggest that the gifts by *pentattis* were made on behalf of brothers, sisters, mothers, or daughters (but never fathers, who remain entirely absent from the limited kin world of the *pentatti*). An eleventh-century inscription from Tiruvisalur, for example, records the gift of temple lamps by a *pentatti* of the Alvar velam for the benefit of her brother Vicchadiran Kunjiramalla and her mother Karoki.[53] Most records, however, do not mention merit-recipients. The great majority of economic and fiscal activities associated with *pentattis* have been recorded in the central region of the Chola empire (Tanjavur, Trichurappalli, and South Arcot districts). They appear to follow the patterns of, or are made in conjunction with, queens and other members of the royal household. They rarely appear in isolation. So during the reign of Aditya II we find separate records of some ten donations by various members of the royal household, including the queen Sembiyanmateviyar, two *pentattis*, and members of five different *kaikkolar* units, apparently donated on the same occasion, to the Anantesvarasvamin temple in Utaiyarkuti, South Arcot.[54] At this stage, we can only speculate that the merit accruing from the "gifts" and donations they made to the temples may have been meant to be shared with the other, more important, donors who sometimes accompanied them. Given the often collective and ritualized nature of religious gifts and the potentially more complex property relations which may have underlain them, it would be hasty to assume that gifts donated by *pentattis* merely represented personally accumulated wealth which could be disposed of at will.

The Reproduction of Devotion

Another way to understand the stratification and advancement of *pentattis* is by exploring the multiple relationships around which *pentatti* lives were structured. Literary texts of the period portray palace women of all ages. In fact, the court literature pays acute attention to the ages of women who formed part of the retinues of Chola kings. The *ula* genre mentioned above is structured around the calibration of a woman's life into seven distinct stages (*elu paruva makalir*) from age five to forty-four.[55] These "stages," which are not attested in pre-Chola literature, notably exclude both infancy and old age, but cross the threshold of sexual maturity. Almost half of these, from the age of five to fourteen, concern prepubescent girls, and the others relate to sexually mature women. This is explicitly recognized in the poetic descriptions of the first three types of young girls (*petai, petumpai,* and *mankai*), which focus extensively on the minutiae of their physical maturation and their impending sexualization. The significant point about these stages is that they seem to reflect a categorization of women not simply as sexual objects, but as *potential* sexual objects—suggesting an unstated transactional economy in which women were scrutinized and valued in relation to the specific degree of their maturity.

Judging from this sexualization of bodies and languages used to describe "palace women" in court literature, the dynamics of favor for women of the *velam* appear to have been closely tied to sexual relationships with members of the royal household. However, the contribution of the literary genres in situating the advancement of female servants through the palace or temple bureaucracy in the language of "favor" and personal "intimacy" should not be overlooked at the same time. Take, for instance, the language of intimacy deployed by the *ula* genre in its treatment of the various generations of women in the king's retinue. The *petai* (ages five to eight), close to the side of their mothers, their bodies "like fresh and tender leaves" and eyes like drops of honey, are not attracted to the king's physical beauty, but become fixated on the garland he wears.[56] The garland (a sign of favor to be bestowed by the king) is extremely difficult to obtain, explain their mothers, and the girls break into tears as the king moves off down the street. With each successive stage, as the sexual maturity of the girl advances, so does the transformation of her desire, until the entire range of emotions of love in separation are experienced by the retinue of waiting women of different ages. Though there is certainly an artificial and formulaic element to the genre, it nevertheless envisions the feminine transition into maturity as at once a romantic fantasy and a quest for intimacy and favor. While these horizons of possibility are suggested by the literati for the young *pentatti,* inscriptional evidence does not corroborate the favor of such intimacy in any precise form.

None of the children of *pentatti*s we find in inscriptions mention their paternity, and we thus have no way of understanding who their fathers were. This absence is significant in itself, for the mothers seem never to have had the benefit of legalized marriage. The corresponding ambiguity and invisibility of the sexual relationships of the *pentatti* makes tracing conjugal and natal kin of these women particularly fraught. Leslie Orr has even suggested that the names of many *tevaratiyar* in the inscriptions may not indicate kinship affiliations of any sort.[57] Name segments aside, in no instances are *pentatti*s explicitly identified as either the daughters or wives of men, even when their own children are mentioned. This absence of male kin remains in stark contrast to the contemporary identification of women from the high-status castes and points markedly to the disconnection from natal and conjugal kin experienced by *pentatti*s.[58] As though in compensation, and underlining the importance of being "related" at all times, many temple slaves were designated "daughters of god" and male palace servants as "work sons" (*pani makan*). Whatever the connotations of this quasi-kin terminology, the men and women of the *velam* did not define themselves through normative natal and conjugal kin relations.

The only kin definitively mentioned in connection with *pentatti*s are their children. In a number of records donors identify themselves as the sons or daughters of *pentatti*s, in some cases making gifts on behalf of or with their mothers.[59] When children do appear in inscriptions, references to their paternity are usually absent. The fate of these children in relation to the complex of institutions surrounding the court is not certain. Young males may have entered the ranks of *kaikkolars*, as we have two instances of *kaikkolars* either making grants on behalf of *velam* women or identifying themselves as children of a *velam pentatti*.[60] This might fit well with the evidence we have from separate records, mentioned above, which identify *kaikkolars* themselves as members of *velams*.[61] But most inscriptional references to *kaikkolars* do not mention *velam* affiliations, but instead note their connection to units within the Chola army—which of course does not preclude their originating from *pentattis*. But *kaikkolars* could rise to higher ranks within the court hierarchy, and we have records suggesting they were sometimes attached to the personal retinues of various members of the royal household and in some cases enjoyed service tenures known as *virabhoga* by order of the king.[62] Whatever the case, there seems to have been some special relationship between *kaikkolars* and *velam* women. They often appear together as donors in clusters of inscriptions at key temples. This seemingly special connection between *velam pentattis* and *kaikkolar* units also seems to fit with the *Kalinkattupparani*'s request to the women of the *velam* that they "open the doors" to the returning soldiery of the Chola army. It is thus likely that one important function of the *velam*, as Nilakanta Sastri hinted at long ago, was to supply the Chola court with a regular source of loyal military retainers whose links (and loyalties) were confined entirely to the extended household and its master.[63]

As for the female children of *pentattis*, they are even more invisible in the epigraphic record, as we come across only occasional references to daughters or sisters in connection with *pentattis*. But this hardly rules out the very likely possibility that the daughters of *pentattis* were born into the same condition as their mothers.[64] The comparative frequency of *pentattis* themselves in the inscriptions across many generations may account for the absence of explicitly identified daughters. The preponderance of females in the *velam* may not be so surprising, for if *pentatti* mothers did not identify themselves with their natal or conjugal kin, being instead identified entirely with the extended household of the royal family, their daughters may have been expected to follow a similar path, while sons would have had the option of pursuing military service and its wider network of affiliations.

Conclusion

In bringing this review of the evidence to a close I would like to summarize a few features of the world of *velams* and *pentattis*. *Velams*, collections of palace servants organized around the daily needs of members of the Chola royal household, seem to have been large institutions which flourished during periods of Chola imperial expansion. They were staffed largely, but not entirely, by women, who were at least in part acquired through tribute and capture during war, but perhaps also through purchase or birth into servile status. The most notable aspect of the identities of these women, known as *pentatti*s, as they appear in the epigraphic record, is a lack of identification with natal and conjugal kin groups. *Velam*s thus seem to have been institutions of those who had been natally alienated through violence or some other process, a very significant fact considering the importance of kin and lineage among the ruling elite in medieval south India. But this may have had its advantages for the royal household, as it made *velam*s ideal reproductive pools for developing a cadre of men loyal to the royal family alone, a fact which may explain their ongoing links with *kaikkolar*s. But natal alienation, combined with their apparently multigenerational presence at the Chola court, their sexualization in contemporary literary sources, their association with tribute and war capture, and even their enjoyment of privileges by virtue of attachment to the royal household, all suggest that the women of the *velam*s were far from voluntary members of the Chola imperial service, as they are sometimes portrayed. While the sources do not allow us to draw more subtle distinctions between *pentatti*s and temple slaves, with whom they seem to have had so much in common, the evidence suggests that both sorts of women participated in a common world of servitude whose lineaments are far wider and more significant than scholars have been willing to admit.

Notes

I would like to thank Sascha Ebeling, A. Murugaiyan, Y. Subbarayalu, S. Swaminathan, and especially Leslie Orr and P. Sundaram for discussions in person and through e-mail of various readings of inscriptions. Leslie Orr was particularly generous in sharing her extensive knowledge of women in Tamil inscriptions. I would also like to thank Indrani Chatterjee for a very careful reading of the essay, which has benefited greatly from her suggestions.

1. See Dharma Kumar, *Land and Caste in South India: Agricultural Labour in the Madras Presidency during the Nineteenth Century* (Cambridge: Cambridge University Press, 1965), 49–55.

2. Some three thousand inscriptions have been published in various journals, including *South Indian Inscriptions* (henceforth *SII*), *Epigraphia Indica* (*EI*), and *Travancore Archaeological Series* (*TAS*), while the remaining unpublished inscriptions have been noted in the *Annual Report on Indian Epigraphy* (henceforth *ARE*), published by the Archaeological Survey of India, and are available in estampage or transcription form only. Citations of epigraphical publications will give the volume number followed by the inscription number or, for citations of the *Annual Report on Indian Epigraphy,* the inscription number followed by the year.

3. See Y. Subbarayalu, *Studies in Cola History* (Chennai: Surabhi Pathippakam, 2001), 92; and Kesavan Veluthat, *The Political Structure of Early Medieval South India* (Bombay: Orient Longman, 1993), 230–31.

4. James Heitzman, *Gifts of Power: Lordship in an Early Indian State* (New Delhi: Oxford University Press, 1997), 69.

5. Ibid., 68.

6. Leslie C. Orr, *Donors, Devotees, and Daughters of God: Temple Women in Medieval Tamilnadu* (New York: Oxford University Press, 2000).

7. See the useful discussion in Orr, *Donors, Devotees, and Daughters,* 52–53.

8. K. A. Nilakanta Sastri, *The Colas,* 2nd ed. (Madras: University of Madras, 1955), 450.

9. Reported originally in the account called *Ling-wai-tai-ta.* See *Chau Ju-Kua: His Work on the Chinese and Arab Trade in the Twelfth and Thirteenth Centuries Entitled Chu-fan-chi,* trans. F. Hirth and W. W. Rockhill (Taipei: Cheng Wen Publishing Co., 1970), 95, 100.

10. See *Manasara,* ed. and trans. P. K. Acharya (Delhi: Oriental Reprints, 1980), 41.10–43.

11. See David Shulman, *The King and the Clown in South Indian Myth and Poetry* (Princeton, N.J.: Princeton University Press, 1985), esp. 303–39; and Velcheru Narayana Rao, David Shulman, and Sanjay Subrahmanyam, *Symbols of Substance: Court and State in Nayaka Period Tamilnadu* (Delhi: Oxford University Press, 1992), 57 ff.

12. See the remarks of Narayana Rao, Shulman, and Subrahmanyam on the utility of inscriptions as historical sources, in *Symbols of Substance,* 31.

13. Cynthia Talbot, *Precolonial India in Practice: Society, Region, and Identity in Medieval Andhra* (New York: Oxford University Press, 2001), 8–9.

14. Noboru Karashima, "Whispering of Inscriptions," in Kenneth R. Hall, ed., *Structure and Society in Early South India: Essays in Honour of Noboru Karashima* (Delhi: Oxford University Press, 2002), 56–57.

15. See Orr, *Donors, Devotees, and Daughters,* 40–41.

16. At least two kings in the tenth century, Parantaka I (907–55) and Uttamacola (979–85), are known to have had at least ten wives each. Notable are the marriages secured with the Malaiyamans of Miladu, the Malavars of Maladu, and the Irukkuvels of Kodambalur, as well as the Vallavaraiyar and Paluvettaraiyar lineages. See George Spencer, "Ties that Bind: Royal Marriage Alliance in the Chola Period," *Proceedings of the Fourth International Symposium on Asian Studies* (Hong Kong: Asian Research Service, 1982), 717–36.

17. Subbarayalu, *Studies in Cola History,* 107.

18. See T. N. Subramaniam, "Glossary," in *South Indian Temple Inscriptions* (Madras: Government Oriental Manuscript Library, 1957), vol. 3, pt. 2, s.v. *velam;* Nilakanta Sastri, *The Colas,* 449–51; B. Venkataraman, *Rajarajesvaram: The Pinnacle of Chola Art* (Madras: Mudgala Trust, 1985), 251; Heitzman, *Gifts of Power,* 149; and most usefully, Y. Subbarayalu, *Tamil Kalvettuc Collakarati* (Chennai: Canti Cathana, 2002), s.v. *velam.*

19. For *velam*s referring to titles of the royal family during the reign of Rajaraja I, see *SII* 2.94; *SII* 2.95; *ARE* 340 of 1927; *ARE* 62 of 1928; *SII* 7.678; *SII* 26.669; *SII* 23.342; *SII* 23.278; and *SII* 23.356.

20. For mention of the Palaiya velam, see *SII* 3.204 and *SII* 5.697. For the Periya velam, see *SII* 17.480; *SII* 19.10; *ARE* 106 of 1925; *SII* 22.291; *ARE* 401 of 1921; and

ARE 424 of 1962. For the Alvar velam, see *SII* 23.45; and on the significance of the term *alvar,* see Nilakanta Sastri, *The Colas,* 142.

21. These are the Pandi velam and the Rajaraja terinda Pandi tirumancanattar velam, both mentioned at Tanjavur (*SII* 2.94; *SII* 2.95), which I take not only as commemorating Chola victories over the rival Pandya dynasty but as indicating that they were at least partly staffed by women captured during these campaigns. Though it is possible (though unlikely) that "Pandi," in the title "Pandi velam," may have referred to a title borne by Rajaraja I, this would seem to be precluded by the title "Rajaraja terinda Pandi tirumancanattar velam," which would be more logically rendered as the "*velam* known as Rajaraja of those from the Pandya kingdom selected for the ceremonial bath."

22. *SII* 19.193; *SII* 22.27; *SII* 8.678; *SII* 2.94 and 95; *ARE* 323 of 1927; *ARE* 142 of 1919; and *ARE* 212 of 1911.

23. See P. Sundaram, "Chola and Other Armies—Organization," in S. N. Prasad, ed., *Historical Perspectives of Warfare in India: Some Morale and Matériel Determinants* (New Delhi: Centre for Studies in Civilizations, 2002), 190–91.

24. L. Thyagarajan has argued this position, and consequently interpreted the *velam* as a military barracks. See Pierre Pichard et al., *Vingt ans après Tanjavur, Gangaikondacholapuram,* 2 vols. (Paris: Ecole française d'Extrême-Orient, 1994), 1:184.

25. Later the term *kaikkolar* came to denote a caste of weavers tracing their origin to military groups of ancient times, but in Chola inscriptions the term referred exclusively to military units. See Nilakanta Sastri, *The Colas,* 454 and passim; also Heitzman, *Gifts of Power,* 150; and Subbarayalu, *Studies in Cola History,* 108.

26. The word is formed by adding the suffix -*al* (a verbal root meaning "to rule, receive, control, or maintain," or a noun meaning "man, servant, slave, laborer") to the noun *pen,* meaning "woman." See Orr, *Donors, Devotees, and Daughters,* 212n5.

27. The spelling is irregular and probably a scribal error; see *SII* 23.278.

28. See *ARE* 88 of 1928 and 69 of 1926; and *SII* 5.700.

29. *SII* 19.98; and *TAS* 1.8.1.

30. It is difficult to know whether the absence of *velam* affiliations for *pentattis* was accidental or indicates a wider usage of the term. In her survey of women in Chola inscriptions, Leslie Orr has identified forty-one instances of *pentattis* in Chola inscriptions, with twenty-six (over 60 percent) mentioning some association with a *velam* (Orr, *Donors, Devotees, and Daughters,* 212n5). My own data suggests a slightly higher number. We also have an instance in the tenth century of two adjacent inscriptions at Utaiyarkuti (South Arcot) commemorating gifts probably made on the same occasion by two women, one identified as "singing" in the Periya velam at Tanjavur and the other simply as a *pentatti, SII* 19.10, 12. The apparently accidental omission of the term *pentatti* in the first inscription may parallel the omission of a *velam* affiliation in the latter.

31. *SII* 22.42; also *ARE* 254 of 1925.

32. *SII* 3.88.

33. *Kalinkattupparani,* ed. Pe. Palanivela Pillai (Chennai: South India Saiva Siddhanta Publishing Works, 1961), vv. 40–43.

34. See C. Ilavaracu, *Parani Ilakkiyankal* (Chidambaram: Manivacakar Nulakam, 1978), 53–54. Ilavaracu contends that among the women of the royal capital depicted in the second canto were contingents of women received as tribute from subordinate rulers or captured during wars in other kingdoms.

35. See especially the *meykkirtti*s of Rajendra I's successors, particularly Rajendra II (1052–64), *SII* 22.80; and Virarajendra (1063–70), *EI* 21.38.

36. The *meykkirtti*s of Virarajendra often boast that the Cholas decapitated the dead body of the Chalukya *mahadandanayaka* Chamundaraja and severed the nose of his only daughter, the beautiful Nagalai, the queen of Irugaiyan, *EI* 21.38; *SII* 3.20. An inscription of Rajadhiraja (1018–54) says the same with regard to a Pandyan king's mother, *SII* 3.28.

37. *SII* 3.29.

38. *EI* 16.11a.

39. "Iracaracacolanula," in *Muvarula,* ed. U. V. Caminathaiyar (Chennai: U. V. C minathaiyar Nul Nilaiyam, 1992), vv. 70–79. Also see the remarks of G. Thirumavalavan, *Political, Social, and Cultural History of the Cholas as Gleaned from the Ula Literature* (Thiruvathipuram: Ezhilagam Publishers, 1991), 134–35.

40. *Mayamata: Traité sanskrit d'architecture,* ed. and trans. Bruno Dagens (Pondichéry: Institut français indologie, 1970), 10.74–75.

41. *Kalinkattupparani,* v. 336.

42. *ARE* 141 of 1922, discussed in Nilakanta Sastri, *The Colas,* 556.

43. As in the case of a *pentatti* of the Melai velam with the single name Raman, *ARE* 340 of 1927. It is also possible that men were given the title *pentatti* (personal communication of P. Sundaram), but this is difficult to confirm.

44. On the practices of naming in medieval south Indian inscriptions, see Noboru Karashima, Y. Subbarayalu, and Toru Matsui's introduction to their *A Concordance to the Names in the Cola Inscriptions* (Madurai: Sarvodaya Ilakkiya Pannai, 1979), 1:ix–lxvii.

45. *SII* 23.278.

46. *SII* 3.201; and *ARE* 424 of 1962.

47. *SII* 22.291l and *ARE* 323 of 1927. On the occurrence of the title among *tevaratiyar,* see Orr, *Donors, Devotees, and Daughters,* 148.

48. *SII* 23.219; *SII* 23.247; and *SII* 4.223.

49. *ARE* 401 of 1921.

50. One At[n]ukkan Mahamalli, of the Utaiyar Iracakesari velam, appears as the mother of a *kaikkolar* donor, *SII* 26.669.

51. *SII* 22.141, discussed along with other cases by Orr, *Donors, Devotees, and Daughters,* 127.

52. *SII* 22.27.

53. *SII* 23.45. See also *ARE* 212 of 1911 and *SII* 17.480.

54. *SII* 19.10 ff.

55. They are *petai* (5–8), *petumpai* (8–11), *mankai* (12–14), *matantai* (15–19), *arivai* (20–25), *terivai* (25–32), and *perilam pen* (32–44). This division is unknown in earlier literature, and is elaborated in the *pattiyal* poetic texts, the earliest of which is the anonymous *Panniruppattiyal,* published with the commentary of K. R. Kovintaraca Mutaliyar (Tinnevelly: South India Saiva Siddhanta Publishing Works, 1963), vv. 131–38. While the specific age spans of each category differ in different *pattiyal* texts, they all embody the logic of progression from sexual immaturity to maturity.

56. "Vikkiramacolanula," in *Muvarula,* vv. 112 ff.

57. Orr's findings suggest that most women did not incorporate the names of their fathers into their own. *Donors, Devotees, and Daughters,* 147, 248n16.

58. Ibid., 154–55.

59. See *SII* 17.530 for a gift by the children (*makkal*) of a *pentatti* of the Kila-natikal velam; *SII* 17.480 for a gift by a man for his elder sister, who is identified as the daughter of a *pentatti* of the Periya velam; and *ARE* 63 and 64 of 1928 for a joint gift by a *pentatti* and her daughter, both residents of the Sivapadasekhara terinta tirumancanattar velam.

60. See *SII* 26.669 for a *kaikkolar* whose mother was a *pentatti* in the Iracakesari velam; and *SII* 23.356 for a *kaikkolar* making gifts for various women in the Kotanta velam. The editors have assumed in the latter case that the women were relatives of the donor, though the inscription does not indicate what relation the donor may have had to the women of the *velam*.

61. We have one tenth-century record of a *kaikkolar* in the *velam* of Peruma-natikal Mateviyar, *SII* 4.536; and four twelfth-century records, *SII* 5.697; *SII* 5.698; *SII* 23.279; and *SII* 23.281.

62. See *ARE* 69 and 72 of 1926, where the village of Kulottunkacolanallur is des-ignated as *virabhoga* for *kaikkolar*s from Merka-natu who were of lesser (*ciruda-nam*) rank and served in the palace at Gangaikondacholapuram.

63. P. Sundaram has also suggested that *velam*s were training establishments for Chola military personnel. "Chola and Other Armies—Organization," 191.

64. This is in fact the implication of the *Iracaracacolanula,* which speaks of gen-erations of women from different lands living by the order of the king.

3

Turkish Slaves on Islam's Indian Frontier

PETER JACKSON

In his *Ta'rikh-i Firuz Shahi*, written in 1357, the Delhi historian Ziya al-Din Barani scathingly contrasts men of illustrious birth with those "bought for money."[1] He was referring to *amir*s (commanders) who had been purchased as slaves, though for him they were just one category of the low-born among many. Elsewhere in this work—as in the *Fatawa-yi Jahandari*, a "Mirror for Princes" in the Persian tradition, which he produced a few years later—he leaves the reader in no doubt that he sees high birth as a prerequisite for office.[2] Yet the Turkish military slave (Arabic *ghulam, mamluk;* Persian *banda*) had a long and venerable history in the Muslim world: when the Delhi Sultanate came into existence in c. 1210–11, such troops had already been active on Islam's Indian frontier for almost three hundred years. In an article published some years ago, I examined the role of Turkish slave-*amir*s in the tangled politics of the mid-thirteenth-century Delhi Sultanate;[3] here I shall confine my attention to the early history of Turkish slaves in India down to the first decades of the sultanate's history.

Historical Background

The ninth-century 'Abbasid caliphs had first recruited Turks from Central Asia as an elite guard corps in their successive capitals, Baghdad and Samarra. To what extent these were technically slaves has been questioned, and it has been proposed that the men who appear in the sources are often free in status and belong more to the tradition of the *comitatus,* the warband.[4] Whatever the individual case, some were certainly *ghulam*s, and the use of slave-soldiers became increasingly widespread. As the 'Abbasid empire disintegrated and real power passed into the hands of hereditary provincial governors, they in turn buttressed their illegitimate rule by recruiting Turkish slave-contingents of their own. A few of these upstarts were themselves *ghulam*s. Both Alptegin, who carved out a quasi-independent principality at Ghazni around 962, and Sebuktegin, the effective founder of the Yaminid or Ghaznawid dynasty (977–1186), which would carry Muslim arms deep into the Panjab, were Turkish slave-officers (see map 1).

The Ghaznawids' nemesis, the Shansabanid or Ghurid dynasty (early twelfth century to 1215–16), also maintained Turkish slaves by the beginning of the reign of Ghiyas al-Din Muhammad b. Sam (1163–1203).[5] His brother and successor, Mu'izz al-Din Muhammad (d. 1206), is said to have been especially keen to acquire them.[6] As the subjugation of the Jamuna-Ganges *doab* gathered pace in the mid-1190s, he largely entrusted his new conquests to his slave-officers, rather than to Ghuris, Tajiks, or other Turks of free status.[7] It was one of these, Qutb al-Din Aybak (d. 1210), who was to lay the foundations of an independent Muslim state in India, and Aybak's own *ghulam*, Shams al-Din Iltutmish (d. 1236), who would be the real architect of the Delhi Sultanate.

Functions

By the eleventh century, then, Turkish slave-regiments formed the nucleus of most armies in the eastern Islamic world. Even Turkish dynasties whose power was initially based on a mass nomadic following, like the Qarakhanids (tenth–early thirteenth centuries) in Transoxiana and Turkestan and the Seljuks (1040–1194) in Iran and the Near East, employed them.[8] *Ghulam* officers might be favored as an instrument of despotism—as a highly disciplined counterweight to an indigenous aristocracy or to tribal leaders for whom a monarch was simply *primus inter pares*.[9] In addition to holding high rank in the military, such as that of military chamberlain (*hajib, amir-hajib*), favored Turkish *ghulam*s filled ceremonial positions at court. Under the Ghaznawids and the early Delhi sultans, we find them serving as cupbearer (*tasht-dar*), holder of the royal parasol (*chatr-dar*), intendant of the royal stable (*amir-i akhur*), and so on. It is true that the Turkish general Ahmad Inaltegin is described as treasurer (*khazin*) to Mahmud of Ghazni.[10] This office was usually entrusted to members of the Persian bureaucratic class, but from a hint by the Ghaznawid historian Bayhaqi that Mahmud was possibly Ahmad Inaltegin's father, there is reason to doubt that he was a first-generation *ghulam*.[11] Ahmad's mother may have been the child of a Turkish slave, or he himself may have been a free-status Turkish immigrant.

The impulse to purchase Turkish *ghulam*s in significant numbers was sometimes clearly a matter of military exigency. The Ghurids, whose own subjects were a people of the uplands (*jibal*) accustomed to infantry combat, presumably bought Turks in order to develop a strong cavalry arm, and in particular to amass a corps of mounted archers.[12] There is no solid evidence regarding the training of Ghaznawid *ghulams*,[13] or indeed of any other slave-troops outside the Mamluk Sultanate of Egypt, and such meager information as the Delhi historian Juzjani (c. 1260) supplies about the training of the sultanate's Turkish slave-commanders amounts to no more than vague allusions to archery (*tir-andazi*) and horsemanship (*sawari*).[14] Yet we should note, at this juncture, that the *ghulams*' value to their employers did not reside in the celebrated skills of the light-cavalry archer. The tradition of fighting as heavy cavalry also existed in certain regions of the steppe, and Turkish slave-troops were trained to fight in this manner, with weapons like the mace (*gurz*), rather than as lightly armed mounted bowmen.[15] It is generally accepted that under the ʿAbbasids relatively small numbers of these heavily armed and highly skilled warriors had supplanted the larger infantry armies of an earlier era.[16] Doubtless their value in the Indian subcontinent lay in the ability of such a small but superb force to tilt the fortunes of an engagement.[17]

Reliable numbers are elusive. Juzjani—a late source in this respect—tells us that Mahmud of Ghazni's court was guarded by four thousand Turkish slave-youths, armed with maces;[18] the figure seems to have been derived from the description by Bayhaqi of a caliphal embassy in 1031–32.[19] The figure of ten thousand actually cited on the authority of a caliphal envoy to Mahmud, and found elsewhere,[20] may well reflect, rather, the total number of Turkish *ghulams* in the army.[21] We are given no indication of how many Turkish *ghulams* were in the service of the later Ghurids at any time or what numbers were maintained by the early sultans of Delhi.

Information as to the equipment and attire of these slave-guards is also non-existent after the Ghaznawid era, when Bayhaqi furnishes detailed descriptions of the ceremonial apparel of the Turkish *ghulams*, with their rich robes, bejeweled belts and sashes, and weapons decorated with gold and silver.[22] The remains of mural paintings found in the audience hall of the Ghaznawid palace at Lashkar-i Bazar are strikingly evocative of Bayhaqi's data. They depict forty-four figures, each clad in a sumptuously decorated kaftan and carrying on the left shoulder the haft of what is probably a mace. The facings, and the fact that various items, including a wallet, are suspended from the belt, are reminiscent of Central Asia; and although the heads are almost totally obscured, the face of a beardless adolescent with evidently Central Asian features has survived in an adjacent room.[23] It is generally assumed, therefore, that the subjects of these paintings are the Ghaznawid sultan's Turkish guards. It would doubtless be hazardous, however, to assume that the military slaves of, for example, the early Delhi Sultanate presented much the same appearance.

Provenance

The tribal background of Turkish slave-soldiers varied considerably. One circumstance that helps to cloud the matter of origin is the tendency of Muslim writers to lump together the non-Muslim peoples of the northern and eastern regions under the general designation of "Turks." Thus several Arabic and Persian geographical works class the Hungarians (*Majar*), Slavs (*Saqaliba*), and Greeks (*Rum*) as Turks. The Arabic narrative sources that furnish us with data about the Seljukid and Ayyubid empires or, later, the Mamluk state distinguish the Slavs, for instance, from the Turks when referring to the background of slaves. But this is not the case with the smaller corpus of Persian authors on whom we are dependent for information about the eastern Islamic world, and for whom the ranks of the Turkish peoples are often swollen also by Tibetans or nomadic peoples of Mongolian ("Tatar") type from eastern Asia.[24] Notable among this last category were the Khitan, a people who had ruled over part of northern China as the Liao dynasty (907–1125), and the Qara-Khitan, refugees from the defunct Khitan regime who had migrated westward: they founded an empire that dominated Central Asia (1128–1218), including Muslim states such as Khwarazm and the fragmented Qarakhanid polity, until it collapsed under pressure from the advancing Mongols and the steppe peoples they had dislodged.

The Ghaznawid slave-contingents had included men from the Qarluq (from whom, possibly, the Qarakhanids themselves had sprung),[25] Yaghma, Tukhsi, and Chigil tribes, all of whom nomadized in the region of the Issik Kul and more or less acknowledged the authority of the Qarakhanid sovereigns; from the Qarakhanid towns of Kashghar and Barskhan (this last town the birthplace of Sebuktegin); and from Khotan, the center of a Buddhist kingdom which in the early eleventh century had only recently been reduced by the Qarakhanids. It should be noted, of course, that at this date by no means all the Qarakhanids' subjects, whether nomads or town-dwellers, would have been Muslims. Slaves are also mentioned from among the Kimek, the Qayi, and the Qirghiz, whose lands lay at a greater distance to the east, toward Mongolia, and who at this stage were undoubtedly pagans.[26] In addition, control of Khwarazm and the Dihistan region gave the Ghaznawid sultans, and subsequently the Seljuks, access to the nomadic peoples of the Pontic and Caspian steppes, who were largely untouched by Islam until the Mongol era. From the mid-eleventh century, these were the grazing grounds of the confederacy known to the Muslims as the Qipchaq, to the Byzantines as the Cumans, and to the Rus as the Polovtsy.[27]

The Pontic and Caspian steppes would attain a greater prominence as a source of Turkish *ghulams* in the first half of the thirteenth century. The Delhi historian Juzjani, compiling his *Tabaqat-i Nasiri* in c. 1260, devotes the penultimate *tabaqa* to biographies of twenty-five Shamsis, i.e., slave-*amirs* of the first Delhi sultan, Iltutmish; the list is by no means exhaustive and the criteria used by Juzjani in his selection are unclear, though his own patron, the future sultan Ghiyas al-Din Balban (1266–86), is naturally accorded the longest biography. In some cases tribal origins are not given. Three, however, are described as *Rumis* (i.e., Greeks or possibly Slavs or Bulgars who had arrived from the Byzantine territories).[28] Two came from the Qara-Khitan;[29] so also, in all probability, did two others, described as "Khitaʾis":[30] in any event, rather than being themselves ethnically Khitan, they may simply have belonged to peoples who were subject to the Qara-Khitan empire. Six other slaves are said to have originated from the Qipchaq confederacy;[31] and three more, including Balban, belonged to Iltutmish's own tribe, the Olberli, a subgroup of the Qipchaq (or possibly of the Qangli, a closely related people who were their eastern neighbors and whose pasturelands extended from the Ural River to the Aral Sea).[32]

Such a high proportion of the Shamsi slaves whose origins are specified came from the Pontic and Caspian steppes because of the upheavals caused by the Mongol campaigns in these regions in 1222–23 and 1236–39.[33] In 1253 the Franciscan missionary William of Rubruck, on his way through the Crimea, would hear an eyewitness describe the pitiful condition of the Qipchaq ("Cumans") who, in terror of the Mongols, had crowded into the peninsula, the living eating the dying in desperation.[34] Many of the fugitives surely ended up as slaves in Anatolia, as did Baybars, the future Mamluk sultan of Egypt (1260–77) and himself (like Iltutmish and Balban) an Olberli, who was treacherously seized by a local chieftain and bundled off to the market at Sivas.[35] A glut in the supply of Qipchaq slaves by the 1240s, which certainly fed the ambitions of the Ayyubid sultan of Egypt and enabled him to build up a corps of mamluks,[36] is just one aspect of the strikingly widespread and prolonged diaspora unleashed by the Mongol conquests. That diaspora, which in part resulted from the Mongols' deliberate dispersal of subject Turkish peoples across the breadth of their empire,[37] also included the migration of numerous Muslim nobles, scholars, and soldiers from Central Asia into India during the 1220s and 1230s; and the westward migration of Qipchaq/Cumans, into Hungary and the Balkans (1239–41), and of Khwarazmians (largely former Qipchaq auxiliaries of the Khwarazm-Shah), first into Persia and thence (from c. 1231) into Mesopotamia and (in 1244) Syria.[38]

Many Turkish slaves who reached India in the late twelfth and early thirteenth centuries, prior to the advent of the Mongols, would have been prisoners captured in the frequent conflicts that involved the Qara-Khitan. Just as Mahmud of Ghazni had repeatedly clashed with the Qarakhanids, so the Ghurid sultans Ghiyas al-Din and Mu'izz al-Din engaged in a bitter struggle with the Khwarazm-Shahs around the turn of the twelfth century, and on occasion the Qara-Khitan came to the aid of their client. In 1198 and 1205 the Ghurid ruler of Bamiyan wrested Balkh and Tirmiz respectively from their Qara-Khitan garrisons,[39] and in 1204 Mu'izz al-Din's attempt to invade Khwarazm itself suffered a decisive check at the hands of the Qara-Khitan and their subordinates near Andkhud (now Andkhoi). After the Khwarazm-Shah Muhammad b. Tekish repudiated the suzerainty of the Qara-Khitan in c. 1208, "Khita'is" would have been taken prisoner in the battles that brought him control over Transoxiana and other regions to the east.[40]

Turkish slaves also reached the Ghurids and their successors, the Delhi sultans, through a flourishing commercial traffic. In the 1330s the Moroccan visitor Ibn Battuta heard that Iltutmish had sent agents to Transoxiana to buy slaves on his behalf;[41] and slave merchants may have followed the sultan as he moved around northern India on campaign, since he bought one future *amir* while investing Mandor, in Rajasthan, in 1227.[42] It was not unknown for tribal nomads to sell their own kin into slavery. Juzjani claims that Iltutmish's brothers, from jealousy of his beauty and his noble qualities, had sold him to a slave merchant, which enables the historian to liken him to the Biblical patriarch Joseph (the Qur'anic Yusuf: *sura* 12:7–20).[43] The same author describes one of Iltutmish's *amir*s as having been enslaved "through the perversity of kindred."[44] He heard rumors that two others were of Muslim parentage and had therefore been enslaved unlawfully.[45] During the reduction of the western steppelands, the Mongols would themselves take part in the slave traffic, selling off those of their captives who were surplus to their requirements, like Balban's younger brother.[46]

It is worth bearing in mind that Turkish slave-soldiers did not necessarily arrive in India directly from the pagan steppe. Where we are told something of the early career of a slave-*amir*, we may find that he had spent several years elsewhere in the Muslim world before being sold again and brought to the subcontinent. Iltutmish passed some years in Bukhara, where his first owner was a kinsman of the Sadr-i Jahan, the effective ruler of the city;[47] and Balban's first owner was based in Baghdad (though Ibn Battuta would later hear that Balban too had been purchased in Bukhara).[48] Clearly, such an interval might furnish the opportunity to learn Arabic, since for a time Aybak was the property of a prominent *imam* in the Khurasanian city of Nishapur, who appears to have taught him to read the Qur'an.[49] In such cases it is conceivable that a *ghulam* had imbibed not merely the rudiments of Islam but also something of the politics and statecraft of the Islamic heartlands; but this can only be a matter for conjecture.

A word needs to be said here about manumission, a subject to which our sources allude very rarely. Balban is one of the few Turkish slave-officers in the early Delhi Sultanate to be described as a freedman.[50] Juzjani tells us that Aybak had manumitted Iltutmish on the express orders of Sultan Mu'izz al-Din.[51] At this time, surprisingly, Aybak himself was still of unfree status, since after Mu'izz al-Din's death he and other Turkish slave-officers are said to have asked the late monarch's nephew and eventual successor, Ghiyas al-Din Mahmud, for deeds of enfranchisement (*khutut-i 'itq*).[52] In the 1330s Ibn Battuta picked up a tale that the jurists had required Iltutmish to furnish proof of his manumission before acknowledging him as their ruler.[53]

We should notice also that the death of the master did not automatically confer freedom, as it evidently did in the Deccan at a later date (see Eaton, this volume). In the Ghaznawid empire the slaves of a dead slave-commander passed to the sultan.[54] If Juzjani's story about Aybak and his colleagues were not enough to demonstrate that this situation still obtained in the early thirteenth century, his description of them as now the slaves (*bandagan*) of Sultan 'Ala al-Din Muhammad (who in 1206 briefly succeeded Mu'izz al-Din in Ghur before being ousted in favor of Ghiyas al-Din Mahmud) would confirm it.[55] In the same way, Juzjani shows us that Iltutmish acquired the *ghulam*s of masters who had died: the fact that in each case the *amir* in question is said to have been purchased from his master's heirs makes it clear that he had not been freed.[56] Another of Iltutmish's Turkish officers had formerly belonged to Mu'izz al-Din himself, though regrettably Juzjani fails to tell us whether he passed to Iltutmish through purchase.[57]

The Perceived Qualities of the Turk

Slave status, then, for Turks, was no barrier to favor, promotion, or eventual rulership; it was, rather, a major pathway to advancement. The Turkish peoples were highly regarded within the Muslim world for their courage, stamina, and military skill, and Turkish *ghulam*s further acquired a reputation for steadfastness and orthodoxy in Islam.[58] Within a very short time after the Seljuk conquest of Baghdad, we find Ibn Hassul (d. 1058) singing the praises of both Turkish tribesman and Turkish slave-soldier for his new masters.[59] Admittedly, the mainly Persian members of the bureaucratic (*dabir*) class who produced our literary sources sometimes impute to the

Turkish military a lack of sophistication. Bayhaqi describes the two *ghulam* generals, Asightegin and Eryaruq, for all their military prowess, as inexperienced and naïvely reliant for advice on a group of worthless individuals they had gathered around them.[60] Almost two centuries later, when one of Iltutmish's *ghulam* officers was accused of financial improprieties, the sultan's *wazir* advised him to entrust the investigation to a Tajik rather than a Turk, on the grounds not of possible bias but of Turkish "brashness [*tahawwur*]."[61] But even this lack of finesse might be turned to good account, as when a veteran slave-commander was brought in to dissuade the Ghaznawid sultan Mas'ud (1031–40) from a particularly rash enterprise and succeeded by dint of his plain speaking where others had failed.[62]

One of the principal virtues of the Turkish *ghulam* (as opposed to the free Turkish immigrant tribesman) was his detachment from family or territorial interest, so that his loyalty was (in theory, at least) to the master who had bought, trained, and—sometimes—manumitted him. This trait, rehearsed by a series of Muslim writers from al-Jahiz (d. 868–69) onward, assumes the character of a topos. In a famous passage cited by the Seljuk *wazir* Nizam al-Mulk, the loyalty and goodwill of the slave toward his master are contrasted with the aspirations of the son, who desires his father's death.[63]

Fakhr-i Mudabbir, in the *Shajarat* (or *Bahr*) *al-ansab,* which he dedicated to Qutb al-Din Aybak at Lahore (c. 1206), was harping on a well-worn theme (if in more highly figurative language than most of his precursors) when he wrote that

> there is no kind of infidel people which is brought over to Islam and does not look with longing at home, mother, father, and kindred. For a time they are bound to adopt Islam, but in most cases they apostatize and relapse into paganism. The exception is the Turkish race, who, when they are brought over to Islam, fix their hearts in Islam so firmly that they no longer remember home or region or kinsfolk. . . . The Turk is like a pearl that lies in the oyster in the sea. For as long as it is in its habitat, it is devoid of power and worth; but when it emerges from the oyster and from the sea, it acquires value and becomes precious, decorating the crown of kings and adorning the neck and ears of brides.[64]

This was an idealized picture, of course. It is undeniable that the Turks who entered India, in sharp contrast with their non-Turkish precursors from the Inner Asian steppes, strongly resisted indigenous cultural influences— whether Hindu or Buddhist—and retained a markedly separate identity which centered on Persian culture and, especially, on the religion of Islam.[65] According to Juzjani, every one of the slaves of the Ghurid dynasty "spread the carpet of justice over the surface of the world and raised palaces of beneficence and liberality";[66] and it was through their rule that "the light of the faith of Muhammad … had remained on the pages of the furthest limits of the empire of Hindustan."[67] Thirteenth-century Turkish slave-sultans and *amir*s are known to have done the Muslim cause signal service by building mosques in territory conquered from the Hindus.[68] What has to be asked, even so, is how far the Turkish military slave—a first-generation Muslim— had really turned his back on the steppe, where the dominant religious traditions were shamanistic or perhaps Manichaean (or sometimes Nestorian Christian).

Two illustrations will suffice. Firstly, Sebuktegin seems to have designated his youngest son as his successor at Ghazni, to the exclusion of Mahmud, the eldest, and it has been proposed that this echoes the tradition, familiar to the Central Asian Turks and Mongols, of ultimogeniture in succession to the "hearthland."[69] And in the second place, the enthronement at Delhi in 1236 of a female sovereign (Iltutmish's daughter Raziyya), an episode without precedent in the Islamic world outside the Yemen, might well hark back to the more prominent political role of royal women in steppe society, particularly among the Khitan and the Qara-Khitan, peoples to which some of the leading *amir*s involved traced their origins.[70] It is possible that a thorough sifting of our sources could identify other pagan "hangovers";[71] though the research so far devoted to the subject has tended to focus on the nomadic Turco-Mongol societies in Inner Asia that had embraced Islam, as opposed to the *déraciné* Turkish *ghulam*s.[72]

So too there were certainly striking instances of fidelity to a master: at Andkhud in 1204 the Ghurid sultan Mu'izz al-Din Muhammad was carried from the battlefield by one of his Turkish *ghulam*s, after being abandoned by a significant number of his Ghurid and Tajik troops.[73] But there had been occasions in the Ghaznawid period when Turkish slave-contingents deserted their master and went over to the enemy, notably prior to the battle of Dandanqan (1040) against the Turkish Seljuks.[74] And just as in the ninth century a number of 'Abbasid caliphs had been killed in risings by their Turkish slave-troops, and as Turan Shah, the last Ayyubid sultan of Egypt, was assassinated by a group of mamluks in 1250, so acts of regicide were not unknown in the eastern Islamic territories. The most notorious instance of disloyalty was that of Mahmud of Ghazni's slave Tughril (immortalized in the sources under epithets such as *kafir-i ni'mat*, "the ingrate"). Having after his master's death joined the Seljuks, he subsequently returned to the Ghaznawids' service, but was finally encouraged by his military successes to murder Sultan 'Abd al-Rashid b. Mahmud in 1051 and usurp the throne.[75] Service in the subcontinent offered an ever-present temptation to revolt against a distant sovereign, as the Turkish general Ahmad Inaltegin demonstrated when he rose against Sultan Mas'ud in 1033 (having, incidentally, sent agents to Central Asia to recruit Turkish *ghulam*s on his behalf and forward them to him in India).[76] Following his disastrous defeat by the Qara-Khitan at Andkhud in 1204, Mu'izz al-Din had to suppress the insurrection of a Turkish slave-officer who had reacted to rumors of his discomfiture by seizing control of Multan.[77] In the circumstances, the tribute paid to the faithfulness of Turkish slaves by successive authors begins to smack of literary affectation.

Turks in thirteenth-century India certainly did not enjoy an unalloyed reputation. Whatever their value as military assets, they were also believed, as a race, to exhibit less desirable characteristics and, with the growth of antipathy toward the Turk on the part of Arab and Persian populations, some of these traits, like an inordinate love of plunder, were aired in Muslim writings further west.[78] The final years of the Ghurid dynasty furnish a couple of incidents which highlight the capacity of Turkish slave-troops to riot when the firm hand of their master was removed. Following the death of Sultan Mu'izz al-Din in 1206, the younger Turkish *ghulam*s had wanted to plunder his baggage and had with difficulty been restrained by his *wazir* and by their own officers.[79] Juzjani himself recalled how, when Mu'izz al-Din's nephew and successor, Ghiyas al-Din Mahmud, died at Firuzkuh in 1210–11, his Turkish slaves raised an "uproar [*ghawgha*]" and put to the sword a number of Ghurid princes, ostensibly in order to safeguard the throne for his infant son.[80]

Similar turbulence would manifest itself in the Delhi Sultanate, first during the brief reign of Iltutmish's son and successor, Rukn al-Din Firuz Shah (1236), when the Turkish slaves massacred a body of Tajik bureaucrats at Tarain.[81] Barani devotes a long passage of his history to the way in which Iltutmish's Turkish slave-commanders—the Shamsi khans and *malik*s, as he calls them—profited from the weakness of his progeny to destroy a host of immigrant Tajik nobles. This is undoubtedly simplistic; but there is nevertheless a substratum of truth beneath his analysis.[82] As had been the case in ninth-century Samarra, the impulse underlying such violent outbreaks was usually fear of hostile action by the ruler and the instinct to maintain a position that was perceived as under threat. Thus it is no accident that Turkish slave-*amir*s deposed Sultana Raziyya in 1240 because she relied inordinately (in their view) on a Black African ("Habshi," or "Abyssinian") slave-*amir*, Jamal al-Din Yaqut; or that they brought down her brother and successor, Sultan Mu'izz al-Din Bahram Shah b. Iltutmish, in 1242 because he was rumored to be planning the wholesale removal of the Turkish slave-elite; or that they set upon and killed their former ally, the *wazir* Muhadhdhab al-Din, in the following year because he sought to concentrate all affairs of state in his own hands at their expense.[83] This is not to deny that other "excluded"

elements—free Turkish grandees, Ghuri military leaders, or even Tajik bureaucrats—joined forces with them on each occasion.[84]

Providence and Panegyric

The obscure origins of the Turkish slave-commanders, lying in the *Dar
al-Harb,* often far beyond the horizons of their future Muslim subjects, rendered it possible—and indeed desirable—for those who catalogued their exploits to indulge in a little historical creativity. At a fairly mundane level, the
slave trader who purchased Sebuktegin was supposed to have seen in him
signs of valor and acumen;[85] and Juzjani, similarly, claims that his patron
Balban had displayed the marks of rectitude and ingenuity (*rushd-u sha-
hamat*) for the benefit of his first owner.[86] More impressively, omens of
greatness were naturally discernible at an early date in those whom God had
destined to fill the highest office. A tale circulated about Iltutmish that when
he was a mere child slave in Bukhara a holy man (*darwish*) had foretold his
rise to power and made him promise to show generosity toward ascetics (although Juzjani, who transmits this anecdote, ascribes it ultimately to Iltutmish himself).[87] Decades later, Ibn Battuta heard a cognate story in which a
faqir in Bukhara conferred the "kingdom of India" on Balban in return for
some trifling service.[88]

Hindsight of this kind was given the fullest latitude, perhaps, when it
remolded slave-officers into the heirs of their dead lords.[89] According to Juzjani, the Ghurid sultan Mu'izz al-Din Muhammad, who had no son, had
intended that his most senior slave, Taj al-Din Yildiz, should succeed him
as ruler of Ghazni,[90] when in fact the material he himself provides, and the
information given by the well-informed Mosuli historian Ibn al-Athir (d.
1233), alike demonstrate that the Turkish *ghulams* at Ghazni regarded
Mu'izz al-Din's nephew Ghiyas al-Din Mahmud as his rightful heir. It was
Ghiyas al-Din Mahmud's failure to move on Ghazni in 1206 that enabled
Yildiz to take control there.[91] In what is possibly a later embellishment of the
legends purveyed by Juzjani, Yildiz was alleged to be Mu'izz al-Din's adopted son.[92]

Juzjani further makes out that Mu'izz al-Din had bequeathed his Indian
dominions to his Turkish slaves. "I have several thousand sons," he supposedly told those who bewailed his lack of male offspring, "whose inheritance
will be my kingdom";[93] and after his death events had duly transpired just as
he had prophesied.[94] This legacy, moreover, had now devolved upon the sovereigns of Iltutmish's line, in the person of the reigning sultan, Nasir al-Din
Mahmud Shah b. Iltutmish (1246–66).[95] What had perhaps made this possible was that Aybak had seen Iltutmish as a future ruler and had adopted

him—or so Juzjani tells us elsewhere.[96] Juzjani seeks, in other words, to fashion some kind of continuity between the extinct Ghurid dynasty and the regime at Delhi under which he was writing. All this was to discount the realities of the master-slave relationship in Islam, whereby the master inherits from the slave and not vice versa.[97] It also conveniently ignored the vicissitudes of the early thirteenth century in which Aybak and Iltutmish had each in turn seized power in default of Ghurid intervention and held it in the face of Turkish competitors.[98]

The panegyrists, moreover, were not above devising a more exalted background for Turkish slaves who attained sovereignty. One tradition had placed Sebuktegin's origins, as we have seen above, in the town of Barskhan, in Qarakhanid territory, close to the shores of the Issik Kul. Yet Juzjani cites a now lost work which traced Sebuktegin's descent, somewhat less plausibly, from Yazdagird III, the last Sasanian king of Persia, who had died in flight from the victorious Arabs in 651.[99] There may have been some reluctance to acknowledge that the Ghaznawids' ancestry lay among subjects of the rival Qarakhanid dynasty; though it is equally possible that the genealogy quoted by Juzjani had arisen in part as a counterblast to the pretensions of other antagonists, the Buyids in central and western Persia,[100] or to the spectacular (and more dangerous) rise of the Seljuks.

Whatever the case, by the mid-thirteenth century, Turkish dynasties—whether founded by nomadic chieftains like the Seljuks or by slave officers like the Ghaznawids and the Khwarazm-Shahs—had governed Persia for several decades, and steppe antecedents were now sufficiently respectable for Turkish slave-rulers to dispense with bogus Iranian pedigrees and to embrace instead an illustrious nomadic Inner Asian ancestry. Thus Juzjani could describe Balban's forebears as "khans of the Olberli and rulers of the Yemek [i.e., the Kimek]," and claim that Balban's father had been khan over some ten thousand families.[101] He referred also to the father of his first patron, Iltutmish, as a khan of the Olberli, with "numerous dependants, kindred, and horsemen [atbaʿ-u aqribaʾ-u khayl-i bisyar]"; but predictably, perhaps, his very vagueness conveys the impression of a less substantial figure than Balban's progenitor.[102] Parallel examples of retrospective promotion are found in connection with the leaders of other Turkish nomadic groups transplanted from their habitat to provide military service for sedentary princes.[103]

Conclusion

Turkish military slavery differed markedly from other kinds of slavery. It did not, properly speaking, hinge on a particular social status but on a relationship to a ruler (or to a series of rulers) and on a career of a particular type. Turkish slaves also differed in terms of their service from the free Turkish tribesmen among whose ranks they had originated. Turkish slave-officers and their troops were not recruited in order to replicate the tactics traditionally associated with the light cavalry of the steppe. Yet in other respects the former *ghulam* who attained high office shared some of the characteristics of his free brethren who came to dominate large swaths of the Islamic world. These included a mixed reputation—for greed and turbulence as well as for martial accomplishments and perseverance in Islam. The Turkish slave-elite were not an unmitigated blessing to their masters; and their actions were not necessarily designed to court popularity among contemporaries at large. But they undoubtedly played a prominent role in the implantation of Muslim rule in India and in the politics of the fledgling Delhi Sultanate. In crafting a more respectable ancestry for such patrons and in seeking, eventually, to rewrite the process by which they had attained power, the Persian literati who dedicated their works to them were perhaps registering a belief that Turkish paramountcy was there to stay. They could hardly have foreseen that it would pass away within two generations of Juzjani's era.

Notes

1. Ziya al-Din Barani, *Ta'rikh-i Firuz Shahi,* ed. Saiyid Ahmad Khan, Bibliotheca Indica 33 (Calcutta: Asiatic Society of Bengal, 1860–62), 27.

2. Irfan Habib, "Barani's Theory of the History of the Delhi Sultanate," *Indian Historical Review* 7, no. 2 (1980–81), 106–108.

3. Peter Jackson, "The *Mamluk* Institution in Early Muslim India," *Journal of the Royal Asiatic Society* (1990), 340–58; idem, *The Delhi Sultanate: A Political and Military History* (Cambridge: Cambridge University Press, 1999), chapter 4, "Turks, Tajiks and Khalaj."

4. C. I. Beckwith, "Aspects of the Early History of the Central-Asian Guard Corps in Islam," *Archivum Eurasiae Medii Aevi* 4 (1984), 29–43; and Hugh Kennedy, *The Prophet and the Age of the Caliphates,* 2nd ed. (Harlow: Longman, 2004), 157–58.

5. Minhaj al-Din Abu 'Umar 'Uthman b. Siraj al-Din Juzjani, *Tabaqat-i Nasiri,* ed. 'Abd al-Hayy Habibi, 2nd ed., 2 vols. (Kabul: Anjuman-i Ta'rikh-i Afghanistan, 1963–64), 1:354–55, uses the term *turkan-i khass;* the translation by H. G. Raverty, *Tabakat-i Nasiri: A General History of the Muhammadan Dynasties of Asia,* Bibliotheca Indica, 2 vols. with continuous pagination (London, 1872–81), 1:371 ("their own immediate Turkish followers"), obscures the sense. The chronological context suggests a date at the very outset of the reign.

6. Juzjani, *Tabaqat-i Nasiri,* 1:410 (trans. Raverty, *Tabakat-i Nasiri,* 1:497).

7. Irfan Habib, "Formation of the Sultanate Ruling Class of the Thirteenth Century," in Irfan Habib, ed., *Medieval India,* vol. 1, *Researches in the History of India, 1200–1750* (Delhi: Oxford University Press, 1992), 4–7.

8. See the evidence analyzed in David Ayalon, "The Mamluks of the Seljuks: Islam's Military Might at the Crossroads," *Journal of the Royal Asiatic Society,* 3rd series, 6, no. 3 (Nov. 1996), 305–33.

9. For a useful introduction to the institution of military slavery, see the various articles by D. Sourdel, C. E. Bosworth, and P. Hardy, "Ghulam," in *Encyclopaedia of Islam,* ed. H. A. R. Gibb et al., new ed., (Leiden: E. J. Brill, 1954–2002), 2:1079–85; and Robert Irwin, *The Middle East in the Middle Ages: The Early Mamluk Sultanate, 1250–1382* (London: Croom Helm, 1986), 3–10. More detailed studies are Patricia Crone, *Slaves on Horses: The Evolution of the Islamic Polity* (Cambridge: Cambridge University Press, 1980); and Daniel Pipes, *Slave Soldiers and Islam: The Genesis of a Military System* (New Haven: Yale University Press, 1981).

10. Abu l-Fadl Muhammad b. al-Husayn Bayhaqi, *Ta'rikh-i Bayhaqi,* ed. Qasim Ghani and 'Ali Akbar Fayyad (Tehran: Bang-i Milli-yi Iran, 1945), 267; Abu Sa'id 'Abd al-Hayy b. al-Dahhak b. Mahmud Gardizi, *Zayn al-akhbar,* ed. Muhammad Nazim, E. G. Browne Memorial Series 1 (London: Luzac, 1928), 97.

11. Bayhaqi, *Ta'rikh-i Bayhaqi,* 401. See generally C. E. Bosworth, "Ahmad Inaltigin," in Ehsan Yarshater, ed., *Encyclopaedia Iranica* (London: Routledge; Costa Mesa, Calif.: Mazda; New York: Bibliotheca Persica and Encyclopaedia Iranica Foundation, 1982–), 1:647.

12. André Wink, *Al-Hind: The Making of the Indo-Islamic World,* vol. 2, *The Slave Kings and the Islamic Conquest, 11th–13th Centuries* (Leiden: E. J. Brill, 1997), 90–94; and Jackson, *Delhi Sultanate,* 11–12.

13. C. E. Bosworth, *The Ghaznavids: Their Empire in Afghanistan and Eastern Iran, 994–1040,* 2nd ed. (Beirut: Librairie du Liban, 1973), 102–103.

14. Juzjani, *Tabaqat-i Nasiri,* 1:416, 443, and 2:27 (trans. Raverty, *Tabakat-i Nasiri,* 1:513, 604–605, and 2:756). At 2:5, he is still vaguer: *harafha-yi jang-u dilawari-u jaladat* ("the discourse of warfare, valor, and courage"; cf. Raverty's translation, *Tabakat-i Nasiri,* 2:725).

15. As pointed out by Yuri Bregel, "Turko-Mongol Influences in Central Asia," in Robert L. Canfield, ed., *Turko-Persia in Historical Perspective* (Cambridge: Cambridge University Press, 1991), 67; cf. also Claude Cahen, "Les changements techniques militaires dans le Proche Orient médiéval et leur importance historique," in V. J. Parry and M. E. Yapp, eds., *War, Technology, and Society in the Middle East* (Oxford: Oxford University Press, 1975), 121.

16. Kennedy, *The Prophet and the Age of the Caliphates,* 158.

17. Wink, *Al-Hind,* 2:91–94. Thus the Khalaj freebooter Muhammad b. Bakhtiyar is alleged to have burst into the city of Bihar in c. 1204 with only two hundred heavily armed (*bar-gustuwan*) horsemen: Juzjani, *Tabaqat-i Nasiri,* 1:423 (trans. Raverty, *Tabakat-i Nasiri,* 1:551–52).

18. Juzjani, *Tabaqat-i Nasiri,* 1:230 (trans. Raverty, *Tabakat-i Nasiri,* 1:83–84).

19. Bayhaqi, *Ta'rikh-i Bayhaqi,* 288.

20. C. E. Bosworth, "An Embassy to Mahmud of Ghazna Recorded in Qadi Ibn az-Zubayr's *Kitab adh-dhaka'ir wa't-tuha*," *Journal of the American Oriental Society* 85 (1965), 405.

21. For a discussion of numbers, see C. E. Bosworth, "Ghaznevid Military Organisation," *Der Islam* 36 (1961), 48; also idem, *Ghaznavids,* 105.

22. Bayhaqi, *Ta'rikh-i Bayhaqi,* 540. For a translation, see Bosworth, *Ghaznavids,* 136.

23. Daniel Schlumberger, "Le palais ghaznévide de Lashkari Bazar," *Syria* 29 (1952), 261–67 and plates xxxi/2–xxxii/1; and C. E. Bosworth, "Lashkar-i Bazar," in *Encyclopaedia of Islam.*

24. So the Rusi (*Urus*), the Slavs (*Saqalai* < *Saqaliba*), the Tibetans (*Tibat*), and the Tatars are listed among the Turkish peoples in c. 1206 by Fakhr-i Mudabbir (Muhammad Mubarakshah b. Mansur al-Qurashi), *Shajarat* (or *Bahr*) *al-Ansab,* partial ed. by E. Denison Ross as *Ta'rikh-i Fakhr al-Din Mubarak Shah,* James G. Forlong Fund 4 (London: Royal Asiatic Society, 1927), 47; and see E. Denison Ross, "The Genealogies of Fakhr-ud-Din, Mubarak Shah," in T. W. Arnold and Reynold A. Nicholson, eds., ʿ*Ajab-nama: A Volume of Oriental Studies Presented to Edward G. Browne. . . . on His 60th Birthday* (Cambridge: Cambridge University Press, 1922), 407. For similar usage by other authors, including Juzjani, see Wink, *Al-Hind,* 2:68–69; also idem, "India and Central Asia: The Coming of the Turks in the Eleventh Century," in A. W. Van den Hoek, D. H. A. Kolff, and M. S. Oort, eds., *Ritual, State, and History in South Asia: Essays in Honour of J. C. Heesterman* (Leiden: E. J. Brill, 1992), 761, 766.

25. Omeljan Pritsak, "Von den Karluk zu den Karachaniden," *Zeitschrift der deutschen morgenländischen Gesellschaft* 101 (1951), 270–300, and repr. in idem, *Studies in Medieval Eurasian History* (London: Variorum, 1981).

26. Bosworth, *Ghaznavids,* 103, 109; cf. also idem, *The Later Ghaznavids: Splendour and Decay; The Dynasty in Afghanistan and Northern India, 1040–1186* (Edinburgh: Edinburgh University Press, 1977), 60; and idem, "Notes on Some Turkish Names in Abuʾl-Fadl Bayhaqi's Tarikh-i Masʿudi," *Oriens* 36 (2001), 309. For the Kimek, a sizable Turkish confederacy in the upper Irtysh basin which dissolved under pressure from the advancing Qipchaq in the eleventh century, see C. E. Bosworth, "Kimäk," in *Encyclopaedia of Islam;* Peter B. Golden, "The Peoples of the South Russian Steppe," in Denis Sinor, ed., *The Cambridge History of Early Inner Asia* (Cambridge: Cambridge University Press, 1990), 277–80; and Linda Amy Kimball, "The Vanished Kimak Empire," in Edward H. Kaplan and Donald W. Whisenhunt, eds., *Opuscula Altaica: Essays Presented in Honor of Henry Schwarz,* Studies on East Asia 19 (Bellingham, Wash.: Center for East Asian Studies, Western Washington University, 1994), 371–92.

27. For the Qipchaq-Cumans, see Golden, "Peoples of the South Russian Steppe," 277–84; and G. Hazai, "Kipčak" and "Kuman," in *Encyclopaedia of Islam,* 5:125–26, 5:373.

28. Juzjani, *Tabaqat-i Nasiri,* 2:5, 24, 42 (trans. Raverty, *Tabakat-i Nasiri,* 2:724, 752, 787). For what follows, see also Habib, "Formation," 10.

29. Juzjani, *Tabaqat-i Nasiri,* 2:13, 19, 22 (trans. Raverty, *Tabakat-i Nasiri,* 2:736, 746, 749).

30. Juzjani, *Tabaqat-i Nasiri,* 2:9, 28 (trans. Raverty, *Tabakat-i Nasiri,* 2:731, 757).

31. Juzjani, *Tabaqat-i Nasiri,* 2:17, 25, 27, 30, 36, 40 (trans. Raverty, *Tabakat-i Nasiri,* 2:742, 754, 756, 761, 775, 788–89).

32. Juzjani, *Tabaqat-i Nasiri,* 2:43, 45, 47 (trans. Raverty, *Tabakat-i Nasiri,* 2:791, 796, 800). For the Olberli, see P. B. Golden, "Cumanica II: The Ölberli (Ölperli); The Fortunes and Misfortunes of an Inner Asian Nomadic Clan," *Archivum Eurasiae Medii Aevi* 6 (1988 [1986]), 27–28. The name appears in the mss. of Juzjani's work as Albari (Raverty's "Ilbari"). On the vexed question of the Qipchaq-Qangli relationship, see Paul Pelliot and Louis Hambis, *Histoire des campagnes de Gengis Khan:*

Cheng-wou Ts'in-tcheng-lou (Leiden: E. J. Brill, 1951, only one volume published), 95–116; and C. E. Bosworth, "Kanghlı," in *Encyclopaedia of Islam*.

33. Thomas T. Allsen, "Prelude to the Western Campaigns: Mongol Military Operations in the Volga-Ural Region, 1217–1237," *Archivum Eurasiae Medii Aevi* 3 (1983), 5–24.

34. William of Rubruck, *Itinerarium*, ed. Anastasius Van den Wyngaert, O.F.M., in *Sinica Franciscana*, vol. 1, *Itinera et relationes Fratrum Minorum saeculi XIII et XIV* (Quaracchi-Firenze: Collegium S. Bonaventurae, 1929), 171; translated by Peter Jackson and David Morgan, *The Mission of Friar William of Rubruck: His Journey to the Court of the Great Khan Möngke, 1253–1255*, Hakluyt Society, 2nd series, 173 (Cambridge: Cambridge University Press, 1990), 70.

35. Qutb al-Din Musa al-Yunini (d. 1326), *Al-Dhayl ʿala Mirʾat al-zaman*, 4 vols. (Hyderabad, A.P.: Dairatuʾl-Maʿarifiʾl-Osmania, 1954–61), 3:240; Salah al-Din Khalil b. Aybak al-Safadi (d. 1363), *Al-Wafi bi l-wafayat*, 10, ed. Ali Amara and Jacqueline Sublet (Wiesbaden: Steiner, 1980), 329, citing Ibn Shaddad (d. 1285), whose informant was Baybars's fellow Olberli, Baysarï; and Peter Thorau, *The Lion of Egypt: Sultan Baybars I and the Near East in the Thirteenth Century*, trans. Peter Holt (Harlow: Longman, 1992), 28.

36. Irwin, *Middle East*, 17–19; and Thorau, *Lion of Egypt*, 16–18. But for an important qualification, see R. Stephen Humphreys, "The Emergence of the Mamluk Army," *Studia Islamica* 45 (1977), 67–100 (esp. 94–99), and 46 (1977), 147–82.

37. P. B. Golden, "'I will give the people unto thee': The Činggisid Conquests and Their Aftermath in the Turkic World," *Journal of the Royal Asiatic Society*, 3rd series, 10 (2000), 21–41.

38. For immigration into India, see Habib, "Formation," 13–14, and Jackson, *Delhi Sultanate*, 39–43; and for the Near East, R. Stephen Humphreys, *From Saladin to the Mongols: The Ayyubids of Damascus, 1193–1260* (Albany, N.Y.: State University of New York Press, 1977), index s.v. "Khwarizmians." For Eastern Europe, see generally James Ross Sweeney, "'Spurred on by the fear of death': Refugees and Displaced Populations during the Mongol Invasion of Hungary," in Michael Gervers and Wayne Schlepp, eds., *Nomadic Diplomacy, Destruction, and Religion from the Pacific to the Adriatic*, Toronto Studies in Central and Inner Asia 1 (Toronto: Joint Centre for Asia Pacific Studies, 1994), 34–62; James Ross Sweeney, "Identifying the Medieval Refugee: Hungarians in Flight during the Mongol Invasion," in Ladislaus Jöb et al., eds., *Forms of Identity: Definitions and Changes* (Szeged: Attila József University, 1994), 63–76; A. Pálóczi-Horváth, "L'immigration et l'établissement des Comans en Hongrie," *Acta Orientalia Academiae Scientiarum Hungaricae* 29 (1975), 313–33; and Nora Berend, *At the Gate of Christendom: Jews, Muslims, and "Pagans" in Medieval Hungary, c. 1000–c. 1300* (Cambridge: Cambridge University Press, 2001), 134–40, 142–47.

39. Ibn al-Athir, *Al-Kamil fi l-taʾrikh*, ed. C. J. Tornberg, 12 vols. (Leiden, 1851–76), 12:88, 134; reprinted with different pagination in 12 vols. (Beirut: Dar el-Sader, 1965–66), 12:134, 206.

40. For the events of this period, see W. Barthold, *Turkestan down to the Mongol Invasion*, 3rd ed. (London: Luzac, 1968), 349 ff.

41. Ibn Battuta, *Tuhfat al-nuzzar fi gharaʾib al-amsar*, ed. Ch. Defrémery and B. S. Sanguinetti, 4 vols. (Paris, 1853–58), 3:171; translated by H. A. R. Gibb and C. F. Beckingham, *The Travels of Ibn Battuta, A.D. 1325–1354*, 5 vols. with continu-

ous pagination, Hakluyt Society, 2nd series, 110, 117, 141, 178, 190 (Cambridge: Published for the Hakluyt Society at the University Press, 1958–2000), 3:633.

42. Juzjani, *Tabaqat-i Nasiri*, 2:36 (trans. Raverty, *Tabakat-i Nasiri*, 2:777–79).

43. Juzjani, *Tabaqat-i Nasiri*, 1:441 (trans. Raverty, *Tabakat-i Nasiri*, 1:599–600); cf. also Juzjani, *Tabaqat-i Nasiri*, 1:440 (trans. Raverty, *Tabakat-i Nasiri*, 1:598), and the remarks about Yusufin Juzjani, *Tabaqat-i Nasiri*, 1:439 (trans. Raverty, *Tabakat-i Nasiri*, 1:596–97).

44. Juzjani, *Tabaqat-i Nasiri*, 2:41, omits the phrase *ba-ʿinad-i aqriba,* which is found in the reliable fourteenth-century British Library ms. Add. 26,189, fol. 211r (and see Raverty's trans., *Tabakat-i Nasiri*, 2:790).

45. Juzjani, *Tabaqat-i Nasiri*, 2:24, 33–34 (trans. Raverty, *Tabakat-i Nasiri*, 2:752, 766).

46. Juzjani, *Tabaqat-i Nasiri*, 2:45 (trans. Raverty, *Tabakat-i Nasiri*, 2:796).

47. Juzjani, *Tabaqat-i Nasiri*, 1:441–42 (trans. Raverty, *Tabakat-i Nasiri*, 1:600–601). For the dynasty of Sadr-i Jahans in Bukhara, see Omeljan Pritsak, "Al-i Burhan," *Der Islam* 30 (1952), 81–96, repr. in his *Studies in Medieval Eurasian History.*

48. Juzjani, *Tabaqat-i Nasiri*, 2:48 (trans. Raverty, *Tabakat-i Nasiri*, 2:801); and cf. Ibn Battuta, *Tuhfat al-nuzzar*, 3:171 (trans. Gibb and Beckingham, *Travels of Ibn Battuta*, 3:633).

49. Fakhr-i Mudabbir, *Taʾrikh-i Fakhr al-Din Mubarak Shah*, 21.

50. Barani, *Taʾrikh-i Firuz Shahi*, 25: *azad shuda.*

51. Juzjani, *Tabaqat-i Nasiri*, 1:443–44 (trans. Raverty, *Tabakat-i Nasiri*, 1:605).

52. Juzjani, *Tabaqat-i Nasiri*, 1:373 (trans. Raverty, *Tabakat-i Nasiri*, 1:398).

53. Ibn Battuta, *Tuhfat al-nuzzar*, 3:164–65 (trans. Gibb and Beckingham, *Travels of Ibn Battuta*, 3:629–30).

54. Bosworth, *Ghaznavids*, 106.

55. Juzjani, *Tabaqat-i Nasiri*, 1:373 (trans. Raverty, *Tabakat-i Nasiri*, 1:398).

56. Juzjani, *Tabaqat-i Nasiri*, 2:5, 7, 9 (trans. Raverty, *Tabakat-i Nasiri*, 2:725, 727, 731).

57. Juzjani, *Tabaqat-i Nasiri*, 2:10 (trans. Raverty, *Tabakat-i Nasiri*, 2:732).

58. C. E. Bosworth, "Barbarian Incursions: The Coming of the Turks into the Islamic World," in D. S. Richards, ed., *Islamic Civilisation, 950–1150,* Papers on Islamic History 3 (Oxford: Oxford University Press, 1973), 6–7, and repr. in C. E. Bosworth, *The Medieval History of Iran, Afghanistan, and Central Asia* (London: Variorum, 1977).

59. Abbas Azzavi, "İbni Hassulʾün Türkler hakkında bir eseri" [*Türk Tarih Kurumu*], *Belleten* 4 (1940), 235–66, plus fifty pages of Arabic text (here 40–43); extracts trans. in Ayalon, "Mamluks of the Seljuks," 314–15.

60. Bayhaqi, *Taʾrikh-i Bayhaqi*, 221.

61. Sadid al-Din Muhammad b. Muhammad ʿAwfi, *Jawamiʿ al-hikayat* (c. 1232–33), British Library ms. Or. 6376, fols. 263v-264r: this is the anecdote listed as no. 1729 in Muhammad Nizamʾd-Din, *Introduction to the Jawamiʿuʾl-hikayat wa lawamiʿuʾr-riwayat,* Gibb Memorial Series, new series, 8 (Leiden: E. J. Brill, 1929), 228.

62. Bayhaqi, *Taʾrikh-i Bayhaqi*, 615.

63. Nizam al-Mulk, *Siyar al-Muluk or Siyasat-nama,* ed. Hubert Darke (Tehran: Bangah-i Tarjama-u Nashr-i Kitab, 1968), 158; translated as Nizam al-Mulk, *The Book of Government, or Rules for Kings: The Siyar al-Muluk, or Siyasat-nama of Nizam al-Mulk,* trans. Hubert Darke, 2nd ed. (London: Routledge and Kegan Paul, 1978), 117.

64. Fakhr-i Mudabbir, *Ta'rikh-i Fakhr al-Din Mubarak Shah*, 35–37. The simile of the pearl is first found in an early eleventh-century work: C. Edmund Bosworth, "Tha'alibi's Information on the Turks," in Rudolf Veselý and Eduard Gombár, eds., *Zafar Name: Memorial Volume of Felix Tauer* (Prague: Enigma, 1996), 61–66 (Arabic text at 63, tr. 64).

65. Wink, "India and Central Asia," 768.

66. Juzjani, *Tabaqat-i Nasiri*, 1:323 (Raverty's trans., *Tabakat-i Nasiri*, 1:310, modified).

67. Juzjani, *Tabaqat-i Nasiri*, 1:415 (Raverty's trans., *Tabakat-i Nasiri*, 1:512, modified).

68. E.g., in the Doab (Sultan Balban): Barani, *Ta'rikh-i Firuz Shahi*, 57–58; in the Badaon and Katehr regions (Taj al-Din Sanjar-i Qabaqulaq): Juzjani, *Tabaqat-i Nasiri*, 2:26 (trans. Raverty, *Tabakat-i Nasiri*, 2:755).

69. C. E. Bosworth, "A Turco-Mongol Practice amongst the Early Ghaznavids?" *Central Asiatic Journal* 7 (1962), 237–40, and repr. in idem, *Medieval History of Iran*. Cf. also Peter B. Golden, "The Karakhanids and Early Islam," in Sinor, ed., *Cambridge History of Early Inner Asia*, 359.

70. Peter Jackson, "Sultan Radiyya bint Iltutmish," in Gavin R. G. Hambly, ed., *Women in the Medieval Islamic World: Power, Patronage, Piety* (New York: St. Martin's Press, 1998), 181–97.

71. Turkish officers continued to observe a taboo well known among Inner Asian nomadic societies—namely, the practice of beating to death in a carpet those of princely status in order to avoid shedding their blood on the ground: see Mehmed Fuad Köprülü, "La proibizione di versare il sangue nell'esecuzione d'un membro della dinastia presso i Turchi ed i Mongoli," in *Scritti in onore Luigi Bonelli*, Annali dell'Istituto Universitario Orientale di Napoli, nuova serie 1 (Rome: Edizioni universitarie, 1940), 15–23. Unfortunately, the only piece of hard evidence from the Delhi Sultanate relates to the murder of Sultan Kayqubad in 1290, when the perpetrator may have been an immigrant Mongol *amir* rather than a Turk: Barani, *Ta'rikh-i Firuz Shahi*, 173.

72. Jean-Paul Roux, "Recherche des survivances pré-islamiques dans les textes turcs musulmans: Le *Babur-Name*," *Journal asiatique* 256 (1969), 247–61; idem, "Recherche des survivances pré-islamiques dans les textes turcs musulmans: Le *Kitab-i Dede Qorqut*," *Journal asiatique* 264 (1976), 35–55.

73. Juzjani, *Tabaqat-i Nasiri*, 1:403 (trans. Raverty, *Tabakat-i Nasiri*, 1:476–78).

74. Bosworth, *Ghaznavids*, 106, points out, however, that a considerable proportion of these *ghulams* had formerly belonged to *amirs* who had fallen foul of the Ghaznawid sultan Mas'ud. For an earlier example of desertion to the Seljuks, see Juzjani, *Tabaqat-i Nasiri*, 1:250 (trans. Raverty, *Tabakat-i Nasiri*, 1:129).

75. Juzjani, *Tabaqat-i Nasiri*, 1:236 (trans. Raverty, *Tabakat-i Nasiri*, 1:99–100). On this version of Tughril's career, however, see the doubts expressed by Bosworth, *Later Ghaznavids*, 42–43.

76. Bosworth, *Ghaznavids*, 105–106.

77. Ibn al-Athir, *Al-Kamil fi l-ta'rikh*, 12:122–23 (Beirut reprint, 12:187–88); he also alleges that a leading *ghulam* commander, Taj al-Din Yildiz, made an unsuccessful attempt to seize Ghazni, though no other source confirms this.

78. Wink, "India and Central Asia," 764–65.

79. Ibn al-Athir, *Al-Kamil fi l-ta'rikh*, 12:140 (Beirut reprint, 12:214).

80. Juzjani, *Tabaqat-i Nasiri*, 1:371–72 (trans. Raverty, *Tabakat-i Nasiri*, 1:395–96); a slightly different version, claiming that the late sultan's widow put them up to it, is in Juzjani, *Tabaqat-i Nasiri*, 1:377 (trans. Raverty, *Tabakat-i Nasiri*, 1:408). See Peter Jackson, "The Fall of the Ghurid Dynasty," in Carole Hillenbrand, ed., *Studies in Honour of Clifford Edmund Bosworth*, vol. 2, *The Sultan's Turret: Studies in Persian and Turkish Culture* (Leiden: E. J. Brill, 2000), 230–31.

81. Juzjani, *Tabaqat-i Nasiri*, 1:456 (trans. Raverty, *Tabakat-i Nasiri*, 1:634–35); see also 2:36 (trans. Raverty, *Tabakat-i Nasiri*, 2:779).

82. Barani, *Ta'rikh-i Firuz Shahi*, 27–28, 550. Cf. Jackson, "*Mamluk* Institution," 345–49; and idem, *Delhi Sultanate*, 65–70. The passage from Barani is translated in Habib, "Formation," 15–16.

83. Juzjani, *Tabaqat-i Nasiri*, 1:460 (trans. Raverty, *Tabakat-i Nasiri*, 1:642–43), for Raziyya; and cf. 1:461 (trans. 1:645) for Yaqut's Habshi origins; and 1:466–67, 469 (trans. Raverty, *Tabakat-i Nasiri*, 1:642–43, 658, 662) for Bahram Shah and Muhadhdhab al-Din respectively.

84. See Jackson, "*Mamluk* Institution," 349; and idem, *Delhi Sultanate*, 68–69.

85. Juzjani, *Tabaqat-i Nasiri*, 1:226 (cf. Raverty trans., *Tabakat-i Nasiri*, 1:71).

86. Juzjani, *Tabaqat-i Nasiri*, 2:48 (cf. Raverty trans., *Tabakat-i Nasiri*, 2:801).

87. Juzjani, *Tabaqat-i Nasiri*, 1:442 (trans. Raverty, *Tabakat-i Nasiri*, 1:600).

88. Ibn Battuta, *Tuhfat al-nuzzar*, 3:171 (trans. Gibb and Beckingham, *Travels of Ibn Battuta*, 3:633).

89. Juzjani, *Tabaqat-i Nasiri*, 1:268–69 (trans. Raverty, *Tabakat-i Nasiri*, 1:169–70), for example, suggests that the great Seljuk sultan Sanjar envisaged his dominions passing into the hands of his slaves because he had no son.

90. Juzjani, *Tabaqat-i Nasiri*, 1:412 (trans. Raverty, *Tabakat-i Nasiri*, 1:500); at 1:393 (trans., 1:438), he is alleged to have entrusted (*sipurd*) Ghazni to Yildiz.

91. Juzjani, *Tabaqat-i Nasiri*, 1:412 (trans. Raverty, *Tabakat-i Nasiri*, 1:501); and Ibn al-Athir, *Al-Kamil fi l-ta'rikh*, 12:140–41, 146 (Beirut reprint, 12:214, 221). For the struggle for Ghazni, from which Yildiz emerged victorious, see Jackson, "Fall of the Ghurid Dynasty," 213–16, 220.

92. Barani, *Ta'rikh-i Firuz Shahi*, 550.

93. Juzjani, *Tabaqat-i Nasiri*, 1:410–11 (Raverty's trans., *Tabakat-i Nasiri*, 1:497, modified).

94. Juzjani, *Tabaqat-i Nasiri*, 1:411, 415 (trans. Raverty, *Tabakat-i Nasiri*, 1:497–98, 508–12).

95. Juzjani, *Tabaqat-i Nasiri*, 1:323 (trans. Raverty, *Tabakat-i Nasiri*, 1:310).

96. Juzjani, *Tabaqat-i Nasiri*, 1:418: *qutb al-dinra nazar-i mulkdari bar sultan shams al-din bud-u ura pisar khwanda bud* (trans. Raverty, *Tabakat-i Nasiri*, 1:530); see also 1:443: *ura farzand khwand* (trans. Raverty, *Tabakat-i Nasiri*, 1:603).

97. Paul G. Forand, "The Relation of the Slave and the Client to the Master or Patron in Medieval Islam," *International Journal of Middle East Studies* 2 (1971), 61; and Patricia Crone, *Roman, Provincial, and Islamic Law* (Cambridge: Cambridge University Press, 1987), 36–38.

98. On all this, see Jackson, *Delhi Sultanate*, 26–27, 31–32; and idem, "Fall of the Ghurid Dynasty," 210–11.

99. Juzjani, *Tabaqat-i Nasiri*, 1:226 (trans. Raverty, *Tabakat-i Nasiri*, 1:69–70). See also C. E. Bosworth, "The Heritage of Rulership in Early Islamic Iran and the Search for Dynastic Connections with the Past," *Iran* 11 (1973), 61, repr. in his *Medieval History of Iran*.

100. On which see Bosworth, "Heritage of Rulership," 57.

101. Juzjani, *Tabaqat-i Nasiri*, 2:43, 45, 47–48, 220–21 (trans. Raverty, *Tabakat-i Nasiri*, 2:791, 796, 799–800, 1295). For the Yemek/Kimek, see above, note 26.

102. Juzjani, *Tabaqat-i Nasiri*, 2:441 (cf. Raverty trans., *Tabakat-i Nasiri*, 1:599).

103. See, for instance, the adoption of the title "daughter of the Emperor of the Cumans" by Elizabeth (consort of István V of Hungary, 1270–72), whose father can only have been chief over one among several Cuman groupings: cited by T. Halasi-Kun, "Ottoman Data on Lesser Cumania: Keçkemet Nahiyesi—Varoş-i Halaş—Kariye-i Kökut," *Archivum Eurasiae Medii Aevi* 4 (1984), 95n19; and by Berend, *At the Gate of Christendom*, 262.

4

Service, Status, and Military Slavery in the Delhi Sultanate: Thirteenth and Fourteenth Centuries

Sunil Kumar

> [W]hen the hearts [of the Turkish slaves] turn to Islam, they do not really remember their homes, their place of origin or their kinsmen . . . the further [they] are taken from their hearth, their kin and their dwellings, the more valued, precious and expensive they become, and they become commanders and generals.[1]

Fakhr-i Mudabbir, a Persian scholar searching for patronage in early thirteenth-century Lahore, included these comments in a text dedicated to Qutb al-Din Aybak, a Turkish slave of the Shansabanid monarch, Sultan Mu'izz al-Din Ghuri (1173–1206). The author tried to explain why Turkish slaves, *bandagan* (singular *banda*), were so important and valuable to Mu'izz al-Din Ghuri. The eulogy was offered to both the master for recognizing the merits of Turks as slaves and to his Turkish slave, Qutb al-Din Aybak, for abiding by the trust reposed in him by his master. According to Fakhr-i Mudabbir, the experience of slavery—what Orlando Patterson described much later as "natal alienation and social death"—never troubled individuals of Turkish origin.[2] Instead, unlike all other slaves, the Turkish *bandagan* seized the opportunities offered by their master and made good in their new homes, where they prospered to eventually become political grandees and governors. This was why, Fakhr-i Mudabbir suggested, Turks were an exceptional people. Indeed, while slaves were a dime a dozen in the north Indian marches, only the exceptional slaves were carefully segregated and trained for armed service. Slaves who could be trusted with independent commands were even

Table 4.1. The Delhi Sultans, 1192–1526. The Delhi sultans ruled over large tracts of north India. This table provides information on three of their five "dynasties" or "regimes." Lineages are listed in chronological order of rule within each "dynasty."

Mamluk Regime	Khalaji Regime	Tughluq Regime
Qutbi Lineage: 1206–10	*Jalali Lineage: 1290–96*	*Ghiyasi Lineage: 1320–51*
Qutb al-Din Aybak: 1206–10	Jalal al-Din Firuz Shah: 1290–96	Ghiyas al-Din: 1320–24
Aram Shah: 1210	Rukn al-Din : 1296	Muhammad Shah: 1324–51
Shamsi Lineage: 1236–66	*ʿAlai Lineage: 1296–1320*	*Firuzi Lineage: 1351–1412*
Shams al-Din Iltutmish: 1210–36	ʿAla al-Din Khalaji: 1296–1316	Firuz Shah: 1351–88
Rukn al-Din Firuz Shah: 1236	Qutb al-Din Mubarak Shah: 1316–20	
Raziyya: 1236–40	*Barwari interregnum*	
Muʿizz al-Din Bahram Shah: 1240–42	Nasir al-Din Khusrau Khan Barwari 1320	
ʿAla al-Din Masʿud Shah: 1242–44		
Nasir al-Din Mahmud Shah: 1242–66		
Ghiyasi Lineage: 1266–90		
Ghiyas al-Din Balban: 1266–86		
Muʿizz al-Din Kaiqubad: 1286–90		
Kayumarth: 1290		

more exclusive. They were the *bandagan-i khass,* a select body of senior, experienced slaves, whose service had been carefully scrutinized. These were the slaves deployed by their master in the central retinue (*qalb*) of the army and trusted to function as governors of strategic territories.[3]

Many scholars have followed chroniclers such as Fakhr-i Mudabbir in associating military slavery under the Delhi sultans almost exclusively with the Turkish *bandagan*. In the historiography of the Delhi Sultanate, it is commonplace to define the years between 1192 and 1290 as the period of the "Turkish" or "Slave (Mamluk)" Sultanate: a period when military slaves of Turkish ethnicity monopolized power and created an extremely authoritarian political system. Historians frequently fuse the three elements—military slavery, Turkish ethnicity, and despotic rule—to encapsulate the nature of the early sultanate.[4] There is also a significant historiographical consensus that structural transitions occurred in the history of the Delhi Sultanate only when the Khalajis deposed the Slave regime in 1290. Amongst other changes that stemmed from administrative and fiscal reorganization in the sultanate, the rule of the Khalajis altered the social and ethnic composition of the military elites: the rulers and their nobility were no longer slaves. Instead, free military commanders, some of whom were of humble origins, became the new ruling elite.[5]

Rather than following in this historiographical tradition, this essay turns the analytic gaze upon the medieval chronicling tradition from the outset. Medieval rhetoric about slaves and slavery, military service and political status can only be understood in the context of its production. As slaves, the *bandagan-i khass* commanded power and patronized many of the chroniclers. The peculiarities of such patronage in turn conditioned the record of the medieval chroniclers, the memory and history of slaves and military service. The dependence of the Persian literati upon the military elite, many of whom were powerful slaves, and their own ideological and social precommitments to an aristocratic social universe created significant elisions in their accounts of the *bandagan* and the Delhi Sultanate political system. These factors also explain the chroniclers' obscuring of a structural feature common to all sultanate regimes—the universal and simultaneous reliance on both free and unfree military personnel.

This chapter has four sections. It begins by contrasting materials produced by court chroniclers—Fakhr-i Mudabbir's troubling eulogy to the loyal Turks, for instance—with a Sufi text to explore the contingent nature of medieval ethnicity and military slavery in the thirteenth century. In the second section, I interrogate the chroniclers' representations of "the loyal, servile slave" by focusing on two episodes in which slave-commanders seized the throne from the sultan's son. The third section analyzes the ways in which the chroniclers represented the reproduction of political authority through the deployment of social menials. This helps us to reenvision the later sultanate regimes (Khalajis and Tughluqs) not as sharp contrasts to the early sultanate (the "Mamluk" regime) but as continuations thereof. The final section of the chapter unravels the contradictions between high political position and slave status, which appear in different ways in the lives of aspiring or able sons of slave-fathers during the history of the Delhi Sultanate. The chroniclers' attempts at erasing the contested transitions within the polity and the corps of the natally alienated draw our attention to the incongruent articulation of social stature and political authority in the early sultanate, as well as to its reproduction. The progeny of slaves struggled to entrench themselves in the corridors of sultanate power even as the Persian chroniclers created new terms for their alienated status.

Remaking Alienation as Ethnicity:
"Turkish" as Sign

With Mu'izz al-Din Ghuri's north Indian campaigns and their consolidation under his subordinates during the last decade of the twelfth century, there was an increase in the number of Turkish *bandagan* in positions of power and influence in north India. By the 1220s, with the emergence of a politically paramount sultanate of Delhi under Sultan Iltutmish, the recently annexed and strategically important military commands were almost without exception given to the monarch's senior slaves, the elite *bandagan-i khass*.[6] As Peter Jackson's chapter in this volume points out, by the end of Iltutmish's reign in 1236, the influence of the Turkish *bandagan* on the political structure of the sultanate was disproportionate to their number and social status.

Although these Turkish slaves had undergone the trauma of natal alienation and had received an introduction to the Islamic creed and the decorum of the court as a part of their training, their Turkish ethnicity remained intact in the representations of all the Persian chroniclers. At one level this was to be expected: the Turkish slaves had only just been uprooted from their homes in the Central Asian steppes. Despite Fakhr-i Mudabbir's claims to the contrary, the *bandagan* did not immediately acculturate to the traditions of their host society. In fact, Fakhr-i Mudabbir's *Ta'rikh* has a large section on the Turks, their culture and traditions. He had, himself, never traveled in Central Asia and he probably culled much of his information from travelers and merchants. But some of his observations on languages, scripts, and religious beliefs of the Turks either came from direct observation or were received first-hand from Turks in north India.[7] Fakhr-i Mudabbir's account suggests that through the first decades of the thirteenth century, the Turks maintained their "racial" and cultural/linguistic separateness in north India. He explains,

> after the Persian language, none is finer and more dignified than Turkish. And nowadays the Turkish language is more popular than it ever was before. This is due to the fact that the majority of Amirs and Commanders are Turks. And it is the Turks who are most successful and most wealthy; and so all have need of that language. And grandees of the highest pedigree [*asilan wa buzurgan wa buzurgzadgan*] are in the service of the Turks ... [and from their success derive] ... peace, prosperity and honour.[8]

Fakhr-i Mudabbir's remarks draw our attention to the linguistic and cultural distance between the lords and the members of the realm they governed, so much so that Persian-speaking secretaries—"the grandees of the highest pedigree"—had to master a "foreign" language to function as their subordinates. These remarks should not be taken to mean that the Turkish slaves of the Delhi sultans knew no Persian. On the contrary, the Turkish slave of Iltutmish, Malik Saif al-Din, functioned as a judge and must have been fluent in Persian with some knowledge of Arabic as well. So remarks like those of Mudabbir refer to the advantages that knowledge of the Turkish language conferred upon a Persian subordinate in the service of the Delhi Sultanate.[9]

To a significant extent, the early Delhi sultans, themselves of Turkic origin, deliberately sought to impart exclusive signs of "Turkishness" to their elite *bandagan*. As a part of the process of divesting the slaves of old relationships and creating new identities and bonds for them, the sultans renamed their *bandagan*. Rather than names of Qur'anic (Arabic) or legendary Persian provenance, both Qutb al-Din and Iltutmish gave their male slaves, without exception, new Turkic names. The former gave his slave Aybak, a compatriot of Iltutmish, the name Tamghaj, and all the Turk *bandagan-i Shamsi* mentioned in Juzjani's twenty-second section were given Turkic names and titles by Sultan Shams al-Din Iltutmish.[10] Turks certainly predominated amongst the *bandagan-i khass,* and by retaining their ethnicity in their names, the Delhi sultans underlined their deracinated, alien quality. A shared Turkish ethnicity reinforced the bonds between the Turk *bandagan-i khass* and the sultan, although it did not imply the distancing of other elite non-Turkish slaves. Instead, the sultan sometimes honored non-Turks with Turkish titles. Iltutmish gave his *banda-i khass* Hindu Khan, who was, as his name suggests, of subcontinental provenance, the Turko-Mongol title of khan and appointed him the *mihtar-i mubarak,* the superintendent of all his slaves.[11]

Persian chroniclers implied that the term "Turk" signaled a cultural divide that ran parallel to the political distinctions between the rulers and the ruled—the "Turks" against the non-Turks. They lauded the stable, powerful political system of the "Turks" for creating a sanctuary for Islam especially when eastern Iran, Central Asia, and Afghanistan were suffering the Mongol apocalypse. Sultan Iltutmish and his *bandagan-i khass* stood united against the foes of Islam. Even as the great sultan's political arrangements unraveled after his death, court chroniclers kept the memory of its homogeneity alive. It was for this reason that Barani was surprised when the Khalajis removed the Turks from political power in 1286. As he put it, "people . . . wondered how the Khalajis had replaced the Turks and seized the throne and how kingship had left the line [*asl*] of the Turks and gone to another."[12] By the middle of the fourteenth century, when Barani was composing his text, he could essentialize the years of slave dominance as a period of Turkish dynastic rule.

But the monolithic character given to the "Turkish" military elite in one set of chronicles created problems for others. The thirteenth-century historian Minhaj-i Siraj Juzjani, for example, found it difficult to explain the innumerable occasions of internal conflict amongst Sultan Iltutmish's *bandagan* later in the century. It would be easier to represent such conflict as exceptional and unnatural to the system rather than inherent to it. Describing a conflict between slave-officers, he noted that

> the armies came close to each other—all brothers and friends of each other, two battalions of one dynasty, two armies of the same capital, [belonging to] the same mansion, two parts of the same [saddle-?] lining [*du jauq az yak batana*]—it was impossible for there to be a more amazing case. They were all of one purse, sharers of salt, partakers of one dish and between them accursed Satan introduced much discord.[13]

In Juzjani's narration, the Shamsi *bandagan* would have never been in conflict with each other had Satan not intervened. Even as the great sultan's political arrangements unraveled after his death, Juzjani continued to dwell upon the ethnic homogeneity of the Turkic military elite.

Although the court chroniclers put a positive spin on their descriptions of this regime, its simple monochromatic appearance also allowed its detractors relatively easy targets to assault. The Chishti Sufi saint Nizam al-Din Auliya, who never otherwise identified individuals according to their ethnicity, seldom noticed the sultan's slaves by name or title; to him they were just anonymous "Turks." The anonymity of the Turk benefactors in the compilation of the shaikh's discourses, the *Fawa'id al-Fu'ad*, might be explained by the fact that they were, finally, incidental agents of God's beneficence. Thus it was through God's intervention, and not the devotion or generosity of "a Turk," that Maulana Kaithali was given twenty *tanka*s, enough money to clear an outstanding debt.[14] Another eminent Sufi, Baba Farid, comforted Shaikh Najib al-Din when he was removed from the mosque, house, and office of *imam* conferred upon him by "a Turk." Shaikh Najib had advised his patron to spend his money on charitable service rather than wasting it on his daughter's wedding. Narrating that episode, Nizam al-Din speculated that the Turk's name was Aitamar because Baba Farid had prophesied that "if an Aitamar departs, God brings forth an Aitakar (in his place)," and indeed, another Turk by the name of Aitakar subsequently became Shaikh Najib's benefactor.[15]

Thus, even when the reader was informed about the identity of "the Turk," he was expected to infer that one Turk benefactor was much like another, the alliteration in the names underlining their incidental nature.[16] Noticeably, the saint's own discourse about other individuals, presumably equally "incidental agents" of God's will on earth, carefully identified them by name, or place of origin, or occupation—military commander (*amir, malik*), merchant (*tajir*), governor (*wali*), or judge (*qazi, hakim*). Only "the Turks" required no further description; the reference to their ethnicity encapsulated the host of qualities understandable to the saint's audience.

Some of these qualities were suggested in Shaikh Najib's story above. But these were more fully worked out in the story Nizam al-Din Auliya told about a Khwaja Hamid, a secretary in the service of a Turkish slave, Tughril. One day, the secretary saw a mysterious face that taunted him. The face reappeared on several occasions and finally explained its reason for harassing the secretary:

> Oh Hamid! Why are you standing before this man? . . . You are wise and he is ignorant, you are a freeman and he is a slave, you are virtuous and he is an uncultured sinner.[17]

Apparently Khwaja Hamid had never perceived his position from that perspective. He promptly left Tughril's service. The Sufi saint thus encapsulated all the qualities of "the Turks" in this anecdote: they were slaves, not learned in the secretarial or Islamic sciences, they were rude, bellicose, and vain, and their military calling undoubtedly led to the unjust killing of innocent people. But the central conundrum in the Chishti Sufi saint's stories revolved around the fact that it was these Turks who possessed the wealth and power that attracted individuals like Khwaja Hamid and Shaikh Najib (and Fakhr-i Mudabbir and Juzjani, for that matter) to their service.

While the chroniclers and Sufi leaders disagreed on the characteristics of the "Turk," their attribution of antithetical values to the ethnonym itself indicated a deeper tension within the polity. Noticeably, too, both Sufi and chronicler agreed that the "Turks" were a homogenous group which was powerful, rich, and "different." This element of "difference" was crucial in the construction of political authority. The possessors of political power could not be "of" the people that they were governing, nor was the recruitment of "aristocrats"—men with enviable "titles" (*laqab*) or genealogies (*nisba, asi-lan*)—ever seized upon as a viable option. Despite the presence of many aristocratic émigrés at court in Iltutmish's reign, the sultan purchased slaves, an extremely expensive body of individuals, trained to serve and fight. Their reliability, at least through the duration of their master's lifetime, made them expensive but worthwhile investments, and it was this positive value that chroniclers like Fakhr-i Mudabbir tried to communicate.

To be sure, such Persian chroniclers were deeply invested in an ideology that conflated majesty with political status, high birth, and cultural upbringing. But since "slavery" hardly carried any of these positive connotations, they had to displace some of its negative elements and graft on others until the Turkish *bandagan* could "pass" as nobles. Deracinated slaves needed, first, to be integrated into their host societies as a "different" group of people, and then endowed with the qualities of command and leadership that demarcated "nobility" to the chroniclers. As we will see in the next section, elite slaves were depicted as sharing a distinctive, royal ethnicity, and some were creatively incorporated into the royal bloodline as well. The transformation of the Turkish slave into a paradigmatic hero of the Delhi sultans and servitor of Islam was a creative sleight of hand which, though contested by contemporary critics of the regime, endured over the long term.

Creating the Loyal Slave: The Chroniclers and the Erasure of Disloyal Acts

When Persian chronicles used generalities like "Turkish slaves," they meant to gesture mainly to a small corps of senior military slaves who had graduated to occupy positions of political responsibility, the *bandagan-i khass*. The chroniclers emphasized the loyalty and obedience of this small and special cadre of slaves and their great value in enforcing the authority of their master over the dispersed provinces of the sultanate. This was significant because it can be read as a response by the literati to a fundamental paradox in the situation of such slaves. The latter were legal agents only when empowered by their master or mistress. The slave's very "agency" was considered to lapse with the death of the master or mistress, which transformed such a slave legally into a "personal possession" and part of the master's or mistress's bequest to heirs. The juridical reasoning was clear enough on the subject. Its implementation was more difficult since, their slave status notwithstanding, governors of provinces and commanders of large armies were not always willing to part with their power, especially if the new heir or heiress was ready to deploy his or her own subordinates in their stead. This is precisely what appears to have happened in the following two episodes of usurpation by highly placed slaves in the Delhi Sultanate. Hence, the treatment of these two breaches of law by the chroniclers also generated a special kind of rhetoric.

The first incident relates to Shams al-Din Iltutmish, the slave of Qutb al-Din Aybak, and the second one concerns Ghiyas al-Din Balban, the slave of Shams al-Din Iltutmish. Both Iltutmish and Balban seized the throne after military conflict with a variety of competitors, not the least of whom were the sons of their masters. In the near-contemporary accounts of Juzjani and Barani there is no discussion of these events as an act of usurpation by slaves. These Persian chroniclers glossed over the violent seizure of royal privileges and obvious display of disloyalty to the memory of the master. Instead, they dwelt upon the honorable conduct of their protagonists and the seamless continuity of the sultanate from one lineage to another.

Shams al-Din Iltutmish was described by Juzjani as a *banda-i khass,* a special, senior, honored military slave of Sultan Qutb al-Din Aybak. Juzjani provided rare details about how Iltutmish was enslaved as a youth in the Central Asian steppes, brought to Bukhara by slave merchants, acculturated to an Islamicate way of life in the household of the pious *sadr-i jahan* (the local governor, head of the judiciary), and sold again to a broker who brought the young slave to Ghazni. (See map 1.) His prior training and personality had made Iltutmish into a precious commodity, so expensive that Sultan Mu'izz al-Din found him to be overpriced. Qutb al-Din eventually purchased and trained him and eased him gradually into the responsibilities of a military command. According to Juzjani, Iltutmish's rise to power occurred when his master noticed that "the signs of rectitude were, time and again, manifest and clear in his actions and thoughts." He was then trusted with public responsibility and kept close (*nazdik*) to the monarch, who called him his son.[18]

References to the trusted slave as "the dear and beloved," "the heart and liver" of the master were standard tropes in Persian literature, used for exceptional slaves to emphasize their proximity to their master and to explain their deployment as commanders and governors in the realm.[19] Such slaves were frequently described as "better than sons," a complex allusion to their (agnatic-like) proximity to their master/father. Slaves were better than real sons, however, because they remained dependent and the favor showered upon them did not promote fractious ambitions to inheritance rights. In Islamic law, the master (and his successors) inherited the slave's property, an asymmetrical relationship not altered by manumission.[20] Hence Nizam al-Mulk advised, "A slave, whom one has brought up and promoted, must be looked after, for it needs a whole lifetime and good luck to find a worthy and experienced slave. Wise men have said that a worthy and experienced servant or slave is better than a son."[21] In Juzjani's narrative, Iltutmish was a special slave and his selfless duty and service to his master was a paradigm of conduct that "real" sons would do well to emulate.

Iltutmish's conduct at his master's death offered a sharp contrast to this image. As a slave, Iltutmish was a part of Qutb al-Din's bequest to his son, Aram Shah. Rather than accept this position, Iltutmish battled with Aram Shah and seized the throne, a usurpation that he sought to consolidate by marrying his master's daughter. This matrimonial union too was an innovation. Hitherto, brides had been given only to peers, both within the Shansbanid family of Ghur and amongst the Mu'izzi *bandagan-i khass.* For example, Sultan Muʿizz al-Din Ghuri had arranged the marriages of his slaves in strictly endogamous fashion: the daughters of his slave-commander, Taj al-Din Yilduz, were married to two of his senior male slaves, Qutb al-Din Aybak and Qubacha; two daughters of the slave Qutb al-Din were married in turn, one after the death of the other, to Qubacha.[22] Iltutmish's marriage with his master's daughter was a break in the patterns of slave-slave endogamy, and the master had not arranged it in his lifetime. Iltutmish planned it carefully, however, and it served to obscure the change in the dynasty that his accession had constituted. These events were obviously a matter of some concern, because Juzjani was extremely diffident in his recollection of them.

Juzjani described the accession of Iltutmish in two different parts of his chronicle: in a section titled "Great Sultan Shams al-Din Iltutmish, the father of victory," and in another section titled more simply "Aram Shah, the son of Sultan Qutb al-Din."[23] While Iltutmish figured prominently in both the sections, Aram Shah did not. In the first of the two sections, the son of Qutb al-Din Aybak was completely absent from the narrative. Instead Juzjani described how Iltutmish was invited to the throne by some Delhi notables on account of having been favored by his master during his lifetime. The slave battled with some discontented commanders—no mention of Aram Shah here either!—and won.[24]

Ironically, in the section whose title recognized Aram Shah as the son of Qutb al-Din Aybak, Juzjani devoted most of the account to the daughters of the sultan and their marriages. This brought the reader's attention back to Iltutmish, whose marriage to the daughter of Qutb al-Din Aybak was mentioned twice, once suggesting that the marriage took place while his master was still alive, the second time suggesting that the marriage occurred after his accession to the throne. Despite such repetition, the awkwardness of the event remained and it was, therefore, embedded within a genealogical frame. Thus the significance of the statement that "Qutb al-Din had Iltutmish in mind as his heir and referred to him as his son." Such language explained the behavior of the *malik*s of the realm who raised the slave to the throne, and elided the marriage of a slave to the (presumably free-born?) daughter of a sultan. Furthermore, when the author described the marriage of the slave, the active agents of the rest of the narrative, Sultan Qutb al-Din and the *malik*s, disappeared from the text. The marriage "happened," as it were, through anonymous agents (*dukhtar-i Sultan Qutb al-Din dar hibalaʾyi o amad*),[25] suggesting an inevitable conclusion to a special relationship between the master and his slave.

Two Persian chroniclers of the late sixteenth century, Nizam al-Din Ahmad and ʿAbd al-Qadir Badaʾuni, successfully elaborated on this "special relationship." They reinterpreted the succession dispute as a conflict between equals: between a son, Aram Shah, and a slave and son-in-law, also called "son" by Sultan Qutb al-Din.[26] Usurpation, the gradual erasure of Aram Shah, and the dynastic change introduced by Iltutmish's succession were all neatly folded into the theme of a genealogical inheritance of power, whereby Iltutmish, as son-in-law and "adopted" son, succeeded the father-in-law. This trope had congealed so well by the twentieth century that some modern historians began to doubt Aram Shah's descent from Qutb al-Din Aybak.[27] Very few were equally skeptical of the "wonderful, attentive, loyal" slave Iltutmish, or wondered about the truth of his "sonship" or his status as son-in-law and heir.

The social and political contexts within which such chronicles were produced, both in the thirteenth and in later centuries, conditioned the creation and maintenance of their elisions. Juzjani's major patron was Ghiyas al-Din Balban, a slave of Iltutmish, who had gradually fought his way through the ranks of the Shamsi *bandagan* to emerge as the primary power broker in the sultanate. We do not know when Balban was manumitted but, like Iltutmish, the freed slave (*mawla*) was still juridically bound in a relationship of dependent servitude to his master's successors. This was how Balban came to be the servant of Sultan Nasir al-Din (1246–66), the youngest son of Sultan Iltutmish, also the patron of the chronicler. In 1255–56 Juzjani had been appointed the chief jurist of the realm, with jurisdiction over the city of Delhi, from Sultan Nasir al-Din.[28] As a client of both the sultan and the slave, Juzjani consistently reported the different stature of the two protagonists in his work: he praised the valor and influence of Balban, but always mentioned that he was a slave and a loyal servant of Sultan Nasir al-Din, the great monarch of the age.[29] It must have been a difficult balancing act for the chroniclers, since Balban controlled the sultan for the better part of his reign, and in 1249, the sultan also married the slave's daughter.[30] Again, the tensions in such an inverse relationship were deflected by Juzjani's reiterations of the slave's loyalty, such as a statement to the effect that Nasir al-Din gave him the status of father (*mansab pidari midad*), but Balban, ever mindful of his actual position, remained more obedient and submissive to his sultan than a thousand newly purchased slaves.[31]

The chroniclers were hardly tender toward all slaves who murdered their masters and usurped the latter's powers. Juzjani's own narrative mentions one Tughril Bozan(?), who had murdered his master Sultan 'Abd al-Rashid in 1053 and seized the throne. Juzjani refers to the slave as Tughril *al-mal'un* ("the accursed") because of his disloyalty and ingratitude to the household of his patrons.[32] But the actual difference between Tughril, Iltutmish, and Balban was that the former was quickly deposed, whereas the latter two

slaves had long, successful reigns and were munificent patrons of chroniclers like Juzjani. So even though Juzjani scrupulously recorded that Sultan
Nasir al-Din had four sons and perhaps a fifth, borne by Balban's daughter
in 1259,[33] his chronicle revealed nothing about these sons in the final years
of the sultan's reign. In fact, when the sultan died in 1266, none of his sons
succeeded to the throne; instead "his slave" and father-in-law inherited the
throne. Meanwhile, Juzjani had tactfully concluded his account six years before the sultan's death and thus avoided having to deal with Balban's accession altogether.

In order to retrieve a fuller account of Balban and his accession to power,
we have to turn to other chroniclers. One of them, Ziya al-Din Barani, started his *Ta'rikh-i Firuz Shahi* with the accession of Balban but provided no details of his succession to the throne. Instead, Barani recalled how famous
rulers, *wazir*s, and secretaries—people with years of administrative experience—adorned the court of Iltutmish. During the thirty years following
Iltutmish's death, the great nobles of the realm were all murdered by the frivolous and cheap slaves (*harzgan wa diram-i kharidgar*), who plunged the
state into crisis.[34] It was in this context that Balban, though himself a slave,
seized the throne, restoring the dignity of the king and an ideal social order
in which the low-born could never aspire to political authority. In several
places in the text, Barani had Balban ruminating on the virtuous quality of
his master's governance, providing examples that illuminated Balban's own
conduct of governance.[35] Hence the enduring impression left by Barani upon
his readers: Balban's accession was not a calamitous usurpation, but a "re-
newal" of the best traditions of monarchical statecraft.

Another chronicler writing in the middle of the fourteenth century,
'Isami, charged Balban with having murdered Sultan Nasir al-Din.[36] Although 'Isami's versified history was replete with details supporting this accusation, sixteenth-century chroniclers like Nizam al-Din Ahmad and 'Abd
al-Qadir Bada'uni ignored these details in their narratives of the sultanate.
Neither of these later historians characterized Balban as a regicide. In their
accounts, Balban's master, the pious sultan of Delhi, fell sick and died.[37]
Moreover, despite Juzjani's information to the contrary, both the sixteenth-
century chroniclers categorically stated that the sultan had no sons.[38] The
erasure of the sultan's sons made it easier to suggest that Balban succeeded to
the throne by virtue of his great military and political experience. In their
accounts, Balban's military and political exploits had raised his stature to
such an extent that the king honored the slave by marrying his daughter. As
a result, they explained, at the death of the monarch, the grandees of the
state invited Balban to the throne. It was Balban's firm administration that

had rescued the sultanate in the past; it was required again, they underscored, to ensure the survival of "Turkish" rule.

Modern historians inherited some of this selective use and interpretation of information. Khaliq Nizami, the only modern historian who took cognizance of Balban's regicide, absolved him thus: "The methods employed by Balban . . . were . . . callous and uncompromising but . . . it can hardly be disputed that through these Draconian measures alone the unruly elements could be forced to submit to the authority of the State."[39] A small detail mentioned by Juzjani helped to consolidate the sense of a Turkish sultanate that could seamlessly incorporate both Iltutmish and Balban within a monolithic dynasty. Certainly Barani and the later Mughal historians had missed it. According to Juzjani, Balban belonged to the Ilbari Turkish tribe, the same one as Shams al-Din Iltutmish.[40] Although the thirteenth-century chronicler had made nothing of the shared natal origins, modern historians seized on this "clan connection" between the two sultans to christen the period "Ilbari."[41] Such a return to genealogical readings of the past marginalized the slave's usurpation of political authority, and rooted it firmly in Balban's clan background—one that had royalty stamped all over it.

Local Memory and Courtly Chronicles of Slave-Sultans

While the contradictions and elisions in these reports reveal a remarkable suppression of senior male slaves' usurpations of power, the account of a fourteenth-century traveler reveals that court chroniclers were dialogically engaged with "popular" discussions of slave delicts. The Moroccan Ibn Battuta visited India sometime between 1333 and 1342 and provided a brief but significant assessment of the rulers of Delhi up to his own host, Muhammad Shah Tughluq (1324–51).[42] It is doubtful if Ibn Battuta personally ever read any of the chronicles of the Delhi sultans or had any read to him.[43] He composed his history on the basis of a variety of oral reports received from diverse informants. Some reports were of indiscriminate provenance; others were received from friends and acquaintances like the chief *qazi* of Delhi (Kamal al-Din Muhammad) or the Suhrawardi shaikh Rukn-i 'Alam.[44] Although the account of the Delhi sultans is a pastiche of anecdotes, these suggest the ways the past was remembered and circulated—at least within the group of jurists in the region willing to speak to the traveler. It is especially significant that a century after the events, of all the other information about Iltutmish and Balban that could have been conveyed by such juridically minded informants, it was only their "just" and "unjust" actions that were distilled in the traveler's account.

Ibn Battuta recorded two anecdotes about Sultan Iltutmish. One was a brief and stereotypical account of the king's munificent justice and the bell that he placed for the oppressed to ring for restitution. The second was a longer anecdote touching on the sultan's slave status and service to his master Qutb al-Din Aybak. Ibn Battuta mentions that on his master's death, when Iltutmish had seized the throne, he was approached by the jurists of Delhi. Iltutmish realized that they doubted the legality of his accession, and the (freed) slave, therefore, showed them his deed of manumission. Since only a free individual could hold a position of public responsibility and command over other free Muslims, it was only after they had perused the document that the jurists rendered their oath of allegiance to the new monarch.[45] The story implied that doubts about the legality of the event had persisted in "popular" memory into the fourteenth century, when the jurists resolved them by the traditional juristic device—the slave's documentary claim to freedom and hence to rule.

Ibn Battuta's account of Sultan Ghiyas al-Din Balban was slightly longer. It also included two anecdotes. One was a brief introduction dilating on the monarch's accessibility to those seeking justice, and a second one focused on the king's slave-antecedents.[46] This story mentioned the "puny, contemptible and ignoble" stature of the young slave, whose precocious character and service led a Sufi *faqir* to bless him with the throne of Hindustan. The same precocious nature of this otherwise unprepossessing slave won the attention of Sultan Iltutmish. After some hesitation, the king purchased Balban and deployed him with the other menial water-carriers. It was a fateful decision; soon afterward court astrologers started warning Iltutmish that one of his slaves would depose his son, seize the throne, and bring his dynasty to an end. The worried sultan asked if they would be able to recognize the murderous usurper and on receiving an affirmative reply, Iltutmish ordered a muster of his slaves. But, as it happened (it was, of course, God's will), Balban escaped scrutiny and continued to rise in stature under Iltutmish's successors, becoming Sultan Nasir al-Din's father-in-law and his deputy. He ultimately killed him, seized the throne, and established his own dynasty, and his sons (they were actually his grandsons) succeeded him on the throne.

Ibn Battuta's accounts of both slaves who became sultans highlighted three aspects of their lives: both had been famous for their justice, both had been slaves, and both seized the throne from their masters to start independent dynasties. Ibn Battuta recounted nothing else from the careers of the two monarchs. His report introduced a perspective on how the seizure of authority by a slave might have remained a subject of considerable discussion amongst the jurists of the realm. Therefore, Ibn Battuta's treatment of the two usurpations did not legitimize these by appeals to the "loyal conduct" of the particular slave, nor by either slave's superior administration, and definitely not by appeals to their kinship to their erstwhile masters. Ibn Battuta's anecdotes recalled and justified the usurpations in distinctly different terms. In one, the slave's seizure of authority could have created a juridical quandary, but Iltutmish escaped censure because he could prove his manumitted status. In the other instance, the murder of the master and seizure of the throne by Balban was only an enactment of God's will; that the slave became sultan was beyond temporal right or wrong.

The difference between the accounts of the court chroniclers and those of Ibn Battuta is not a simple one of dissenting perspectives. The difference marks the space between the efforts of chroniclers to contour the past for their audience and the creative reception and transcreation of these contours. Jurists concerned about the maintenance of a higher "law" (implicit in the *shari'a*) made no attempt to gloss over the unfree condition of military slaves, irrespective of the earthly political stature of the protagonist. Chroniclers, clients of such slaves, were concerned with more mundane social hierarchies and thus more sensitive to the need to tame the threats posed by the actions of some military slaves. In order to comprehend the significance of the chroniclers' achievements, as well as to situate military slavery itself within the historiographic context, we need to briefly outline a polity in which many different kinds of natally and socially alienated beings played significant roles. Like the *bandagan*, the free-born of "mean and base lineages" were integral to sultanate political authority but, unlike the "valorous Turks," they were never metamorphosed into nobles. It is to such groups that we now turn.

Remaking Alienation through the Free-Born: "Afghans," Menials, and Sultans

During the reign of Sultan Iltutmish, the governorships of some of the most strategic provinces located far from Delhi (Uch, Multan, and Lakhnauti, for example) were entrusted to elite slaves.[47] But some governorships were also given to a few free *amir*s and to those of the sultan's children who were old enough to hold command. Thus we learn about three of Iltutmish's sons. Malik Nasir al-Din, who predeceased his father, had at different times been given the command of Hansi, Awadh (1226), and Lakhnauti (1227). Rukn al-Din Firuz Shah was appointed to Badayun (1228) and then Lahore (1233).[48] A third son, Ghiyas al-Din, probably had the command of Awadh when he was killed soon after his father's death (1236).[49] The princes had independent retinues, military slaves, and administrative staff. Despite Juzjani's ambiguity on the matter, Iltutmish seems to have made a deliberate effort to indicate that his eldest surviving son, Rukn al-Din, should succeed him to the throne.

By Juzjani's and Barani's accounts, Iltutmish's sons were incompetent wastrels, more given to pleasure and merriment (*lahw wa tarab*) than to the serious affairs of governance.[50] Rukn al-Din, in particular, was singled out as a prince more generous in giving grants than any preceding monarch. This would not have been a problem in itself but for the fact that the recipients of his largesse were musicians, jesters, and catamites (*matraban wa maskhara-gan wa mukhannasan*), not the ideals of masculinity fit to command an army, and even less to rule a kingdom. Though Juzjani was prepared to commend the prince for his easy-going nature, the chronicler suggested that the prince's consorting with the base and the impure (*najinsan wa khabisan*) cost him the kingdom.[51]

Yet Juzjani's own account provided details that contradicted the picture of a weak-kneed, pleasure-seeking prince. It is from his text that we learn that soon after Iltutmish's death, Rukn al-Din launched campaigns against his father's slaves, had a younger male sibling, Qutb al-Din, executed, and alarmed two others into rebellion.[52] During his father's reign, Rukn al-Din had already gained considerable experience as a governor and discharged his duties creditably enough to warrant his appointment as heir. As governor he also raised his independent military retinue. Juzjani provides few details of the prince's political dispensation, but we do have the intriguing reference to Beg-Timur or Khan Rukni, who was, as his "Rukni" *nisba* indicates, a slave of Sultan Rukn al-Din.[53] Beg-Timur Rukni might have been a part of the prince's personal slave-retinue, which certainly also included a sizable following of Persian administrators, whom we know about only from their moment of massacre at the hands of Iltutmish's slaves.[54]

Rukn al-Din's attempts to challenge the stifling control of his father's slaves and establish his own independent political base led him into conflict with the Shamsi *bandagan* and directed the prince's patronage in unexpected and interesting directions. In his description of Rukn al-Din's "immoral" qualities, Juzjani noted the great favor he showed to mahouts (*pil-banan*), the pleasure that he derived from spending time with them and riding elephants through the city. Apparently, through his gifts and kindness (*az daulat wa ahsan-i o*), their fortunes multiplied. Much to Juzjani's chagrin, the mahouts became important in Rukn al-Din's court.[55]

In the wide-ranging conflict between the Ruknis and the Shamsis, there seems to have been little in the way of a rapprochement between the two competing dispensations. Juzjani does mention in passing, however, that Rukn al-Din approached the junior Shamsi slave, Ikhtiyar al-Din Yuzbeg Tughril Khan, and tried to win him over by offering him the position of commandant of the elephants (*shahnagi pilan*).[56] The consistency in the prince's patronage of the elephant drivers and the management of his elephant corps is especially significant given that war horses and elephants were crucial military resources in the armed forces of the sultanate. Elephants were the "battle tanks" of medieval warfare.[57] If elephants were important in the military forces of the sultanate, they were valuable only with their mahouts. Rukn al-Din understood this, and acted accordingly.

But in doing so, he extended his patronage to groups outside the circle of personnel accustomed to high office in the sultanate. While the mahouts were undeniably individuals of low social standing, considered "foreign" by the entrenched and pedigreed elites of sultanate society, their elevation was as pragmatic as the deployment of military slaves, individuals without any social status and roots. Like slaves, they derived their political status from the sultan's patronage, and like the military slaves, they were, because of their social (if not natal) alienation, utterly dependent upon their master.

It may even be surmised that the chroniclers' negative portrayal of the prince and his companions rested on an acute sensitivity about the opposition to Shamsi slaves represented in the maneuvers of the prince. Later chroniclers who were less dependent on Shamsi slave patronage than Juzjani were therefore also more forthright in their description of the prince. For instance, 'Isami characterized Rukn al-Din's intentions thus: "within three or four months rather than following his father's customs he followed his own conclusions.... I have heard that towards his father's slaves, each of whom was a world conqueror, he adopted an angry and arrogant demeanour."[58]

But the historian Barani went much further than Juzjani in holding both "cheap slaves" and "social menials" alike responsible for the unstable conditions of the sultanate. For Barani, it was part of a larger lesson in statecraft: it highlighted the disasters that befell a regime which did not appoint people of impeccable genealogy and social background (like himself) to positions of public authority. Barani's exemplar of "great" government was none other than Balban's sweeping away of the "base-born" (*bad asli wa na kas*): he had the genealogies of court officers scrutinized and declared that he would not associate with or patronize anybody of suspect lineage and character irrespective of their accomplishments (*hunarmandi*).[59] As Barani put it, Balban did not want to sully the dignity of sovereignty or his own pure Afrasiyabi lineage through association with people of indiscriminate backgrounds.

The ironies of situating these ideas as part of an apocryphal conversation that the sultan had with two of his old compatriots, individuals who were, like Balban himself, *khwaja tash,* or slaves of the same master, were not obvious to the chronicler.[60] This was because Barani, like Juzjani before him, did not consider slaves like Balban or his close associates to be "base-born" (*bad asli wa na kas*) or "frivolous and cheap" slaves (*harzgan wa diram-i kharidgar*). Instead, he regarded these slaves as having displayed their "innate" high pedigree through their stated preferences for a "conventionally" stratified social order.

The passage of time, according to Barani, was not kind to these people and, ever so gradually, first during ʿAla al-Din Khalaji's reign (1296–1316) and then during that of Muhammad Shah Tughluq (1324–51), the number of social menials increased until they held some of the highest positions in administration.[61] In Irfan Habib's analysis this process was described as the "plebianisation of the nobility," in which the "sluggish nobility resting on its hereditary claims" could not keep pace with the dynamic expansion of the political sphere and the complex economic life of the sultanate under the great Khalaji and Tughluq monarchs. In his argument: "The ambitions, fed on the immense opportunities, now brought in those who could gain the sultan's confidence in their loyalty by their very lack of any hereditary following, and so their complete dependence upon his favours. The *plebianisation of the nobility* was an inevitable product of the political development of the sultanate."[62] In resurrecting the strands of evidence from the *Taʾrikh-i Firuz Shahi* to formulate a linear progression of material change and economic expansion in sultanate history, Irfan Habib ignored the circularity in Barani's argument. Just as Balban provided some degree of social harmony after the anarchic rule of Iltutmish's successors, Barani argued, Firuz Shah Tughluq (the best of all sultans) was the restorer of social order after the tyrannical rule of Muhammad Shah Tughluq.[63] The negative depiction of Muhammad Shah Tughluq's reign was vital to the didactic intent of his history, and the sultan's patronage of the base-born was integral to the creation of the sultan's tyrannical and unbalanced character.

If we are sensitive to the discursive attitude of the Persian chronicles toward individuals without any "hereditary following," then Muhammad Shah Tughluq's recruitment of social menials—ʿAziz Khummar the wine distiller, Firuz Hajjam the barber, Manka Tabbakh the cook, Ladha and Pira the gardeners—can be placed in a larger context.[64] They no longer appear as novel manifestations of strategic choices made by Delhi sultans. As already discussed, natal alienation and contingent incorporation helped to persuade the early sultans to deploy slaves in military positions. They were also important considerations in the patronage extended by Rukn al-Din, the son of

Iltutmish, to social menials. And if we ignore Barani's discourse on Sultan Balban's fixation with aristocrats for a moment, his reign provides a wonderful example of the recruitment of people who could be called the "lowest and basest of the low and base-born" (*sifatarin wa razalatarin-i siflagan wa razalagan*).[65]

Such information was first given by Juzjani in his account of Ulugh Khan's (the future Sultan Balban's) 1260 campaigns in the Mewat region, to the south of Delhi. During these campaigns Juzjani noticed the deployment of a new body of military personnel. These were the Afghans, a body of people who were perhaps used earlier in some sultanate campaigns but must have been demustered quickly enough to escape the notice of the chroniclers of the time. That they were not a regular presence in sultanate armies is evident from the awe-struck manner in which Juzjani described their fearful, strange presence:

> each one of them, one could say, is like an elephant with two braided manes [*du ghazhgha*] on [their] broad shoulders, or is like a bastion [*burji*] . . . and each one of them would seize a hundred Hindus, [whether] in the mountain or the jungle, and on a dark night would reduce a demon to helplessness.[66]

Balban continued to use Afghans in his armies after he became sultan. In fact they were deployed in the strategic areas of the Ganges-Jamuna *doab* soon after his accession and then further afield in the areas of Haryana and western Panjab. Forts were built in these newly pacified areas, old military cantonments were refortified, and it was the Afghans who were given charge of these strategically important regions.[67] Just over a decade after their first recorded deployment, Afghans controlled the cantonments that encircled the capital of the sultanate. Balban gave them rent-free lands and settled them in territories that had seen some of the most violent conflicts between the monarch and his competitors in the preceding decade. These were the most strategic areas in the sultanate. In appointing Afghans to these sites Balban displayed the extent of his regard for this group. Such trust was greeted with ambivalence by the residents of Delhi. Sometime around 1280 the famous poet Amir Khusrau wrote about the salient features of the Afghans residing in the near vicinity of the capital thus:

> In this (?) fortress live the Afghans—nay man-slaying demons, for even the demons groan in fright at their shouts. Their heads are like big sacks of straw, their beards like the combs of the weaver, long-legged as the stork but more ferocious than the eagle, their heads lowered like that of the owl of the wilderness. Their voices hoarse and shrill like that of a jack-daw, their mouths open like a shark. Their tongue is blunt like a home-made arrow, and flings stones like the sling of a battering ram. Well has a wise man said that when speech was sent to men from the sky, the Afghans got the last and least share of it.[68]

Although Sultan Balban's Afghan recruits were hardly "new" to the sultanate, their novel fearsome qualities had not been smoothed over since Juzjani first noted their presence. The Persian literati of the time looked with horror at these military heroes of the sultanate; these were not a body of people to whom could be ascribed the status of nobles. Yet they were systematically patronized and deployed by Balban, the one sultan whose supposed aversion to the low-born was so celebrated by Barani.

Beyond Barani's didactic moralizing, however, it is not difficult to note how the huge social chasm between the Afghans and other elites in sultanate society was extremely valuable to the Delhi sultan. They could be patronized and given high political positions, but they would always remain the creatures of the monarch. Like the mahouts of Sultan Rukn al-Din, or the wine distillers, gardeners, barbers, and cooks of Muhammad Shah Tughluq, Afghans were menial enough to be considered "the meanest of the base-born." Ironically, it was exactly this quality that made them valuable to their patrons. The Delhi sultans systematically deployed slaves and "plebian" groups in their efforts to segregate political authority. This development was not unique to the fourteenth century. In the sultanate political system, political and social statuses were seldom congruent. But in contrast to what was done for the slaves, no effort was made to discursively reengineer the status of mahouts and Afghans into nobles, and the bad press lingered.

Maulazadgan and the "Debris of Political Dispensations"

The "low and base-born" personnel raised to high positions by the Delhi sultans did not usually survive beyond a single generation. While military slaves continued to be important well into the fourteenth century, their careers, and often their lives, seldom outlasted their master's reign. During the second half of ʿAla al-Din Khalaji's rule his most trusted and influential subordinate was the slave Malik Kafur Hazar Dinari. He was killed soon after his master's death. During the reign of the next Khalaji monarch, Qutb al-Din Mubarak Shah (1316–20), the chief notable was also a slave, Nasir al-Din Khusrau Khan. He murdered his master and seized the throne, but was deposed and killed before the year was out.[69] The rapid turnover of the deracinated personnel can be associated with their "one-generational" quality: they were deployed and empowered because they were "aliens," a persuasive argument against any transmission of their positions to their children.

However well the structuralist-functionalist reading of slave-master relationships captures the rationale for the creation of political elites from the "socially dead and natally alienated," its synchronicity does not help us explain how political empowerment remade the lives of deracinated groups in time. The *bandagan* of the Delhi sultans married, had children, and established households; those with high military commands recruited slaves and other military personnel, hired administrators, and patronized litterateurs. As Fakhr-i Mudabbir noted, they possessed considerable wealth and power, and had managed to translate some of their political accomplishments into social capital. Did the change of a political dispensation erase this lifetime of work? Even if they lost their lives during the maelstrom of a political transition, what became of their children and their households?

In his *Ta'rikh-i Firuz Shahi*, Barani used the term *maulazadgan* (singular *maulazada*), a neologism, to describe the "sons of [freed] slaves" of Ghiyas al-Din Balban. It was supposed to refer to a very narrow group of people who were quite distinct from the *bandagan* retinue of the sultan. But given the forty-years-long domination of sultanate politics by Balban and the numbers of slaves who died in his service, the numbers of the *maulazadgan* must have been substantial enough.[70] The sultan certainly recruited some of these to his service. The most famous *maulazada* was Ikhtiyar al-Din ʿAli Sarjandar (also known as Hatim Khan), the commander of Amroha and later Awadh. He had considerable influence and wealth and was a munificent patron with enough literary discrimination to patronize Amir Khusrau when the poet was just starting his career.[71] Similarly, despite the indiscretions of the slave Malik Baq Baq, his son Malik Qerabeg was favored in 1277 with the command (*iqtaʿ*) of Sonepat.[72] These examples should not lead us to assume that Balban was bound by any emotional attachment to the memory of his slaves; the Delhi sultan did not recognize status that was claimed as a birthright, and he was remarkably circumspect in the selection of his subordinates. This was more than apparent in the case of the *maulazadgan*, not all of whom won his patronage.

Such discretion, though difficult of explanation, was apparent in the case of Kamal Mahiyar, recommended to the office of financial administrator (*khwaja*) of Amroha. The sultan rejected Kamal Mahiyar's application for the post. Barani suggested that it was because he was the son of a Hindu (domestic?) slave. It is extremely doubtful that Balban discriminated amongst his *maulazadgan* on the basis of "poor lineage and background" (*kam asli wa kam bizaʿat*) as suggested by Barani.[73] Nor is it entirely plausible that Kamal Mahiyar was of impoverished origins, since any aspirant to the office of *khwaja* would have had knowledge of Persian, mathematics, and accountancy, not easy skills for the ordinary unlettered slave to acquire.[74] Barani's description of the event—from the rejection of Kamal Mahiyar, the ban on recruitment of all low-born to administrative positions, the recollection of Sultan Iltutmish's moralization on the issue, to the investigation and discovery of the Shamsi *wazir* Nizam al-Mulk Junaydi's humble weaver origins and his dismissal—is completely didactic.[75] As we have already seen, Balban showed no hesitation in deploying "plebeians" throughout his reign; they were, in fact, some of his important subordinates. On the other hand, the rejection of Kamal Mahiyar does serve as a salutary reminder that all aspirants to high political office—slaves, "plebeians," *maulazadgan,* and the highest lords of the land—had to gain the sultan's support and protection (*himayat-i Balbani*) before they could be included in his dispensation.

These incidents reveal that some of the *bandagan* had successfully managed to transfer their crucial political connections to their children, enabling their recruitment into the sultan's retinue. Others had provided their children with the training, skills, and ambitions to seek high office. The sons of freed slaves were not regarded as a part of the *bandagan* cadre because they were no longer socially dead or natally alienated. By Balban's reign, these *maulazadgan* wanted to seize the high ground in the political affairs of the sultanate. They were recruited by Balban's successor, Mu'izz al-Din Kaiqubad (1286–90), in his effort to counter the baleful influence of the Balbani slaves. Such patronage provided the *maulazadgan* the space to consolidate their position, and Barani noted how they emerged as great *malik*s with large garrisons in Kaiqubad's reign. The "sons of slaves" networked and established matrimonial relations with the Mongols (another new entry in sultanate politics) to emerge as a threat to their patron.[76]

It is important to keep in mind that Barani used the term *maulazadgan* in a relatively narrow context to refer only to the sons of those slaves who had served Balban. Yet his description of the *maulazadgan* in Balban's reign does force us to consider the *bandagan* as a part of a social unit whose lives stretched beyond the immediate context of their master. Did they have a life of their own without a patron? Barani, himself, was only concerned with the *maulazadgan* because they remained involved and were important participants in the post-Balbanid politics of the sultanate. But what became of the *bandagan* and their families that were defeated or marginalized by new dispensations of power? Once these people were outside the realm of the court and political authority they were of marginal interest to sultanate chroniclers, and we have to reconcile ourselves to the fragmentary nature of the available information.

Juzjani provides us with sparse but important details to reconstruct a rudimentary history of a slave household from the early half of the thirteenth century. The evidence concerns Baha al-Din Tughril, a slave of Mu'izz al-Din Ghuri, who was given the command of Thangir in the Bayana region in 1196. Tughril was an obviously favored and powerful Mu'izzi *banda* who had great ambitions for his command of the Bayana region. He gave grants to attract commerce and traders into his territory, built up a vast retinue which included slaves, embellished towns with mosques, and built a new capital for his principality at Sultankot. His ambition attracted the jealousy of Qutb al-Din Aybak, the commander of Delhi, and the two had a falling out over who should annex Gwalior. Sometime after the death of his master, Tughril placed an inscription in his congregational mosque where he had taken the title of the exalted monarch, *padishah wa al-sultan*.[77]

Tughril did not long outlive his master. He died sometime during the first decade of the thirteenth century, probably around the same time as Qutb al-Din (c. 1210). But the control of Bayana stayed, at least for a while, with his sons. Their fortunes declined fairly rapidly, in inverse proportion to the expansion of Delhi's authority through the 1220s. Tughril's sons were apparently hard pressed financially and militarily and were forced to sell their father's slaves to Iltutmish. This might have served the purpose of raising vital funds for the family, but the loss of important military personnel, especially to a political competitor, underlined their inability to withstand Delhi's political encroachments into the area. Iltutmish finally annexed Bayana and, in 1234–35, appointed his slave Malik Nusrat al-Din Ta'isi to the command of Bayana/Thangir and the superintendency, *shahnagi*, of the region of Gwalior.[78]

It is interesting to note that the influence of Baha al-Din Tughril's descendants was incorporated into the Shamsi regime through a revival of the "endogamous" marital alliance building that Iltutmish had abjured in his own marriage. The Delhi sultan arranged the marriage of one of his trusted manumitted slaves, Taj al-Din Sanjar Arsalan, to Baha al-Din Tughril's daughter. Juzjani ascribed to Taj al-Din's matrimonial relations the influence that led to his appointment as *muqti* of Bayana under a later sultan (Nasir al-Din Mahmud, 1246–66).[79] Whatever other reasons existed for this appointment, the chronicler clearly believed in the political weight of affinal relationships between freedmen's families. It was equally significant that despite the loss of political control nearly two decades earlier, Baha al-Din's descendants carried sufficient symbolic potency for a social relationship with the daughter to be regarded as advantageous to her husband. That they were marginalized from court politics and incidental in the historical narratives of the time did not mean that they were redundant in local politics. Their importance in their local milieu was evident in the Delhi sultan's efforts to seek their incorporation by linking a member of his cadre with them.

If the example of Baha al-Din's family touches on the period from the early into the middle of the thirteenth century, Ziya al-Din Barani provides us with information about Shamsi slaves and their descendants from the middle into the later half of the century. These were years of intense conflict between rival camps, but these slaves, of a far humbler stature than Tughril and his progeny, were equally successful in establishing roots and in consolidating and transmitting their gains and privileges from one generation to the next. Iltutmish's central contingent (*qalb*) included about two thousand cavalrymen. Barani does not provide any precise details about their social backgrounds, but Juzjani consistently mentions that the central contingent of the early sultanate army included military slaves.[80] It is also likely that at least some of the cavalrymen (their leaders certainly) were slaves, because they were given revenue assignments (*iqta*) by Iltutmish in the strategic vicinity of the capital, in the still largely unsettled region of the Ganges-Jamuna *doab*. By Balban's reign these cavalrymen had aged, and most were unfit to fulfill their contracted obligations to the state; some had died and their assignments had been inherited by their sons as if they were outright grants. Corruption and collusion between these assignees and the officers in charge of the muster were rife. Balban intervened and tried to revoke these assignments but relented on account of the men's emotional appeal to past service. Eventually a compromise was reached between Balban and the Shamsi assignees.[81]

Barani's emotional narrative of the incident, the plight of the Shamsi cavalrymen and its resolution, was interlinked with his own history. It carried a veiled appeal to Firuz Shah Tughluq to abide by the great traditions of Sultan Balban and honor the service of old servants of the sultanate like himself.[82] But the significance of this episode in a discussion of the households of the *bandagan* is that it illustrates how they altered revenue assignments with specific military obligations into outright grants. They escaped sultanate scrutiny for over two decades, and it was only after Balban intervened militarily in the region (deploying the Afghans) that he made any effort to discipline this group. As it happened, the effort at coercion altered into a settlement in which Balban allowed all the old Shamsi servants to retain their original assignments. In Barani's narrative this was because Balban relented on humanitarian grounds. But from a different perspective, we can also appreciate the ability of the Shamsi cavalrymen to negotiate the perpetuation of all their inherited advantages from an aggressively inclined monarch. Certainly, contrary to the traditional practices associated with the *iqta*'s, which were always supposed to be one-generational and transferable, Balban "enforced" a settlement where revenue assignments in the *doab* passed from father to son.[83]

Barani's and Juzjani's account of the *maulazadgan* draws our attention to a new body of personnel in the politics of the Delhi Sultanate. These are the second-generation descendants of slaves, the "debris of [past] dispensations." They vied with old and new parvenus for the spoils of appointment.

The ambitions of some of the *maulazadgan* might have gone much further, for some remained outside the realm of the state in order to establish local bases. Yet the term "debris" captures the distance of this group from that which the chroniclers wished to champion; in this the term represented the scattered residue of past political formations. But considering them en bloc is also analytically useful because it captures their shared historical background and the impact that the recruitment of military slaves had on the Delhi Sultanate in the long duration.

We still lack a social history of political elites in the sultanate and the focus on the deracinated character of its servants only enlarges upon contexts of their deployment and the authoritarian character of governance that they enabled. The narratives that emerge from this history are not very distant from the cyclical arguments of the fourteenth-century Arab intellectual Ibn Khaldun, who argued for an ebb and flow in state formations and group solidarities (*asabiyyat*), so that the rise and decline of authoritarian regimes depended on the transference of support from old to new groups.[84] The evidence of the *maulazadgan* suggests that the history of the Delhi Sultanate was not quite that cyclical. The survival of this group depended upon its ability to transfer the advantages gained through service as slaves to their descendants, to restore a sense of natality and social life outside the coming and going of political patrons. It points to processes whose origins lie in the earliest moment of the formation of the Delhi Sultanate but whose history followed a genealogy that was not determined by the fortunes of the state.

Conclusion

Military slaves were integral to the reproduction of the authority of the Delhi Sultanate. Yet Persian chroniclers were extremely wary of discussing how the reproduction of sultanate authority affected the reproduction of slavery. The efforts of the natally alienated to incorporate themselves into networks of power, establish households, and bequeath power to a second generation not only challenged the logic of their original deployment; it also contradicted a hierarchical ordering of society idealized by the Persian literati. Yet sultans, their important military commanders, and many of the patrons of the litterateurs of the time were slaves or of slave descent. Narrating the history of how the excluded, natally alienated slaves went beyond their brief and seized vital dimensions of the political life of the sultanate was a delicate exercise that Persian chroniclers chose not to attempt. Their narratives instead explained succession to (seizure of) high office as a result of a supernatural, mystical dispensation, or a product of innate, ethnic characteristics. Historical agency was removed from the lives of slaves as Persian chronicles explained the ways in which masters rewarded their more trusted subordinates with regard befitting a son or a son-in-law.

The critics of the sultanate political system challenged these representations as well, and their interrogation explained, as Sean Stilwell puts it, how slavery was "fundamentally about conflict: conflict over reproduction, conflict over autonomy, conflict over who belonged and who did not."[85] The *bandagan-i khass* were deployed because they were "outsiders," but they seized the opportunities offered by their deployment to take control of the social and political realm, an arrogation whose juridical details remained subjects of debate for nearly a century. Between the seizure of political initiative by slaves and its divergent representations lay the contested terrain where the natally alienated challenged their prescribed submissive roles.

It is possible to penetrate the elisions in the treatment of military slaves in the writings of the Persian chroniclers by studying other social menials deployed by the Delhi monarchs. Like slaves, these individuals were utterly dependent upon their master and their genealogies distanced them from high society. They were recruited by the Delhi sultans through the thirteenth and fourteenth centuries, a recruitment that underscored the structural continuities in the formation of the sultanate's power over this period.

Their deployment also generated more anxious and visible reactions from the Persian chroniclers. Although Persian court chroniclers noticed but found it politically uncomfortable to comment on the opportunities for independent political action available to the *bandagan-i khass,* they had less compunction in criticizing the patronage shown to mahouts, Afghans, wine distillers, barbers, cooks, gardeners, and the sons of slaves. We have to look beyond their commentaries, however, to appreciate the reliance of the Delhi sultans upon a pool of deracinated military personnel to consolidate political authority—even if the natally alienated came in different guises. The anxieties of the Persian chroniclers about the challenge to their idealized aristocratic social order were not misplaced. The natally and socially alienated personnel of the Delhi sultans made a constant effort to translate their political gains into social capital. This was an unending struggle, and although they did gain social roots, the circuits of enslavement were difficult to shake off. Despite the high political status achieved by the slaves, their progeny often had to live with the epithet of *maulazadgan* as a reminder of their slave origins. Certainly, despite the earnest efforts of Juzjani and Barani to invent noble pedigrees for the Delhi sultans, it was Iltutmish's slave status that was reported to Ibn Battuta nearly a century after his death. Iltutmish was remade into an individual of aristocratic birth, a noble-like figure within the narrow ambit inhabited by the court chroniclers; slavery under the

Delhi sultans, on the other hand, was the subject of discussion and reflection by a variety of other spatially and temporally dispersed observers. We can only grasp its more textured features, the violence and conflict that it sublimated, when we read the two together.

Notes

This essay has profited immensely from discussions with Anjali Kumar. I am grateful to Richard Eaton and Indrani Chatterjee for their careful comments; to Indrani for help in tightening and finessing my arguments. To John F. Richards, friend and mentor: many thanks for all your support, introducing me to Orlando Patterson and helping me rethink much of my medieval history.

1. Fakhr-i Mudabbir, *Ta'rikh-i Fakhr al-Din Mubarak Shah,* ed. E. Denison Ross (London: Royal Asiatic Society, 1927), 36.

2. Orlando Patterson, *Slavery and Social Death: A Comparative Study* Cambridge, Mass.: Harvard University Press, 1982).

3. On the *qalb,* see Minhaj-i Siraj Juzjani, *Tabaqat-i Nasiri,* ed. ʿAbd al-Hayy Habibi, 2nd ed. (Kabul: Anjuman-i Taʾrikh-i Afghanistan, 1963–64), 1:403, 456.

4. See, among many possible examples, R. P. Tripathi, *Some Aspects of Muslim Administration* (reprint, Allahabad: Central Book Depot, 1978); A. B. M. Habibullah, *The Foundation of Muslim Rule in India: A History of the Establishment and Progress of the Turkish Sultanate of Delhi, 1206–1290 A.D.,* 3rd ed. (Allahabad: Central Book Depot, 1976); and André Wink, *Al-Hind, the Making of the Indo-Islamic World,* vol. 2, *The Slave Kings and the Islamic Conquest, 11th–13th Centuries* (Leiden: E. J. Brill, 1997).

5. Among many examples, see Mohammad Habib, "Introduction to Elliot and Dowson's *History of India,* vol. II," in Khaliq A. Nizami, ed., *Politics and Society during the Early Medieval Period* (Delhi: People's Publication House, 1974), 1:103–10; Irfan Habib, "Economic History of the Delhi Sultanate—an Essay in Interpretation," *Indian Historical Review* 4 (1978), 287–303; and idem, "Barani's Theory of the History of the Delhi Sultanate," *Indian Historical Review* 7, no. 1–2 (July 1980–Jan. 1981), 99–115.

6. For details see Sunil Kumar, "When Slaves Were Nobles: The Shamsi *Bandagan* in the Early Delhi Sultanate," *Studies in History* 10, no. 1 (Jan.–June 1994), 23–52.

7. See Fakhr-i Mudabbir, *Ta'rikh-i Fakhr al-Din Mubarak Shah,* 38–46, where the description of Turkistan was probably culled from the reports of travelers and merchants and the account of the language, poetry, and religious beliefs fleshed out by the information received from émigrés.

8. Ibid., 43–44. I have followed E. D. Ross's translation of this passage, with minor modifications. See E. Denison Ross, "The Genealogies of Fakhr-ud-Din, Mubarak Shah," in T. W. Arnold and Reynold A. Nicholson, eds., *ʿAjab-nama: A Volume of Oriental Studies presented to Edward G. Browne . . . on His 60th Birthday* (Cambridge: Cambridge University Press, 1922), 405.

9. For details on Malik Saif al-Din see Juzjani, *Tabaqat-i Nasiri,* 2:40–42. The later testimony of Amir Khusrau confirms Fakhr-i Mudabbir's observations on the

efforts by Taziks to learn Turkish. See Amir Khusrau, *Dibacha-i Diwan Ghurrat al-Kamal*, ed. Sayyid ʿAli Haidar (Patna: Institute of Postgraduate Studies and Research in Arabic and Persian Learning, 1988), 40: "I have seen many Persians, not Turks, who have learnt Turkish studiously and industriously, in Hindustan. And they speak [Turkish thus] that (when) the eloquent speakers of that language come from [Turkistan] they are astonished."

10. On Aybak/Tamghaj see Juzjani, *Tabaqat-i Nasiri*, 1:442–43; on the Shamsi slaves refer to table 1 in Kumar, "When Slaves Were Nobles," 32–35, bearing in mind the fact that a large number of the titles mentioned by Juzjani were given to the Shamsi slaves by Iltutmish's successors. Balban, for example, received the title Ulugh Khan, "Great Khan," only in 1249 (Juzjani, *Tabaqat-i Nasiri*, 2:60), and we have no information concerning his earlier name or title. It needs to be noticed in passing that one of the important historiographical accomplishments of Peter Jackson in his *The Delhi Sultanate: A Political and Military History* (Cambridge: Cambridge University Press, 1999) is the careful restoration of the Turkish names and titles of Iltutmish's and Balban's slaves. Jackson performed this task diligently without asking why Turkish names and titles were given to members of the political elite operating within a Persianate world, or why there was so much corruption in the transcription of Turkish names and titles by the Persianate literati. The subject has received a fuller treatment in my "The Ignored Elite: Turks and Mongols in the Early Delhi Sultanate," in preparation.

11. On Hindu Khan see Juzjani, *Tabaqat-i Nasiri*, 2:18–19. Juzjani described Hindu Khan as a slave especially close to the monarch, *qurbat tamam dasht* (2:19).

12. Ziya al-Din Barani, *Taʾrikh-i Firuz Shahi*, ed. Saiyid Ahmad Khan, Bibliotheca Indica 33 (Calcutta: Asiatic Society of Bengal, 1860–62), 175.

13. Juzjani, *Tabaqat-i Nasiri*, 2:73.

14. Amir Hasan Sijzi, *Fawaʾid al-Fuʾad*, ed. Khwaja Hasan Sani Nizami (Delhi: Urdu Academy, 1990), 112–14.

15. Ibid., 134.

16. The play with names takes on an additional, wonderful twist if we recall that *najib* literally means a cultured person with excellent noble qualities.

17. Sijzi, *Fawaʾid al-Fuʾad*, 343.

18. Juzjani, *Tabaqat-i Nasiri*, 1:441–43.

19. For its usage in Abu al-Fazl Bayhaqi, *Taʾrikh-i Bayhaqi*, see Marilyn R. Waldman, *Towards a Theory of Historical Narrative* (Columbus: Ohio State University Press, 1980), 188. See also Nizam al-Mulk, *The Book of Government, or, Rules for Kings: The Siyar al-Muluk, or Siyasat-nama of Nizam al-Mulk*, trans. Hubert Darke, 2nd ed. (London: Routledge and Kegan Paul, 1978), 104, 105.

20. For a useful discussion of manumitted slaves and their legal status, see Patricia Crone, "Mawla," in *Encyclopaedia of Islam*, ed. H. A. R. Gibb et al., new ed. (Leiden: E. J. Brill, 1954–2002), 6:874–82; and for master-slave relationships, see Paul G. Forand, "The Relation of the Slave and the Client to the Master or Patron in Medieval Islam," *International Journal of Middle East Studies* 2 (1971), 59–66.

21. Nizam al-Mulk, *Siyasat-nama*, 117.

22. Juzjani, *Tabaqat-i Nasiri*, 1:411, 418.

23. Ibid., 1:440, 418.

24. Ibid., 1:444.

25. Ibid., 1:418.

26. Khwaja Nizam al-Din Ahmad, *Tabaqat-i Akbari*, ed. B. De, Bibliotheca Indica Series, no. 223 (Calcutta: Asiatic Society of Bengal, 1927), 1:55. See also ʿAbd al-Qadir Badaʾuni, *Muntakhab al-tawarikh*, ed. Maulavi Ahmad ʿAli, Bibliotheca Indica n.s. no. 131 (Calcutta, 1868), 1:61.

27. See Muhammad Aziz Ahmad, *Political History and Institutions of the Early Turkish Empire of Delhi* (reprint, Lahore: University of the Punjab, 1987), 152–55; Tripathi, *Some Aspects of Muslim Administration*, 24–25; Habibullah, *Foundation of Muslim Rule in India*, 76–77; S. L. Rathor, "A Plea against the Charge of Usurpation by Iltutmish," *Islamic Culture* 32 (1958), 262–67; Gavin Hambly, "Who Were the *Chihalgani*, the Forty Slaves of Sultan Shams al-Din Iltutmish of Delhi?" *Iran* 10 (1972), 60; and, most recently, Peter Jackson, *Delhi Sultanate*, 29.

28. This could have been a confirmation of the position given to Juzjani by the *wazir* the year before. See Juzjani, *Tabaqat-i Nasiri*, 1:488, 489.

29. See, for example, ibid., 2:48 and 52.

30. Ibid., 1:483 and 2:59.

31. Ibid., 2:85.

32. Ibid., 1:236. See also Jackson's chapter in this volume.

33. Juzjani, *Tabaqat-i Nasiri*, 1:475, 487, and for a reference to the son borne by Balban's daughter, see 1:496.

34. Barani, *Taʾrikh-i Firuz Shahi*, 27; see also another edition ed. Shaikh Abdur Rashid (Aligarh: Aligarh Muslim University, Department of History, 1957), 33.

35. Ibid., edited by Khan, 31; edited by Rashid, 37.

36. ʿAbd al-Malik ʿIsami, *Futuh al-Salatin*, ed. A. S. Usha (Madras: University of Madras, 1948), 163.

37. Nizam al-Din Ahmad, *Tabaqat-i Akbari*, 1:77; ʿAbd al-Qadir Badaʾuni, *Muntakhab al-tawarikh*, 1:94.

38. Nizam al-Din Ahmad, *Tabaqat-i Akbari*, 1:77; ʿAbd al-Qadir Badaʾuni, *Muntakhab al-tawarikh*, 1:94.

39. See Khaliq A. Nizami, *Some Aspects of Religion and Politics in India during the Thirteenth Century*, 2nd ed. (Delhi: Idarah-i Adabiyat-i Delli, 1974), 143; idem, "Balban, the Regicide," in *Studies in Medieval Indian History and Culture* (Allahabad: Kitab Mahal, 1966), 41–53.

40. For the Ilbari background of Iltutmish and Balban see Juzjani, *Tabaqat-i Nasiri*, 1:441 and 2:47 respectively. Jackson, in *Delhi Sultanate*, 57n63, and his essay in this volume, cites the research of P. B. Golden to identify the Ilbari with the Olberli tribe, a part of the Qipchaq-Cuman people in the eleventh century. I cannot agree with Jackson (*Delhi Sultanate*, 56–57) that Juzjani wanted to draw attention to the Ilbari connection between Iltutmish and Balban. He mentioned the Ilbari backgrounds of Iltutmish and Balban in separate contexts, never once drawing the reader's attention to the shared natal origins of the two monarchs.

41. See, for example, Tripathi, *Some Aspects of Muslim Administration*, chapter 3, "Experiments of the Albari Turks"; and S. B. P. Nigam, *Nobility and the Sultans of Delhi, A.D. 1206–1398* (Delhi: Munshiram Manoharlal, 1968), chapter 2, "The Ilbari Nobility as King-makers."

42. Ibn Battuta, *Rehla*, trans. Agha Mahdi Hussain (Baroda: Oriental Institute, 1976), 32–55. For a review of the chronology of Ibn Battuta's visit to India see Peter Jackson, "The Mongols and India, 1221–1351" (Ph.D. diss., Cambridge University, 1976), 219–30.

43. Ibn Battuta, *Rehla*, 39. Ibn Battuta refers to the anonymous text entitled *Liqa al-sa'dain*. As Mahdi Hussain pointed out, this is probably an incorrect reference to Amir Khusrau's *Qiran al-sa'dain*, about which the traveler may have been informed. There is nothing in the travelogue to suggest that he was familiar with the content of this or another sultanate chronicle.

44. Ibn Battuta, *Rehla*, 32, 47, 55 for references to the *qazi* and the shaikh. For a note that begins "An Indian narrated to me," see ibid., 39.

45. Ibid., 33.

46. Ibid., 36–37.

47. For details see Kumar, "When Slaves Were Nobles."

48. Juzjani, *Tabaqat-i Nasiri*, 1:453–54, 438.

49. Ibid., 1:454. Space limitations prevent a discussion of Iltutmish's daughter in this chapter. I have dealt with her reign separately: "The Woman in the Accounts (*hisab*) of Men: Sultan Raziyya and Early Sultanate Society," in preparation.

50. According to Juzjani, at least, barring Nasir al-Din, the only other able successor of Sultan Iltutmish was his daughter, Sultan Raziyya (1236–40). Juzjani, *Tabaqat-i Nasiri*, 1:457–58.

51. Ibid., 1:457.

52. Ibid., 1:455–57.

53. Ibid., 1:490 and 2:29.

54. Ibid., 1:456.

55. Ibid., 1:457.

56. Ibid., 2:30.

57. Simon Digby, *War Horse and Elephant in the Delhi Sultanate: A Study of Military Supplies* (Karachi: Orient Monographs, 1971), 55–82.

58. 'Isami, *Futuh al-Salatin*, 130.

59. Barani, *Ta'rikh-i Firuz Shahi*, edited by Khan, 33–39; edited by Rashid, 39–47.

60. Ibid., edited by Khan, 37, 39; edited by Rashid, 44, 47.

61. For a review of these materials in Barani, see Mohammad Habib, "Governing Class," in Mohammad Habib and Afsar U. S. Khan, *The Political Theory of the Delhi Sultanate* (Allahabad: Kitab Mahal, n.d.), 144–51; and Habib, "Barani's Theory of the History of the Delhi Sultanate," 104–10.

62. Habib, "Barani's Theory of the History of the Delhi Sultanate," 109, my italics.

63. Barani, *Ta'rikh-i Firuz Shahi*, edited by Khan, 575.

64. Ibid., 505.

65. This was Barani's description of the kinds of people patronized by the Tughluq monarch. Ibid.

66. Juzjani, *Tabaqat-i Nasiri*, 2:80.

67. For the garrisons in the *doab* see Barani, *Ta'rikh-i Firuz Shahi*, edited by Khan, 57–58; edited by Rashid, 66–68.

68. Amir Khusrau, *Tuhfat al-Sighar*, IOL Persian Ms 412, fols. 50–51, quoted in Wahid Mirza, *The Life and Works of Amir Khusrau* (reprint, Delhi: Idarah-i Adabiyat-i Delli, 1974), 51–52.

69. For details see Jackson, *Delhi Sultanate*, 175–77.

70. Prior to his reign, Balban (1266–86) was the dominant political broker in the court of the preceding Delhi sultans. He was appointed the commander of Hansi in 1242 by Sultan 'Ala al-Din Mas'ud, and then the court chamberlain. By 1244–45, he

was deputy to the state (*na'ib*) under Sultan Nasir al-Din and, barring a brief hiatus during the years 1253–55, remained in power through the duration of the monarch's reign (1266–86).

71. Barani, *Ta'rikh-i Firuz Shahi*, edited by Khan, 24, 36, 118–19; edited by Rashid, 29, 43, 138–40; and Mirza, *Life and Works of Amir Khusrau*, 66–73.

72. Barani, *Ta'rikh-i Firuz Shahi*, edited by Khan, 40; edited by Rashid, 48. See G. Yazdani, "The Inscriptions of the Turk Sultans of Delhi—Mu'izz al-Din Bahram, 'Ala al-Din Mas'ud, Nasir al-Din Mahmud, Ghiyathu-d-Din Balban, and Mu'izz al-Din Kaiqubad," *Epigraphica Indo-Moslemica* (1913–14), 27–28, no. 11, plate 10b (in mosque attached to the tomb of Imam Nasir, Sonepat).

73. Barani, *Ta'rikh-i Firuz Shahi*, edited by Khan, 36–37; edited by Rashid, 42–43.

74. There is considerable confusion regarding the *khwaja* in modern historiography. Tripathi, *Some Aspects of Muslim Administration,* 251, noted the presence of the accountant, *khwaja,* together with the military commander, *muqti,* for the first time in Balban's reign. He suggested that this was a new development in which greater administrative control from the center checked the autonomy of the governor. Irfan Habib, "Iqta's," in *Cambridge Economic History of India,* vol. 1, *c. 1200–c. 1750,* ed. Tapan Raychaudhuri and Irfan Habib (Cambridge: Cambridge University Press, 1982), 70, followed Tripathi; and Jackson, *Delhi Sultanate,* 100, followed Habib. On the other hand, Juzjani, *Tabaqat-i Nasiri,* 1:284, clearly provided an example from Iltutmish's reign in which a *malik* (Karim al-Din Hamza) and a *khwaja* (Najib al-Din) were appointed together to Nagaur in 1221. Nor was this a novelty: Juzjani was obviously quite familiar with the deployment of the two officers together and provides another, more detailed, example from Tulak in Afghanistan, where the military and fiscal duties of the two functionaries were clearly spelt out (see 2:134).

75. Barani, *Ta'rikh-i Firuz Shahi,* edited by Khan, 36–39; edited by Rashid, 43–46. Barani's narration of the Kamal Mahiyar incident needs to be contextualized with the author's own negative sentiments regarding the "base-born." The need to distance individuals of such background from political power was the theme of the twenty-first *nasihat* (advice) of his normative text, *Fatawa'yi Jahandari,* and Barani transposed these didactic ideas into his history as well. Ibid., edited by Khan, 29–30, 34; edited by Rashid, 34–35, 40. See also Ziya al-Din Barani, *Fatawa'yi Jahandari,* ed. Afsar Salim Khan (Lahore: Idarah-i Tahqiqat-i Pakistan, 1972), 295–304, where the ideas contained in the *Ta'rikh* are repeated in similar episodes with new characters. Contemporary scholars have assimilated Barani's moralizations into "Balban's theory of kingship." See, for example, K. A. Nizami, "Sultan Balban and Kaiqubad: (iii) Theory of Kingship," in *A Comprehensive History of India: The Delhi Sultanat (A.D. 1206–1526),* ed. Mohammad Habib and K. A. Nizami (reprint; New Delhi: People's Publishing House, 1982), 280–84; Tripathi, *Some Aspects of Muslim Administration,* 34–37; Ahmad, *Political History and Institutions,* 260–63; and more recently, Wink, *Al-Hind,* 1:22. Jackson, *Delhi Sultanate,* 79, 79n106, doubted Barani's account of the Kamal Mahiyar incident as well, but for its independent confirmation in Sayyid Ashraf Jahangir Simnani, *Maktubat-i Ashrafi,* BL ms. OR. 267, fol. 66b. I am not questioning the veracity of the Kamal Mahiyar incident, but the spin put upon it by Barani. Moreover, the anecdote could have rhetorical salience for authors in different contexts across generations, as in the previously discussed case of Aram Shah and Iltutmish and, in a different context, Sultan Raziyya and Yaqut.

76. Barani, *Ta'rikh-i Firuz Shahi,* edited by Khan, 134; edited by Rashid, 155. The text in Rashid's edition varies, but is clearer.

77. Juzjani, *Tabaqat-i Nasiri,* 1:421; for a transcription of Tughril's inscription see Mehrdad Shokoohy and Natalie H. Shokoohy, "The Architecture of Baha al-Din Tughrul in the Region of Bayana, Rajasthan," *Muqarnas* 4 (1987), 115. For Tughril more generally, see also Sunil Kumar, "Qutb and Modern Memory," in Suvir Kaul, ed., *Partitions of Memory* (Delhi: Permanent Black, 2001), 154–57.

78. No date is explicitly given for the annexation of Bayana. In fact, Thangir is not mentioned in the list of Iltutmish's conquests in Habibi's edition of the *Tabaqat-i Nasiri,* 1:452. But this list varies substantially in the various manuscripts (see ibid., 1:452n5), and Habibi notices its presence in other manuscripts. The earlier edition of the *Tabaqat-i Nasiri,* edited by W. Nassau Lees (Calcutta: College Press, 1864), 179, includes Thangir in its list of Iltutmish's conquests. On the appointment of Malik Nusrat al-Din Ta'isi, see ibid., edited by Habibi, 2:10.

79. Juzjani, *Tabaqat-i Nasiri,* edited by Habibi, 2:34.

80. For references to slaves in the *qalb* see ibid., 1:403, 456.

81. For details see Barani, *Ta'rikh-i Firuz Shahi,* edited by Khan, 60, 61–64; edited by Rashid, 70, 72–76.

82. According to Barani, when Balban revoked the grants, the old and infirm soldiers appealed to Fakhr al-Din Kotwal, who interceded on their behalf. The plea was that old servants should not be cast away when their utility was ended, and it succeeded in its intent. The story was very close to Barani's own experience—he was a close confidant of Sultan Muhammad Shah and had lost everything when Firuz Shah succeeded. The story carried Barani's plea for patronage from Firuz Shah, the sultan to whom the *Ta'rikh-i Firuz Shahi* was dedicated. In Barani's story, Balban was moved to tears, and although he did demand that the young and able should perform military service, the old and the infirm were allowed to keep their grants. This was much what Barani would have liked Firuz Shah Tughluq to do as well.

83. Barani, *Ta'rikh-i Firuz Shahi,* edited by Khan, 64; edited by Rashid, 76; and on the traditional practices associated with the *iqta',* see Irfan Habib, "Iqta's," in *Cambridge Economic History,* 1:68–69. See also Kumar, "When Slaves Were Nobles," 28–29.

84. See Ibn Khaldun, *The Muqaddimah: An Introduction to History,* trans. Franz Rosenthal, ed. and abridged by N. J. Dawood (reprint, Princeton, N.J.: Princeton University Press, 1974), 123–52.

85. Sean Stilwell, *Paradoxes of Power: The Kano "Mamluks" and Male Royal Slavery in the Sokoto Caliphate, 1804–1903* (Portsmouth, N.H.: Heinemann, 2004), 248.

5

The Rise and Fall of Military Slavery in the Deccan, 1450–1650

Richard M. Eaton

> One obedient slave is better than three hundred sons; for the latter desire their father's death, the former his master's glory.
>
> Nizam al-Mulk (d. 1092)

Between the mid-fifteenth and mid-seventeenth centuries, streams of Ethiopians—known in the Arab world as "Habshis"[1]—turned up in slave markets in the Middle East. From there they entered elite households as servants, or they were reexported to India's Deccan plateau to meet that region's insatiable demand for military labor. The appearance of these slaves in western India at that time in South Asian history raises a number of issues of race, class, and gender, in addition to important issues related to the institution of slavery. What explains the appearance of military slaves in the Deccan between the fifteenth and seventeenth centuries? How did this type of slavery compare or contrast with military slavery in the Delhi Sultanate? Why was Ethiopia the major source for India's military slaves after the fifteenth century? How did these slaves become assimilated into the society into which they had been introduced, over time evolving from slaves, to clients, to patrons, even to slaveholders themselves? And what ultimately happened to them?

One way of exploring these issues is to trace the career of one of the most famous slaves—and Africans—in South Asian history. This is Malik Ambar, a man whose earlier name, "Chapu," points to his origins in the Kambata region of southern Ethiopia (see map 2). Born in 1548, Chapu as a young man had fallen into the hands of slave dealers then operating between the Ethiopian highlands and the coasts of eastern Africa. Possibly he was

captured in war, or perhaps he had been sold into slavery by his impoverished parents. In any event, Chapu joined streams of other Ethiopians who
turned up in slave markets in the Middle East and were then reexported to
the Deccan. He also appears to have been sold and resold several times after
his initial entry into slavery. A contemporary European source relates that
he was sold in the Red Sea port of Mocha for the sum of eighty Dutch
guilders[2]—information confirming the presence of commercialized slave
markets in Arabia in the decades following the Ottoman conquest of the
Arab Middle East. A near-contemporary Persian chronicle reports that he
was then taken to Baghdad and sold to a prominent merchant named Mir
Qasim Baghdadi. Recognizing Chapu's superior intellectual qualities, Mir
Qasim raised and educated the youth, converted him to Islam, and gave him
the name "Ambar" (Ar. 'anbar, "ambergris").[3]

Although Islamic Law prohibits Muslims from enslaving Muslims, Ambar's conversion to Islam in no way affected his status as a slave or as a mar-
ketable commodity. The matter had already been settled by the time he
reached Baghdad. In a case specifically involving an Ethiopian who had converted to Islam after his enslavement, the Moroccan jurist Ahmad al-Wansharisi (d. 1508) took up the issue of whether the man in question, though a
Muslim, could still be bought and sold as a slave. In his legal decree (fatwa),
al-Wansharisi ruled that the man's conversion to Islam after his enslavement
did not automatically set him free, since slavery was a condition arising from
his previous unbelief; hence, his servile status persisted after conversion.[4]
Likewise with Ambar. Although Mir Qasim had taken him into his household in Baghdad, nurtured him, renamed him, and facilitated his conversion
to Islam, the Ethiopian was returned to the slave market and sold, though
doubtless at a higher price than the eighty Dutch guilders for which he had
originally been purchased.

From Baghdad Ambar was taken to the Deccan, where he was purchased
by Chengiz Khan, the peshva (chief minister) of the Nizam Shahi Sultanate
of Ahmadnagar (1496–1636), which was the westernmost of the five succes-
sor-states to the Bahmani Sultanate (1347–1510).[5] He was one of a thousand
Habshi slaves purchased by the peshva, himself a Habshi and a former slave.[6]
As a black African, then, Ambar would hardly have stood out amidst the mosaic of ethnic groups then inhabiting the western Deccan. Moreover his
master, Chengiz Khan, was only one among many high-ranking Nizam
Shahi servants who were systematically recruiting Habshis as military slaves
in the sixteenth century. In this respect, officials at Ahmadnagar were following a practice that their parent dynasty, the Bahmanis, had already established in the fifteenth century. Like the Bahmanis, the Nizam Shahi sultans
of Ahmadnagar and the 'Adil Shahis of Bijapur controlled the important

seaports along the Konkan coast. This gave them ready access to slave markets in the Middle East, since it took Arab dhows sailing down from the Red Sea or Persian Gulf only several weeks to reach India's western ports.

Slaves and Regional Networks of Exchange

Malik Ambar is usually remembered for having rescued the Nizam Shahi Sultanate of Ahmadnagar from annexation by the imperial Mughals, or for having at least postponed that fate.[7] In order to understand his career as a slave, however, we need to step back into the land of his birth—the remote highlands of sixteenth-century Ethiopia. Ever since the fourth century the ancient Christian kingdom of Ethiopia, cut off from the Mediterranean world by the rise of Islam in the seventh century, had evolved along its own distinctive path, creating a remarkable synthesis of Semitic and northeast African (i.e., Cushitic) cultures. Nobles, patriarchs, priests, monks, and a dynasty of sacred kings believed to be descended from the biblical Solomon presided over a predominantly agricultural society. Although Jesuits of the seventeenth century would denigrate the Ethiopian Church as a Jewish-pagan corruption of "true," that is, Latin, Christianity,[8] earlier European assessments were far more favorable. Beginning in the twelfth century, rumors circulated through European capitals of a mighty Christian monarch named "Prester John" whose kingdom was thought to lie somewhere beyond the Muslim world, in "the Indies." In the following centuries, however, Europeans gradually lost hope of finding this great monarch in Asia. But in the early sixteenth century Portuguese navigators, reaching the Arabian Sea by sailing around the Cape, encountered the Solomonic kingdom of Ethiopia, whose Christian emperor was now identified as the long-sought Prester John.[9] Hoping to forge an anti-Muslim strategic alliance with this Christian king and his kingdom, Portuguese explorers and officials, as well as Catholic clergy, probed the possibilities presented by their discovery of this Christian kingdom.

In the course of their explorations in the Horn of Africa, the Portuguese also learned that Ethiopia was the principal source of slaves taken from eastern Africa to Arabia and points east. In 1516 the Portuguese official Tomé Pires noted that Arabs would "make raids on horseback, in the course of which they capture large numbers of Abyssinians [i.e., Ethiopians] whom they sell to the people of Asia."[10] Some slaves were obtained directly by Arab raiding parties coming from beyond the Red Sea, in the manner that Pires described. Others were captured in internal wars between local communities and then bartered to long-distance merchants. Still others were sold into slavery by impoverished parents.

Between the fourteenth and seventeenth centuries both Muslims and Christians obtained most of their slaves from amongst pagan communities that lay along the western and southern fringes of the Christian kingdom, in regions such as Damot, Kambata, or Hadya. In 1520 Father Francisco Alvares, a member of the first Portuguese mission to reach the Ethiopian highlands, kept a journal in which he sketched the broad contours of the Christian kingdom's slave-extraction system. As he approached its southern frontiers, he encountered semi-independent pagan states that paid tribute to the Solomonic dynasty. With reference to Damot, one of these kingdoms, Alvares wrote,

> The slaves of this kingdom are much esteemed by the Moors, and they do not let them go at any price; all the country of Arabia, Persia, India, Egypt, and Greece, are full of slaves from this country, and they say they make very good Moors and great warriors. These are pagans, and among them in this kingdom are many Christians.[11]

That is to say, although some Christians were to be found in this non-Christian kingdom—a tributary satellite of the Ethiopian state—those enslaved in Damot were pagans who, like Malik Ambar, were converted to Islam and sent to serve as warriors in lands far beyond Arabia.[12] Kambata, the region from which Malik Ambar appears to have come, lay directly south of Damot.

Although Arab slave raiding readily caught the attention of foreign observers, the less conspicuous forces of international commerce seem to have played a more important role in Ethiopia's slave-extraction system. In one town in the northeastern highlands, Father Alvares found "merchants of all nations," including "Moors of India." Noting the importance of Indian textiles in the regional economy, and more particularly in the kingdom's clerical hierarchy, Alvares wrote that Ethiopian priests wore white cloaks made of Indian cotton. The emperor himself ("Prester John") presented Alvares and five other Europeans with fine Indian cloths. Alvares also noted the enormous quantities of Indian silks and brocades consumed by the Ethiopian court, acquired both by gifting and by purchase.[13] Writing a century later of a small pagan state in southwestern Ethiopia, the Jesuit priest Manuel de Almeida observed that whenever the king of that state bought foreign cloth from merchants, the price would be fixed in slaves, which the king would then procure and use to settle the transaction.[14]

This evidence points to an active Arabian Sea commercial system in which Indian textiles and African slaves were vital: cotton goods manufactured in India were reaching the Ethiopian highlands in exchange for Ethiopian exports, which included gold and ivory in addition to slaves. As the Ethiopian highlands became more tightly integrated into Indian Ocean trading networks in the course of the fifteenth and sixteenth centuries, huge caravans of long-distance merchants, most of them Muslims, pushed ever deeper into the hinterland, exchanging goods brought from the coasts for goods extracted from the interior. The outflow of Ethiopian slaves was thus responding to forces of supply and demand that spanned the larger Indian Ocean trading world. African demand for Indian textiles, however, appears to have been the principal engine behind Ethiopia's slave-extraction process, in this respect anticipating by several centuries the much better known slave trade from West Africa to the Americas.[15]

Facilitating Ethiopia's slave-export system were the mutually supportive ties between the Solomonic dynasty and the long-distance Muslim merchants that connected the Christian kingdom with the outside world. Ethiopia's "Law of the Kings" (*Fethä Nägäst*), a law code dating to the thirteenth century, sanctioned the enslavement of non-Christian war captives and the ownership of children of slaves by their parents' owners, basing such sanctions on Hebrew scripture (i.e., Leviticus 25:44–46). It also prohibited Ethiopians from selling Christian slaves to non-Christians, although they were not in principle prevented from capturing and selling pagans to others to enslave. Taken together, these sanctions and prohibitions had the effect of leaving Ethiopia's entire export slave trade in non-Christian, that is, Muslim, hands.[16]

In fact, the Christian kingdom seems to have collaborated with long-distance Muslim traders in exporting slaves to the wider world. Jealously claiming sovereignty over the trade routes that connected the interior with the sea, the Ethiopian state imposed taxes on all Muslim commercial activity in its domain.[17] Court officials therefore protected an activity from which they benefited financially. In 1556, when Malik Ambar would have been just eight years old, a Jesuit account recorded that owing to the taboo against enslaving Christians, the Solomonic kingdom actually refrained from baptizing neighboring pagan communities. This allowed the Christian kingdom to capture and send such peoples down to the coasts, there to be sold as slaves to Arab brokers and shippers, evidently in exchange for Indian textiles. In this way, from ten to twelve thousand slaves annually left Ethiopia, according to this account.[18]

The extraction of slaves from the Ethiopian highlands forms only part of the story; the other is the demand for slaves in the various hinterlands behind the ports that rimmed the Arabian Sea. The Habshis drawn into the Indian Ocean trading world were not intended to serve their masters as menial laborers, but, as Tomé Pires had observed already in 1516, as military specialists—"knights," as he put it.[19] As in most other forms of slavery, military slaves were severed from their natal kin group, rendering them dependent upon their owners. But unlike domestic or plantation slaves, military slaves were intended to perform the purely political task of maintaining the stability of state systems, since in most cases their masters were themselves high-ranking state servants. Dating from ninth-century Iraq, the institution of military slavery was based on the assumption that political systems can be corrupted by the faction-prone webs of kinship in which such systems are embedded. A solution to this problem was thought to lie in the recruitment of soldiers who were not only detached from their own natal kin, but were total outsiders to the state and the society it governed—circumstances that in principle guaranteed their political loyalty. As the Seljuk minister Nizam al-Mulk (d. 1092) aptly put it, "One obedient slave is better than three hundred sons; for the latter desire their father's death, the former his master's glory."[20]

Although military slavery is often considered an "Islamic" institution, its appearance in the Muslim world was in fact more often the exception than the rule. Yet the institution did seem to thrive in politically unstable and socially fluid conditions. Historian André Wink has proposed that "élite slavery was and always remained a frontier phenomenon."[21] Perhaps more precisely, it seems to have occurred wherever hereditary, aristocratic authority was either weak or fractious (as is often the case on frontiers). Such was certainly the case in the northern Deccan from the fifteenth through seventeenth centuries, where incessant struggles between the region's two main power groups—the "Deccanis," or Muslims born in the Deccan, and "Westerners" (*gharbian*), or immigrants from the Middle East or Central Asia—had produced conditions of chronic political instability. With neither faction able to achieve permanent dominance over the other, state officials of one faction sought to strengthen their position over those of the other by recruiting to their service slave-soldiers whose loyalty lay in principle with the state, but in practice with their legal owners.

On either side of the Arabian Sea, then, two very different kinds of markets—one commercial, the other political—were driving the slave trade. On the Ethiopian side, African manpower was extracted and exported in exchange for Indian textiles that were consumed by elite groups in the Christian kingdom. In the Deccan, a chronic instability caused by mutually antagonistic factions, the Deccanis and Westerners, created a market for culturally alien military labor. The other ingredient to the system was an increasingly commercialized international trading system in which goods, including slaves, were exchanged for cash, or for other goods calculated in cash, at agreed-upon prices.

The life of a Habshi man took a dramatic turn after he had been transplanted to the Deccan, where he was termed a *ghulam* (Ar.) or *banda* (Pers.), both terms meaning "slave." It was a life very different from what he would have known in Africa. The buyers of such men fed them, housed them, edu-cated them in the ways of household life and duties, and in all respects pro-tected them, receiving in return an absolute and unswerving loyalty. This intimate relation between African slave and Indian master was both asym-metrical and complementary. That is, the Africans possessed power but lacked kin and inherited authority, whereas their Indian masters possessed kin and inherited authority, but lacked sufficient power. Such an interde-pendence engendered lasting bonds of mutual trust, which explains why court officials, administrators, and high-ranking army commanders were willing to entrust the most delicate and important official duties to their Habshi slaves, and to them alone. Already in Bahmani times, Habshis in the court of Sultan Firuz (1397–1422) served as personal attendants, body-guards, and guards of the harem. Sultan Ahmad Bahmani II (1436–58) also assigned to Habshi slaves his most trusted posts, such as key governorships and keeper of the royal seal. The great Bahmani prime minister Mahmud Gawan appointed a Habshi as his personal seal-bearer,[22] and in 1481, when that same minister was executed, it was a Habshi—one of the sultan's slaves—who was the executioner.

Slavery in the Making of Regional Societies: Deccani versus Mughal

As slaves, however, Habshis found their status in Deccan society neither fixed nor permanent. On the death of their masters, Habshi slaves generally became freedmen, continuing their military careers as free lancers in the ser-vice of powerful commanders. In this way they exchanged a master-slave re-lationship for a new patron-client one. The humbler sorts sought out and served commanders as paid troopers; the more talented managed to attract their own troopers (frequently other ex-slaves), obtain land assignments, and enter the sultanate's official hierarchy as ranked commanders (*amirs*). As this happened, Habshi ex-slaves generally allied themselves both cultur-ally and politically with the Deccani class. For unlike the Westerners, who after several generations of living in the Deccan continued to cultivate the Persian language and nourish close family or commercial ties with the Mid-dle East, Habshis had no option of returning to Ethiopia. Their ties with Africa having been permanently severed, these men adopted the Deccan as their only home, readily embracing the regional culture and its vernacular languages. Many, in fact, became fiercely loyal to the region. As is suggested by the career of Malik Ambar, upon acquiring their freedom from their mas-ters, Habshi ex-slaves seem to have transferred their loyalties from their for-mer masters to their adopted land.

The importation of Ethiopian slaves into the western Deccan profoundly altered the region's society and culture, which in turn diverged sharply from the society and culture of contemporary north India under the imperial Mughals (1526–1857). In Deccan sultanates like Ahmadnagar or Bijapur, there emerged a heterogenous ruling class that consisted of Ethiopian military slaves and former slaves; a Westerner class composed of Iranian, Central Asian, or Arab nobles; an old Deccani nobility descended from fourteenth-century Indo-Turkish settlers transplanted from north India (now thoroughly accommodated to Deccani culture); and Maratha chieftains and their clients, these latter being the indigenous warriors of the Marathi-speaking Deccan. This motley collection of communities contrasted with the more homogenous ruling class of Mughal north India, which throughout the sixteenth and seventeenth centuries received continuous infusions of blue-blooded Persian-speaking immigrants—mainly Iranians or Persianized Turks—from nearby Iran and Central Asia. As a result, dominant sections of the Mughal ruling class cultivated a posture of racial arrogance, a strong sense of pedigree, and a sense of hereditary aristocracy not found in the Deccan.

A key source of the north-south contrast was the presence of military slavery in the Deccan, and its absence in the Mughal realm. As a living institution, military slavery had largely disappeared in north India since the early days of the Delhi Sultanate; by the Mughal period it survived only in a vestigial, rhetorical form.[23] High-born Mughal officials, all of them free men, would swear their loyalty to the emperor by styling themselves "slaves of the court" (e.g., *bandagan-i dargah, bandagan-i hazrat zill-i Allah,* or *ghulaman-i 'alam-panah*). In the Deccan, by contrast, military slavery as an actual institution still very much existed, especially in the western Deccan, where Ahmadnagar and Bijapur enjoyed access to Arabian Sea commerce. Moreover, among Ahmadnagar's fighting men there were also large numbers of Habshi ex-slaves whose African background gave them no purchase on political power, and to whom appeals to Iranian ethnic or cultural solidarity would have had no meaning whatsoever. For such former slaves, as for other groups in Nizam Shahi service, oaths of political loyalty were based on the ethnically neutral notion of salt, and specifically on "eating the salt" of a political superior. "Eating the salt" or "fidelity to salt" refers to the oath that bound a patron and client through mutual obligations of protection and loyalty. Although such an ideology is also found in Mughal political thought and practice, for free Habshis of Ahmadnagar, the metaphor expressed the new ethically based patron-client relation into which these men had entered, replacing the earlier, legally based master-slave relation they had known since childhood.[24]

The political and ideological confrontation between these contrasting societies—the more homogenous north Indian one structured largely around Persian culture and Iranian ethnicity, and the more mixed Deccani one informed by loyalty to salt—came to a head in the late sixteenth century. By this time the Mughals had swollen into a vast imperial formation, which under Akbar (1556–1605) exhibited a seemingly insatiable appetite for territory. Sooner or later, every state of the Deccan had to deal with this colossus of the north. Ahmadnagar, occupying the Deccan's northwestern corner, was the first. In fact, the same internal ferment and instability that had been drawing military labor from Africa into Ahmadnagar also invited interference from the aggressive and expanding Mughals. When the sultan of Ahmadnagar died in 1595, disputes over his succession reignited the deadly and always-latent factional struggle between Westerners and Deccanis. When one of the two parties unwisely invited Akbar's son, Prince Murad, to march south and intervene on its behalf, Mughal armies, now possessing the very excuse they wanted, promptly reached Ahmadnagar and laid siege to the fort. The northerners' conquest of the Deccan might well have begun then and there, had it not been for the gallant and spirited defense of the citadel led by Chand Bibi, the sister of the late sultan.

In March 1596, with the military situation at Ahmadnagar's fort stalemated, representatives of the two sides met just beyond the city walls to discuss a settlement. In these talks we can glimpse something of the vast chasm separating the culture of the Mughal ruling class from that of the various groups, including Habshi slaves, then ruling Ahmadnagar. The meeting opened with Ahmadnagar's diplomat, Afzal Khan, challenging the Mughals' right to make demands on Deccani territory. Whereupon Sadiq Khan, one of the Mughal officers, with Prince Murad at his side, exploded in rage:

> What nonsense is this? You, like a eunuch, are keeping a woman [i.e., Chand Bibi] in the fort in the hope that she will come to your aid. . . . This man [i.e., Prince Murad] is the son of his Majesty the Emperor, Jalal al-Din Muhammad Akbar, at whose court many kings do service. Do you imagine that the crows and kites of the Deccan, who squat like ants or locusts over a few spiders, can cope with the descendant of Timur and his famous *amirs*—the Khan-i Khanan and Shahbaz Khan, for example—each of whom has conquered countries ten times as large as the Deccan? . . . You, who are men of the same race as ourselves, should not throw yourselves away for no purpose.[25]

One notes the different strategies by which Sadiq Khan attacked his Ahmadnagar counterpart. First, the haughty Mughal challenged Afzal Khan's manliness. Second, he contrasted the lofty dignity of Akbar and his illustrious ancestor Timur (a.k.a. Tamerlane, d. 1405) with the mere "insects" of the

Deccan. Third and most importantly, he played the race card, reminding the Ahmadnagar diplomat that, in the end, all the assembled negotiators for both sides of the conflict were Westerners. That is, they all were of the same, proud Persian stock, in contrast to the assortment of Marathas, Habshis, and Indo-Turks—contemptuously dismissed by Sadiq Khan as "the crows and kites of the Deccan"—then defending Ahmadnagar's fort against the advancing tide from the north.

Afzal Khan, however, yielded no ground to the arrogant Mughal. Instead, he replied, calmly and boldly,

> For forty years I have eaten the salt of the sultans of the Deccan. . . . There is no better way to die than to be slain for one's benefactor, thereby obtaining an everlasting good name. . . . Moreover, it should be evident to you that the people of this country are hostile toward Westerners. I myself am a Westerner and a well-wisher of the emperor [Akbar], and I consider it to be in his interest to withdraw the Prince's great *amirs* from the neighborhood of this fort.[26]

By invoking the ancient metaphor of "salt," the Ahmadnagar envoy articulated a conception of socio-political solidarity very different from his counterpart's baser appeal to a common Iranian ethnicity.

The Rise of Malik Ambar

It was in precisely this context—of a Mughal military presence in the northern Deccan, and of sharply opposed visions of socio-political solidarity represented by the two sides—that Malik Ambar rose to prominence. We have seen that, during his travels from Ethiopia to Baghdad to India, Ambar had been sold and resold several times before finally entering Nizam Shahi service in the early 1570s as a slave of Chengiz Khan, the peshva of Ahmadnagar. In 1574–75, Chengiz Khan died. Freed by the widow of his former master,[27] Ambar now became a free lancer. He also acquired a wife, though her identity is not known. Abandoning Ahmadnagar, for some time the Habshi served the sultan of neighboring Bijapur, who placed him in charge of a small contingent of troops and gave him the title "Malik." But in 1595, complaining of insufficient support, he quit Bijapur and, with his corps of 150 loyal cavalrymen, returned to Ahmadnagar, where he entered the service of another Habshi commander, Abhang Khan. This was the moment when Mughal armies were besieging the capital with a view to annexing the Nizam Shahi kingdom to Akbar's vast and still-expanding empire. In August 1600, Ahmadnagar's fort finally fell to the determined and heavily armed Mughals, who carried into captivity the state's reigning sultan. Nonetheless, Mughal authority extended no further than the immediate hinterland of

Ahmadnagar's fort; the countryside teemed with troops formerly employed by the crippled Nizam Shahi state.

Foremost among those picking up the pieces of the Nizam Shahi state was Malik Ambar, whose own cavalry swiftly grew from 150 to 3,000, and then to 7,000 men.[28] Finding a twenty-year-old scion of Ahmadnagar's royal family in neighboring Bijapur, he promoted the cause of this youth as future ruler of a reconstituted Nizam Shahi state. To bind his royal candidate more closely to him, Ambar gave him his own daughter in marriage, and in 1600 the two were married at Malik Ambar's headquarters at Parenda, a fort located seventy-five miles southeast of Mughal-occupied Ahmadnagar.[29] When the wedding ceremonies were concluded, Ambar presided over the installation of his new son-in-law as Sultan Murtaza Nizam Shah II.[30] Governing as the regent of the new sultan, Malik Ambar also had himself made peshva of the Nizam Shahi Sultanate. It is notable that a Habshi ex-slave, for a quarter century a free man, had married not only into the Deccan's non-slave society, but even into a royal family.

But the Mughals would not retire. On the contrary, after Akbar's death in 1605, a new emperor, Jahangir, came to the Peacock Throne determined to consolidate Mughal authority over territory the northern imperialists regarded as already conquered. Despite repeated Mughal invasions against Ambar and his puppet sultan, however, Malik Ambar's strength continued to grow. In 1610, he even managed to expel the Mughals from the Ahmadnagar fort. This triumph emboldened him to transfer the Nizam Shahi court to Daulatabad, the spectacular hill-fort that had been capital of the Yadava dynasty of kings before the Tughluqs made it their own regional capital in the early fourteenth century. As such, the impressive city and citadel had for long been a focus of both Marathi regional sentiment and centralized political rule.

Notwithstanding these geopolitical triumphs, Malik Ambar now found himself beset by knotty domestic problems. For one thing Sultan Murtaza II, by this time a mature thirty years of age, refused to play the role of docile puppet and had begun meddling in affairs of state that Ambar, as peshva, considered his own. What is more, high up in Daulatabad's lofty royal palace, a family quarrel broke out between the sultan's senior and junior wives. A contemporary Dutch traveler records that in 1610 a fair-skinned "Persian" wife (*een witte Parsianse vrouwe*) from an earlier marriage reproached her younger co-wife, who was Malik Ambar's own daughter, slandering the latter as a concubine and even "a mere slave-girl" (*maer een cafferinne*). The altercation appears to have involved issues of race and of slave status. Malik Ambar's daughter was probably darker than the sultan's "Persian" co-wife, described by the outsider as white-skinned. Then too, since she had been born after Malik Ambar's own manumission, the daughter would have been born free and could not have been anybody's slave. In the heat of the outburst, moreover, the sultan's senior wife defamed Malik Ambar himself, calling him a former rebel against the state. When the daughter informed her father of the altercation, an angry Ambar ordered his secretary to poison both the meddlesome sultan and his quarrelsome senior wife.[31] In the former ruler's place, Ambar enthroned the sultan's five-year-old son by his "Persian" wife.[32] Crowned as Sultan Burhan III, the youth now became the second Nizam Shahi prince installed by Malik Ambar as his puppet sultan.

We need to take stock of the socio-political changes that lay behind these dramatic events. For one thing, under Malik Ambar's rule the revitalized Nizam Shahi kingdom had acquired a distinctly African character. As peshva, Ambar himself held undisputed control over Ahmadnagar's military and civil affairs, and his daughter had been assimilated into the Nizam Shahi royal household for twenty years. His family had also merged with the African component of the ruling class of neighboring Bijapur. In 1609, with a view to shoring up relations with this powerful sultanate to the south while taking on the Mughals in the north, Ambar had married off his son, Fath Khan, to the daughter of Yaqut Khan, a free Habshi and one of Bijapur's most powerful nobles.[33] Here we see networks of free Ethiopians engaging in interstate marital relations at a level immediately below that of the dynastic houses, at the same time mimicking the pattern of interdynastic marriages practiced by those houses.

By this time, too, entire armies of Habshi warriors were fighting for the revitalized kingdom of Ahmadnagar. The English merchant William Finch, who happened to be in the region in February 1610, reported that Malik Ambar's army consisted of ten thousand men "of his own caste," in addition to forty thousand Deccanis.[34] In an engagement with the Mughals six years later, he is said to have brought to the field ten thousand Habshi youths (*bachigan*), age seventeen or eighteen, mounted on Persian horses. The chronicler of this event also mentioned that many of those killed by the Mughals had been "slaves" of Ambar.[35] This suggests a pattern of Ethiopians entering India in considerable numbers as military slaves, with some of them, on becoming freedmen, subsequently purchasing large numbers of their own Habshi slaves. Malik Ambar had arrived in the Deccan as one of a thousand slaves belonging to Chengiz Khan, then peshva of Ahmadnagar, who himself had been brought to the Deccan as a Habshi slave. One sees, then, a diachronic process of movement from slave, to free lancer, to commander, to slave-owning commander—a remarkable pattern of upward mobility that echoed a pattern already witnessed in thirteenth-century north India. Indeed, Malik Ambar's career shares distinct parallels with that of Balban (d. 1287), a freed slave (Ulugh Khan) who, having accumulated his own slaves along with other supporters, went on to seize control of the Delhi Sultanate. The careers of the two men differed, however, in that whereas Balban eventually seized the Delhi throne and began his own dynasty, Malik Ambar never took the final step of declaring himself sultan. Yet Habshis, whether freedmen or slaves, were everywhere dominant in Ahmadnagar, especially as commandants of the many hill-forts and plains-forts that dotted the Nizam Shahi portion of the western Deccan.

Indeed, the African character of the restored Nizam Shahi Sultanate appears to have energized the race-conscious Mughals in their efforts to annihilate Malik Ambar and annex the kingdom he ruled. We have already noted the contempt with which Akbar's officers viewed their Deccani adversaries when Prince Murad attacked the Nizam Shahi Sultanate in 1595–96. Such attitudes were heightened during the reign of Jahangir (1605–27), who was simply obsessed with Malik Ambar. Unable to defeat the African in battle, the emperor instead spewed imprecations on his adversary. In his memoir for the year 1612, Jahangir calls him "'Ambar, the black-faced"; in 1616, he is "the ill-starred 'Ambar" and "the rebel 'Ambar"; in 1617, "'Ambar of dark fate" and "that disastrous man"; in 1620, "'Ambar, the black-fated one," while his men are "the rebels of black-fortune"; in 1621, he is "the ill-starred one" and "the crafty 'Ambar."[36] It is significant that darkness, specifically the color black, dominates Jahangir's thinking about Malik Ambar. Indeed, both the memoirs and the art commissioned by Jahangir point beyond the Mughal-Deccan conflict to a deeper tension between light-skinned Westerners—personified by the emperor himself—and dark-skinned Deccanis, especially Habshis, personified by Malik Ambar.[37]

But the emperor's judgment of the Ethiopian was not the only one to be found at the Mughal court. It is instructive to contrast Jahangir's negative assessment of Malik Ambar with the unambiguously positive one made by Mu'tamad Khan, who completed the emperor's memoirs when his patron fell too ill to continue writing them. In 1626, only a year before the emperor's death, news reached north India that Malik Ambar, the Mughals' long-time nemesis, had died, evidently of natural causes. "This 'Ambar was a slave," recorded the chronicler. "But," he added, "an able man."

> In warfare, in command, in sound judgment, and in administration, he had no rival or equal. He well understood that predatory (*kazzaki*) warfare, which in the language of the Dakhin is called *bargi-giri*. He kept down the turbulent spirits of that country, and maintained his exalted position to the end of his life, and closed his career in honour. History records no other instance of an Abyssinian slave arriving at such eminence.[38]

Two things are notable in this extraordinary tribute. The first is the range of opinion it shows to have existed within the Mughal establishment about Malik Ambar and, by extension, about black Africans generally. If Jahangir himself saw Ambar through a racial lens tinted by Iranian or Central Asian chauvinism, Mu'tamad Khan viewed him through the lens of raw ability and practical achievement. The contrast is revealing. Inasmuch as both the emperor and his chronicler were Muslims, their opposing views of Malik Ambar refute the contention, still heard today, that Islamic civilization since the eighth or ninth century nurtured a racially motivated bias against black Africans.[39]

Also notable in Mu'tamad Khan's tribute is the reference to Malik Ambar's mastery of guerrilla warfare. Refusing to engage in pitched battles against the Mughals' imposing façade of artillery, infantry, and heavy cavalry, Ambar made surprise night attacks, harassed enemy supply lines, and drew Mughal forces into wooded hills and rugged ravines where they could be hacked to pieces by his light cavalry. The Mughal term for such tactics, *bargi-giri*, referred to units of Marathas who were trained and paid by the Ahmadnagar Sultanate. Light and swift, Maratha cavalrymen in Malik Ambar's service had a deadly effect on the Mughals' cumbersome armies; on occasion they pursued Mughal troopers clear up to their regional headquarters at Burhanpur.[40] Although Ahmadnagar was not the first Deccani sultanate to make use of Maratha cavalrymen—they, like Habshi slaves, had also served Bahmani sultans in the fifteenth century—the Nizam Shahi state under Malik Ambar's leadership made more extensive use of Maratha troopers than did any other Deccani kingdom. Under him, the units of Maratha cavalry in Ahmadnagar's service grew from ten thousand in 1609 to fifty thousand in 1624.[41] In fact, the Ahmadnagar Sultanate under Ambar's direction had effectively become a joint Habshi-Maratha enterprise.[42]

The Eclipse of Military Slavery

But the nature of this enterprise gradually changed in the course of the seventeenth century. In the late sixteenth century, both Westerners and Deccan-born Muslims receded in relative importance in the state's political system, largely because of their long history of mutual antagonism, even civil war. As we have seen, slave and free Ethiopians steadily filled the power vacuum created by this discord. But theirs was a brief moment of prominence, to be followed by the rise of Maratha warrior-clans, who were the ultimate beneficiaries both of Nizam Shahi patronage and of Nizam Shahi decline. By the mid-seventeenth century, military slavery as an institution had come to an end in the Deccan; and by the eighteenth century, the Habshis as a distinct Deccani group and military caste had nearly disappeared. What best explains these developments?

In the first place, in 1636, just a decade after Malik Ambar's death, the Mughals finally swallowed up the Nizam Shahi Sultanate. This abruptly ended the patronage system that for several centuries had been geared to recruiting Ahmadnagar's military slaves from overseas. For as a matter of policy, the imperial Mughals did not recruit military slaves into their armies. Second, since few Ethiopian females were recruited to the Deccan, African men necessarily married local women, as did their male offspring. As a result, African males became mainly absorbed in the local society, an outcome quite different from that found in the Americas, where the introduction of both male and female African slaves created a self-reproducing and enduring black population.[43]

A third factor behind the Habshis' disappearance as a distinct community involved their transition from kinless aliens to native householders. This socio-historical process directly counters characterizations of slavery as a permanent state of "social death."[44] From the remarks of seventeenth-century foreign travelers we know that African slaves in the Deccan were tied to their masters by close and affectionate bonds.[45] Indeed, throughout the Middle East, the recruitment of slave-soldiers from beyond the borders of the Muslim world was followed by their integration first into the central government and ultimately into their host society.[46] The Ottoman historian Dror Ze'evi has drawn particular attention to the role of the master's household as an agent in the slave's socialization and as a springboard for his career. It was "meaningful integration into the household, as a special son of the master," writes Ze'evi, that "enabled the slave to complete the metamorphosis from slave to lord." Living in the same surroundings and eating the same food as their masters, military slaves not only became fictive kin of their masters, but they did so, Ze'evi argues, even before being manumitted.[47] The same appears to have been the case in the western Deccan.

Conclusion

Several conclusions emerge from this discussion of Malik Ambar and military slavery in the early modern western Deccan. For one thing, the just-cited argument by Dror Ze'evi suggests that military slavery was a self-terminating process, and not an enduring condition. This position is amply supported by evidence from seventeenth-century Ahmadnagar, where men who had begun their careers as culturally alien slaves without kin over time became integrated into their host society, acquired kin, and embraced a Deccani regional identity.[48] This points to a theme that one encounters repeatedly in studies of slavery in South Asia, namely, its evolving, rather than static, character. The movement from alien slave to socially and culturally integrated freedman could explain why we seldom hear of the formal manumission of Habshi slaves in Nizam Shahi service. The transition from a master-slave to a patron-client relationship appears to have been so smooth that, on the death of the patron, a former slave emerged as a de facto freedman, with or without a letter of formal manumission. This process was so common as not even to have warranted notice in contemporary Persian chronicles. In Malik Ambar's own case, it was only the Dutchman Van den Broecke who mentioned the Ethiopian's manumission by Chengiz Khan's widow. But he, of course, was an outsider whose own culture drew a sharp distinction between the categories of slave and free. Persian chroniclers took no notice of Malik Ambar's manumission, nor of that of other Habshi slaves.

On the other hand, both Europeans and chroniclers of Iranian origins were well aware of the Habshis' African ethnicity, which to them—if perhaps not to long-time residents of the Deccan—persisted despite their slave or non-slave status. To immigrant chroniclers of Deccani history like ʿAli Tabataba or Qasim Firishta, non-slave commanders of African origin, even those who were themselves slaveholders, were referred to not as "*amirs*," but as "Habshi *amirs*" (*umra-yi Habshi*), or as simply "the Habshis" (*Habush*).[49] In the same way, to contemporary Europeans Malik Ambar's Ethiopian identity persisted throughout his career. Whereas on official documents the Ahmadnagar leader referred to himself as "Malik Ambar," Englishmen in the Deccan continued to call him by the Ethiopian name he had borne before his enslavement—"Chapu"—as well as by the name given him by Mir Qasim, the merchant who had bought and trained him in Baghdad. In 1610 William Finch referred to him as "Amber-champon," and William Hawkins, another Englishman who was in India between 1608 and 1612, called him "Amberry Chapu."[50] Clearly, to race-conscious Iranian or European outsiders, an essential aspect of Malik Ambar's African identity remained intact fully forty years after his arrival in the Deccan.

In the last analysis, the appearance and disappearance of military slavery in the Deccan must be seen as a product of circumstances quite specific to the western Deccan between the mid-fifteenth and mid-seventeenth centuries—e.g., Ethiopian demand for Indian textiles, factional politics in the western Deccan, the Mughals' termination of a particular kind of military recruitment, and the gradual assimilation of Ethiopians into Deccan society. The phenomenon certainly had nothing to do with Islam. Nor does it illustrate "Islamic slavery," an illusory category that continues to appear in slavery studies. Like any other historical phenomenon, instances of military slavery are best explained by placing them in their specific and unique historical contexts, rather than by invoking essentialized ideologies or religious traditions.

Notes

Material in this chapter is derived from Richard M. Eaton, *A Social History of the Deccan, 1300–1761: Eight Indian Lives* (Cambridge: Cambridge University Press, 2005), chapter 5.

1. A note on terminology: "Ethiopia" is the ancient Greek term for Abyssinia. I am using "Ethiopian" and "Habshi" to refer to members of various ethnic communities from either the Abyssinian highlands or the regions immediately surrounding those highlands. Contemporary Indo-Persian accounts referred to slaves in the Deccan by the term "Habshi," while sixteenth-century Portuguese accounts called them Abyssinians. In Dutch records of the seventeenth century they were known by the term *caffer,* which referred more generally to blacks from Africa.

2. W. Ph. Coolhaas, ed., *Pieter Van den Broecke in Azië,* 2 vols. (The Hague: Martinus Nijhoff, 1962), 1:148.

3. Hashim Beg Astarabadi, *Futuhat-i-ʿAdil Shahi* (London: British Library, Add. 26,234), cited in D. R. Seth, "The Life and Times of Malik Ambar," *Islamic Culture* 31 (1957), 142.

4. Bernard Lewis, *Race and Slavery in the Middle East: An Historical Enquiry* (New York: Oxford University Press, 1990), 57.

5. Radhey Shyam, *Life and Times of Malik Ambar* (New Delhi: Munshiram Manoharlal, 1968), 35.

6. Jadunath Sarkar, *House of Shivaji: Studies and Documents on Maratha History; Royal Period,* 3rd ed. (Calcutta: M. C. Sarkar and Sons, 1955), 6.

7. Prominent biographies include Jogindra Nath Chowdhuri, *Malik Ambar: A Biography Based on Original Sources* (Calcutta: M. C. Sarkar and Sons, ca. 1933); Seth, "Life and Times"; Shyam, *Life and Times;* and B. G. Tamaskar, *The Life and Work of Malik Ambar* (Delhi: Idarah-i Adabiyat-i Delli, 1978).

8. Mordechai Abir, *Ethiopia and the Red Sea* (London: Frank Cass, 1980), 215.

9. See Manuel Joao Ramos, "Ethiopia in the Geographical Representations of Mediaeval and Renaissance Europe," in Jessica Hallet and C. Amaral, eds., *Cultures of the Indian Ocean* (Lisbon: Comissao Nacional para as Comemoraçaoes dos Descobrimentos Portugueses, 1998), 44–54.

10. Tomé Pires, *Suma Oriental,* trans. Armando Cortesao, 2 vols. (London: Hakluyt Society, 1944), 1:14.

11. Francisco Alvares, *The Prester John of the Indies: A True Relation of the Lands of the Prester John, Being the Narrative of the Portuguese Embassy to Ethiopia in 1520,* trans. C. F. Beckingham and G. W. B. Huntingford, 2 vols. (Cambridge: Hakluyt Society, 1961), 1:455.

12. By the mid-1600s the Ethiopian state had extended its slave-raiding expeditions to its western frontier with Sudan. Some non-Christian slaves were integrated into the Ethiopian state apparatus as palace guards or cavalrymen. See Richard Pankhurst, *A Social History of Ethiopia: The Northern and Central Highlands from*

Early Medieval Times to the Rise of Emperor Tewodros II (Trenton, N.J.: Red Sea Press, 1992), 111–12.

13. Alvares, *Prester John,* 1:187, 270; 2:359, 429, 434, 447–48.

14. C. F. Beckingham and G. W. B. Huntingford, trans. and ed., *Some Records of Ethiopia, 1593–1646: Being Extracts from the History of High Ethiopia or Abassia by Manoel de Albeida* (London: Hakluyt Society, 1954), 162.

15. At its height in the eighteenth century, this trade was likewise driven mainly by African demand for Indian textiles. Herbert S. Klein, "Economic Aspects of the Eighteenth-century Atlantic Slave Trade," in James D. Tracy, ed., *The Rise of Merchant Empires: Long-Distance Trade in the Early Modern World, 1350–1750* (Cambridge: Cambridge University Press, 1990), 290–93.

16. Pankhurst, *Social History,* 64.

17. Taddesse Tamrat, *Church and State in Ethiopia, 1270–1527* (Cambridge: Clarendon Press, 1972), 85–88; and Harold G. Marcus, *History of Ethiopia* (Berkeley: University of California, 1994), 19.

18. Richard Pankhurst, *The Ethiopian Borderlands: Essays in Regional History from Ancient Times to the End of the 18th Century* (Lawrence, N.J.: Red Sea Press, 1997), 252–53.

19. Pires, *Suma Oriental,* 1:8.

20. Nizam al-Mulk, *The Book of Government, or Rules for Kings: The Siyar al-Muluk, or Siyasat-nama of Nizam al-Mulk,* trans. Hubert Darke, 2nd ed. (London: Routledge and Kegan Paul, 1978), 117.

21. André Wink, *Al-Hind: The Making of the Indo-Islamic World,* vol. 2, *The Slave Kings and the Islamic Conquest, 11th–13th Centuries* (Leiden: E. J. Brill, 1997), 181.

22. Richard Pankhurst, "The Ethiopian Diaspora to India: The Role of Habshis and Sidis from Medieval Times to the End of the Eighteenth Century," in Shihan de Silva Jayasuriya and Richard Pankhurst, eds., *The African Diaspora in the Indian Ocean* (Trenton, N.J.: Africa World Press, 2003), 195.

23. As Peter Hardy notes, "The Mughals did not, as did the Ghurids, win north India with the aid of large contingents of military slaves; they relied upon mainly free forces of often quarrelsome and sometimes disloyal Mughals, Turks, and Iranians; Akbar found it necessary to put Indian-born Muslims and (after he had subdued the principal chiefs of Rajasthan) Rajputs in the balance against his immigrant followers." Peter Hardy, *Muslims of British India* (Cambridge: Cambridge University Press, 1972), 14.

24. In the ancient Mesopotamian world, the Akkadian phrase meaning "to eat the salt of (a person)" expressed the act of making a covenant with a person or of permitting a reconciliation with another individual. See Daniel Potts, "On Salt and Salt Gathering in Ancient Mesopotamia," *Journal of the Economic and Social History of the Orient* 27, no. 3 (Oct. 1984), 228. The phrase "not worth his salt" is traceable to Petronius Arbiter (*Satyricon,* first century AD), but the political sense of an oath of salt entered modern English through Britain's imperial connection with India. This is reflected, for example, in the doggerel poems of Rudyard Kipling: "I have eaten your bread and salt, I have drunk your water and wine; The deaths ye died I have watched beside, and the lives ye led were mine." *Departmental Ditties,* 1886, Prelude, st. 1.

25. Sadiq Khan's "You, who are men of the same race as ourselves," reads in the original *shuma mardum ki ibna-yi jins-i ma'id.* Saiyid ʿAli Tabataba, *Burhan-i*

ma'asir (Delhi: Jam'i Press, 1936), 629–30. It has been translated by Wolseley Haig as "The History of the Nizam Shahi Kings of Ahmadnagar," *Indian Antiquary* 52 (Nov. 1923), 343–45. I have modernized the language of Haig's English translation.

26. Haig, "History of the Nizam Shahi Kings," 344–45.

27. Coolhaas, *Van den Broecke*, 1:148.

28. Sarkar, *House of Shivaji*, 6–7.

29. For an excellent description and account of the fort, see G. Yazdani, "Parenda: An Historical Fort," *Annual Report of the Archaeological Department of His Exalted Highness the Nizam's Dominions* (1921–24), 17–36.

30. Shyam, *Life and Times*, 38–39.

31. Coolhaas, *Van den Broecke*, 1:149.

32. It is not known whether Malik Ambar's daughter had any offspring. See Pieter Gielis van Ravesteijn, "Journal, May 1615 to Feb. 1616," in Heert Terpstra, *De opkomst der Westerkwartieren van de Oost-Indische Compagnie (Suratte, Arabië, Perzië)* (The Hague: Martinus Nijhoff, 1918), 176–77. The earliest text of the journal is in Leiden, National Archives, "Journal of Pieter Gillisz van Ravesteijn on his Journey from Masulipatam to Surat and Back, 8.5–29.10.1615," VOC 1061, fol. 239v. I am indebted to Gijs Kruijtzer for his assistance in interpreting the texts of both Ravesteijn and Van den Broecke.

33. Radhey Shyam, *The Kingdom of Ahmadnagar* (Delhi: Motilal Banarsidass, 1966), 257–58.

34. William Foster, ed., *Early Travels in India, 1583–1619* (reprint, New Delhi: S. Chand and Co., 1968), 138.

35. Astarabadi, *Futuhat-i 'Adil Shahi*, fol. 278b, cited in Sarkar, *House of Shivaji*, 17.

36. Jahangir, *The Tuzuk-i-Jahangiri, or Memoirs of Jahangir*, trans. Alexander Rogers, ed. Henry Beveridge, 2 vols. (1909–14; reprint, Delhi: Munshiram Manoharlal, 1968), 1:220, 312, 313, 368, 373, 2:155, 156, 207, 208.

37. The Mughal emperor's obsession with Ambar is tellingly revealed in an extraordinary portrait of the two men commissioned by Jahangir and painted around 1616 by the renowned Mughal artist Abu'l-Hasan. In this painting Jahangir stands atop the globe and, holding a bow and arrow, takes aim at the severed head of Malik Ambar, which is impaled on the tip of a spear. Rich in symbolism, the painting repeatedly associates the emperor with light and justice, whereas the head of Malik Ambar, surrounded with owls both dead and alive, is associated with night, darkness, and usurpation. Persian captions on the painting also play on Ambar's dark color—e.g., "The head of the night-coloured usurper has become the house of the owl." Above all, the portrait reveals the emperor's profound frustration with his failure ever to vanquish Ambar. It appears that he fantasized in art what he could not accomplish on the battlefield. See Linda York Leach, *Mughal and Other Indian Paintings from the Chester Beatty Library*, 2 vols. (London: Scorpion Cavendish, 1995), 1:398–405.

38. Mu'tamad Khan, *Iqbal-nama-yi Jahangiri*, quoted in Henry M. Elliot and John Dowson, eds. and trans., *History of India as Told by Its Own Historians*, 8 vols. (Allahabad: Kitab Mahal, 1964), 6:428–29.

39. See Lewis, *Race and Slavery*, 26, 41, 55.

40. Shyam, *Life and Times*, 96–98.

41. Ibid., 147. In 1610 when William Finch described Malik Ambar's army as consisting of ten thousand Habshis and forty thousand Deccanis, it is likely that the latter figure actually referred to the forty thousand Marathas that he had by this time recruited and trained. Foster, ed., *Early Travels,* 138.

42. Some of the more important Maratha chiefs in Ambar's service were Shahji, Sharofji, Maloji, Parsoji, Mambaji, Nagoji, Trimbakji, Hambir Rao, Chavan, Madhji, Nar Singh Raj, Ballela Tripul, Vithal Raj, Kavata, Dattaji, Naganath, Nar Singh Pingle, and Sunder Jagdev. Shyam, *Kingdom of Ahmadnagar,* 277.

43. The scattered communities of so-called Siddis that survive in western India today appear to be descended not from Habshi military slaves of the fifteenth through seventeenth centuries, but from male and female domestic slaves brought from East Africa by European or Arab dealers in the eighteenth and nineteenth centuries. On the African diaspora eastward, see Shanti Sadiq Ali, *African Dispersal in the Deccan* (New Delhi: Orient Longman, 1996); Edward A. Alpers, "Recollecting Africa: Diasporic Memory in the Indian Ocean World," *African Studies Review* 43, no. 1 (Apr. 2000), 83–99; Helene Basu, *Habshi-Sklaven, Sidi-Fakire: Muslimische Heiligenverehrung in westlichen Indien* (Berlin: Das Arab Buch, 1995); idem, "The Siddi and the Cult of Bava Gor in Gujarat," *Journal of the Indian Anthropological Society* 28 (1993), 289–300; Rudy Bauss, "The Portuguese Slave Trade from Mozambique to Portuguese India and Macau and Comments on Timor, 1750–1850: New Evidence from the Archives," in *Camoes Center Quarterly* 6–7, nos. 1–2 (1997), 21–26; D. K. Bhattacharya, "Indians of African Origin," *Cahiers d'études africaines* 10, no. 40 (1970), 579–82; Jyotirmay Chakraborty and S. B. Nandi, "The Siddis of Junagadh: Some Aspects of Their Religious Life," *Human Science* 33, no. 2 (1984), 130–37; R. R. S. Chauhan, *Africans in India: From Slavery to Royalty* (New Delhi: Asian Publication Services, 1995); Joseph E. Harris, *The African Presence in Asia: Consequences of the East African Slave Trade* (Evanston, Ill.: Northwestern University Press, 1971); Jayasuriya and Pankhurst, eds., *African Diaspora;* T. B. Naik and G. P. Pandya, *The Sidis of Gujarat: A Socio-economic Study and Development Plan* (Ahmadabad: Tribal Research and Training Institute, Gujarat Vidyapith, 1981); T. C. Palakshappa, *The Siddhis of North Kanara* (New Delhi: Sterling Publishers, 1976); Jeanette Pinto, *Slavery in Portuguese India (1510–1842)* (Bombay: Himalaya Publishing House, 1992); Kiran K. Prasad, "The Identity of Siddis in Karnataka," in B. G. Halbar and C. G. Husain Khan, eds., *Relevance of Anthropology: The Indian Scenario* (Jaipur: Rawat Publications, 1991), 215–38; Vasant D. Rao, "The Habshis, India's Unknown Africans," *African Report* (Sept.–Oct. 1973), 35–38; and Markus Vink, "'The World's Oldest Trade': Dutch Slavery and Slave Trade in the Indian Ocean in the Seventeenth Century," *Journal of World History* 14, no. 2 (2003), 131–77.

44. See Orlando Patterson, *Slavery and Social Death: A Comparative Study* (Cambridge, Mass.: Harvard University Press, 1982).

45. John Fryer, *A New Account of East India and Persia, Being Nine Years' Travels, 1672–1681,* ed. William Crooke, 2 vols. (London: Hakluyt Society, 1912), 2:52.

46. Miura Toru and John Edward Philips, eds., *Slave Elites in the Middle East and Africa: A Comparative Study* (London: Kegan Paul, 2000), x.

47. Dror Ze'evi, "My Son, My Lord: Slavery, Family, and State in the Islamic Middle East," in Toru and Philips, eds., *Slave Elites,* 74, 76.

48. On the integration of slaves into their masters' households, see Paul G. Forand, "The Relation of the Slave and the Client to the Master or Patron in Medieval Islam," *International Journal of Middle East Studies* 2 (1971), 59–66. See also Sumit Guha and Indrani Chatterjee, "A Slave's Quest for Selfhood in Eighteenth-Century Hindustan," *Indian Economic and Social History Review* 37, no. 1 (2000), 53–85.

49. See, for example, Tabataba, *Burhan-i ma'asir,* 632; translated in Haig, "History of the Nizam Shahi Kings," 346.

50. Foster, *Early Travels,* 100, 138.

6

Drudges, Dancing Girls, Concubines: Female Slaves in Rajput Polity, 1500–1850

Ramya Sreenivasan

This essay explores the forms of female slavery and servitude among the Rajput ruling clans of Rajasthan between the sixteenth and early nineteenth centuries. The twenty-first-century historian seeking to recover such a history faces the obstacle of sparse information, given the nature of the archive. Uneven record-keeping practices were compounded by norms of "respectability" that proscribed the discussion of women in public.[1] The biased nature of the historical record is apparent in Varsha Joshi's rich exploration of polygamy and *purdah* among Rajput women.[2] Joshi pieces together an intricate history of concubinage and domestic servitude in elite Rajput households between the sixteenth and early twentieth centuries. However, she echoes her sources' emphasis on the distinctions between "concubine" and "wife," based on an assumed and asserted "purity" of the Rajput lineages from which "wives" were drawn.

Nor have the continuous histories of boundary marking between lineage, clan, and *jati* ("caste") been kept in sight by other historians of medieval Rajasthan. While B. D. Chattopadhyaya demonstrates the mixed-caste origins of the Rajputs of Rajasthan between the seventh and twelfth centuries, he argues that a distinctive Rajput clan structure was in place by the end of this period.[3] Most historians have treated such "Rajput" identity as changeless in the period between the twelfth and early nineteenth centuries. They have focused instead on specific strategies for consolidating power employed by particular lineages within the broader understanding of "state," such as intermarrying with other Rajput clans, establishing monopolies over resource extraction, and acquiring the trappings of kingship, such as patronage of temple centers, public works, and monumental architecture.[4] Such an emphasis on state formation has led historians to pay less attention to continuing histories of *jati* formation, in which Rajput elites and their chroniclers defined evolving boundaries for the *jati* through an ideology of "purity."[5]

This essay demonstrates that the boundaries of lineage, clan, and *jati* asserted in the Rajput courtly sources and assumed in the historiography were not absolute, but were interwoven with a history of slavery in Rajput polities between the seventeenth and the nineteenth centuries. Constructions of lineage, clan, and *jati* evolved during this period, as much through the management of slave labor in elite households as through the oft-rehearsed network of marriage alliances among the Rajputs.

The Historical Moment

Little is known of the political history of modern Rajasthan during the fourteenth century, after ʿAla al-Din Khalaji's conquests in the region. It was during the fifteenth century that several new lineages became prominent, such as the Sisodiyas in Mewar and the Rathors in Marwar, with their capitals in Chitor and Jodhpur respectively (see map 3). By the mid-sixteenth century, rulers in these new lineages were attempting to shift the basis of their power away from their clans toward a more hierarchical monarchical polity, built on patron-client relationships rather than kin networks.[6] Members of the clan networks of course contested these new claims by the rulers, so that kings and clan chiefs continued to assert their respective (and often mutually incompatible) rights. The intense politicization of the Rajput lineages and clan networks also coincided with the growth of Mughal power in the same period. However, Mughal intervention had complex consequences for the various Rajput kingdoms. On the one hand, service in imperial military campaigns during the period of Mughal territorial expansion brought independent rewards for both Rajput rulers and chiefs, in the form of increased assignments of rights to revenue from other parts of the empire. On the other hand, by the late sixteenth century, the Mughal emperor became overlord and arbiter of conflicts between the Rajput rulers and chiefs.

It was in this context that a variety of genres emerged for narrating the past in the Rajput courts, partly because of the Mughal emphasis on record keeping. Simultaneously, the Mughal emphasis on "illustrious ancestry" as a stated basis for political favor reinforced the Rajput drive to assert glorious genealogical pasts. Through the late sixteenth and seventeenth centuries, therefore, the Rajput kingdoms of Rajasthan witnessed another spurt in the redefinition of the boundaries of clan, lineage, and ultimately *jati*. Both internal and external stimuli impelled ruling lineages to redefine, regulate, and narrow the conditions for "belonging" that determined access to entitlements within this ruling elite. Crucial to this enterprise was the articulation of an ideology of "purity" of descent.

The chief sources used in this account are chronicles produced in the Rajput courts of Jodhpur and Udaipur between the seventeenth and nineteenth centuries. Bureaucrats and scholars in the Rajput courts, such as Munhata Nainsi (*Nainsi ri khyat*, c. 1660) and Kaviraj Shyamaldas (*Vir Vinod*, c. 1880), retold the history of their princely patrons' lineages with a view to asserting the latter's grandeur to an audience of other Rajput elite lineages and imperial overlords. Chroniclers dependent upon courtly patronage were as invested as their princely patrons were in affirming the socio-political hierarchies underpinning Rajput power.[7] Such sources thus described slavery in terms of the same ideology of "purity" that belonged to their Rajput masters, not the slaves and servants themselves.

Enslavement and Its Narrations

Evidence on the procurement of slaves from just before our period suggests that women in particular were vulnerable to capture and enslavement during battles and raids. An inscription on the Kirtistambh pillar, erected to commemorate the victory of Rana Kumbha of Mewar over Sultan Qutb al-Din Ahmad Shah of Gujarat in 1454, declares that the *rana* (king) "stole Nagaur from the sultan, demolished the fort there, captured many elephants and took many Muslim women prisoners, and then turned Nagaur into a pasture for grazing."[8] Similarly, Malu Khan—*subedar* (governor) of Ajmer on behalf of the Mandu sultan—brought an army against the principality of Merta around 1490, "looting and burning villages and taking prisoners."[9]

While comparable information is not available for the sixteenth and seventeenth centuries, evidence from the late eighteenth century suggests that the practice may have continued. During this period, the principality of Alwar (in eastern Rajasthan) emerged as a Rajput state, partly through the subjugation of Meo pastoralists within its declared "territories." Meo memory recorded how, during one raid upon their fortress, the chief minister of Alwar captured and imprisoned two hundred girls, nine hundred cows, and seventy men.[10] Similarly, during the Jodhpur state's conflict with Jaipur in 1807, "first the Jaipur forces caught and sold the women of Marwar for two *paise* each; then in the same way the forces of Singhvi Indraraj [of Jodhpur] and Nawab Amir Khan caught the women of Dhundhar and sold them for one *paisa* each."[11]

The availability of the "women of the vanquished" as spoils of war seems to have been widely assumed in the region. It is clear that not all such captives were of the same kind. As we discuss below, some female captives were skilled artisans, while others were kinswomen and lesser servants and clients of defeated warriors. However, it is not always possible to determine which captives were retained exclusively by the victorious chiefs or military commanders, and which, if any, became shares in the "loot" distributed among ordinary soldiers. Courtly chronicles concerned with celebrating the preeminence of their princely patrons were not likely to record the disbursement of captives to humble-born soldiers. Nevertheless, these chronicles hint at the fact that all captives were not always sold as slaves; some women perceived to be of higher social rank were incorporated into the harems of their conquerors, with or without "marriage."

In his chronicle, dating to around 1660, Nainsi recounts how in the early fifteenth century Rao Rinmal of Jodhpur exacted vengeance upon the Sisodiya Rajputs of Mewar for murdering their ruler, Rana Mokal. After a successful siege of Chitor and the killing of those responsible for Mokal's murder,

> Rinmalji cut off the heads of the Sisodiyas and planted them on stakes to create an enclosure [*chokya kivi*]. Then he created a wedding pavilion [*mandap*] with those stakes. And he wedded the daughters of the Sisodiyas to the [victorious] Rathors. The weddings continued throughout the day.[12]

Again, the chronicler recounts how, in 1529, Sekho Sujavat enlisted the military support of Daulat Khan of Nagaur against his nephew Rao Gango of Jodhpur, by invoking similar expectations of the spoils of war: "If we win, there are many Rinmals [i.e., the ruling Rathor Rajputs in Jodhpur]; we will marry two of their girls [to the two khans]."[13] Of note here is the fact that even as Nainsi recounts such transfers of women to victors in battle, he is scrupulous to assert the legitimizing mechanism of marriage while describing the transfer of Rajput women.

The mechanisms for incorporating female captives seem to have followed similar hierarchies into the eighteenth century. Thus among the two hundred Meo girls mentioned above who were captured by the Alwar forces was Musi, the daughter of a Meo chief. In Meo oral traditions narrating their resistance to the Rajput state of Alwar, Musi protested strongly upon being captured and "put into a *dol* (palanquin) by the Rajputs": "I am the daughter of Mansa Rao, and vow three times, I will not embrace you as long as I live, why have you violated my faith?"[14] The various accounts of Musi's subsequent life reveal more about their authors than about their subject. Meo tradition is silent about her life as the concubine of Bakhtavar Singh, the Raj-

put ruler of Alwar. Upon his death, she immolated herself on his pyre, a phenomenon explored later in this essay. A red sandstone cenotaph was constructed near the palace in Alwar city, and is still known locally as *Musi Ma-
harani ki chhatri* (the cenotaph of Queen Musi). The mode of her death
(through immolation) seems to finally have elevated Musi's perceived status.

In keeping with this postmortem "upward" mobility that was accepted
locally, a later bardic account produced under Rajput patronage ascribed
different origins to her, calling her "an orphaned Rajput girl who was bought
up by a prostitute and given a home and protection by the king." The bardic
account thus recuperates both Musi and the Rajput ruler simultaneously,
providing Rajput status to her and benevolent magnanimity to him.[15] However, other, later Rajput accounts adamantly denied her such status. The
chronicler Shyamaldas, patronized by the Mewar court, who, around 1880,
attempted to compile an "accurate" history of the Rajputs, recorded Musi's
immolation but not her origins. In doing so he suppressed the history of her
capture and reinscribed her perceived illegitimacy as "the whore Musi"
(*Musi randi*).[16] For the seventeenth-century chronicler Nainsi, the mechanism of "marriage" was vital in distinguishing Rajput women from other females captured during battle. For the nineteenth-century Shyamaldas, writing when the Rajput princely states had become vassals of the British, Rajput
status was asserted as inhering in birth alone. Since birth identities had become the sole basis for determining access to entitlements during the colonial regime, Rajput status could not be represented as "indiscriminately"
achieved by disparate members of the harems of the ruling elites—even in
retrospect.

Enslavement occurred in other circumstances as well, in addition to war.
While we have little evidence in the courtly chronicles for this, James Tod—
Resident Agent of the British East India Company in the princely state of
Udaipur and author of the definitive colonial "history" of the Rajputs—
recorded in 1829 how "thousands were sold in the last great famine" in
Mewar.[17] When the sale of people occurred on such a scale, it is reasonable
to speculate that non-Rajputs may also have engaged in the purchase and
transfer of slaves.[18] As for the Rajput elite in this later period, another steady
source of slaves seems to have been the chiefs' "illegitimate" progeny by
women of "lower" caste, such as Gujar, or of "tribal" origins, such as the
Bhils.[19]

Transfers and Gifts: The Value of a Slave

Skilled slave-performers were in greater demand because they were more
difficult to come by. In one index of their greater value, the transfer of such

slaves between chiefs could often provoke conflicts, as the instance of Haji Khan Pathan reveals. In 1556, Rana Udai Singh of Mewar sent two of his chiefs to Ajmer to demand payment from Haji Khan in exchange for supporting him against Rao Maldeo of Jodhpur. In Nainsi's words, the *rana*'s message was

> I supported you against Rav Malde. [In payment] give me several elephants [and] some gold, [and] you have a band [of women]; in it is the dancing girl (*patar*), Rangray, so give [her] to me.[20]

Udai Singh's chiefs advised him that since the Mewar *rana* had provided refuge to Haji Khan in his distress, demands for repayment of the favor were inappropriate. Udai Singh persisted, however, and while Haji Khan agreed to send the elephants and the gold, he refused to send Rangray Patar, since she was his "woman."[21] In the ensuing battle at Harmaro in 1557, Haji Khan defeated Udai Singh's forces with the assistance of Rao Maldeo of Jodhpur.

How Rajputs and their chroniclers in the seventeenth century construed the significance of a *patar*'s transfer becomes clearer when we consider another such instance recounted in Nainsi's *Khyat*. Recounting an episode from the early fourteenth century, Nainsi describes how 'Ala al-Din Khalaji's chiefs Mamusah and Mir Gabhru took refuge with Raval Kanadde of Jalor. They entered the *raval*'s service and were rewarded with generous grants and opportunities for service. However, Kanadde was reluctant to let them continue in Jalor. One of his advisors suggested that he ask for their *patars* Dharu and Varu; rather than accede to the request, the chiefs would leave of their own accord. In Nainsi's account, the king's advisor had anticipated events well; Mamusah and Mir Gabhru replied to Kanadde's emissary,

> the *ravalji* has set out to build a temple to Mahadevji; we would have presented him with the *patars* of our own accord. But the *ravalji* has demanded the surrender of the *patars* from us; it appears that he wishes to expel us.[22]

In Nainsi's account, the Khalaji chiefs leave Jalor rather than surrender the women. The episode is all the more striking when we consider that it is entirely absent from the earliest available account of 'Ala al-Din's siege of Jalor, Padmanabha's *Kanadde Prabandh* (c. 1450). In that account, the conflict between 'Ala al-Din and Kanadde originated in the latter's denying free passage to the sultan's armies on their way to Gujarat, and in his subsequent rescue of the Somnath idol, along with prisoners, from the camp of 'Ala al-Din's victorious commander. Where the fifteenth-century account articulated a contest between the rival sovereignties of the Jalor chief and the

Delhi sultan in its own distinctive terms,[23] Nainsi inserted an additional episode involving the sultan's chiefs that reveals the conflict latent in the potential transfer of such slave-performers. By the seventeenth century, therefore, the mode of transfer of such slaves signified the relationship between the "donor" and the "recipient," in a practice common to elites across "religious" or "ethnic" affiliations. As Nainsi's accounts reveal, the voluntary transfer of such performers signified a relationship of vassalage to an overlord; in contrast, their forced surrender signified subjugation and the loss of sovereignty. Thus rulers and overlords could demand such slave-performers from vassals or lesser chiefs, as Ram Singh of Jodhpur (b. 1730) was said to have done from Sher Singh, the chief (*thakur*) of Riya.[24]

The provenance, duration, and modes of training in such skills are largely uninvestigated in the courtly narratives of these regimes. Varsha Joshi, working from records of the nineteenth century, points out that in Jaipur state, such performers were trained by professional artists in *patar khana*s (or *gunjan khana*s—"houses of *patar*s" or "houses of melody"), owned by the state as well as by individual Rajput queens.[25] Though it is not clear when such *patar khana*s were established in the different Rajput chiefdoms, Nainsi's seventeenth-century accounts of Rangray, Dharu, and Varu suggest that such a trained *patar* would not be easily or lightly transferred to another chiefly household or state. These accounts then draw attention to the investments of time, labor, and resources "embodied" as the skilled performer (perhaps comparable to those invested in recruitment of soldiers by the same regimes). These investments made such figures "speak" of the wealth and prestige of the holder. In the seventeenth century, then, Nainsi's *Khyat* could render the stature of Salivahan Bhati of Jaisalmer (c. twelfth century) transparent to the cognoscenti by representing him as a commander of ten thousand infantry (*payakka*) as well as the proud possessor of a gymnasium (*akhara*) filled with beautiful, slender-waisted women who danced for his pleasure at all hours of the day.[26]

Rajput rulers in the seventeenth century went to some lengths to obtain skilled performers. The *Jodhpur hukumat ri bahi* (Register of Jodhpur State) takes care to record that when Jaswant Singh, the ruler of Jodhpur, was sent to Jamrod (in modern Afghanistan) by the Mughal emperor, he obtained ten fine singing women (*gayin*) there between 1668 and 1672. He then sent these women—Pransantosh, Chutrarekha, Anuprang, Surasrai, Rangopa, Pransaman, Vidasarup, Vidaparvin, Hulasrai, and Dhana Gujaratan—back to his *zanana* in Jodhpur. The transaction highlights many different aspects of this social history. The women themselves were clearly uprooted from their kin-based and *jati*-based communities at the point of their entry into slavery, and might have experienced a change of location yet again. Unlike wives from the Rajput lineages, who continued to be known by their natal names after marriage, these female slaves were given new names by their masters that effectively erased all other identities and affiliations. Thus Jaswant Singh named one of the singing women he acquired from Jamrod Survilas ("she who dallies in music").[27] Names such as this were entirely conventional and refocused the identity of the newly acquired slave around the new master, who asserted absolute power through such renaming.

Looking at the transaction from the new master's perspective, it appears that Jaswant Singh was attempting to "jumpstart" his quest for status by acquiring these already-skilled women from elsewhere. On the other hand, it is also striking that the *Jodhpur hukumat ri bahi* does not record any subsequent transfer of any of these performers to the Mughal emperor, in the conventional acknowledgment of Jaswant Singh's vassalage to his overlord. Such silence may suggest either Jaswant Singh's favored status within the hierarchy of the Mughal court, or the Jodhpur chronicler's subtle assertion of his ruler's autonomy: an autonomy marked by his ability to acquire such skilled slave-performers and retain them for his own "use," even when on imperial assignment.

Other chiefs perhaps had already devised ways to acquire such figures, sometimes by acquiring lesser kinds of slaves and retainers. We might better understand the shifts and swings within each lineage's strategies if we run our eye over the layers of services and skills that each chief was expected to command.

Skills and Services

The multiple functions performed by slaves in Rajput chiefly households are indicated by the profusion of terms to denote different kinds of service. We have already encountered the *patar*s, skilled female slave-performers, usually dancing girls; other female slave-performers who sang were termed *olagani*. A woman "elevated" to the rank of concubine was referred to as a *khavasin* (masc. *khavas*) or *pasvan* (alt. *pasban*). The same terms denoted their progeny, as well as male servants and retainers in general. *Davri* denoted female domestic slaves, while a *badaran* (alt. *vadaran*) was a senior female slave-retainer in the women's quarters, the *zanana*. Such terminology was multivalent; it denoted different functions or skills, as well as different positions in the hierarchy of the household, based on degree of proximity to or intimacy with the Rajput ruler or queen. Thus the *davri*s would have occupied a far lower position than the *patar*s or *olagani*s, who in turn would have been considered lower in rank than the *vadaran*s, while the *khavas* or *pasvan* would have been ranked higher still. At the top of this slave pyramid were the *pardayat*s: women permitted to wear the veil like their "superiors," the Rajput queens. *Chakar* denoted any individual in a relationship of service to a superior; the latter term could thus be used for a vassal as well as for a slave. More derogatory terms included *gola* (fem. *goli*) and *daroga* (fem. *darogi*), each suggesting descent from the illegitimate union of Rajputs and their "inferiors."

These differences of rank within the chiefly household were instituted formally, and sustained by hierarchies of entitlements as well. In the early seventeenth century, Sur Singh of Jodhpur (d. 1619) brought all of Jodha's descendant lineages into a single, hierarchically ranked order under his control. At the same time, he forbade his brothers and sons and the women of his chiefs (*umrav*) to enter the royal *zanana*. He also established a hierarchy of ranks for *khavas* and *pasvan*.[28] Sur Singh thus asserted his monarchical authority by reordering not only the chiefly lineages within "his" realm, but also the slave-women in his household.

Such *chakar*s included entire families from particular occupational groups, such as wet nurses (*dhai*), tailors (*darji*), cooks (*vari*), washer-women (*dhoban*), and Brahman women. Male slaves (*khavas, pasvan*) accompanied their masters on military campaigns. The *Jodhpur hukumat ri bahi* indicates some of the tasks assigned to such *pasvan* men in Jaswant Singh's entourage when he was camped at Peshawar (c. 1673). Khichi Mukanddas Kalavat was responsible for keeping his master's lance and tying his sword. Sahni Raghunath worked around the camel stables. Asaich Bhagchand Vaga and Gehlot Jugraj Bhojrajot both worked around the camp stores (*kothar*), while Gujar Lakhman Narsinghdasot and Gujar Udairaj Narsinghdasot were personal attendants of Jaswant Singh.[29]

Female slave-servants or slave-performers could be "elevated" to the rank of concubine (*khavas, pasvan*) if they caught the ruler's fancy. Joshi describes the ceremonial initiation into concubinage, as the ruler and the women of his *zanana* marked the new woman's entry into their ranks by the giving of gifts. At this point of entry, the concubine was also granted the right to wear ivory bangles and anklets of silver and gold. The ritual marking entry into concubinage was clearly differentiated, however, from the rituals marking marriage, which were reserved for women from isogamous Rajput clans entering the chiefly household as wives. Even at the point of entry, therefore, ritual served to demarcate boundaries and hierarchies between "concubine" and "wife." For the concubine, upward mobility within the *zanana* depended upon her degree of intimacy with the chief. An especially favored *pasvan* could be further elevated to the ranks of *pardayat*. *Pardayat* women lived in independent quarters within the *zanana*, like the ruler's wives. While female slave-servants (*davri*) were paid in cash and kind (grain after the harvest twice a year), *pardayat* women were comparable to the Rajput queens in that they had independent allowances through revenue grants for "personal expenses" (*hath kharch ki jagir*), and their own personal attendants maintained by the state.[30]

The consequences of such intimacy with the chief were varied. In a polygynous household where proximity to, and intimacy with, the chief was the primary avenue to political power and influence, co-wives from isogamous Rajput clans were already competing for the husband's attention and affections. In this fraught environment, female slaves who gained intimacy with the chief could provoke queenly ire. Umade, the Bhati queen of Rao Maldeo of Jodhpur, relocated to her stepson's residence in Mewar a mere year after her marriage in 1537. Remembered in the chronicle traditions as the "angry queen" (*roothi rani*), she never returned to Jodhpur during Maldeo's lifetime. Jodhpur traditions record that her anger grew out of Rao Maldeo's pronounced favor for a slave (*davri*) Bharmali, who had been part of Umade's dowry from her father.[31]

By the late sixteenth century, we find a female slave occasionally taking her master's son under her wing, becoming his mother by nurture, as it were. Suraj Singh, who succeeded to the Jodhpur throne in 1595, had been "adopted" when young by Harbolan, a singing woman (*olagani*) of his father, Mota Raja Udai Singh. Suraj Singh later had a stepwell built in Harbolan's name near the Balsamand lake in Jodhpur.[32] Such commemoration suggests a degree of affection between young boy and slave foster-mother in the chiefly household that challenges our modern association of affective nurture exclusively with biological kinship.[33]

Even where the relationship was not necessarily one of nurture, a concubine's favor for one of her master's sons over another could shape the succession, especially in a polity where primogeniture was not ossified as the norm. Before his death, Gaj Singh of Jodhpur (d. 1638) asked the emperor Shahjahan to let his younger son Jaswant Singh succeed him. According to Shyamaldas's later reconstruction, the Jodhpur chronicles are said to have ascribed the passing over of the elder son Amar Singh to the influence of the *patar* Anara, Gaj Singh's concubine (*khavas*). Amar Singh is said to have hated her (*nafrat*) for her inferior status (*kam darja*). So once, when Jaswant Singh placed her slippers before her, she praised him before the king, and on her urging, Gaj Singh nominated his younger son as his heir.[34] Shyamaldas's account was written in the late nineteenth century, when the British had finally established primogeniture as the principle of succession in the Rajput princely states; because of this, the passing over of an elder son to the succession in the seventeenth century required particular explanation. His ascribing this to intrigue and the (undue) influence of a *patar* is striking, however, when compared to the explanation offered by the Bikaner chronicles, which ascribed Amar Singh's being passed over to his own weaknesses and errors. Independent testimony of Anara's influence is provided by the Anasagar lake in the environs of Jodhpur, believed to have been excavated by a grateful Gaj Singh or Jaswant Singh.[35]

Consolidations and Shifts of the Eighteenth Century

Given the outline above, we can now resituate the older historiography of elite Rajput marriages within broader structures of labor exchanges that were heightened during the eighteenth century. This century was characterized by many subtle shifts in the imperial and subimperial political order within the region. With the inability of the Mughal authorities in Delhi to arbitrate in contests over status and entitlements, competitive displays of wealth in the form of dowry gained additional importance within these chiefdoms. Since marriage dowries were addressed to fellow chiefs and subjects alike, renewed attention to the numbers and composition of such dowries in courtly chronicles sponsored by chiefly patrons was thus a significant addition in itself. Thus we find it recorded that at the marriage of Chandrakunwar Bai, the daughter of Rana Amar Singh II of Mewar, to Maharaja Jai Singh of Amber in 1708, the bride's dowry included

> two elephants laden with articles of silver, forty-five horses, one chariot, jewelry, utensils of gold and silver, twenty thousand rupees in cash, eight hundred ceremonial robes for men and 616 such [robes] for women. In addition, the bride was given jewelry, clothes, male and female slaves [*das aur dasiyan*] and many other items in dowry.[36]

Such marriage dowries sustained Rajput chiefly households and their claims to prestige. The transfer of entire families of *chakar* in dowries by the eighteenth century thus transferred substantial groups of dependents from wife-giving chiefly households to wife-taking households and in turn reinforced long-standing indices of rank within the Rajput *jati* hierarchy. Since the giving of such servants in dowry became more emphatic, and it is said that chiefs without enough slaves of their own to give in dower purchased the requisite number,[37] it may be surmised that the need for dowries especially spurred the sales of young female humans.

At the same time, the absence of an imperial overlord also intensified factional struggles and intrigue within Rajput courts. Through this period, concubines close to the ruler seem to have wielded more power. This is apparent from the instance of Gulabrai, a *pasvan* from the Oswal (Jain) *jati* during Vijay Singh's reign in Jodhpur (1752–93). According to Shyamaldas, Vijay Singh followed her bidding so implicitly that they were like Jahangir and Nurjahan. When the Jodhpur forces were defeated badly by the Shindes, the king sent his household and children to Jalor, while Gulabrai stayed with him. In 1790, the king paid a tribute of six hundred thousand rupees and ceded Ajmer to the Marathas, thus freeing himself from their control. However, Gulabrai's willfulness (*jo chahti kar baithti thi*) upset the chiefs (*sardaron ke dil bigde*), and they turned away from Jodhpur. In 1792, the king's grandson seized control of the Jodhpur fort and Gulabrai was murdered. Shyamaldas recounts that Vijay Singh was grief-stricken at her murder and died the next year.[38] Gulabrai's influence can be discerned from the fact that she had the lake of Gulabsagar excavated within the precincts of Jodhpur city. Subsequently she had a second tank, Krishnakund, constructed outside the city for the use of cattle and livestock.[39]

Some concubines continued to wield greater power into the early nineteenth century, before the British established their authority as the new overlords in the Rajput princely states. Raskapur was an intimate of Jagat Singh of Jaipur (r. 1803–18), elevated to the status of his Rathor and Bhati Rajput wives. Jagat Singh made over half the kingdom's resources to her, and demanded that the Jaipur chiefs give her the respect due to the queens, including gifts of the appropriate rank. Coins were issued in her name and she would appear in royal processions on the same elephant as the king. When one chief, Chand Singh of Duni, refused to attend any ceremonies or festivities at which she was present, he was fined two lakh rupees, which amounted to four years' income from his lands. However, Raskapur's prominence was short-lived: she fell out of favor and was imprisoned. Her subsequent fate is not known. The courtly chronicler's ire at the concubine for her elevation above the Rajput queens and clan chiefs is apparent from the abuse that Shyamaldas reserves for her, calling her a "base whore" (*adna kasbi*).[40]

In the same period, other concubines used their proximity to rulers for significant material gain. Traveling through Mewar in 1820, Tod crossed the village of Bahmania, "having a noble piece of water maintained by a strong embankment of masonry," and with "no less than four thousand *bighas* [of land] ... attached." The village was in the hands of Moti *pasvan*, "the favorite handmaid of 'the Sun of the Hindus' [as the ruler of Mewar was known]. This 'Pearl' [*moti*] pretends to have obtained it as a mortgage, but it would be difficult to show a lawful mortgager."[41]

From the eighteenth century, then, in keeping with the greater powers assumed by concubines in matters of inheritance and succession, one can decipher a reordering of the older service hierarchies within the same polities. Other and lesser female servants rose to wield great authority and influence within both household and realm. They accessed this authority, not through the male rulers, but through their queens. Ram Pyari, a slave of Rana Ari Singh's Jhala Rajput queen Sardar Kanwar in Mewar, was her trusted confidante when the queen governed the state during the minority of her sons after her husband's death in 1773. From an inscription recording Ram Pyari's munificence on the occasion of a ritual that she performed publicly, we know that she was the daughter of Gujar Rama and Rukma. While the precise mode of her entry into slavehood is not mentioned, the inscription invokes her "great authority" in the *zanana* (*antahpur mein bado adhikar liya*).[42] Known for her verbal skills (*zaban daraz*), she wielded enough influence over the queen regent to have one prime minister dislodged and another installed. As a negotiator, she was successful in defusing the tensions between the queen and the powerful Chundawat faction of Rajput chiefs within Mewar.[43] She had her own retinue of soldiers (*risala*), and personally persuaded the Mewar chiefs to accept Maratha demands for payments in order to avoid military confrontation.[44]

Another senior female servant (*badaran*) wielded great power in Jaipur state between 1818 and 1836. Rupa *badaran* was one of the slaves (*laundi*) of Jagat Singh of Jaipur (r. 1803–18). When he died at the age of thirty-two, the succession was contested and eventually passed to the infant Jai Singh III, born to Jagat Singh's Bhati queen four months after his death. Through the minority of the new ruler, the administration was run from the *zanana,* and all orders were communicated to the court through Rupa. The Bhati queen mother died in 1833, and shortly afterward her son Jai Singh died at the age of sixteen, of suspected poisoning. Shyamaldas suggests that the treacherous minister Jhootha Ram was responsible. As the infant Ram Singh II was anointed successor, Rupa's influence continued: as she had earlier been the "life" (*jan*) of the Bhati queen mother, she now became the voice (*zuban*) of the new Chandravat queen mother, also regent during her son's minority. When Jhootha Ram returned to the city after cremating Jai Singh III, the people rose in revolt; a rumor had spread that the treacherous minister and Rupa *badaran* had murdered the king. While the minister suppressed this rebellion forcibly, he fell out of favor later and died in prison. With the support of her *badaran* slaves, the Chandravat queen mother resisted British attempts to undercut her authority during her son's minority. The British were forced to send an armed force of several hundred men against the queen's servants when they incited a mob to murder an English official investigating Jai Singh's death. After two aborted attempts to arrest her, Rupa was finally taken into captivity and sent away. The British held an enquiry into the affair, where her testimony was recorded; however, she was never prosecuted and died in captivity in Pushkar more than a decade later, in 1849.[45]

The careers of Ram Pyari and Rupa reveal that female slaves in the *zanana* were a valuable resource to queens engaged in intrigues and factional struggles for power and influence. Rajput queens typically had indirect influence—through favor and intimacy with their chiefly husbands; through the prominence of their natal lineage and the significance of that alliance in their marital household; as mothers of declared heirs; and through their alignment with particular factions within the ruling household and among the chiefs of the realm. Such indirect influence, centered as it was on the queen's perceived proximity to the ruler, waxed and waned depending upon the nature of her relationship to him. When an infant son succeeded a ruler, his mother became unusually powerful, governing on behalf of her son during his minority. The instability inherent in such succession would have been magnified in the eighteenth century, with the disappearance of an imperial overlord who could ratify the succession in the Rajput chiefdoms. The rise of Ram Pyari and Rupa was tied to the rise of their mistresses, who governed on behalf of infant sons. Still, Rupa's ability to survive several reigns over eighteen years and to gain the trust of several queens testifies to her extraordinary skills—all the more remarkable given the generational shifts in the royal household with the death of every ruler. In the case of such *badaran*s, it is also apparent that slaves moved inward and upward through the political hierarchies of both *zanana* and realm with age: both Ram Pyari and Rupa were older women, older than their mistresses and masters, and older than the new recruits joining at the "outer" fringes of the household. Age and experience thus added value to slaves, as much as talent and the ability to exploit opportunities within factionalized and riven chiefly households.

Dying to Make a Difference

When a ruler died his female associates—wives, concubines, and their respective slave and slave-born entourages—were replaced by the successor's intimates. This loss of authority and power was accompanied by a reduction in, or even loss of, entitlements. Domestic servants around the household (*davri*) who were not associated closely with any one center of power seem to have weathered such transitions better, with little change in either tasks or entitlements. The queens of the deceased ruler could retain their jewelry and cash resources, unless the successor expressly decreed otherwise. Entitlements in land and revenue grants were, however, revoked or reduced substantially. As Jodhpur state records of the seventeenth century reveal, the entitlements of concubines were subject to more sweeping revo-

Table 6.1. List of Immolations of Queens, Servants, and Slaves upon the Death of Their Ruler

Date	Kingdom	Queens	Slaves named	Unnamed
1573	Bikaner	4	Pohaprai *olagani; patar* Jivu, Jaimala, Budhrai, Kamasena, Rangrai, Padmavati, Sughadrai, Manavati, Rupamanjari, Rangmala	3 *khavas*
1611	Bikaner	3	*Patar* Rangrai, Nainajiva, Kamarekha	
1614	Jaipur			60 including queens
1620	Mewar	10		9 *khavas*, 8 *saheli*
1621	Jaipur			2 queens, 8 *saheli*
1669	Bikaner	8	*Khavas* Kamodakala, Ramoti, Meghmala, Kisanai, Gunamala, Champavati, Rupkali, Pemavati, Kunjkali, Mrdangrai	
1678	Jodhpur	1	*Gayin* Survilas, Alaprekha; *khavas* Moti; Survilas's *chhokri* Gomati; *gayin* Pransantosh, Chutrarekha, Anuprang, Surasrai, Rangopa, Pransaman, Vidasarup, Vidaparvin, Hulasrai, Dhana Gujaratan; Pransantosh's *chhokri* Mohandasi and Shyamrangi; Anupranga's *chhokri* Kishankali and Mathuradasi; Sarasrai's *chhokri* Devaki; Rangopa's *chhokri* Champa; *chhokri* Ramgari, Bhagvandasi	
1698	Bikaner	2	*Khavas* Sughadrai, Rangrai, Gulabrai; *patar* Jaimala, Narangi, Saraskali, Anarkali; *khalisa* Rupkali, Kapurkali; Jaisalmeriji Sahiba's (queen) *saheliya* Ruprekha, Hararekha, Gunajot, Motirai; Tunwarji Sahiba's *saheli* Harmala; *khavas's saheli* Kamodi, Dagli	
1710	Mewar	5		2
1720	Kota			2 queens, 5 *pasvan*
1724	Jodhpur			66 women; queens, *khavas, laundi, nazir*, etc.
1735	Bikaner	1	*Patar* Garudrai, Rangrai, Nainsukhrai, Gumanrai; *badaran* Harjotrai; *khalisa* Hasti, Chainsukh	
1735	Mewar	12		8

Date	Kingdom	Queens	Slaves named	Unnamed
1746	Bikaner	2	*Khavas* Sadanji; *patar* Gora, Sarupa, Gulaba, Tantarang, Rangnirat, Fattu, Vana, Sukhvilas, Raja, Gumani, Viji, Mahtab; *khalisa* Ramjot, Kapurkali; *vadaran* Gunajot; *saheli* Rahi, Fattu, Sakami; *patar*'s cooking woman Brahmani Rahi	
1749	Jodhpur	6		2 *khavas*, 11 *pardayat*, 14 *khalisa* and *patar*
1751	Mewar	3		16
1752	Jodhpur	5		10 *patar* and others
1754	Mewar	2		
1761	Mewar	2		
1773	Mewar	2	*Pasvan* Manbhavan, Sajjanrai, Kamalrai, Vraijkunwarrai	
1778	Mewar			3 *pasvan*
1793	Jodhpur			1 *patar*
1803	Jodhpur	8		19 *khavas*, *patar*, and *vadaran*
1815	Alwar		Musi	
1828	Mewar	4	*Pasvan* Gunarai, Moti, Sainarup; *vadaran saheli* Jamuna	
1838	Mewar	2	*Pasvan* Jamunabai, Udabai, Daibai; *saheli* Pravinrai, Hira, Manbhavan	
1842	Mewar	2	*Khavas* Lacchubai	
1843	Jodhpur	1		6 *khavas* and *pardayat*
1861	Mewar		*Khavas* Aijankunwar	

cation upon the death of the chief. Not only were their entitlements in land and revenue grants withdrawn, they were required to return all their jewelry to the treasury as well.[46]

Both queens and concubines of the deceased ruler were also required to move out of the *zanana* in the chief's palace. For the female *khavas-pasvan,* their physical removal from the main *zanana* effectively severed them from all further chiefly or royal patronage. Many such *khavas-pasvan* immolated themselves upon the death of their chief. In chronicle traditions authored by bardic clients and celebrating their Rajput chiefly patrons, many female slaves were rendered visible only at this point, when they burnt themselves on the pyre of their dead master. Table 6.1 lists the concubines recorded as having immolated themselves upon their master's death.[47]

Among the slaves listed in table 6.1 are the ten singing women that Jaswant Singh of Jodhpur had acquired in Afghanistan and sent back to his *zanana* between 1668 and 1672; within a decade of their arrival in Jodhpur, these performers immolated themselves upon his death in 1678. Chroniclers of these momentous occasions maintained the differences between "wives" and "concubines" in death and beyond. While the immolation of queens was termed *sati*, the immolation of concubines was often termed just *bel* (burning).[48] Further, while a *sati* "wife" occasionally achieved the status of a clan or local goddess, concubines who immolated themselves never did.

The scale of this phenomenon—in which female slave-performers, concubines, and attendants immolated themselves upon the death of their masters—raises questions about their motives. For women whose status depended upon proximity to a ruler or queen, the sudden loss of patronage and reduction in entitlements, and the potential for humiliation in such loss of status, may have been powerful considerations. At the same time, women who had survived only through such patronage and support within chiefly households were also perceived to have incurred a "debt of food" to their holder and his descendants[49]—debts that were perhaps repaid through their sacrifice of themselves upon their holder's death. Where the ubiquitous norm for social relationships was loyal *chakri* (service) in exchange for sustenance, the incurring and repayment of such "debt" would have functioned as an equally powerful normative aspiration. It is not clear, however, whether the immolation of such female slaves affected the fortunes of their progeny in any way.

Slave-Progeny and the Reproduction of Hierarchy

The "debt of food" incurred by slaves was held to be "inherited" by their children as well, so that chiefly households typically appropriated the offspring of their slaves to their own perceived needs. The available evidence suggests that between the sixteenth and eighteenth centuries, the offspring of concubines were not typically bought and sold; daughters in particular served as tokens of exchange in political negotiations (including expressions of vassalage to an overlord). Rukhmavati, the daughter of Rao Maldeo of Jodhpur by his *patar* Tipu Gudi, was sent in *dolo* to the Mughal emperor Akbar.[50] The chief had the right to dispose of not only his own offspring by his concubines, but his father's slave-progeny as well. Thus in 1622 Gaj Singh of Jodhpur gave his half-sister—his father Sur Singh's daughter by Mohini *patar*—in marriage to Bhati Chandrasen, and retained the latter in his service with a revenue grant (*patta*).[51]

The sons of such concubines, while identified in the courtly chronicles as *khavas* or *pasvan*, were identified by their fathers' names as well. The *Jodhpur hukumat ri bahi* lists the "brave warriors" (*chidhad*) who died at the battle of Dharmat (1657), between the forces of Jaswant Singh and Aurangzeb. Along with ninety-seven Rajput chiefs listed by clan names (Kumpavat, Jaitavat, Rupavat, etc.), four ministers, three Brahmans and one Charan, the *Bahi* also lists four *khavas-pasvan*: Gehlot Pragdas Champavat, Jaswant Isardasot, Sahaso Sanvaldasot, and Sarang Hingolavat.[52]

The sons of wet nurses, in particular, were incorporated into the household as putative foster-brothers (*dhaibhai*) of the chief. In the turbulent eighteenth century, again, such slave foster-brothers could provide critical assistance to embattled rulers.[53] In the 1770s, when a young and inexperienced Vijay Singh of Jodhpur was struggling to assert his authority over the lineage chiefs in his kingdom, he was aided by Jaga, his *dhaibhai*. Since Vijay Singh had no armed men of his own with whom to confront the chiefs, Jaga hired a band of seven hundred mercenaries to guard the person of the king. He was also able to gather a small army with fifty thousand rupees that he extracted from his mother, the king's wet nurse, by threatening to commit suicide. The *dhai*, or wet nurse, had been given that money by the king in acknowledgment of her service. The lineage chiefs promptly gathered their forces for military confrontation, and forced Vijay Singh to accept the disbanding of both Jaga's troops and the king's personal bodyguard. While Vijay Singh acceded to these demands, he had the leaders of the chiefs murdered treacherously by Jaga's men shortly after, thus finally establishing his authority.[54]

Male slave-progeny who thus served their holders or Rajput kin loyally were acknowledged in the courtly traditions. Their own prospects for upward mobility were limited, however. Chatterjee, Guha, and Eaton have shown how, between the sixteenth and eighteenth centuries, enterprising waifs, slaves, or slave-progeny could rise to rule kingdoms in the Deccan and Bengal.[55] The rise of male slave-progeny to the status of clan member, or even chief, was rarer in the Rajput chiefdoms. One known exception was Raval Man Singh, the son of Raval Pratap Singh of Banswada (c. 1550–79) by the *baniya khavas* Padma. Nainsi recounts how Raval Pratap had no other son, and Man Singh was an accomplished (*sulakhano*) man. The Rajput chiefs of Banswada therefore anointed him ruler. Subsequently, the Chauhans "sent him the [ceremonial] coconut," indicating their desire to wed their daughter to him. However, he was killed shortly after the wedding in a conflict with the Bhils.[56] Although Man Singh's "mixed" parentage does not seem to have affected his prospects, it must be noted that there were no other, competing heirs to challenge his rise.

Some four decades earlier, however, another *pasvan*'s son was less successful in Mewar. Banvir, the son of Rana Sanga's elder brother Prithviraj by his *pasvan* Putalde, had been expelled from Mewar by his uncle Sanga; he had found service with Muzaffar Shah of Gujarat, before returning to Mewar after Sanga's death. In 1535, he murdered Rana Vikramaditya (Sanga's son, who had succeeded him in Mewar) and ruled in his stead for a little over a year. The Mewar chiefs rallied around Vikramaditya's younger brother and heir Udai Singh at Kumbhalmer. After Udai Singh seized control of Chitor, Banvir's fate is unknown. In the seventeenth-century account of the *Rawal Ranaji ri bat* (Anecdotes of the Rawals and Ranas [of Mewar]), Udai Singh is said to have spared his life because he had been crowned king of Mewar; Banvir is thus said to have left the fort of Chitor with his household and belongings (*janano saj baj*).[57]

A similar dynamic is apparent in the late seventeenth century, in the instance of Banmalidas—the son of Raja Karan Singh of Bikaner by a *pasvan*—who found favor with Aurangzeb. The latter assigned half the kingdom of Bikaner and the appropriate *mansab* (rank, status) to Banmalidas, and sent Mughal forces with him to help claim his share. As Shyamaldas recounts, Karan Singh's successor Anop Singh gave the appearance of agreeing to surrender half his kingdom to his half-brother for fear of Aurangzeb's ire. Banmalidas fortified the fortress of Changoi and wished to make it his capital. Anop Singh's father-in-law Sonagara Lakshmidas expressed a desire to give a daughter in marriage to Banmali. He sent a slave-girl disguised as his daughter, who poisoned Banmali's drink on their wedding night and killed him.[58] Like Udai Singh in Mewar a century earlier, Anop Singh also benefited from the support of the Rajput chiefs, who in both instances rallied around the successor descended from Rajput lineages both paternally and maternally. The histories of Banvir and Banmalidas indicate how the resources of the queens' natal lineages thus gave their sons an invaluable edge over the claims of *pasvan* offspring. In these instances and in the case of the *dhaibhai* Jaga in late eighteenth-century Jodhpur, the Rajput chiefs moved swiftly to counter challenges to their authority from slave-progeny within chiefly households.

Between the sixteenth and eighteenth centuries, an ideology of *jati* "purity," which empowered sons born of Rajput mothers over their half-brothers born of slave-mothers, grew progressively stronger. In the turmoil of the eighteenth century, with the collapse of imperial authority, the gradual intrusion of Maratha raids into the Rajput chiefdoms, and the increased factionalism of the Rajput courts, slaves wielded potentially greater authority, as we have seen. These circumstances may have impelled the ruling lineages to police the boundaries of the Rajput *jati* more closely, by insisting on "purity" of descent as a precondition for access to contested and dwindling resources.

Conjunctions of the Nineteenth Century

It is possible to see such insistence on "purity" of descent as a strategic response to the shrinking "markets" and expanded prestige claims within yet another political-ideological order. On the one hand, the gradual establishment of British supremacy in the region from the nineteenth century meant that the warfare typical of Rajput polity in the precolonial period waned dramatically. Given the absence of frequent battles and the raiding economies that they sustained, and a gradual squeeze upon the more visible "slave markets" in the region through the nineteenth and early twentieth centuries, the chiefly households became ever more reliant on reproducing servility within themselves. Hence it was in these centuries that a custom, hitherto unmarked, began to be associated with elite marriage prestation: the custom of a bridegroom's clan providing "unmarried boys equal to the number of unmarried *davri*s [female domestics] who were being dowered."[59] Such servants given in dowry then settled with the Rajput bride in her marital household. This coming together of Rajput labor and prestige systems and colonial concerns can be glimpsed in the actions of the British Resident, Major Ludlow. In the 1840s, he encouraged the Jaipur court to declare both the giving of extravagant dowries and the buying and selling of slaves (*laundi ghulam bechna*) criminal offenses, along with widow immolation.[60]

This conjuncture of prestige and property came to rest therefore almost entirely on the "inherited" status of children born of slaves. Tod had attested in the early nineteenth century that "the offspring of a *goli* or *dasi* must be a slave."[61] As is obvious from the remark, East India Company officials in the early nineteenth century found contemporary elite Rajput male concerns about "purity" of lineage comprehensible mainly in terms of the British plantocratic concepts of "miscegenation" and the ideology of the "family."[62] The colonial observers could not, however, immediately impose a new and additional layer of signification on the practices of slavery among the Rajput elite. Company officials and the latter concurred in perceiving slave-progeny as infringing upon the rights of "lawful inheritance," as is apparent in Alwar when its chief, Rao Raja Bakhtavar Singh, died in 1815 and his concubine Musi (discussed above) burnt herself on his pyre. The chief had had a daughter and a son, Balvant Singh, by Musi. However, he had also kept his brother's son Vinay Singh with him since the latter's boyhood. Upon Bakhtavar Singh's death, the Alwar notables regarded Vinay Singh as his son for all purposes, even though formal procedures of adoption had not occurred.

The status of Musi's son Balvant Singh provoked disagreement; one faction of notables considered him "illegitimate" (*najayiz*), while the other faction argued that by virtue of being Bakhtavar Singh's son, he was entitled to a share with Vinay Singh. Company officials, led by the Resident, Charles Metcalfe, agreed with the faction that regarded the nephew Vinay Singh as the appropriate heir. Yet, noticeably, neither faction of notables had insisted that Balvant Singh was his father's legitimate heir; his supporters were only emphatic that the entitlements of the concubine's son should not be abrogated entirely. Hence, they asked that Balvant Singh be given some unspecified share in his patrimony. The British were forced to accede to these claims: Vinay Singh was declared the successor but Balvant Singh was made responsible for the administration. Metcalfe presented robes of honor on behalf of the Company to both contenders, and Vinay Singh was forced to accommodate Balvant Singh by granting him a *jagir* yielding two lakhs and two lakhs in cash annually. Balvant Singh lived in his *jagir* of Tijara for the next twenty years. When he died without heirs, Tijara was reincorporated into Alwar, together with its significant wealth.[63]

The British, however, introduced new constructions of concubinage into their discussion of the Rajput polity. Inasmuch as the term "concubine" represented "licentious" and "illicit affection" in societies that had overvalued monogamous conjugality, the prevalence of concubines among Rajputs was believed to place them among the "semi-barbarous nations" of the Orient.[64] Similarly, slaves who rose to wield influence within the factionalized chiefly household and realm were now attacked as "interlopers" corrupting those exclusively Rajput domains. Thus J. Stewart, sent by the East India Company to investigate Jaipur's political affairs in 1821, complained of the influence of "two Female slaves" upon the Bhati Rajput queen regent.[65] One of these slaves was Rupa Badaran, whom the British government in Calcutta subsequently described as exercising an "all powerful and pernicious influence over the Rannee's mind," to the detriment of the administration of the realm.[66]

Such characterizations were to have momentous consequences for the histories written in the later centuries of these very households and figures. Witness the treatment given by the chronicler Shyamaldas in the late nineteenth century to the Banvir episode discussed above. Reemphasizing the importance of "pure" lineage in the Rajput past, Shyamaldas condemned those female slaves and their progeny who aspired to compete with the Rajput chiefs and their queens. Thus he described the few chiefs of Chitor who supported Banvir at first as "self-interested" (*khudmatlabi*). He also established Udai Singh's legitimacy and Banvir's lack of it through the idiom of commensality. In his account, while the chiefs in Kumbhalmer partook of food from Udai Singh's own plate, signaling their acceptance of his kingship, the chiefs in Chitor refused to eat from Banvir's plate, ostensibly because he was "less pure" (*kam asl*). Shyamaldas's account presents a contrast with seventeenth-century accounts of Banvir's career, even within the Mewar chronicle traditions, from which such details on commensality were absent. Shyamaldas thus presented recent norms of the boundaries of kinship and the Rajput *jati* as having been always in place, thereby reshaping the past in the light of present imperatives.

Conclusion

This essay has explored the history and narrations of female slavery in Rajput courts and elite households between the sixteenth and early nineteenth centuries. During the fifteenth and sixteenth centuries, particular Rajput lineages consolidated their authority in the region. Frequent battles during a period of territorial expansion produced a steady flow of war captives who were enslaved, with women being particularly vulnerable. Other circumstances in which enslavement occurred included famine and debt. Such slaves fulfilled the labor needs of elite Rajput households asserting their status in a competitive polity and evolving *jati* hierarchy. The proliferation of slave labor by the seventeenth century is suggested by the reordering and regulation of slaves' entitlements in this period, both within and after the lifetimes of particular chiefs. Their utter loss of material and political resources after their holder's death may have prompted female slave-performers and slave-concubines, in particular, to immolate themselves on his pyre —a phenomenon that was also widely perceived to demonstrate such women's "love of" and "loyalty to" their "lord."

The establishment of Mughal overlordship, with the emperor functioning as arbiter of disputes among the Rajput chiefs, accentuated the latter's need to engage in competitive displays of status. Such needs were fulfilled partly by courtly chronicles, authored in this period by bardic and bureaucrat clients, that legitimized the authority of their chieftain patrons by asserting "ancient" and "illustrious" descent while articulating an emerging ideology of *jati* "purity" as the basis of Rajput hegemony. We also find the emergence of other modes of transfer of slaves (including slave-progeny), in this period, as part of the dower from bride-giving to bride-taking households. Throughout, skilled slave-performers were in great demand as markers of elite status for their holders; in an idiom shared across elite groups in this period, the transfer of such slaves was one of the mechanisms initiating a hierarchical relationship between the "donor" and the receiver.

The collapse of Mughal authority in the eighteenth century intensified the factional nature of Rajput courts and households; succession struggles also became more frequent. The turmoil offered opportunities for slaves to wield a greater degree of power as favored concubines, attendants, and advisors. At the same time, the Rajput elite may have responded to diminished opportunities for expansion through imperial military service, and the consequently diminished potential for upward mobility, by redrawing boundaries that determined access to entitlements within their courts and households. A stronger ideology of lineage "purity" emerged in this period, restricting the rise of slave-progeny in particular. As the Rajput chiefdoms became "subsidiary" powers under the British by 1819, colonial envoys and administrators thus found in Rajput polity familiar preoccupations with lineage and descent that de-legitimized slave-progeny. Rajput elites and the colonial state thus collaborated in reducing the entitlements and power of slaves in an altered political and moral economy in the nineteenth century.

Notes

I am grateful to Richard Eaton, Michael Fisher, and especially Indrani Chatterjee for their comments on a draft version of this essay. Their criticisms have helped me to sharpen and clarify the argument significantly. I remain responsible for any errors.

1. Marzia Balzani and Varsha Joshi, "The Death of a Concubine's Daughter: Palace Manuscripts as a Source for the Study of the Rajput Elite," *South Asia Research* 14, no. 2 (autumn 1994), 142.

2. Varsha Joshi, *Polygamy and Purdah: Women and Society among Rajputs* (Jaipur: Rawat Publications, 1995).

3. Brajadulal Chattopadhyaya, "Origin of the Rajputs: The Political, Economic, and Social Processes in Early Medieval Rajasthan," in *The Making of Early Medieval India* (New Delhi: Oxford University Press, 1994), 57–88.

4. See, for example, G. N. Sharma, *Mewar and the Mughal Emperors,* 2nd ed. (Agra: Shiv Lal Agarwal, 1962); G. D. Sharma, *Rajput Polity: A Study of Politics and Administration of the State of Marwar, 1638–1749* (New Delhi: Manohar Publishers, 1977); Norman P. Ziegler, "Rajput Loyalties during the Mughal Period," in John F. Richards, ed., *Kingship and Authority in South Asia* (New Delhi: Oxford University Press, 1998), 242–84; Frances Taft, "Honor and Alliance: Reconsidering Mughal-Rajput Marriages," in Karine Schomer, Joan L. Erdman, Deryck Lodrick, and Lloyd I. Rudolph, eds., *The Idea of Rajasthan: Explorations in Regional Identity,* 2 vols. (New Delhi: Manohar and American Institute of Indian Studies, 1994), 2:217–41; Nandini

Sinha Kapur, *State Formation in Rajasthan: Mewar during the Seventh–Fifteenth Centuries* (New Delhi: Manohar Publishers, 2002); and Norbert Peabody, *Hindu Kingship and Polity in Precolonial India* (Cambridge: Cambridge University Press, 2003).

5. In contrast to the historiography of Rajasthan, several scholars have demonstrated the open-ended and assimilative nature of Rajput identity in northern and central India, as well as ongoing histories of "Rajputization" throughout this period. For examples, see Surajit Sinha, "State Formation and Rajput Myth in Tribal Central India," *Man in India* 12, no. 1 (1962), 35–80; and Dirk H. A. Kolff, *Naukar, Rajput, and Sepoy: The Ethnohistory of the Military Labour Market in Hindustan, 1450–1850* (Cambridge: Cambridge University Press, 1990).

6. For the Rathors in Jodhpur, see Sharma, *Rajput Polity;* for the emergence of patron-client relationships in the seventeenth century, see Zeigler, "Rajput Loyalties during the Mughal Period."

7. For a discussion of such "bardic" chroniclers and genealogists, see Norman P. Ziegler, "Marvari Historical Chronicles: Sources for the Social and Cultural History of Rajasthan," *Indian Economic and Social History Review* 13, no. 2 (Apr.–June 1976), 219–50. For the consequent perspective of such courtly narratives, see Ramya Sreenivasan, "Honoring the Family: Narratives and Politics of Kinship in Pre-colonial Rajasthan," in Indrani Chatterjee, ed., *Unfamiliar Relations: Family and History in South Asia* (Delhi: Permanent Black; New Brunswick, N.J.: Rutgers University Press, 2004), 46–72.

8. Richard D. Saran and Norman P. Ziegler, *The Mertiyo Rathors of Merto, Rajasthan: Select Translations Bearing on the History of a Rajput Family, 1462–1660,* 2 vols. (Ann Arbor: Centers for South and Southeast Asian Studies, University of Michigan, 2001), 2:440, their translation.

9. Ibid., 2:338.

10. For this raid and the subsequent fate of one of the captured girls, see Shail Mayaram, *Against History, Against State: Counterperspectives from the Margins* (New York: Columbia University Press, 2003), 248–52.

11. Mahamahopadhyay Kaviraj Shyamaldas, *Vir Vinod: Mevad ka itihas,* 4 vols. (1944; reprint, New Delhi: Motilal Banarsidass, 1986), 2.2.864. All translations from Rajasthani sources are mine, except where indicated otherwise.

12. Nainsi, *Munhata Nainsi ri khyat,* ed. Badariprasad Sakariya, 4 vols. (1960; reprint, Jodhpur: Rajasthan Oriental Research Institute, 1984), 2:337.

13. Saran and Ziegler, *Mertiyo Rathors,* 1:195, their translation.

14. Mayaram, *Against History, Against State,* 165, 184. The practice of *dolo* served to mark the "lower" status of those women, Rajput or other, who were incorporated into the harems of Rajput chiefs without "marriage."

15. Ibid., 165–66, 186.

16. Shyamaldas, *Vir Vinod,* 2.2.1385.

17. James Tod, *Annals and Antiquities of Rajasthan or the Central and Western Rajput States of India, by Lieut.-Col. James Tod,* ed. William Crooke, 3 vols. (1920; reprint, New Delhi: Low Price Publications, 1995), 1:207.

18. For the sale and holding of slaves among craft groups in eighteenth-century Marwar, see Nandita Prasad Sahai, *Politics of Patronage and Protest: The State, Society, and Artisans in Early Modern Rajasthan* (Delhi: Oxford University Press, forthcoming). I am grateful to Sahai for permission to cite her unpublished work.

19. Joshi, *Polygamy and Purdah*, 155.

20. Saran and Ziegler, *Mertiyo Rathors*, 2:84.

21. Saran and Ziegler translate Nainsi as describing Rangray as Haji Khan's "wife." Nainsi's word *bair* is more ambiguous, however, denoting either "woman" or "wife."

22. Nainsi, *Khyat*, 1:208.

23. Richard H. Davis, *Lives of Indian Images* (Princeton, N.J.: Princeton University Press, 1997); and Ramya Sreenivasan, "The 'Marriage' of 'Hindu' and '*Turak*': Medieval Rajput Histories of Jalor," *Medieval History Journal* 7, no. 1 (2004), 87–108.

24. Shyamaldas, *Vir Vinod*, 2.2.849.

25. Joshi, *Polygamy and Purdah*, 134.

26. Nainsi, *Khyat*, 2:37.

27. Satish Chandra and Raghubir Sinh, eds., *Marwar under Jaswant Singh (1658–1678): Jodhpur hukumat ri bahi* (Meerut: Meenakshi Prakashan, 1976), 77.

28. Shyamaldas, *Vir Vinod*, 2.2.818.

29. Chandra and Sinh, eds., *Marwar under Jaswant Singh*, 83–84.

30. Joshi, *Polygamy and Purdah*, 119–21.

31. Ibid., 151.

32. Saran and Ziegler, *Mertiyo Rathors*, 2:45.

33. For similar instances of affective (as opposed to biological) kinship in eighteenth-century Bengal, see Indrani Chatterjee, *Gender, Slavery, and Law in Colonial India* (New Delhi: Oxford University Press, 1999), 57–60.

34. Shyamaldas, *Vir Vinod*, 2.2.820–21.

35. Y. D. Singh, *Rajasthan ki jhilen aur talaben: Jodhpur ke sandarbh men* (The Lakes and Tanks of Rajasthan: In the Context of Jodhpur) (Jodhpur: Maharaja Man Singh Pustak Prakash, 2002), 137–38. I am grateful to Keith Goyden for this citation.

36. Shyamaldas, *Vir Vinod*, 2.2.771.

37. Joshi, *Polygamy and Purdah*, 158.

38. Shyamaldas, *Vir Vinod*, 2.2.856–57.

39. Singh, *Rajasthan ki jhilen*, 98–99, 148–49. For the ability of slave-women to sponsor public works and buildings as a sign of their authority, see Chatterjee, *Gender, Slavery, and Law*, 58.

40. Shyamaldas, *Vir Vinod*, 2.2.1316–17.

41. Tod, *Annals*, 3:1630–31.

42. Shyamaldas, *Vir Vinod*, 2.3.1771–72.

43. Ibid., 2.3.1692, 1706–11.

44. Joshi, *Polygamy and Purdah*, 165.

45. Shyamaldas, *Vir Vinod*, 2.2.1320–23.

46. Joshi, *Polygamy and Purdah*, 122.

47. Collated from Nainsi's *Khyat*, the anonymous *Jodhpur hukumat ri bahi*, Shyamaldas's *Vir Vinod*, and a list of immolations in Mewar between 1710 and 1842 in Joshi, *Polygamy and Purdah*, 150. The predominance of information on the kingdoms of Mewar, Jodhpur, and Bikaner reflects the sources I have used.

48. As Indrani Chatterjee points out, the scholarship on *sati* has focused exclusively on "familial" relationships framed in biological terms; scholars and activists alike have thus ignored the phenomenon of immolation by female slaves in the premodern period, and the alternative structure and boundaries to the family that they suggest. Chatterjee, introduction to *Unfamiliar Relations*, 9–14.

49. For the idiom of feeding as a mechanism of incorporation into affective kin in eighteenth-century peninsular India, see Indrani Chatterjee and Sumit Guha, "Slave-Queen, Waif-Prince: Slavery and Social Capital in Eighteenth-Century India," *Indian Economic and Social History Review* 36, no. 2 (Apr.–June 1999), 168.

50. Saran and Ziegler, *Mertiyo Rathors,* 2:35.

51. Nainsi, *Khyat,* 2:81.

52. Chandra and Sinh, eds., *Marwar under Jaswant Singh,* 23.

53. For the reliability of slaves and their progeny in the face of conflict within the kin group among ruling elites, see the essays by Sunil Kumar and Richard Eaton in this volume; also see Chatterjee and Guha, "Slave-Queen, Waif-Prince."

54. Tod, *Annals,* 2:1067–71.

55. See Eaton's essay in this volume; and Chatterjee and Guha, "Slave-Queen, Waif-Prince."

56. Nainsi, *Khyat,* 1:65–66.

57. *Mewar Rawal Ranaji ri Bat,* ed. Hukam Singh Bhati (Udaipur: Pratap Shodh Pratishthan, 1984), 56–63.

58. Shyamaldas, *Vir Vinod,* 2.1.498–99.

59. Joshi, *Polygamy and Purdah,* 159.

60. Shyamaldas, *Vir Vinod,* 2.2.1323.

61. Tod, *Annals,* 1:207.

62. Chatterjee, *Gender, Slavery, and Law.*

63. Shyamaldas, *Vir Vinod,* 2.2.1385.

64. Tod, *Annals,* 2:1075.

65. Letter from J. Stewart to George Swinton, secretary to govt. in the Secret and Political Dept., Fort William, May 18, 1821, in Narendra Krishna Sinha and Arun Kumar Dasgupta, eds., *Selections from Ochterlony Papers, 1818–1825, in the National Archives of India* (Calcutta: University of Calcutta, 1964), 153.

66. Sinha and Dasgupta, eds., *Ochterlony Papers,* 391.

7

Slavery, Society, and the State in Western India, 1700–1800

Sumit Guha

Introduction: Enslavement and Compulsion in Eighteenth-Century India

In the 1970s Miers and Kopytoff sought to remedy deficiencies in the comparative data on slavery as well as the social sciences' lack of general theory of that institution with a path-breaking volume on the African continent. Its editorial introduction warned against taking Atlantic plantation ideologies of slavery and freedom as the norm against which other societies and practices could be calibrated. Miers and Kopytoff called, instead, for histories of slave practices that assessed them on their own terms and in their own historical and social contexts.[1]

Nothing comparable to Miers and Kopytoff's work has yet appeared for the Indian subcontinent, and the present volume seeks to remedy and understand this silence as well as to fill out and correct the models developed elsewhere. My chapter will examine the institution and practices of slavery in western and central India from the mid-seventeenth through the early nineteenth century. This region witnessed the crumbling of Mughal imperial power at the turn of the eighteenth century, and it was replaced by a loosely united confederacy of Maratha rulers who gradually extended their power into northern and southern India before succumbing to British colonialism in 1818.[2] This is a region and period for which abundant documentation has survived, documentation that enables us to recover the names, lives, and fates of many among the least fortunate in that society.[3]

In order to clarify the distinctions between slavery and other forms of coercion and labor in the region at the time, it is useful to begin with Orlando Patterson's ambitious comparative study of slavery in world history. Patterson's study characterized the institution as one type of power relation in society. "All human relationships are structured and defined by the relative power of the interacting persons." Slavery in Patterson's view forms a limiting case in which the power imbalance approaches its maximum, and is also distinguished by the qualities of coercion that bring the master-slave relationship into being and subsequently sustain it.[4] Western India in the early modern period was familiar with many varieties of coercion, as H. K. Fukazawa showed in his analysis of eighteenth-century documents.[5] The exaction of forced labor (*veth-begar*) by the powerful was a common incident of rural life, both before and after the onset of colonial rule. Thus documents from the eighteenth century often specify the number of bundles of grass-fodder that specific villages had to cut and supply.[6] The baggage of traveling dignitaries had to be carried by the residents of one village to the next one, where under normal circumstances it would be the responsibility of the unprivileged residents of that village.[7] Brahmans, officials, and local worthies were usually exempt from these demands.[8] It therefore appears that either village jurisdictions and borders, or higher authorities, restricted the labor services due from each village, or groups within each. On one occasion, the peshva (chief minister) was moved to issue a general order stipulating that village Mahars (members of a lower *jati,* or caste) were not required to do more than fifteen days' work annually, and they were to be fed while performing this duty.[9] Men could trade on their proximity to the powerful to make unprecedented demands. Yet, when hangers-on of the peshva's court who frequently made such demands on the villagers of Ambodi (west of Pune) did so one time too many, the villagers protested to the government. They secured an order authorizing them to arrest anyone who exacted forced labor without a written order from the court.[10]

Within such a structure, all dependents could be maltreated alike, but retained some ability to protest. Impressed laborers could be coerced by beating and abuse, but they could flee. For example, 250 laborers conscripted by the peshva's government in 1785 to carry an English envoy's baggage to Pune dropped their loads half-way and fled.[11] The movements of British officials and armies in the early colonial era enlarged demands for this kind of forced labor; some British officials then reinvented what they imagined was "tradition" in order to have these demands met. S. J. Thackeray, principal collector of Dharwar in the early years of the British regime, wrote in 1824,

> As very few coolies are to be found here, and the class of Dhers and other Pariahs is quite insufficient to supply the demand, the Amildar's [local administra-

tor's] peons often press into service men who have never carried loads in their lives until the officers of our Government impressed them. When two or three hundred coolies are required, and only a day's notice is given for procuring them, the peons often seize upon inhabitants (with the exception of Brahmans and soucars [big businessmen]), indiscriminately drive them in a herd to the place of rendezvous and pen them like cattle until the arrival of the baggage.

Thackeray sought to revive what he believed was old usage and issued a proclamation requiring that

the village officer is on no account to press the ryuts [peasants] for coolies but is to procure them without violence from the lower classes of Bedurs, Dhers, Dhungurs and other similar castes accustomed to carry burdens. Should there be not sufficient number of such persons, the deficiency shall be supplied from the neighbouring villages.[12]

While forced or impressed labor knew some bounds of time and place, local usage distinguished slavery as a distinct status. A number of different terms were used for such servile dependents, though we cannot always decipher the finer distinctions among them. Male slaves are commonly described by the Arabic loan-word *ghulam;* the Persian loan-word *banda* also appears occasionally in the Marathi records of the eighteenth century. The *Rajavyavaharkosa,* a Sanskrit lexicon compiled under the patronage of the first Chatrapati Shivaji in 1676, gave *dasa* (a masculine noun) as the classical equivalent of both *banda* and *ghulam.*[13] There were several different terms for women; they included *dasi,* but *batik* and *kunbini* were more common. I cannot establish a clear etymology for *batik,* but *kunbini* is probably derived from *kutumbini,* household woman. As has been found for both Asian and inner African social histories, servile women and children were often identified by kinship-derived or genealogical terms. So a Marathi document uses "daughter" (*muli*) and "slave-woman" (*batik*) interchangeably.[14] While it is difficult to tease apart precise symbolic registers for the words that referred to "the slave," it is worth registering the historicity of such symbolic meanings in the region.

Slaves alone were spoken or written of—by hopeful masters rather than by themselves—as examples of "surrender" and devotion. Several of the most popular given names in the subcontinent intimated that their bearers were the slaves of a god, of 'Ali, of the Prophet Muhammad, of a guru, and so on. Nor, it would appear, were the Roman Catholic Portuguese resident on the west coast exempt from incorporating these symbolic meanings into their own ritual circumstances. On November 20, 1681, Donna Paula appeared at the convent of Our Lady of Remedies in Damao (modern Daman, see map 3) and stated that her daughter Donna Maria had been seriously ill.

She vowed that, if the girl recovered, she would give her as a slave to the convent. The girl was then auctioned for 150 *xerafins*, which were paid into the treasury of the convent and shown as gifted by the mother. Antonio Moniz, who published the record of this event, noted that he found five such "redemptions" in the convent's records of 1682 and 1683.[15] Donna Maria might have made a brief symbolic transition through a status in which many lived and died, and others exited via redemption or social incorporation—processes that we will outline in this chapter. Yet in real terms of sex and age, Donna Maria also definitely represented the majority of such persons, who were predominantly young and female.

On the other hand, records of other regimes suggest that it was not the infant daughter, but the mature, destitute, and effectively kinless woman within a household who gave the image of the "female slave" its particular and subtle shades. For instance, when the Koli tribesmen of Nhavi village killed two Gujarati men and detained their sister undiscovered for five years, the report of it described this as "they shoved her into the house."[16] It is perhaps this feature of female slavery that allowed a term like *kunbini,* which originally perhaps meant "domestic female," to come to approximate "slave."

Origins

As the lexicon and the variety of symbolic meanings indicate, slavery had varied "originating" circumstances. A first-generation slave's life in that status necessarily began in social processes. Hence we shall begin there too. People of various ages could fall into the condition as a result of a variety of circumstances. Casual robbery, sometimes hard to differentiate from kidnapping, could lead to a status approximating to slavery. In the example cited above, in 1759–60 two brothers and Keshri, their married sister, went on a pilgrimage to Saptashrngi, a shrine in the mountains of Nasik district. On the way they halted for the night in the Koli tribal village of Nhavi. The Kolis robbed and murdered the men and kept the woman. It was five years before her husband, Joita Gujar, could find out where she was and secure an order for rescue.[17] It is possible to read between the lines here and see a five-year-long stint as a "slave." More commonly, descent into this status could result from capture in war rather than clandestine robbery.

Along the west coast the practice of detaining, and ultimately enslaving, women for arrears of taxes or fines owed by their households appears to have been of old provenance, as can be inferred from the following evidence. One Dhondbhat had been the tax farmer of Madki, a village in Anjanvel subdivision. During a civil suit about the ownership of an estate in the village, eighteen villagers deposed about the circumstances in which

Dhondbhat had been executed by Sidi Sat, the hereditary Mughal governor of Janjira, about fifty years earlier. Ten of them claimed that Dhondbhat had a liaison with Venu, sister of Tandeva Harshe, and was summoned to answer for his conduct. He spat in the face of the emissary and was killed, and both his wives were taken away and enslaved by Sidi Sat. Seven villagers deposed that he and his wives were arrested because he failed to pay his taxes in full; he died of maltreatment in custody, and the women were enslaved. Finally, one villager attested to the enslavement but could not say why it happened.[18] Evidently either of these scenarios was deemed probable by an eighteenth-century audience looking back on the past.

It is therefore not entirely surprising to find that the practice of enslavement for tax arrears permeated into the political administration of western Maharashtra in later centuries. In 1800 Peshva Raghunath Bajirao wrote to the administrator of the coastal district of Ratnagiri that there were many women enslaved on account of tax arrears. "Select from them the best ones, those well-suited to government needs, and retain them. Then carefully sell the rest. If some are so elderly or unfit that no one will pay for them, then release them, but only in consultation with the auditors."[19] The governor of Kalyan (near Bombay) also held various slave-women taken in the course of administration—one of these was Eshi, who came from Gorat subdivision and was given a chintz cloth valued at one and a half rupees. In 1773 he also bought two other women from Sashti for 185 rupees.[20]

The interweaving of judicial procedures with mercantilist practice and prescriptions of moral conduct led to some of the more vulnerable members of society being first imprisoned, then auctioned or sold, and then enslaved to private individuals. Such processes of judicially authorized enslavement may have evolved on the west coast of India in parallel with those on the early Atlantic at the same time. For instance, a record of 1677 reveals that the English administration on the island of Bombay arrested eleven men (for kidnapping several Maratha subjects for ransom) and condemned them to death. But only three were hanged; the rest experienced a literal "commutation of death" when they were shipped off as slaves to the East India Company settlement on St. Helena.[21] In comparative terms, however, the peshva administration appears to have turned more female wrongdoers into slaves than males of the same age. This is what we gather happened to the young wife of a goldsmith of Goregaon, left destitute upon her husband's death. When she came to the city of Pune, the officers in charge of the district arrested her and kept her in prison; then they gave her to Govind Joshi of Revadanda in payment of a religious grant due to him. He brought her to the city of Pune, where her caste-fellow Ganesh, a leading goldsmith, charitably paid him a hundred rupees to release her and told her to go to her parents' home. She remained in the city and worked as a prostitute, so she was arrested and sent to work in the storehouse of the fort of Cakan.[22]

The implementation of social regulation in gender- and caste-differentiated ways led to the same results.[23] A report from the central Indian town of Nagpur of 1813 thus said, "it is the practice in the court [*adalat*] to fine women detained for sexual immorality; if they cannot pay they are sold."[24] Lower-caste widows sometimes faced the same hazard under *rajbeti* (lit. "daughter of the state," approximating to wardship) regulation. Richard Jenkins's assistant, Vinayakrao, reported from Nagpur that

> a woman whose husband dies becomes daughter of the state (*sarkar*)—he who marries her agrees to pay a fee (*nazar*) to the government—such is the custom. In many cases the caste-people do not allow women to remain *rajbetis* as it diminishes the *jati*. So some wealthy and respectable man stands before the government, fixes a fee and marries her. If the woman is attractive then it is profitable to the state—if one says fifty [rupees], another says a hundred. This is possible because the fee is not a fixed one—it depends on what the buyer (*khariddar*) is prepared to give. Women of the following castes are liable to be made *rajbetis*: Dhivar, Kalar, Koshti, local Mahar (*Mahar jhadiche*).[25]

So the judicial aspects of the regime ensured that particularly vulnerable women and children became slaves, and these were the same groups that bore the brunt of famines, when some peasants were pushed into selling their children. A 1792 plaint from subjects of the Baroda state asked for a grain loan, stating that they had survived so far only by "selling their cattle and children," presumably into more prosperous households of the vicinity.[26]

Only second-generation slaves were "born" into the condition. Typically these would be the children of slave-women by nameless fathers—like the sickly eight-year-old son of Umi, a slave-woman imprisoned in Sinhgad for consorting with European men. His mother died in the fort and the peshva's government ordered that he be sold if anybody would pay twenty rupees for him.[27] It is perhaps an interesting coincidence that when male slaves are mentioned in these records, a large number of them belong to this category and appear as "home-born." A census taken of Chimur, a township in the Nagpur kingdom in 1820, thus found forty-three female slaves and twenty-two males described as *Vidura gulam*. The latter were clearly illegitimate descendants of Brahmans, probably kept within their natal households. The total population of the town was 4001.[28] Similarly in the village of Loni, near Pune, which had a total population of 557, the surgeon Thomas Coats found eighteen slaves in 1819, about a year after the British annexation of the region. Of these slaves he said,

The present race are all home-born; but some of them are the descendants of women made prisoners, and brought from Hindoostan and the Carnatic. . . . Traffic in slaves is not thought respectable, and is not much practised: boys are rarely brought to market; but this is more frequent with female children, who, if beautiful are bought by the rich as mistresses, or by courtezans to be taught to dance and sing; they are sold for from 100 to 500 rupees.[29]

British officials who inquired about slave holding in the early nineteenth century were often informed correctly, as in Nagpur in the 1820s, that in "Hindu families, the children of female domestics by any of the relations or inmates of the house, are considered as a kind of personal property."[30] The ambiguity of this status may well explain the general absence from the records of mother-son pairs of slaves. It might also help to illuminate another document from the same period and region (made up of replies to a series of detailed queries) whose attempts to outline both the gendered and generationally shifting nature of slave status can be dimly glimpsed:

Men are not usually enslaved in this region. One born to a slave-woman in the house becomes a slave; or a small boy bought in a period of famine also does. . . . In some jurisdictions a woman arrested for immoral conduct becomes a slave to the government; they are also captured in war, and purchased during hard times. Sometimes they sell themselves.

. . . Men are not seized when villages are being plundered; only women and girls may be carried off. They are not returned by agreement. Captured women become slaves and are sold upon the captors' return to their own country.[31]

Transactions in Slaves

Theories that emphasize the element of kinlessness or "social death" as crucial to the condition of enslavement highlight the significance of transactions in slaves as a way of deepening and complicating the intergenerational and gendered nature of kinlessness.[32] In eighteenth-century western India, some transfers were straightforward while others, especially those involving women and children, were often complex and could lead to disputes over title. Transfer to a completely new habitat or social group consolidated the alienation of a slave. Consequently border regions—such as the west coast— showed a high frequency of such transactions. Many of our records do indeed come from there, and not merely because of the trade in African slaves in earlier periods.

Through the seventeenth and eighteenth centuries, Europeans and other sea-borne traders bought slaves for their own use and for export. In 1685, the English settlement at Surat was arranging to supply three pairs of dwarfs to the court of Charles II. The English factors at Karwar were also instructed to buy twenty to forty slaves for fifteen rupees a head. The Surat Council added, "[b]ut you may obtain them cheaper, being such troubles, we know at such times they may be had at a pagoda [3 to 4 rupees] a head."[33] English envoys and travelers often did a little personal shopping while on their excursions, in ways reminiscent of the Rajput chief Jaswant Singh (mentioned in Ramya Sreenivasan's essay in this volume). So English envoys and officials such as Charles W. Malet and Thomas Mostyn purchased slaves in Pune, and also secured an exemption from the usual sales tax on these transactions.[34]

Internal boundaries, such as the trijunction of the Nizam's territories, Mysore, and the Southern Maratha appanages, provided sites for important slave markets. Suppliers were often itinerant herdsmen-carriers such as Vanjaras or Carans.[35] Gajra Naikin of Dharwad, an entrepreneur in sexual entertainment, testified that she bought her girls from them. She paid up to two hundred rupees for them, but in times of famine also bought them for anything from one to ten rupees each. She wanted young, trainable girls, so her purchases ranged from infants to twenty-year-olds. But she added that those who wanted them for domestic work would buy even women who were thirty or forty.[36]

Slaves—especially women and children—were highly acceptable gifts and often circulated from household to household. We find Peshva Balaji Bajirao acknowledging the gift of a European musical instrument and "two women of the best quality" from Jayappa Desai of Nargund. He also demanded a list of the valuables that had presumably accompanied them.[37] Unsurprisingly, many of the women in the household list of the peshvas seem to have been received as gift-tribute of this kind. Thus we find mention of "Mohni from Samsher Bahadur," "Radhi from Musafarjang [sic]," "Tulsi from Ragho Govind," "Jivi from Vasudev Joshi," and so on. The occasions for such gift-giving are seldom listed, whether ritual occasions or secular or diplomatic ones.[38] Perhaps the most famous such "gift" was Mastani, received by Balaji Bajirao from the Bundela ruler Chatrasal and reputed to be the slave-born daughter of the latter.[39]

Lesser folk also received living gifts on important occasions. The ruling family gifted slaves to favored servants: the Diary for 1750–51 records an order that Yashvantrao Bhaskar was to receive two good slave-women of respectable caste (from the stables at Kavdi or elsewhere).[40] In 1783 Naro Visvanatha Jogdanda paid Martanda Yadav a hundred rupees for a slave-woman who was to be included in the gifts (*dakshina*) made to Brahmans at the funeral of Jogdanda's father.[41]

However, in order to make a gift of a slave, the gift-giver had to own one or acquire one from elsewhere. Owners pressed for money, or tempted by a good price, could and did transfer their slaves to others. Direct sales occurred, like the one in which Saguni, a dancer-prostitute of Pune, bought a four-year-old girl from Dattaji Sabla.[42] Joining this skilled entertainer was the apex of the state, the peshva himself, who also purchased slaves on his personal account. This can be inferred from the note of Peshva Balaji Bajirao to one Damodar Mahadev in 1743, which said,

> At the time that you were dispatched to Delhi you were instructed to buy and send me two beautiful ten-year-old Hindu girls. Despite this you have not sent them. Let this suffice as reminder—now buy and send two beautiful ten-year-old girls. Do not make excuses. Know this! So definitely send on [my] personal account the following sort—two high-quality, pure Hindus of good caste, ten-year-olds. When dispatching them, do not outfit them extravagantly. Know this![43]

This kind of purchase would be identified by late imperial regimes as the only kind of domestic traffic in humans. But in the eighteenth century, at least, such traffic was only part of a larger series of sales, as is illustrated by the sale of two slave-women by Sadashiv Ram Damle to Ramaji Mahadev for 185 rupees. The latter, it is said, had earlier acquired an East African (Siddi) man and young girl from Sashti subdivision—he sold the latter for twenty rupees.[44]

The motives of masters who wished to transfer their slaves were often extremely complex. Sometimes masters were anxious to be rid of unsatisfactory slaves, and looked out for unwary buyers. Thus in 1787 the prior of the convent of Santa Rita in Damao stated that the *cafre* (African slave) Manoel had turned out to be excessively vicious and there were endless complaints about him, and he proposed that Manoel be sold to the French when they next visited the coast in search of *cafre*s. Two years later the convent discovered that the *cafrinho* (little *cafre* boy) purchased for 125 *xerafins* in January 1789 was turbulent and badly inclined and had "a great aversion to labor." Fortunately for the convent, he was sold in November for 315 *xerafins*.[45]

The nature and form of the transaction in a slave was determined by the owner-seller's economic circumstances. Transfers could be intended as short-tenure hire, mortgage with possession, or permanent sale. Any arrangement was acceptable to a desperate Brahman who wrote to Gadgil of Amsure in the later eighteenth century,

> There are only five measures of grain left in the house—after that we have nothing. So I have sent my wife to you: you must give me a hundred rupees. If I cannot return you the money with interest by the month of Shravan then I shall give you my slave-woman Mani together with her ornaments. If you do not trust this offer, then give me a hundred and twenty-five rupees and take the slave and her ornaments this very day. In the month of Shravan I shall repay the

money and take back the woman, or, if you wish, pay me the money and keep her. But if you do this for me today you will have bought and nurtured me and my whole family—that is the good fame that you will earn.[46]

As valuables, slaves could be taken in settlement of their owners' tax arrears or debts, such as the sixty rupees a Brahman named Murarbhat owed to Bhaskar Gopal, against which he transferred his slave-woman to his creditor.[47] But slaves acquired thus could also be sold: Sarjekahn sold a slave, first acquired in repayment of a debt, to Ganeshpant Patankar.[48]

Such a series of transactions—either short-term or more permanent—could lead to disputes. The pattern of repeated transfers often led to complexities in issues of "title." For instance, a slave-woman was sold by Anaji, a goldsmith, to Govindset, an Agarvala trader, who in turn sold her to Ramaji Jivaji, a (Brahman?) official. But then Bayaji Shelar (a peasant?) came and complained that she belonged to him. So Anaji was summoned to explain his transaction.[49] Similarly, a lease or a slave mortgage could lead to a dispute, especially if the terms of the transaction were unclear. According to a complainant, Tryambak Abhyankar, a man called Tavji Jadhav had "kept" Abhyankar's slave-woman, and then began negotiations to marry off her son and daughter.[50] The form of the slave-woman's transfer was unclear, and the dispute reveals that such unclear transactions could lead to indeterminacy of "title" over other slaves as well.

Title over the slave was an aspect of property-right that the state could be asked to clarify and defend. This was obvious especially in the case of the "home-born" child slave. Usually the owner of such a child was also the owner of the child's mother, even if such an owner was an entertainer-prostitute herself. So when a *qazi* (hereditary Muslim judge) of Pune city agreed to officiate at the marriage of the daughter of a slave-woman belonging to an entertainer-prostitute of the city, the latter protested to the government. Although the government warned the *qazi* to desist, he performed the marriage rite. In retribution, the peshva's government seized all the lands and perquisites attached to the *qazi*'s office.[51]

Functions and Careers

Eaton's contribution to this volume discusses the important role of military slaves in the sultanates of western India in the sixteenth and seventeenth centuries, when it would appear that most imported Habshi slaves were men. The Maratha regime does not seem to have used slaves, nor African imports to any significant extent, in such roles. Both infantry and cavalry units drew on freelance soldiers, local and foreign. This preference may be due to the Maratha regime's base among the autochthonous *watandar* gentry of western Maharashtra, a social group that would reject the sort of centralized royal authority associated with mamluk regimes.

By the eighteenth century, however, the records reveal the employment of female slaves in auxiliary military services. Fortresses had a complement of female slaves attached to them as a matter of course. Thus the commander of the Bahula fort was instructed to give the slave-women their grain ration according to the usual practice when the budget was drawn up.[52] The grain store—where the laborious task of husking, winnowing, and grinding grain had to be performed daily—probably employed many women, and we know that the preparation of mortar and building material was also assigned to them.[53] Cavalry units frequently had slave-women attached to them: the stables at Kavdi had fourteen slave-women, and the palace stables in Pune had four. We also find one Jamali attached to the elephant stable.[54] Female slaves also worked in fort arsenals preparing gunpowder, like Krishni, who worked in Sinhgad until she injured her back and arm when she fell from a plank.[55] It is notable that work involving grinding, sifting, and so on resembled the domestic processing of cereals and was thus classified as "women's work." But when thirty African slave-women were employed on the task in the Konkan and complained of the heaviness of their work to a governor visiting the factory in 1765, he ordered that each of them be given a gratuity of one rupee.[56]

We can only wonder whether or not the peshva's regime differentiated between different kinds of female slaves and allocated tasks accordingly. For while some slave-women labored in fortresses, cavalry stables, and military camps, many of their tasks imitated or magnified the tasks performed by female and male slaves in the wealthiest households. The records of the peshva's household in Pune in the mid-eighteenth century reveal that of the 197 slave-women who received gifts of clothing on the festival of Dashara, no fewer than thirty-five were attached to the kitchen. One of them may have been a water-carrier. Others, like "Bhimi washerwoman" and "Tuki washerwoman," probably received their names from their function. Gani of the shepherd caste worked in the menagerie. Many others were attached as servants to more favored slave-women, such as the dancer-concubines referred to as *natakshala*. Several of the latter had as many as five slave-women associated with them.

In lesser households, there would naturally be less specialization of tasks, and a single woman might be expected to perform all the significant domestic chores. Thus a woman who had originally been an upper-caste Prabhu was a slave in the household of Balaji Mahadev, a Brahman administrative officer in charge of Shivner. She swept and plastered the house, scrubbed the pots and pans, peeled and chopped vegetables, made the beds, and performed other such tasks.[57]

In the village of Loni, similar domestic tasks were carried out in Brahman households by their slave-women. The importance of the sexual and domestic services slaves supplied is shown by the predominance of women in their ranks: in Nagpur city an incomplete count in 1825–26 found 843 female slaves as against 445 males.[58]

As households could be stratified by wealth and social authority, the contours of the "domestic" labor asked of slaves could also vary. The talented and adroit could overcome the disadvantages of gender and slavery and rise to wield authority on behalf of their masters, whether those were rustic Brahmans or great rulers. Consider the unnamed Rangdi (Rajput) woman belonging to a village Brahman near Saswad. At harvest time he sent her out with a horse to collect his customary dues from the peasants' crops, and she went to the threshing floors and grabbed more than was customary. The farmers' protests were met with coarse abuse. When the headman of the village went to complain to her owner, the latter threatened him with a flogging.[59] What made some slaves better qualified than others to combine coercion with extraction on behalf of their masters?

It would appear that proximity to owners was a key element in such deployment. The proximity of the "socially dead" and their owners was often discussed when the issue was that of "caste status." Patterson argues that caste societies were not incompatible with slavery, and slaves could retain their caste status despite the social death that consigned them to a servile status.[60] The caste (*jati*) status of slave-women was frequently discussed, perhaps because their higher-caste masters had to be reassured that the touch of the often lower-caste slave did not degrade them. Thus two of the slave-women acquired by a Brahman peshva in 1746 were described as follows:

> Radhi slave-woman Hatkar-Dhangar *jati;* good Kunbis drink water from their hands and eat with them—from the village of Brahmangaon, subdivision Umarkhed, age 25; Kasi slave-woman of Rajput *jati* of good caste; brought from the house of Dipchand Hazari in the village of Babhulwadi subdivision Dhule age 30.[61]

The proximity of the socially "kinless" and the well-born often required indirect explanations that tamed the various threats implicit in such placements. Such narrative strategies can be seen in Ramarao Citnis's biography of the Maratha king Shahu (1682–1749). Shahu, while in detention in the Mughal camp, had been married to the daughters of Rustamrao Jadhav and Shinde of Kannarkheda.

One day, some time later, the padshah said, "The marriages have taken place, let me see the brides." But the Maratha decision was that this was not proper. So Yesubai Saheb [Shahu's mother] discussed this with the begam [Aurangzeb's daughter] and selected a beautiful slave-born girl who had come with the bride from the Shinde household, dressed and adorned her, and sent her with Shahu to the emperor . . . [who] blessed them, saying, "You two will rule together for many days." . . . Shahu had two regularly wedded wives. But because the emperor had blessed him jointly with Virubai, had placed his hands on their heads and blessed them, he took Virubai into a special relationship and favored her above the two wives.[62]

Virubai dominated the king's household until her death: this fact was widely known at the time and is supported by many contemporary documents. Citnis's story may be a post facto attempt to explain this, but it is plausible only if we grant the possibility of such substitutions.[63]

Citnis's account of Virubai allows us to glimpse what such a biographer might consider a significant qualification for "trust" between owner and slave. Virubai had come into the household as a second-generation slave, as part of a bridal dowry. In other words, she might be considered to have lost some of the most obviously threatening signs of her "alien-ness," unlike those characterizing a freshly acquired slave. This kind of indirect explanation of Virubai's qualifications for her administrative authority was probably historically valid as well. It explains the use of such slave-born children in most regimes of the region, and especially the character of "palatine" slavery here.

Such slave-born slaves were especially useful to counter other hereditary officials who presumed upon their status or grew refractory. So in the mid-eighteenth century a hereditary minister challenged the authority of Jijabai, the dowager queen of Kolhapur, with the remark that women's intelligence was unstable. The queen dismissed the minister and snubbed him at the same time by comparing him to her slave-women: she remarked that any of her slave-women could perform his functions. She then entrusted her affairs to Yesajirao Shinde, son of a slave-woman in her natal house, and selected five slave-women to administer five subdivisions of the state. Administrative letters from one Gangi, whom tradition identifies as one of these women, have been published.[64] The fact that she styles herself simply "Gangi," without any village or clan or patronymic last name, confirms her status. So, under particular circumstances, the determined dowager queen of Kolhapur could draw on both kinds of slave-domestics—male and female, first-generation and second—to fill important positions in an administrative regime which combined military and civil functions. The slaves thus selected then combined intimate or private roles and public administrative ones in one package, and often became indistinguishable from the well-born themselves.

Slaves could therefore be often found in close proximity to—and indeed were sometimes indistinguishable from—the powerful and well-born. Such proximity to the powerful enabled some slaves, especially women, to accumulate property in the shape and form valued in the markets of the time— in immovables like lands and houses, and in movables like jewelry, cattle, and slaves. Some enterprising women used the business opportunities arising out of their proximity to the powerful to accumulate a little capital. Putli, a "government woman," farmed the taxes of the village of Vaddare for ten years in Sakarkheda subdivision, and lent money to its headman.[65] A former concubine of one of the peshvas, Gultarang, died in Benaras in 1793. Her dying wish was that her money be used to build a house for a Brahman in the holy site of Panchvati, and that he should inherit the land yielding seventy-five rupees that she had formerly held from the state. This was permitted.[66]

Such slaves were perhaps well on their way out of slavery, and might indeed plan to use their property to emancipate themselves. But it was when slave-women themselves acquired other humans that they made explicit the reproduction of the slave-using regime, as did two slave-women (attached to ladies of the ruling family) who paid 140 rupees for two slave-girls in 1773– 74.[67] Like other accumulations of wealth, wealth in human form made the purchaser's own emancipation possible. In this, too, there were precedents, such as Sakhi, a female slave attached to the stables, who earned her release by presenting the government with a substitute female slave. The possibility of a slave-woman basing her "freedom" on the enslavement and ownership of another female slave seems to have raised no ethical or economic concerns for Sakhi's owners, or for the ruling authorities. In another example, Meghi and her daughter Krishni worked in Sinhgad fort from 1775 to 1786. When the latter was crippled by a fall, the pair offered a young slave-woman in their place and were emancipated.[68]

Yet the access to resources that some female slaves had raises questions about the denial of such resources to others, often males. When we encounter Eshi, a slave-woman belonging to Ramaji Mahadev, governor of Kalyan, who had been purchased for 125 rupees but freed herself by paying 150 rupees,[69] we can quickly attribute to her some entrepreneurship in the matter of capital accumulation in the household of a governor. But by the same token we should understand the actions of the male slave Vagha, accused of participating in a robbery in another house, as engaged in a similar economic activity of accumulation, perhaps of a nest egg toward his own emancipation.[70]

This must be allowed for, especially since the relation of slave-born and slave owners was always extremely tenuous, varying according to the gender and generation of the slave, the slave-born, and the slave owner alike, as well as the era and the household in question. So while, in some households, an entrepreneurial slave-woman's son could be treated as an important part of the retinue, through whom alliances could be arranged, there were others in which slave-born sons were treated with great cruelty. Sometimes the two behaviors occurred in the same household, in different generations. So in the household of the peshvas, we hear of the slave-woman Yesu, whose son Babu Singh (his father is not mentioned) was married at state expense to a daughter of Sultanji Darekar, hereditary village headman of Karandi, in 1771–72. The latter was paid four hundred rupees, and almost the whole cost of the marriage was borne by the groom's side—that is, the peshva's household. The bride's family spent 610 rupees; the groom's costs came to 3137 rupees. But the pleasures of the young peshva Savai Madhavrao (1772–96) included watching his slave-born male dependents box with each other. If one fell down from exhaustion he was caned by the mace-bearers until he got up and resumed the contest. The boys were forced to continue even when they bled from the nose and mouth. "Two or four" of them were badly injured.[71] The matter was disapprovingly reported by the household official, but we do not know if anything was done to stop it. To sum up, all that we can infer is that it is likely that for each Yesajirao Shinde, Babu Singh, and Virubai there were many more slave-born boys who were not happily situated. The median position might have been the one represented by the ruling household at Nagpur, where slave-born male children were allowed to bear the dynastic surname "Bhosle" but were listed separately in state records as *kharchi* or cheap (the word literally means "expendable").[72]

Freedom, Slavery, and Agency

In the last pages of his magisterial comparative analysis of slavery in world history, Orlando Patterson came to a startling idea: that freedom as such was something that could only be conceived and desired by the enslaved. "Before slavery people simply could not have conceived of the thing we call freedom. Men and women in pre-modern non-slaveholding societies did not, could not, value the removal of restraint as an ideal. Individuals yearned only for the security of being anchored in a network of power and authority. Happiness was membership." So "an ideal cherished in the West beyond all else emerged as a necessary consequence of the degradation of slavery and the effort to negate it."[73]

By this logic, western India in the eighteenth century appears to have been a region where the consciousness of "freedom" already existed because the significance of social relationships had already been established. This impinged on the bodies and fates of each generation of slaves and non-slaves in very distinct ways. Consciousness of the values of kinship as well as of freedom is evident in a letter issued from the secretariat (*Citnisi Daphtar*) to one Eshi in 1741–42:

> You were living in the hill-fort of Purandhar [*sic*] when the noble Ranoji Bhosle claimed to the royal court that you were the daughter of his slave-woman. You were brought before the court and your history was examined. It emerged that the above-mentioned [Bhosle] had arranged your marriage (*lagna*) and there-fore he could not now thrust you into slavery (*kunbinit ghyave aise nahi*). Therefore his ownership (*warsa*) does not extend over you. Live happily wher-ever you choose.[74]

It is evident that the daughter of a slave-woman was owned by the mother's owner: but the claim was annulled by marriage. Marriage created a set of af-final kin, and therefore was deemed emancipation. The content of such free-dom was also indicated: the right to move and reside according to her will.[75] We do not know what social connections the slave-born Eshi had made be-yond those with her husband's house; perhaps these reinforcements were necessary to win for the female a successful evasion of a demand to "return" to her former condition.

The regime's readiness to uphold the freedom of an erstwhile female slave simultaneously underscored the importance of marriage and wifehood for such a woman. This would become especially significant in matters of life and death. Though it is likely that most slaves, both men and women, died as humble inmates of some great house, some—both men and women —undeniably met the fate of Bharattee (or Bharati), whose murder has been so carefully analyzed elsewhere in this volume (see chapter 9). Yet it was the punishment that was meted out to non-slaves who violated the husband's and affinal kin's claims in such "freed" or slave-wives that really indicated the regime's privileging of kinship over claims of property. There are many records which establish that murderers of non-slave females were punished more stringently than slave owners who abused their own female slaves. For example, in 1786–87, Malhar Babaji Mahajan beat his slave-woman so se-verely that she died the next day. He was prescribed a purifying penance (he seems to have been a Brahman) and fined twenty-five rupees. We may con-trast this with what happened to Panduranga Parad, who hit his daughter-in-law in the face, whereupon she killed herself with an overdose of opium. He was fined the sum of five thousand rupees.[76]

The security of "conjugal right" in a wife, even when the husband was himself adjudged a criminal, was characteristic of the peshva's government. So an owner could mistreat his or her own slave with impunity, but not destroy either a daughter-in-law or, for that matter, another man's wife mortgaged or pawned to him. One case that illustrates the vulnerability of such pawns or hostages, as well as the state's attitude toward the destruction of a third person's claims in such human beings, should illustrate the point. Ranoji Mali was found in 1788 to be in league with local Koli bandits and fined twenty-five rupees. He left his wife as a surety (*ol*) in the hands of Bhikaji Gopal, promising to return in a week with the money. He then disappeared, and Bhikaji kept the woman as his mistress. Some disagreement caused him to strangle her with a rope. This being proven, he was fined the very considerable sum of nine thousand rupees.[77]

The privileging of the life of a non-slave over that of a slave could also sometimes imply a denial of "responsibility" for the slave. While such a characteristic may have infantilized a slave, it might also save her from physical death, especially if she would otherwise have to bear the same punishment as a free person for causing the death of a non-slave. For instance, an unnamed slave-woman in the house of Hari and Ramachandra Yadav of Pimplagaon quarreled with the mother of the two men and provoked the old lady into drowning herself. The state punished the brothers, not the slave, for the suicide, making them undergo expensive purification ceremonies; the slave-woman's fate is unknown.[78]

But a slave was not equally exonerated from all responsibility, and this was most evident in instances of sexual liaisons between female slaves and non-slave men. A slave-woman would certainly be made to feel the ire of either her master or the kinsmen of the non-slave if either was offended by such a relationship. Thus when Narayan Venkatesh became attached to Gangi, a slave-woman, the man's mother got the government to imprison the slave-woman in the fort of Birvadi.[79] However, in another instance, the owner of the slave-woman apparently consented to such a relationship. Sambhaji, a blacksmith resident in the village of Pise, developed a relationship with a wife of Budhsa Tamboli; the local administrator, a zealous moralist (and eager fee-seeker?), arrested them both for investigation. Sambhaji exonerated himself by securing the testimony of the village headman and (the absent) Budhsa that the woman was in fact not a wife, but a slave-woman. This led to Sambhaji's being released and told that he could live unmolested.[80] It is likely that the affair had the tacit consent of Budhsa, the nameless woman's owner, and therefore lay in a private domain outside the jurisdiction of the local official. It was equally likely that the same principle was at work here as in the differential punishment for murdering a slave and a non-slave woman; the principle was that an owner of a slave could do as he or she wished with the slave.

Though we cannot read the evidence above for a direct sign of the "agency," "choice," or "freedom" of a slave-woman to live with a non-slave male, it is clear that where the master or owner was either absent or complaisant, female slaves could cohabit with non-slave males in ways that were absolutely barred to non-slave married women. In comparative terms, one may state the case thus: wherever an owner allowed it, a female slave could cohabit with slave and non-slave male alike, while a non-slave female could not cohabit with any male other than the one chosen for her by her natal kinsmen. Similarly for male slaves: wherever an owner allowed it, a male slave could live with the female slave of another owner, as we learn from the following instance from 1782. One Krishnaji Vartak came to Tasgaon from Rajapur and brought a slave-woman with him. Visaji Pant Behre bought her and sent her to Wai. She had a relationship with the male slave belonging to Mundgauda, headman of Nandre, who came and took her away. A month later it was discovered that she was in Nandre, and that the couple had taken shelter in the headman's house. But the headman rebuffed all enquiry. So another potentate was asked to issue a stern warning to the headman that he would have to answer for his slave's doings. The complainant assessed his loss at a hundred rupees, and demanded his money or the woman. The letter ends with some detail to corroborate the headman's complicity: "The male slave had previously gone away to Wai [to visit the woman]—the headman's servants came, beat him and took him back. So the next time he went and brought back the woman."[81]

While it is easy to surmise that an evident lack of solidarity among slave owners favored some slaves and mitigated the worst aspects of their alienation, the cohabitations of slave with slave or non-slave were significant aspects of slave sociality that often veered toward "emancipation." Though our records seldom allow the voice of the slave and slave-born to be heard, they do allow us to detect, through the slave's actions, a certain kind of "voice" or "will." For instance, even though the records themselves are silent on this, one can infer that in some instances a slave-woman changed masters by fleeing from one to another, leaving the matter of title to be settled between the two. This is implicit in the instance of the slave-woman belonging to Birajlal Golandaz, who went to live in the house of Ramji Bhatia, who then murdered her owner. Another slave-woman merely eloped with one Bhavani Pyada.[82] Some special relationship clearly existed between the nephew of Bhavani, a coppersmith, and the slave-woman belonging to a minor royal functionary, as they were seized while eloping together, even though it was the coppersmith who had to pay the fine of sixty-six rupees for his ardent nephew's escapade.[83]

But such cohabitations of slave with non-slave and slave alike then explain a peculiar feature of some caste groups in the region: the coexistence of two sections, one of slave heritage and one of free, within the same caste group. An instance of the latter was the Kadu ("bitter") section of the tailor caste. In 1768 the headman of the community of tailors resident in the Pune suburb of Shahapur complained to the court that a tailor belonging to the slave-descended section of the *jati* had gone to another district and negotiated a marriage with a tailor family of "good" lineage. The government summoned the leaders of the community and inquired into prevailing custom. Finally an order was issued prohibiting intermarriage between the two sections.[84]

Flight and Freedom?

By now, it should be obvious that rather than being antagonistic states, the existence of one of which would cancel the possibility of the other, slavery and freedom, like slavery and agency, coexisted in a variety of cases. How then should one interpret the numerous documented cases of flight—as attempts at seeking total and absolute individual freedom, or as attempts to improve one's lot and circumstance as a slave? It would appear that some slaves simply sought the latter, like a runaway slave who was found in the government stables at Chakan. She was then gifted by the state to Bahirav Joshi; but her master Mahadevbhat sought compensation. Hence the peshva ordered Jivaji Ganesh to find a slave-woman who would be content to stay in a poor man's house in the Konkan and give her to Mahadevbhat in exchange.[85] This order suggests that the woman was not seeking to escape from captivity altogether, for that would cast her friendless into a harsh world. Instead she sought slavery in a bigger, presumably wealthier, establishment. The stables would have a large community of slave-women associated with them and might afford a better life than isolated labor in a poor Brahman household, where one slave would bear the burden of all the varied tasks of subsistence.

It appears that slave flights from smaller households often worked to the advantage of the bigger households as well as to that of the state. For instance, three slave-women and a child fled from the house of Krishnarao Mahadev and were concealed in the mansion of the banker Lala Caturbhuj of Burhanpur. The latter was promptly accused of harboring them; the records suggest that such an accusation allowed for "milking" the banker. For two officials are recorded as having gone to him; he surrendered the fugitives and paid a fine of 960 rupees to atone for his misdeed.[86] While the banker may not have had the boldness to keep his newly acquired slaves, others did. Therefore, it appears that before flight, slaves considered how likely their new protector would be to resist the demands of their former masters and state officials. Sometimes the protector they fled to had been wisely chosen: so we find Dattaji Thorat of Sadas, near Pune, complaining that his slave-woman had fled to the royal capital of Satara and taken shelter in the house of an important person there. The latter refused to surrender her and threatened violence when pressed. He also apparently denied that the woman in question was the slave being sought. Dattaji now abjectly pleaded with Sadashivrao, the peshva's brother, to intercede in the matter.[87] Similarly, a slave-woman belonging to Rayaji Gaikwad fled from Vathad and was sheltered in the house of Tryambak Gosavi, a holy man resident in the village of Caphal. The owner traced her but was not allowed to take her away. In 1724 he secured an order from the noble Fatehsingh Bhosle requiring her return.[88] Appeals from former owners to more politically powerful figures—like the peshva's brother as well as the noble Fatehsingh Bhosle—could not be made without a "gift" payment alongside. So, though this is rarely stipulated, such recoveries of slave-fugitives cost the owners something, and again favored the more substantial and powerful officials over the lesser owners.

The more powerful the official and the more prosperous the household, the greater the slave's success in securing protection. The fear of such flight in turn might lead lesser masters to mitigate the living conditions of individual slaves. A letter from 1763–64 has hints of this. The complainant, Bapuji Govind, states,

> My daughter [*muli*] ran away; I searched and found her in the local administrative officer's house. He then agreed to pay me sixty rupees after a week. When I went to him for the money he refused payment, saying that the slave-woman [*batik*] had run away. He is acting deceitfully and refusing to either restore the woman or give me the money. The government should issue an order in this regard.[89]

The alacrity with which local regimes seized and appropriated slave-fugitives can thus be understood as part of a silent but ongoing tussle between the bigger households and the state's "workshops" or fortresses over such slave bodies. Thus two Muslim women, Maini and Surupi, were arrested as runaway slaves and put to work on government buildings. Another woman was arrested on her way to the Karnataka: quite possibly she had originally been kidnapped from there during one of the numerous Maratha raids in that region.[90] But the eagerness with which escaped slaves were sought for arrest conditioned the suspicion of all women who traveled alone, even if they were slaves deputed by their masters to travel without escorts.

Thus two officials posted at Jambgaon detained two slave-women belonging to the noble Trimbakrao Sivdev who were traveling with their master's knowledge. The latter had to secure a government order for their release.[91]

Conclusion

In conditions where flight was a favored method of improving the contours of one's slave condition rather than of ending it, it is to be expected that transitions out of slavery occurred most often with marriage, with self-redemption, or with death. Despite the demands for exemplary devotion made of most slaves, it is therefore not surprising to find that seldom was manumission offered as a reward. The British observer Thomas Coats mentioned a household in Loni whose members may have been beneficiaries of an informal manumission thus: they had, "virtually though not formally yet, got their freedom from their masters, in consequence of their good conduct, and occupy a separate house, and cultivate on their own account."[92] However, since his description did not specify in what ways a non-slave cultivator might be distinguished from a slave-cultivator on his way to the standing of a freedman, we are left pondering whether this was a case of mistaken identity.

On the other hand, as established earlier, masters in the region were acutely conscious about the status of, and the title to, the slave-born. The second generation of slaves, both men and women, might sometimes be emancipated via marriage (though this might not preclude further claims on them). In other cases the doubtful boon of emancipation only came when the slaves were old and unfit for work, like the nameless slave-woman in the stables administered by Baba Mahat, who was released in 1763–64.[93] Some children sold by their parents during famines were released by way of "charity" by their owners when grain became cheaper. For instance, Richard Jenkins wrote that in Nagpur in 1818–19 peasants who had sold their children came to reclaim them, "when they were either gratuitously relinquished by the purchasers, or for a trifling compensation."[94] For at least these lucky few, the time spent in slavery was a brief interlude. But most premodern lives were short: for many, if not most, slaves, death came before freedom did.

Notes

I am deeply indebted to Dr. Indrani Chatterjee for several close readings of successive drafts and many useful suggestions. I have also benefited from the comments and suggestions of Dr. Sylvia Vatuk and three anonymous referees. Any remaining errors are my responsibility. I have translated all sources in Marathi, Sanskrit, and

Portuguese. I have written retroflex and palatal sibilants as "sh" in order to distinguish them from the dental sibilant "s."

1. Suzanne Miers and Igor Kopytoff, eds., *Slavery in Africa: Historical and Anthropological Perspectives* (Madison: University of Wisconsin Press, 1977), xv, 4–6.

2. An excellent narrative history is Ananta R. Kulkarni and Ganesha H. Khare, eds., *Marathyancya itihasa,* 3 vols. (Pune: Published by Continental Prakashan for the Maharashtra University Book Production Board, 1985). Govind S. Sardesai, *A New History of the Marathas,* 3 vols. (Bombay: Phoenix, 1947–58) is an English summary of Sardesai's research findings. A brief English history that (unlike some) makes effective use of Indian-language records is André Wink, *Land and Sovereignty in India* (Cambridge: Cambridge University Press, 1985), 66–153.

3. There has been significant earlier work in this field. Ganesha C. Vad included many documents on slavery in the important selection of government records that he compiled at the turn of the nineteenth century. With characteristic insight, he placed them immediately after documents dealing with forced labor. See G. C. Vad, comp. and ed., *Selections from the Satara Raja and Peshwas' Diaries,* 9 parts (Pune: Deccan Vernacular Translation Society, 1902–11), hereafter cited as *SSRPD.* Many other documents were subsequently printed, notably in Govind S. Sardesai, ed., *Selections from the Peshwa Daftar,* 46 vols. (Bombay: Government Central Press, 1931–35). An early discussion of the issue was published by Hiroshi K. Fukazawa in Japanese in 1961; I refer to the 1974 English version, "Some Aspects of Slavery (Ghulam and Kunbina)," reprinted in Hiroshi K. Fukazawa, *The Medieval Deccan: Peasants, Social Systems, and States, Sixteenth to Eighteenth Centuries* (Delhi: Oxford University Press, 1991), 114–30. P. A. Gavli's *Peshvekalina gulamgiri va asprshyata* [Slavery and Untouchability in the Peshva Era], 3rd ed. (Kolhapur: Anjish Commercial Art Printers, 1990), which first appeared in 1983, has been widely discussed in the Marathi-language press. Kulkarni and Khare, eds., *Marathyancya itihasa,* which is a college textbook, has a brief discussion of slavery: 2:324–27. The subject also receives a chapter in Shankarrav Kharat's survey of social life in the eighteenth century: *Athravya shatakaktila Maratha kalkhandat samajika paristhiti* (Kolhapur: Shivaji University, 1992), 57–64.

4. Orlando Patterson, *Slavery and Social Death: A Comparative Study* (Cambridge, Mass.: Harvard University Press, 1982), 1–2.

5. H. K. Fukazawa, "A Note on the Corvee System (*Vethbegar*)," 1971, reprinted in Fukazawa, *Medieval Deccan,* 131–47.

6. *SSRPD,* pt. 7, vol. 2: 317–18; 8, 3: 245–46.

7. See *SSRPD,* pt. 8, vol. 3: 259 for an example from 1777.

8. See Rajaram V. Oturkar, *Peshwekalina samajik va arthik patravyavahara* (Pune: Bharata Itihasa Samshodhak Mandala, 1950), 45, for a case where vegetable vendors who sold their goods in the village street were pressed into forced labor merely because there were no Mahars available.

9. Cited in Kharat, *Samajika paristhiti,* 54.

10. Oturkar, *Patravyavahara,* 3.

11. *SSRPD,* pt. 8, vol. 3: 247–48.

12. Printed in R. D. Choksey, ed., *Period of Transition (1818–1826)* (Poona: The author, 1945), 202, 204.

13. *Rajavyavaharakosha,* a Sanskrit text composed c. 1676, in D. V. Apte and N. C. Kelkar, eds., *Shivacaritrapradipa* (Pune: Shiva Caritra Karyalaya, 1925), 146.

14. Maharashtra State Archives, Pune (hereafter MSA), Citnisi Rumal 10, Pudke 2, doc. 5211.

15. Antonio Francisco Moniz, *Noticias a documentos para a historia de Damao, antiga provincia do norte,* 4 vols. (Bastora: Tipografia Rangel, 1910–17), 3:225–26.

16. MSA, Sanika Rumal 24, Pudke 4, doc. 15365.

17. MSA, Sanika Rumal 28, Pudke 4, doc. 15365.

18. MSA, Parasnis transcripts, vol. 9, fols. 79–80.

19. *SSRPD,* pt. 5: 247.

20. N. G. Capekar, "Kalyanachya subhedaranche jamakharcha," in *Bharata Itihasa Samshodhaka Mandala Traimasik* 8, nos. 1–2 (1927): 57.

21. Narasimha C. Kelkar and Dattatraya V. Apte, eds., *English Records on Shivaji, 1659–1682* (Poona: Shiva Caritra Karyalaya, 1931), 2:128.

22. *SSRPD,* pt. 8, vol. 3: 252–53.

23. See Sharmila Rege, "The Hegemonic Appropriation of Sexuality: The Case of the *Lavani* Performers of Maharashtra," in Patricia Uberoi, ed., *Social Reform, Sexuality, and the State* (New Delhi: Sage Publications, 1996), 23–38.

24. British Library, Oriental and India Office collection, Mss. Mar D.31, fol. 110.

25. Ibid., Mss. Mar D.31, fol. 100.

26. State Records Department, *Historical Selections from Baroda State Records,* 5 vols. (Baroda: State Press, 1934–36), 3:358.

27. *SSRPD,* pt. 8, vol. 3: 253–54.

28. British Library, Oriental and India Office collection, Marathi Mss. D.44 fol. 67a. Vidura in the *Mahabharata* is the biological son of the Brahman *Rshi* Vyasa, begotten on a slave-woman.

29. Thomas Coats, "Account of the Present State of the Township of Lony," *Transactions of the Literary Society of Bombay* 3 (1823): 225–26.

30. Richard Jenkins, *Report on the Territories of the Raja of Nagpur* (1827; reprint, Nagpur: Government Press, 1923), 32. Note the term "domestic"—it is almost certainly used to translate *kunbini,* or slave-woman. He added that the head of the family could not "sell them or hire them out to another." This claim is not borne out by contemporary documents cited below.

31. Sardesai, ed., *Selections from the Peshwa Daftar,* 42:32–43.

32. Patterson, *Slavery and Social Death,* 8–10.

33. Factory records cited in Jadunath Sarkar, *House of Shivaji: Studies and Documents on Maratha History; Royal Period* (1940; reprint, Hyderabad: Orient Longman, 1978), 201.

34. Cases cited in Gavli, *Peshvekalina gulamgiri,* 74.

35. *SSRPD,* pt. 8, vol. 3: 248–49 records several sales by Charans.

36. Sardesai, ed., *Selections from the Peshwa Daftar,* 42:56–57.

37. Ibid., 27:37.

38. *SSRPD,* pt. 7, vol. 2: 318–23.

39. Her history is discussed in some detail in Pramod Oak, *Peshve gharanyaca hakikat,* rev. ed. (Pune: Continental Prakashan, 1991), 207–22.

40. *SSRPD,* pt. 2, vol. 2: 190.

41. *SSRPD,* pt. 8, vol. 3: 252.

42. *SSRPD,* pt. 8, vol. 3: 251.

43. Visvanath K. Rajvade, *Marathyanchya itihasachi sadhanen,* vol. 6 (Kolhapur: The author, 1905), 277.

44. Capekar, "Kalyanachya subhedaranche jamakharcha," 57–58.

45. Moniz, *Noticias,* 4:107–108 and note 108. *Cafre* clearly derives from the Arabic *kafir,* "infidel," as applied to the indigenous African population.

46. *Bharatiya Itihasa Samshodhaka Mandala Varshika Itivritta* (Shake: Bharata Itihasa Samshodhaka Mandala, 1835 [1923]), 191.

47. *SSRPD,* pt. 7, vol. 2: 325.

48. Capekar, "Kalyanachya subhedaranche jamakharcha," 57–58.

49. Oturkar, *Patravyavahara,* 132.

50. *SSRPD,* pt. 8, vol. 3: 251.

51. *SSRPD,* pt. 8, vol. 3: 259.

52. *SSRPD,* pt. 9, vol. 1: 389.

53. *SSRPD,* pt. 8, vol. 3: 251–52.

54. The complete list is in *SSRPD,* pt. 7, vol. 2: 319–23.

55. *SSRPD,* pt. 8, vol. 3: 253.

56. *SSRPD,* pt. 7, vol. 2: 324.

57. *SSRPD,* pt. 8, vol. 3: 267.

58. Jenkins, *Report on the Territories,* 33–34.

59. Oturkar, *Patravyavahara,* 65–66.

60. Patterson, *Slavery and Social Death,* 49–50.

61. Sardesai, ed., *Selections from the Peshwa Daftar,* 45:86.

62. R. V. Herwadkar, ed. *Thorle Shahu Maharaj yance caritra* (Pune: Venus Prakashan, 1976), 6.

63. For a full discussion of this and similar cases, see Indrani Chatterjee and Sumit Guha, "Slave-Queen, Waif-Prince: Slavery and Social Capital in Eighteenth-Century India," *Indian Economic and Social History Review* 36, no. 2 (Apr.–June 1999), 165–86.

64. Balaji P. Modak, *Kolhapur va Karnatak prantatil rajyen va sansthanen yancha itihasa-uttarardha* (Pune: V. B. Modak, 1924), 44n, 50; and Appasaheb Pavar, ed., *Jijabaikalina kagadpatren* (Kolhapur: Shivaji University, 1978), 138, 144.

65. *SSRPD,* pt. 1: 131.

66. *SSRPD,* pt. 1, 254.

67. *SSRPD,* pt. 8, vol. 3: 249.

68. *SSRPD,* pt. 8, vol. 3: 253.

69. *Bharata Itihasa Samshodhaka Mandala traimasik* 8, nos. 1–2 (1926–27): 57.

70. *SSRPD,* pt. 2, vol. 2: 325, 217.

71. "Aitihasik Tipanen," *Itihasa Sangraha* 1, no. 1 (1908): 1.

72. British Library, Oriental and India Office collection, Mss. Mar D.31, fol. 220b.

73. Patterson, *Slavery and Social Death,* 341–43.

74. *SSRPD,* pt. 1: 213. We do not know if Eshi's husband was alive at this time: I think it likely that he was not, or the claim would have been brought against him.

75. This freedom of movement is often the only explicit marker of freedom: an order releasing the slave-woman Badi says, "Have no fear; go wherever your heart wishes." *SSRPD,* pt. 7, vol. 2: 318.

76. Vithal Trimbak Gune, *The Judicial System of the Marathas: A Detailed Study of the Judicial Institutions in Maharashtra, from 1600–1818 A.D.* (Pune: Deccan College Postgraduate and Research Institute, 1953), appendix B-4, 354.

77. Ibid., appendix B-4, 356.

78. *Bharata Itihasa Samshodhaka Mandala traimasik* 11, no. 4 (1932): 181.

79. *SSRPD,* pt. 7, vol. 2: 343–49 and 223–24 respectively.

80. MSA, Citnisi Rumal 4, Pudke 1, doc. 1750, dated Suhur 1207, or 1806–1807 CE.

81. Vasudeva V. Khare, *Aitihasika lekha sangraha,* 26 vols. (Miraj: The editor, 1910–25), 7:3690.

82. *SSRPD,* pt. 7, vol. 2: 218, 213 respectively.

83. Gune, *Judicial System,* appendix B-4, 363.

84. *SSRPD,* pt. 7, vol. 2: 337–39.

85. *SSRPD,* pt. 2, vol. 2: 190.

86. *SSRPD,* pt. 2, vol. 2: 60–61.

87. MSA, Citnisi Rumal 59, Pudke 4, doc. 31440. This letter is damaged in places, and I could not read the name of the alleged protector.

88. S. S. Deva, ed., *Shrisampradayaci kagadpatren* (Dhule: Satotkarshi Sabha, 1930), 353.

89. MSA, Citnisi Rumal 10, Pudke 2, doc. 5211.

90. *SSRPD,* pt. 7, vol. 2: 223, 229.

91. MSA, Citnisi Rumal 10, Pudke 2, doc. 5188 (date unclear, late eighteenth century).

92. Coats, " Account of the Present State of the Township of Lony," 225.

93. *SSRPD,* pt. 2, vol. 2: 324.

94. Jenkins, *Report on the Territories,* 32.

8

Bound for Britain: Changing Conditions of Servitude, 1600–1857

Michael H. Fisher

Introduction

Indian servants and slaves formed a substantial component of the extensive movement to Britain by Indians (totaling in the tens of thousands by the mid-nineteenth century). The living and working conditions of Indians in various forms of servitude in Britain shifted with the expansion of colonialism, and differed significantly from those they endured in India. Many endured great hardship but a few became Anglicized, achieved emancipation, married, and settled in Britain. Studying their lives collectively and individually enables us to consider from the perspective of such Indians the processes of colonialism and the meaning of slavery as they changed over time in Britain as well as India.[1]

Most studies to date of Britain, India, and the colonial relationships between them have not sufficiently considered such people on the margins. British imperial history has conventionally concentrated on the movement of elite male Britons out into the colonies. The recent magisterial five-volume *Oxford History of the British Empire* reflects this tendency, although its emerging Companion series and other responses partly redress this by highlighting issues of gender, race, and class.[2] Even most studies critical of European "Orientalism" and other cultural imperialisms stress the lives and actions of Europeans, although a small but growing body of literature has begun to consider lower-class Europeans and the ways that their particular experiences shaped British identities generally.[3]

Nor have Indian national narratives historically included many non-elite Indians, at home or abroad. Progressive scholarship, including the *Sub-*

altern Studies series, has done much to highlight non-elites in India.[4] The histories of Indians, particularly non-elite Indians, traveling and settling abroad, however, have only begun to emerge.[5]

The English East India Company, for 250 years from the time of its establishment in 1600, formed the main vehicle for the transit of Indians to Britain, as it did for Europeans sailing to India. The Company was also the institution charged by the British government with controlling, protecting, and representing Indians once they reached Britain. As the British commercial, and then political, presence in India extended, increasing numbers of Indians sailed to the metropole, many of them the servants or slaves of Britons returning home. This venture transformed each Indian's life in distinctive ways, depending on his or her background, gender, and individual circumstances.

Indians, Servitude, and Initial English Attitudes of the Seventeenth Century

Indians have sailed to England virtually as long as Britons have sailed to India, from about 1600 onward. Almost from its inception, the East India Company's court of directors sought to enforce its monopolistic control over the movement of all people between India and England, but its initial concerns were not people entering England but rather those entering India. In 1657, the directors ordered that all people going to India apply and pay £12 (equivalent to £1,214 today) for the Company's license or "permission."[6] While primarily intended to exclude from India unwanted European rivals, the indiscriminate comprehensiveness of this regulation nevertheless meant that it also applied to Indians of all classes returning home, including many designated in the Company's records as "Black servants." This category included men and women in various degrees of servitude and of either Indian or mixed Indian and European descent. Some had been sold or gifted and worked without wages throughout their lives. Others worked without or with wages for fixed terms. Yet others simply had contracted employment as a servant in exchange for wages and other customary benefits like food, lodging, and clothing. In any case, this regulation created an expensive barrier to the repatriation of Indians of all classes, providing a powerful incentive for the masters of Indians to keep them in England once there.

When Indians first arrived in England during the early seventeenth century, they entered a society with its own history and changing practices of many degrees of servitude but virtually no direct experience of India or Indians. While the East India Company had only just begun to visit India and transport Indians to England, Englishmen had already been participating in the Atlantic slave trade in Africans for decades. Initially, some Englishmen sought to enslave alien-looking working- and lower-class Indians in England, treating them as they treated many Africans. Nonetheless, the earliest Indians—like the few Africans in England at that time—were rare and costly objects who, by their very visible and also imagined differences from Europeans, as well as by the sheer cost of importation, added a distinguishing cachet to aristocratic households and public pageants.[7] For example, in 1683, as an adornment to the royal court, King Charles II commanded the East India Company to provide him from India with "one Male, and two Female Blacks, but they must be Dwarfs, and of the least size that you can procure."[8] Other elite households paid much for Indians to serve them, occasionally commemorating their service by including them as carefully delineated individuals in joint portraits of the family.[9]

From the beginning, the largest proportion of Indians in England were lascars (Indian seamen), who sailed as wage laborers to England on East India Company and private ships (some twenty thousand or more lascars had reached Britain by the mid-nineteenth century). Most lascars had voluntarily entered into a maritime labor gang for whom an Indian *sarang* (gang boss) negotiated a collective contract with the European ship captain or owner. Yet, once in England, many lascars found themselves in one or another kind of servitude. Like British seamen, some were unwillingly conscripted ("pressed"), often by force, into the Royal Navy.[10] While this meant they received wages, their term of service was involuntary, indefinite, brutal, and often fatal.

Other lascars in England were forced into chattel slavery for life in the Americas, on the model of African slaves there. In one early example in which lascars barely escaped such enslavement, the ship *St. George* under Captain Lord returned to London from Surat late in 1667 (see map 3). Typically, Captain Lord, on departure from India, had supplemented his diminished European crew with Indians, contracting with a *sarang* for a labor gang of ten Indian seamen. On disembarking in London, the *sarang* complained to the Company's directors that Lord had denied the wages due them and had also sold some of them into slavery for shipment to America. The directors consistently exerted the East India Company's right and duty to supervise, protect, and manage Indians in England. The directors thus immediately created a subcommittee of its leading members to investigate the complaints of the *sarang*.[11] Two days later, this committee reported that, while slightly exaggerated, the *sarang*'s assertion had substance. A dockside ale-house keeper in Shadwell had sold two of the lascars as slaves to Captain Tilman of the ship *Constant Friendship*, which had already left London on its voyage to Virginia. The committee dispatched an urgent message to the royal collector of customs at the Downs, off the Kent coast, to forbid the ship its final clearance to sail. When Tilman refused to relinquish these men without reimbursement of his purchase price, the company paid him. It also purchased clothes, food, and lodging for all of the lascars during their time in London, and arranged for them to be employed on one of its ships, the aptly named *Return*, sailing back to Surat that spring. Ever careful of its own balance sheet, the company charged Captain Lord £42 3s. 8d. (worth £4,603 today), which it had laid out to redeem and maintain these lascars.[12] Similarly, in 1737, a letter "from a Black Fellow born in Bengal called Pompey, and brought to Britain by Captain Benfield, and since a servant to Major Woodford at Virginia who now detains him as a Slave" led to an investigation and intervention by the Company to return him to India.[13] Not all Indians were able thus to free themselves from slavery in the Americas by an effective appeal to the East India Company, however.

While protecting their interest in India, the directors also participated in slaving overseas, through the Company and as individuals. The Company's strategically located base at St. Helena (first acquired by the Company in 1659) served the vast transatlantic slave trade. The Company also purchased, transported, and sold Asian and African slaves throughout Asia, albeit on a far smaller scale than other British merchants did in the Atlantic world.[14]

Yet many of the Company's directors, in addition to being merchants, were also committed evangelical Christians. Indeed, one of the central issues of national identity in Britain, and one that affected Indians there particularly, was that of Protestant Christianity.[15] By custom, but not by law, many Britons believed that slavery and being Anglican in Britain were incompatible.[16] (Similarly, in many lands, Muslims regarded being Muslim and being enslaved as inappropriate, although this was not uniform in practice and many Muslims held Muslim slaves.) Hence, an Indian's conversion to the Church of England, especially if domiciled in Britain, could bring a degree of freedom. Accordingly, as early as 1670, the Company's court of directors ordered "that a Clause be inserted in the letter to the Governor General of St. Helena, declaring it to be the sense of this Court; that if any Blacks who now and hereafter shall be sent by the Company to serve on this said island, shall through the Ministry of God's word, be converted to the Christian Fayth (Which is much to be desired) and shall so evidence it in their conversation, that then, seven years after such real conversion, they shall have the benefit of being Free Planters on the Island."[17] While this by no means emancipated large numbers of slaves there, it reflected a growing English sense that sincere Christians should not be enslaved. As we will see below, the ability of Indians to transform themselves in British eyes through conversion and other forms of Anglicization occasionally provided some degree of emancipation, at least during the early period considered here.

Changed Conditions for Indians in British Society in the Eighteenth Century

The developments in British law and society and in Company legislation in the eighteenth century can be better understood against the backdrop of the previous century. As the number of Indians in servitude who lived in Britain grew markedly, their roles and values shifted. Less rare, they became somewhat less valuable as ornaments in elite households, and were more commonly found in middle-class families, particularly those with connections to expanding colonialism. Nonetheless, the value of their labor and the substantial costs of transporting them to Britain meant that their owners went to some lengths to retain possession. In this period, therefore, it is hardly surprising to find parallels between Atlantic and Indian Ocean slave systems. Some Indians in Britain at that time were subjected to chattel slavery for life, with no wages, and with the prospect of being resold without recourse. Specifically for Indians in Britain (as opposed to in India or for people in or from the other colonies), the East India Company established a complex system of bonds which precluded Indian servants (whatever their degree of servitude) from escaping their masters in Britain, or being abandoned by them.

So from the beginning of the eighteenth century, English newspapers included advertisements seeking the recovery of Indians who had fled. These advertisements not only demonstrate their value but also reveal their deportment and accomplishments. For example, in July 1702, an employer sought the return of an

> Indian Black Servant: Went away from his master's house in Drury-Lane upon Monday . . . and has been since seen at Hampstead, Highgate, and Tottenham-Court, an Indian black boy with long hair, about 15 years of age, speaks very good English; he went away in a brown fustian frock, a blue waistcoat, and scarlet shag breeches, and is called by the name of Morat [perhaps Murad]: Whoever brings him to, or gives notice of him, so as he may be brought to Mr. Pain's House in Prince's Court, Westminster, shall have a guinea reward, and the boy shall be kindly received.[18]

Rather than "oriental" dress, Morat wore the English-style clothing of men of his servant class (although on formal occasions he may have been dressed by his master to highlight his exotic origins). The payment of a guinea (equivalent to £112 today) simply for information about Morat suggests his value to his master.[19] Such advertisements were common for British run-aways as well, suggesting that class—not necessarily ethnic—conflict impelled many to flee. Nonetheless, their Indian features strongly marked them out as identifiably different within British society, and made them therefore more recoverable by their masters.

In some cases, British masters made efforts to return Indians to India through public advertisement, seeking a new master bound there to whom they could be transferred. One owner placed the following advertisement in 1775 offering her Indian "Slave girl":

> Any lady going to the East Indies, having occasion for a maid servant may be advantageously supplied with one who is lately come from thence; she is a Slave Girl, and the mistress who brought her over having no occasion for her will give her over to any Lady to attend her in the passage to India and to serve her for three years after the arrival there without wages, provided the lady engages at expiration of the Term to give her freedom. She is a good servant, perfectly good natured, and talks English well. She may be heard of by sending a line to . . .[20]

While designated a "Slave" and receiving no wages, this Indian woman clearly had entered into a limited term of indenture, after which she would have earned her release. Such indenture might result from an advance payment to the slave's family, to be paid off by her or his labor. In this instance, the current master seems to have offered to forego three years of service in exchange for not having to pay the slave's passage back to India.

Three brief examples spread through the eighteenth century suggest how British society pressured Indian slaves in its midst to become Christian, and illustrate three different results for their status if they did. Sometimes resistance to Anglicization lasted too long for it to offer emancipation. One Indian from Madras had been purchased in his early teens by Captain Dawes, brought to Britain around 1720, and then given to Mrs. Elizabeth Turner, who called him "Julian." (See map 2.) He reportedly resisted learning English and becoming Christian, despite Mrs. Turner's repeated orders. Yet, simultaneously, she did not wish him to give up completely his "oriental" identity, which gave him special value in her eyes over her British servants. Using him to display her possession of the "exotic" before her guests at parties, Mrs. Turner made him dance and sing in "Indian style." Although Mrs. Turner denied any awareness of his discontent, after four years he rebelled by stealing twenty guineas and setting fire to her house (on August 8, 1724).[21] In prison awaiting execution for theft and arson, he finally accepted Christianity and was baptized "John," allegedly in the vain hope that this would lead to his release. Instead, he was hanged at Tyburn. While the English judge appreciated this execution-eve conversion as saving the Indian's soul, it did not abrogate the theft and destruction of property for which he was condemned.

In some instances, an Indian becoming Christian might become "free." But emancipation could then expose her or him to hardships all too common among the British poor. A ten-year-old Indian girl was purchased in Bengal and then brought to London around 1741 as the slave of Mr. Suthern Davies, who passed her on to a relative, Mrs. Ann Suthern. After four years in London, this Indian converted to the Church of England and was christened "Catherine Bengall" at fashionable St. James Church, Westminster, on November 26, 1745.[22] Liberated by this, she left Mrs. Suthern's household (either voluntarily or perforce) and lodged at the Ship tavern. Her ongoing sexual relationship with a Briton, William Lloyd, however, left her pregnant, unmarried, and destitute. When her pregnancy became evident in July 1746, she had to appear before the local magistrate, who ordered her lodged in the local parish workhouse.[23] As a Christian member of that parish, she had the right to food and shelter; as an unmarried mother, she was subject to the discipline of the parish. In the workhouse two months later, she gave birth to a son, christened with the father's name, William, on September 22, 1746. Like so many women of her class, Indian and British, she and her son then disappeared from surviving British records, so we cannot know how (or if) her life, or that of her son, continued.

In our third instance of the variable status of an Indian slave, reflective as well of these British beliefs about how conversion to Christianity and residence in Britain could be "emancipating" despite repeated resistance to authority there, we can reconstruct the life of an Indian later called Rippon. He had been born in the 1760s in Allepee, Travancore, one of the princely states that, although nominally independent, was coming under British indirect rule. He had been enslaved, either from birth or in his youth, and had been purchased (along with two others) by Captain Richard Field of the Bombay Marine (naval) service. Field brought him to Bombay and then sold (or perhaps gifted) him to John Canning, also a naval officer, in 1774 at Surat. Five years later, around 1779, Canning brought the teenager to Britain, where he lived with Canning's family in Fingringhoe, a small village south of Colchester, Essex.

The Cannings had him educated and expected him to convert to Christianity. He was apparently baptized into the Church of England there, with the Anglicized name "Rippon." The Canning family, however, found Rippon extremely uncooperative. After several years, they sent him, as a servant to Captain James Douglas, back to the East Indies, where he served in 1782–83. It is not clear if the Cannings sold Rippon or just passed him on to Douglas, but they clearly retained a moral interest or financial responsibility. After his voyage back to England, Rippon allegedly robbed Douglas's home in London. Douglas sent him back to Canning's family rather than prosecute him for theft. Presumably, Douglas demanded back any money he had paid for Rippon. The Canning family next gave or sold him to Mr. Charles Hays, an attorney based in the Manchester Building, Westminster, London, but again Rippon was charged with theft and returned to the Canning family. Evidently still feeling proprietary or paternalistic toward Rippon, John Canning testified that "to prevent his starving or coming to an untimely end, I gave him to Mr. Charles Moore," an East India ship officer, to take to St. Helena for sale in 1784, the sale money covering his passage costs there. Canning believed "a small island or a prison was the only suitable situation for him." Moore eventually sold Rippon in St. Helena, and then he was sold twice more, once for £48.

A dozen years later, in 1797, Rippon petitioned the governor of St. Helena for release, claiming to have been born in Bombay Presidency and illegally enslaved.[24] As we saw, the directors had in 1670 made provision that sincere Christians there would be emancipated. In support of his case, Rippon submitted statements from fellow slaves and shipmates, which are admittedly ambiguous about his actual status. In the current British climate of heated public debate about abolition, the governor asked for an investigation. Despite Canning's testimony that Rippon had indeed been a slave, the governor general of India ordered him released and returned to India, expressly on the grounds that he was a Christian and had lived in Britain sufficiently long to be emancipated.[25] Once the issue of conversion to Christianity which had brought him to prominence had been decided, he, like Catherine Bengall, disappeared from the official record.

Thus, Indians who lived in Britain during these early centuries of colonialism endured a range of degrees and types of servitude. Depending in part upon their adaptation to British values, particularly conversion to the Church of England as a member of a British parish, their condition could change significantly. Their current status therefore varied by their domicile, ostensible religious community of the time, and individual circumstances. Throughout, their relationship to the East India Company, and its assertions of control over them, remained one of the most salient factors in the lives of all Indians in Britain.

Whose Bonds? Regulation by the Company of Indian Servants

The number of Indian slaves, runaways, and indigent abandoned servants in Britain rose over the latter half of the eighteenth century and into the early nineteenth century. Their numbers particularly increased during the years following the first major British territorial assertions in Bengal (marked by the battle of Plassey in 1757). While the Company's enforcement of all regulations remained inconsistent in the eighteenth and subsequent centuries, the archival records of its attempts to monitor the movements and identities of Indian servants and slaves illuminate the ways in which marginalized groups actually enable us to "read" colonial history.

In consequence of these growing numbers of Indians, especially of indigent Indians, in Britain, the Company's directors (and the Company itself) became politically vulnerable to, and morally embarrassed by, widespread charges in Parliament and newspapers that they were responsible for clearing them off the streets of London (and, to a lesser extent, the rest of Britain). This coincided with parliamentary attempts to control the Company's fortunes and influence. It was in this context that the British government required the Company to shelter and return all needy Indians to India, or find some other responsible person to do so. This was a financial as well as moral check on the Company; the Company had to pay two shillings per day to a London lodging-house keeper plus at least £15 to a British ship-owner for the cheapest return passage for each indigent Indian. This was a significant expense for the Company, which, for example, paid £370,487 (equivalent to almost £20 million today) for food, maintenance, medicine, clothing, and passage money home for over ten thousand Indians during the period 1803–13 alone.[26]

In order to reduce these expenses, the directors devised new regulations to ensure that British masters who brought Indian servants to Britain had an economic incentive to retain control over them and to return them to India as quickly as possible at no expense to the Company.[27] These injunctions were also symptomatic of the ongoing efforts by the directors to assert their authority over Company officials in India. Thus, in 1769, the directors first complained to their governor in Calcutta about this perceived growing problem of indigent Indians in Britain. As a solution, the directors ordered the bonding of all Indian slaves and other servants leaving India for England, thus shifting financial responsibility onto individual British masters:

> It has happened of late years amongst the many Natives of India, who have been sent to England as Servants to Gentlemen or their Families returning home, that several have been forsaken entirely by the Persons in whose Service they engaged, and these poor Creatures from their destitute Circumstance in this distant Land, have Petitioned us for going back at the Company's Expence, on board their Ships, which not only from the distress of these Indigents, but to

prevent reflections on us in this respect from the People of India, we have been induced to grant. In order therefore to remedy these Grievances in future you are hereby directed not to permit any Person whatever on returning to England to take with them a Native of India, without giving Security for every such Native in the Sum of £50—for preventing their being Chargeable to the Company in any manner whatever—and you must send us such Bonds in the Packets of the Ships whereon any Indian Servants embark, that in case of necessity we may put the same in [law-]suit here.[28]

The rhetoric of care for Indians notwithstanding, the directors were apparently attempting to do more. These were also indirect attempts at social engineering within British society of the time. On the one hand, these rules implied more stringent monitoring of the households and incomes of individual Britons in colonial service, especially since many of the latter were reputed to have earned huge profits in "private" ventures and were sneered at as "nabobs" in the British press of the time.[29] Further, suggesting how central class, rather than "race" alone, was to the directors' concerns, in 1797 they extended this requirement, insisting that European women—usually the wives of European private soldiers—who worked their way from India to Britain as servants be bonded in the same way as Indians.[30] In this sense, the directors' words referred indirectly to this incipient set of "class conflicts" within the British elites of the late eighteenth century. The directors thus extended their effort to control upwardly mobile Britons through commercial "bonds" and "security" and by using the British judicial system to enforce their authority. On the other hand, the directors' gesture to public opinion in India can also be read as a "trace" of Indian servants' attempts to transform commercial contracts into a more familiar "nurturant" relationship—the historical inheritance of such laborers by the late eighteenth century. In other words, one can see in the directors' own regulations contradictory agencies—their own, and those of the indigent servants as well.

These contradictory agencies and desires explain the persistence of such efforts as well as their ambivalent and complex consequences. The directors repeatedly exhorted their officials in India to institute controls upon British men in Company service. In 1782, they even directed their subordinates' attention to ships with non-British European registry, frequent evaders of the bond system.[31] In deference to repeated injunctions from the directors, the three presidencies (Bengal, Bombay, and Madras) each experimented ineffectively with a range of procedures and levels of bonds—which ranged in different times and presidencies from five hundred to a thousand rupees per Indian servant (£50–100, equivalent to £4,000–8,000 today).[32]

While this bonding requirement did discourage some Britons from bringing Indians to Britain, the extent of that discouragement is difficult to measure today.[33] Perhaps it is a reflection of the wealth or influence of individual British officials serving the Company that, despite these regulations, the number of Indian slaves and other servants—even the officially reported number—rose annually in Britain. By the early nineteenth century, well over a thousand bonded and unbonded Indians arrived annually in Britain (many as servants but more as sailors); by the mid-nineteenth century, this number had risen many-fold. The presence of unbonded servants allows us to surmise that many masters evaded the requirement of a bond. Masters leaving India simply bribed or used their influence on the inspector, hid the Indian slaves or other servants, or boarded them once out of port. On approaching the British coast, many left their ships on local fishing vessels, thus evading government customs and other controls. Professional smugglers of people and goods proliferated. Thus, despite the Company's efforts at surveillance and control, many slaves and other servants continued to leave India and enter Britain without bonds.

For Indians, the implications of such bonds were contradictory—as were other judicial changes of the time. In British legal terms, the existence of a bond established the proprietary claims of a master, which were enforceable in court. This implied, therefore, the bonded servant's continued servitude and inability to find alternative employment. At the same time, bonds also served somewhat to protect Indians from being discarded in Britain. While the substantial number of bonded and unbonded Indians who applied as indigents for succor from the Company indicates that this protection against abandonment often proved inadequate, nonetheless the bonding system also implies that the directors saw abuse of Indian servants as a "wrong" and acted to enforce the servants' claims upon their employers.[34] Perhaps we can also see as evidence of the occasional victories of Indians the fact that, from the end of the eighteenth century well into the nineteenth, the Company maintained barracks for Indian indigents in London, where they received free shelter, food, and clothing. The Company also arranged free passage for them back to India, paid for either by the Company or by the employer who originally brought them. Similarly, in 1772, when African-descended James Somerset resisted return from Britain to slavery in Virginia, he won a judicial ruling that a fugitive slave in Britain could not be forced to return to slavery in the colonies. Many Britons and slaves—both Indian and African—prematurely understood this to mean an end to slavery in Britain. From the perspective of Indians in bondage, then, the evidence suggested by the bonds permits us to wonder whether British

Table 8.1. Bonded Servants by Gender and (Apparent) Community (1792–1856)

	European/ Christian	Muslim	Hindu	Other	Total
Male	23%	15%	5%	3%	46%
Female	28%	15%	7%	4%	54%
Total	51%	30%	12%	7%	n=1,324

Note: These figures are based on the names given for the servants in bonds in the British Library. Although they indicate only the "official" identities of these bonded servants, and constitute only an incomplete listing, they suggest the relative proportions of each group. Almost all bonds were eventually redeemed. On winding up its affairs, the Company found it held only seven unredeemed bonds, totaling Rs. 3,600, one dating as far back as 1792. *Times* (London), November 28 and 30, 1857, 1b.

elite and commercial households were not imperceptibly shaped by Indian slave-servants.

The many hundreds of surviving bonds from this date also allow us to compile a broad collective profile of such Indians. Based on 1,324 of those whose names have survived in the Company's archives, table 8.1 gives us a general sense of their composition.

Over half of those bonded served under "European" names, regardless of their background. This indicates many who took "Christian" names in order to adapt to their masters' culture; others had such names imposed on them by their British master to suit that master's cultural values. Indians who converted to Christianity, either out of conviction or nominally to suit their European employers, also conventionally adopted European names. Further, people of partial European descent, which was usually on the father's side, often took a European name. Some women were Indian or mixed-ancestry wives of British private soldiers or non-commissioned officers, working their way back to Britain in the service of a higher-ranking European. Thus, going to Britain for many Indians correlated somewhat with adopting, accepting, or inheriting a Europeanized identity.

Of these bonded people, over 45 percent retained Indian names, usually identifiable as Muslim, Hindu, or Parsi. Those who retained Muslim names were disproportionately numerous compared to the Muslim proportion of the population in South Asia. Fewer than one out of eight served using Hindu names. This was a disproportionately small number compared to the Indian population generally. Together, they reflect the reluctance of respectable Hindus to travel over the "black water," in contrast to the greater willingness of Muslims to sail overseas, and indicate the cultural preferences of

British masters for Muslim over Hindu personal slaves or servants. Of the small remaining number, some were Parsi (most of whom traveled to Britain in the service of a Parsi merchant). Some cannot be identified by community, usually because only the name of the master, and not the servant, appeared on the bond, or because the name is ambiguous as to community. Finally, well over half of the bonded people were female. However incomplete, the evidence from the bonds becomes much more significant if we read into them the potential for manipulation displayed by the extended accounts of two Indians—Nabob and Munnoo—including the dramatic changes in their lives resulting from their passages in servitude to England and the more subtle changes in the life of their common master as a result of their actions.

Two Indians and One Master

Both Nabob (born circa 1770) and Munnoo (born circa 1795) had their lives recounted by their often frustrated master, the notorious Anglicized Irish lawyer based in Calcutta, William Hickey (1749–1830).[35] As a young boy in Bengal, Nabob had probably been purchased from his distressed family by a British private citizen living in Calcutta, John Lewis Auriol.[36] As was common, Auriol named his young slave with the elevated title of a distinguished office, "nawab," that parodied his enslaved status.[37] Auriol apparently also taught him functional English, so that he could serve better. When Auriol's friend, William Hickey, was looking for a young servant to accompany him back to England late in 1779, Auriol turned Nabob over to Hickey as "a present."[38] Interestingly, Nabob does not appear on the list of servants for whom a bond was posted upon leaving India. It seems, therefore, that Hickey simply brought him out of India unbonded, another indication that the Company's administrative machinery for collecting such bonds was not always effective.

A careful reading of Hickey's autobiographical narrative reveals that Nabob gradually rose in status during their passage to England. In India, Nabob was a slave, subject to transfer at his master's whim. Over the long journey via the Cape and Holland, Nabob took on a personal identity in Hickey's account. Although Nabob was apparently Hickey's only companion on the long voyage from India to the Cape of Good Hope, Hickey in his memoir never mentioned Nabob by name until they left the Cape together. There Hickey first referred to "my little pet boy, Nabob."[39] On their voyage to Holland, Hickey began to mention Nabob more frequently. For example, when Hickey asked him to observe and report the weather at sea, Nabob allegedly replied, "'No much ee wind, but too much ee smoke.'"[40] Hickey found Nabob's English description of fog childishly amusing. After reaching Holland, Hickey began to permit Nabob to ride inside the carriage as something of a companion-servant, instead of outside in a menial servant's position.[41] On landing in England, Hickey even paused on his journey to accommodate Nabob's wants, although Hickey still described these wants in crude terms: "next to Ingatestone, at which place Nabob complaining of hunger, I stopped that he might appease his craving and, not to be quite unemployed, I took a sandwich."[42] Thus, Hickey's shifting characterizations of Nabob seem to reflect how the nine-month passage from Calcutta to England and the asymmetrical personal interactions between them brought Nabob and Hickey closer together.

After Hickey reestablished himself with his family in England, he reported that they treated Nabob more as a family pet than as a working servant. As Hickey recounted, Nabob made himself "quite at home, [Hickey's sister] Emily having taken a great liking to him. Indeed, he was a little pet with all the ladies, being an interesting-looking, handsome boy."[43] Hickey used Nabob as an ornament to his own status: "I dressed him, too, very smart as a husar. As a servant, he was not of the least use to me." This must have appeared, from Hickey's perspective, a significant shift in the relationship, since he was using Nabob's attire to signal not "oriental" remoteness but European-style proximity.

During his two years in England, Nabob sought and received "improvement" in his condition. Hickey's father sent Nabob "to school to be taught reading and writing, which he did, the boy making rapid progress in both. At the end of a few months he expressed a great desire to become a Christian. I therefore, after he was duly instructed, caused him to be baptized at St. James's Church."[44] In Hickey's mind, becoming a Christian and living in Britain automatically emancipated Nabob, transforming him into a free man. This was not, in fact, a legal provision at this time, which Hickey must have known in his capacity as a lawyer. Nevertheless, it reflected the popular identification of slavery with paganism and its distance from Christianity (i.e., Anglican Protestantism), as well as the transforming power of residence in Britain.

As a mark of Nabob's changing social standing, he began to wear garments indicating a rise in status. For example, Hickey remembered that he had some new English-style clothes made for himself, but then, dissatisfied by their appearance on him, paid handsomely to have these "three or four suits of clothes . . . altered to fit my little Bengally," Nabob.[45] Since the sartorial style worn in England marked one's social status, Nabob would have appeared dressed almost as Hickey himself would have been, although perhaps without the expensive accoutrements (for example, the watch, fob, and other jewelry) of a true gentleman.

While Hickey claimed credit for Nabob's upward mobility, Nabob seems not to have accepted it gratefully and submissively as the always egocentric Hickey presumed he would. Rather, on two instances, Nabob displayed strong resistance to Hickey's paternalism. In the first, after his return to England Hickey had incurred debts and faced imprisonment. To discover Hickey's hiding place, his creditor and the bailiff summoned one of Hickey's father's English servants and offered him a guinea for information on Hickey's whereabouts. This servant indignantly rejected the offer. When Nabob soon thereafter overheard him boasting of his loyalty to Hickey, Nabob reportedly rushed out of the house and over to the inn where the creditor and bailiff waited. Nabob then offered to take up the reward and bring them to Hickey's distant hiding place: "'If you please I'll go with you and show you the house.'" Nabob asserted that he knew full well what doing so would mean, allegedly telling the creditor, "'you would send [Hickey] to prison because he would not give you money.'"[46] Hickey claimed that the creditor was so shocked at this "base and unfeeling conduct in the little urchin, knowing as he did full well, the extraordinary and uniform kindness with which he had been treated by me during the voyage, and which had been continued by every one of my family since I had reached England," that he instead beat Nabob and refrained from arresting Hickey. Meanwhile, Hickey paid the debt but did not learn about "this black rascal's scandalous ingratitude" until after their return to India.[47]

While Hickey thus recounted his increasingly kind treatment of Nabob over their passage from India to England, he ended his account of their sojourn there with this instance of Nabob's alleged incapacity to accept such elevation. Hickey explained this incident as the result of Nabob's greed and inability to appreciate kindness and respond with gratitude, both of which were incomprehensible to Hickey. Nevertheless, Hickey clearly misjudged many of his interpersonal relationships. In his memoirs, he repeatedly reported betrayals—by people whom he considered friends or lovers—that he found equally unexpected and incomprehensible. Thus, we should not rely on Hickey's interpretation of Nabob's motives.

We can posit that Nabob's perspective on their relationship differed fundamentally from Hickey's. His reported initiative and eagerness in betraying Hickey to the law and imprisonment may reveal deep resistance to his patronizing master and a newly developed sense of his own agency in Britain. We can speculate that Nabob saw this as a way to escape Hickey's control and use the guinea reward to begin a new life. That this effort by Nabob garnered him instead a beating and diminished standing within Hickey's father's household seems to have precluded any further effort to leave Hickey's employ and remain in England. Therefore, Nabob's first rejection of Hickey's assumption that he would be grateful and obedient to Hickey's interests must be considered deeply, even though our information must necessarily come primarily from Hickey's narrative.

The second and more successful instance of Nabob's rejection of Hickey's patronage came after their return to India together in 1783. There, Hickey, always self-centered, presumed that Nabob would continue to serve him faithfully, bound no longer by law but rather by ties of gratitude and economic necessity. Nabob, however, seems to have been less grateful and more autonomous than Hickey expected. On reaching Calcutta, Auriol asked Hickey for his slave back. Hickey found this incredible because he believed Auriol had given Nabob to him completely as "an absolute and unconditional gift," rather than temporarily as a loan. Hickey further was convinced that he was a far better master for Nabob than Auriol: "a niggardly, parsimonious fellow in all his pecuniary transactions." Hickey determined to prove his possession of Nabob by leaving the decision of which master to serve up to him. He explained to Nabob,

> Mr. Auriol now desires to have you back, claiming you as his exclusive property. This he undoubtedly has no right to do, nor shall he have you unless you should be desirous of changing masters. Now therefore, what say you? Will you stay with Mrs. Hickey and me, or do you prefer going to Mr. John Auriol?

To Hickey's further dismay, Nabob determined to rejoin Auriol: "Without a moment's hesitation, and with an exulting smile, he answered he had rather go to Mr. Auriol." Hickey described himself "somewhat vexed at so unexpected and unjust a claim. . . . Nabob had . . . been treated by myself and the whole of my family with the utmost generosity and kindness, which he repaid with the basest ingratitude." Hickey's parting admonition to Nabob was that he would be sorry for his choice of masters, and to Auriol that "the boy in question . . . being now a Christian he (Mr Auriol) could no longer be justified, nor would the law permit him, to treat him as a slave." Thus, the perception of the master evidently did not always accurately gauge the will of the servant-slave. Nor did Nabob, apparently, elect to remain in England as a free but dependent man by fleeing his master there, as other Indians (especially unbonded ones like Nabob) attempted to do, and sometimes succeeded. We can only speculate about the relative quality of life in Auriol's and Hickey's households, or other considerations that may have influenced Nabob's decision. Nonetheless, Nabob apparently submitted to living in India as a slave, yet he did so under a master of his own choosing.[48]

Another slave or servant of Hickey's remained with him for more than twenty-five years, also rising in status over their passage from India to England. At the end of Hickey's colorful career in Calcutta, he purchased the services of a thirteen-year-old boy called "Munnoo" (an affectionate diminutive for a male child). Munnoo had already worked since age nine for Hickey: "a remarkable, smart, good-tempered boy . . . his chief occupation being to make the other servants laugh by his monkey tricks when waiting at table and standing at the back of my chair."[49] In 1808, Hickey bought or transferred Munnoo from his family in exchange for money: "[Munnoo's] mother, who doted upon the boy, would not for a long time consent to let him go to Europe, until an offer of five hundred sicca rupees [£50] which I made her proved irresistible; she accepted the money and agreed to part with her favourite Munnoo, and a more attached and faithful creature never existed than he proved to me." While this transaction suggested the sale of Munnoo, Hickey seems to have regarded the boy rather as a servant than a slave, designating him "Sirdar [chief] bearer," although Munnoo was Hickey's only servant on the voyage.[50]

Hickey apparently smuggled Munnoo, like Nabob, unbonded from India, nor does Munnoo appear in the ship's official logbook.[51] Munnoo's departure from his home proved heart-wrenching. On first sailing, Hickey locked "the wretched boy" in their cabin: "[Munnoo] fixed himself at the quarter gallery window where he sat looking the very image of despair. . . . there he remained as long as the vessel that was rapidly conveying his old friends from him was discernible, leaving the poor fellow in the midst of strangers and in a scene as uncouth as it was novel to him."[52] While sympathetic in his description of Munnoo's condition from Munnoo's perspective, Hickey clearly asserted his control over him throughout their voyage.

Once in England, Munnoo lived, as Nabob had done, with Hickey's family. The aging Hickey treated Munnoo paternalistically, desiring to impress him with England's glory: "I had anticipated some pleasure from the delight I expected Munnoo would betray upon first beholding the splendid capital of England."[53] While Hickey may have purchased Munnoo, he came to treat him as a ward, calling him "my friend" and considering him someone, albeit a social inferior, who shared Hickey's sense of being an outsider in England because of their mutual domicile in Bengal.

Whatever his legal condition, once in England Munnoo felt free to express some of his own feelings. When Hickey warned his carriage drivers that they were going too fast, Munnoo desired they go even faster: "my friend Munnoo was exceedingly indignant, saying to me with much earnestness, when I was calling to the boys not to drive at such a rate, 'Mud Monakurra mud monakurra! Saheb, kiswastee ni Geldee Jata! bote atcha Geldee

Jata!'" (Hickey's garbled recollection of Munnoo's words probably tells us less about the words Munnoo actually used than Hickey's recollection of Munnoo's intent.) Hickey very loosely translates this for his Anglophone readers as "Don't prevent their going on, it is very pleasant to go fast."[54] Hickey nonetheless made sure they slowed down.

Hickey eventually retired to Beaconsfield, Buckinghamshire. There, Munnoo studied and Anglicized himself, as had Nabob. Hickey credited Munnoo with the full initiative in his conversion to the Church of England in 1809:

> my favourite Munnoo, without the least hint or solicitation on my part upon the subject, expressed an earnest desire to be made a Christian. I had upon first coming to Beaconsfield put him to school to be taught to read and write; his schoolmaster, having made the Catechism the first object, probably turned his thoughts that way. . . . as the boy was extremely zealous, he soon entitled himself to receive baptism.

Yet it was Hickey who determined "to anglify his name a little, and therefore instead of Munnoo, I had him designated in the parochial register, 'William Munnew.'"[55]

While he remained Hickey's servant, Munnew also created his own life and family. Around 1813, Munnew married (or began living with) an Englishwoman, Anne. They had a daughter, christened Anne in 1814 at the Beaconsfield parish church.[56] In 1817, Hickey, with Munnew and Munnew's family, moved to London, taking rooms in Westminster.[57] There, in 1819, Hickey commissioned the prominent artist William Thomas to paint a joint portrait of him, Munnew, and Hickey's dog.[58] This painting displays Munnew dressed not in oriental or servant's garb but rather in the clothes of a British gentleman (or gentleman's gentleman), complete with stylish cravat and waistcoat, much as Nabob seems to have been dressed, plus a gold watch-fob and other jewelry.

Around 1820, Hickey, Munnew, and Munnew's growing family moved to Richmond, Surrey. There, Munnew and Anne christened their newborn son, William.[59] Hickey returned to London sometime before his death in February 1827.[60] Around then, Munnew rose from servant to "licenced victualler," before he himself died in the 1830s. His family settled in Westminster. His eldest son, William, became a skilled pianoforte tuner and maker. In 1840, he married Elizabeth Mills (1816–?), the daughter of a Kent horse dealer, soon after the birth of their son, William, the first of at least ten children.[61] The family had merged into British society, associated by neither name nor deportment with India. This was a long way from Munnoo's birth in Calcutta and life there. Like so many other Indian slaves and servants,

Munnoo found that conversion to Christianity, other forms of Anglicization, and marriage with a British woman proved ways of settling successfully in Britain and altering his condition from slave to lower-middle-class
publican.

Conclusion

This chapter has examined the changes in the unequal power relationships between British masters and Indian servants and slaves as they moved
between India and Britain during the pre- and early colonial periods. Over
time, colonialism in many ways constrained Indians generally. Nevertheless,
expanding numbers of Indians, from a variety of backgrounds and classes,
made the voyage from colony to metropole, and sometimes back, within the
new arena created by the burgeoning British empire. Collectively, Indians in
Britain constituted a "counterflow" that increased modestly in velocity and
volume over the 250 years considered here, although it never matched the
far larger and more powerful flow outward from Europe of colonialism.
Tracing their lives, collectively and individually, enables us to consider expanding colonialism from the perspective of these marginalized peoples,
rather than from the conventional perspective of British or, to a lesser extent,
Indian elites.

Changes occurred in the status of the small but growing numbers of Indian servants and slaves who went to Britain over these centuries, including
in the attitudes of Britons toward them. From the beginnings of colonialism,
Indians in various degrees of servitude both faced new threats there and also
encountered opportunities not available to them in India. Living in Britain
also created new pressures and issues of identity, since the host culture expected considerable conformity to British cultural assertions by these Indians in their midst. Yet, by accepting Christianity and other forms of Anglicization, some could obtain emancipation. Of those who settled there, high
proportions married Britons.

In the seventeenth century, the relatively few Indian servants and slaves
in Britain could be valuable symbols of the exotic "oriental" that orna-
mented the households of the rival classes of "nabobs" and British aristocrats both. In some ways, Britons tended to regard them as similar in status
to Africans. Over that century and the next, however, as the numbers of Indians in Britain increased, they became less rare and their presence more
contentious. Both the British legal system and the East India Company's directors offered some types of protection, but also constraints on their movement, both to and from India. The systems of "permissions" and of "bonds"
served the directors as means of social control over these Indians as well as

over various classes of Britons. Especially by the early nineteenth century, for the East India Company's directors, these increasingly numerous Indians in Britain increasingly appeared to pose both moral and financial "problems."

By the mid-nineteenth century, the more rigid "racial" distinctions that had developed earlier in the colonies haltingly permeated the British homeland. By the late nineteenth century—beyond the scope of this chapter—the conflicts of 1857 in India and of 1865 in Jamaica, as well as the growth of Darwinian concepts in Britain, made "racial" difference appear to many Britons everywhere as biological, hereditary, and therefore immutable. This reduced the scope for agency available to Indians bound for Britain, especially those in various degrees of servitude.

Notes

I would like to thank Indrani Chatterjee and Paula Richman for valuable comments on earlier drafts of this chapter. The material in the chapter derives from my larger project, *Counterflows to Colonialism: Indian Travellers and Settlers in Britain, 1600–1857* (Delhi: Permanent Black, 2004).

1. For changes in slavery in India during the nineteenth century, see Indrani Chatterjee, "Abolition by Denial: The South Asian Example," in Gwyn Campbell, ed. *Abolition and Its Aftermath in the Indian Ocean, Africa, and Asia* (New York: Routledge, 2005), 150–68.

2. William Roger Louis, gen. ed., *Oxford History of the British Empire,* 5 vols. (Oxford: Oxford University Press, 1998–99). To date, the Companion series includes Philip D. Morgan and Sean Hawkins, eds., *Black Experience and the Empire* (Oxford: Oxford University Press, 2004); Philippa Levine, ed., *Gender and Empire* (Oxford: Oxford University Press, 2004); Kevin Kenny, ed., *Ireland and the British Empire* (Oxford: Oxford University Press, 2004); and Norman Etherington, ed., *Missions and Empire* (Oxford: Oxford University Press, 2005). For another effort at redress, see Kathleen Wilson, ed., *A New Imperial History: Culture, Identity, and Modernity in Britain and the Empire, 1660 1840* (Cambridge: Cambridge University Press, 2004).

3. Edward W. Said, *Orientalism* (New York: Vintage, 1978); and Mary Louise Pratt, *Imperial Eyes: Travel Writing and Transculturation* (London: Routledge, 1992). See also David Arnold, "European Orphans and Vagrants in India in the Nineteenth Century," *Journal of Imperial and Commonwealth History* 7 (1979), 104–27; and Linda Colley, *Captives* (New York: Pantheon, 2002).

4. This volume, and much other recent work by its various contributors, has deepened our understanding of non-elites by incorporating gendered identities as well as those of class and ethnicity. On "subalterns" generally, see Ranajit Guha et al., eds., *Subaltern Studies,* 11 vols. to date (Delhi: Oxford University Press, 1982–2000; Delhi: Permanent Black, 2000), particularly Indrani Chatterjee, "Colouring Subalternity: Slaves, Concubines, and Social Orphans under the East India Company," in Gautam Bhadra, Gyan Prakash, and Susie Tharu, eds., *Subaltern Studies X* (Delhi: Oxford University Press, 1999), 49–97.

5. For works considering Indians in Britain over the earlier period, see Rozina Visram, *Ayahs, Lascars, and Princes* (London: Pluto, 1986); idem, *Asians in Britain* (London: Pluto, 2002); and Michael H. Fisher, *Counterflows to Colonialism: Indian Travellers and Settlers in Britain, 1600–1857* (Delhi: Permanent Black, 2004). For the late nineteenth century and thereafter, see Antoinette Burton, *At the Heart of the Empire: Indians and the Colonial Encounter in Late-Victorian Britain* (Berkeley: University of California Press, 1998); Gauri Viswanathan, *Outside the Fold: Conversion, Modernity, and Belief* (Princeton, N.J.: Princeton University Press, 1998); and Shompa Lahiri, *Indians in Britain: Anglo-Indian Encounters, Race, and Identity, 1880–1930* (London: Frank Cass, 2000). For extensive studies of "Blacks" in Britain, but with a prime concern with people of African descent, see Peter Fryer, *Staying Power: The History of Black People in Britain* (London: Pluto, 1984); and Norma Myers, *Reconstructing the Black Past: Blacks in Britain, c. 1780–1830* (London: Frank Cass, 1996). For Indians, including those who were indentured laborers, elsewhere in the British Empire, see Crispin Bates, ed., *Community, Empire, and Migration: South Asians in Diaspora* (New York: Palgrave, 2001) and the works of that volume's contributors.

6. Exempt were Company officials and "menial servants" (almost all Europeans rather than Indians). This licensing continued for "natives of India" until 1813 when the Company lost its monopoly on trade with India. Court Minutes, October 17, 1651, and November 16, 1657, to April 14, 1813, British Library (hereinafter BL). For monetary equivalences see Lawrence H. Officer, "Comparing the Purchasing Power of Money in Great Britain from 1264 to 2002." Economic History Services, 2004, http://www.eh.net/hmit/ppowerbp/.

7. See Fryer, *Staying Power*.

8. Court Letters, May 4, 1683, cited in William Hedges, *Diary,* ed. Henry Yule, 2 vols. (London: Hakluyt Society, 1888), 2:357.

9. See the illustrations in Fisher, *Counterflows to Colonialism*.

10. While the Royal Navy generally regarded Asian seamen as lacking sufficient physical and moral strength to plunge themselves into battle, in practice the Navy impressed and hired substantial numbers of Indians, although this reflected its frequent desperation for manpower rather than its preference. Thus, for example, in 1749 at the end of the War of Austrian Succession, the Navy discharged and consigned to the Company for repatriation fifty-six Indian seamen who had survived its service. Court Minutes, November 1–8, 1749, December 6, 1749. This practice would continue. Court Minutes, May 27, 1807; Shipping Committee Minutes, August 21, 1813, to January 11, 1826, BL.

11. Court Minutes, December 31, 1667, BL.

12. E.g., Court Minutes, January 2–15, 1668, February 22, 1668, March 27, 1668, November 13–27, 1713, BL; and Officer, "Comparing the Purchasing Power."

13. Court Minutes, August 31, 1737, BL.

14. E.g., Court Minutes, January 13, 1671, BL.

15. See Catherine Hall, *Civilising Subjects: Metropole and Colony in the English Imagination, 1830–1867* (Chicago: University of Chicago Press, 2002); and Linda Colley, *Britons: Forging the Nation, 1707–1837* (New Haven: Yale University Press, 1992).

16. For discussion of conversion to Christianity as emancipating, in the case of two Africans, see Randy J. Sparks, *The Two Princes of Calabar: An Eighteenth-Century Atlantic Odyssey* (Cambridge, Mass.: Harvard University Press, 2004), 108–10.

17. Order of December 7, 1670, B/31 Court Book of Committees, April 1670 to April 1672, fol. 76, BL.

18. *Flying Post,* July 11–14, 1702, cited in A. F. Scott, *Every One a Witness* (London: White Lion, 1974), 231–32.

19. Officer, "Comparing the Purchasing Power."

20. *Daily Advertiser,* February 1, 1775, quoted in Visram, *Ayahs, Lascars, and Princes,* 13. For other advertisements see *Daily Advertiser,* July 12, 1777, March 3, 1775, August 26, 1776; *Morning Post and Daily Advertiser,* July 11, 1777.

21. Old Bailey Proceedings, October 14, 1724, http://www.oldbaileyonline.org, ref. t17241014-79; and Arthur L. Hayward, *Lives of the Most Remarkable Criminals* (London: Routledge, 1927), 175–77.

22. Baptism, November 26, 1745, St. James, Westminster, Westminster Archives Centre (hereinafter WAC).

23. Testimony of Catherine Bengall of St. Martin-in-the-Fields, July 23, 1746, in Jill Barber, *Celebrating the Black Presence* (London: Westminster Archives Centre, 2000), 2:25–34.

24. Petition of John Rippon, October 20, 1797, Home Public Consultations, May 1, 1798, no. 10, National Archives of India (hereinafter NAI).

25. Governor, St. Helena, to governor general, India, December 26, 1797, and reply, July 26, 1798, Home Public Consultations, May 1, 1798, nos. 9, 5, NAI.

26. Lascar Papers, vol. 1, fol. 120, BL; Officer, "Comparing the Purchasing Power."

27. The directors tried comparable bonds and other regulations to ensure that Indian seamen would depart Britain rapidly.

28. Court of directors to Fort William, March 17, 1769, para. 74 in NAI; and *Fort William—India House Correspondence,* 17 vols. (Delhi: NAI, various) 5:186.

29. See Tillman W. Nechtman, "Nabobs: Defining the Indian Empire and the British Nation in the Late Eighteenth Century" (Ph.D. diss., University of California, Los Angeles, 2005).

30. Home Public Consultations, January 5, 1798, no. 55, Extract Proceedings of Military Department, December 22, 1797, NAI; and Court Minutes, July 29, 1807, BL.

31. Court of directors to Fort William, July 12, 1782, para. 45, in *Fort William— India House Correspondence,* 9:58–59. See also Minutes of the Committee of Shipping, July 31, 1816, Resolution, BL; and Indrani Chatterjee, *Gender, Slavery, and Law in Colonial India* (New Delhi: Oxford University Press, 1999), especially chapter 5.

32. Officer, "Comparing the Purchasing Power."

33. Officers complained of the impossible financial hardship of taking a servant from India, especially for a junior or unwell or widowed European leaving India. Letter to editor from "Madras Subaltern," *Asiatic Journal and Monthly Register* 27 (Jan.–June 1829), 150–51. For a similar unsuccessful request for smaller bonds, see Bengal, General Proceedings, February 14, 1838, no. 58, West Bengal State Archives.

34. See Minutes of the Committee of Shipping for the extensive nature of this "problem." L/MAR/1 series, BL.

35. While Hickey's accounts must be read carefully and tested against other sources, his descriptions of these two men, and his quotations of their words, provide much of our evidence about them. His complete manuscript autobiography is MSS EUR G.118, BL. This was extensively edited and published as William Hickey,

Memoirs of William Hickey, ed. Alfred Spencer, 4 vols., 3rd ed. (London: Hurst and Blackett, 1919–25). I quote the manuscript, but for ease of access, I use the pagination of the published edition.

36. Auriol held posts under the East India Company's Bengal administration, but does not seem to have been a formal member of its civil or military service. Letter from court, June 25, 1793, and letter to court, May 15, 1795, in *Fort William—India House Correspondence*, 12:62, 463.

37. Interestingly, Hickey was jealous of many of the "nabobs," or Britons who returned from India excessively rich, whom he met in England. Yet Hickey's own memoirs reveal that many of the people he met in England regarded Hickey himself as a "nabob."

38. Hickey, *Memoirs*, 3:150.

39. Ibid., 2:228.

40. Ibid., 2:232.

41. Ibid., 2:238–39.

42. Ibid., 2:246.

43. Ibid., 3:150.

44. Ibid., 2:275.

45. We should note that these were new clothes made for Hickey, but ones that did not meet his standard of workmanship and quality. Ibid., 2:281.

46. Ibid., 2:292–93.

47. Ibid., 2:293.

48. Ibid., 3:150–51.

49. We should remember that Hickey wrote his memoirs with Munnoo in attendance, so their continuing relationship may have shaped his perspectives on Munnoo favorably. Ibid., 4:376, 398.

50. Ibid., 4:399.

51. Journal of Castle Eden, L/MAR/B/296D, BL.

52. Hickey, *Memoirs*, 4:405–406.

53. Ibid., 4:467.

54. Ibid., 4:467–68.

55. Ibid., 4:473; *Beaconsfield Parish Register*, February 27, 1809, 112.

56. She was christened exactly five years after Munnew. Beaconsfield parish church, baptismal records, February 27, 1814.

57. At 19 Manchester Building, Parliament Street. See M. Boyle, compiler, *Boyle's Fashionable Court and Country Guide* (London: Saunders and Otley, various) for those years; Westminster Ratebook, 1818; and Westminster Poll Book 1820, WAC.

58. This portrait was displayed in a Royal Academy exhibition of 1820; it is presently hanging in the halls of Parliament, on loan from the National Portrait Gallery. See Richard Walker, *Regency Portraits*, 2 vols. (London: National Portrait Gallery, 1985), 1:249; 2:574.

59. William Munnew, born December 10, 1820; christened January 5, 1821, St. Mary Magdalen, Richmond, Surrey, International Genealogical Index.

60. Burial certificate, St. John Evangelist, Smith Square, February 10, 1827, WAC.

61. They lived at 93 Norton Street and then settled for many years at 41 Foley Street. Marriage certificate, June 7, 1840, Trinity Church, St. Marylebone. While living there, they had six daughters and four sons. See Great Britain, 1851–81 Census; International Genealogical Index; and Great London Records Office.

9

Bharattee's Death: Domestic Slave-Women in Nineteenth-Century Madras

Sylvia Vatuk

On the 28th of January, 1828, a Muslim noblewoman, a close relative of the nawab of the Karnataka,[1] was charged with having beaten to death—with the help of three young slave-girls—another of her slaves, a somewhat older woman named Bharattee (Bharati).[2] The three girls—Nekqadam, Nargis, and Gulshabs—were immediately taken into custody, while their mistress was allowed to remain free on bail, though ordered to be kept under close watch within the confines of the nawab's Chepauk Palace until the trial. On April 21 of that year the case, *The King vs. Fakr Unnissa Begum and Others*, was heard before Chief Justice Ralph Palmer of the Supreme Court at Madras.[3] (See map 2.) By this time the original charge of murder had been reduced to manslaughter. At the trial, the prosecution presented a number of witnesses to testify to the events leading up to the slave-woman's demise, the disposal of her corpse in a shallow grave on the beach, its discovery and disinterment by an officer of the nawab's police force, his reporting of this to the town police, and the examination of the badly decomposed body by the acting coroner of the town and a local medical doctor.

The advocate general of the presidency, Herbert Compton, was instructed to defend the accused slave-girls, for whom he submitted a plea of not guilty. But he called no defense witnesses nor put the accused girls themselves on the stand.[4] The jury[5] deliberated for two hours and returned a guilty verdict, creating "some surprise among the audience,"[6] but further recommended the girls "to the merciful consideration of the Court." Justice Palmer complied. From the outset, he had hesitated "to proceed with the trial [of the slave-girls] on account of [their] extreme youth,"[7] "the eldest of the prisoners appearing to be about the age of 14, the second about 10 or 11 and the youngest not exceeding 7 or 8 years."[8] The three were held until noon of the following day and then "discharged"—whether to the custody of their erstwhile mistress (or someone else) or simply to fend for themselves is not clear.[9]

Fakhr al-Nissa Begam herself did not appear before the tribunal. Thomas Teed, the East India Company solicitor appointed to defend her, had initially asked that, as a strictly secluded woman of elevated rank, she be tried in absentia. The justices refused, finding no precedent in British law for according her such special treatment. So, on the advice of the advocate general, he had her submit a plea of guilty and then, within a day of receiving the court's verdict on the slave-girls, he forwarded through James Lushington, Government Agent to Chepauk, a petition from the begam to King George IV in which she protested her innocence of the crime.[10] She explained that she had pled guilty simply in order to avoid the shame of being "forced from the Sanctuary" of seclusion in which she had always lived and exposed "to the unhallowed gaze of men" at a public hearing.[11] In regard to the substance of the charge, she acknowledged that she and her alleged accomplices had indeed "chastised" Bharati on the day in question but denied that the "gentle blows" they inflicted could possibly have caused the slave's demise. That actually was the result of a fatal illness from which, unbeknownst to the begam at the time, she had long been suffering. Whether the king of England found Fakhr al-Nissa's explanation convincing or simply considered it politically expedient to accede to her plea, the pardon she sought was granted within the year.[12]

This case raises a multitude of fascinating issues, but I have chosen here to focus on what it reveals about the on-the-ground realities of domestic slavery in India in the early nineteenth century, something about which, recent contributions to the literature notwithstanding, we still know very little.[13] In contrast to the circumstances under which another now well-known "subaltern" woman met her end twenty years later,[14] the events surrounding Bharati's death are comparatively well and richly documented. This is not because Bharati herself was of any intrinsic importance to those responsible for producing and preserving the relevant records but rather because she, unlike Chandra, had been victimized by a member of the extended family of the Karnataka nawabs, by someone of at least indirect political consequence to the government of the Madras Presidency. I will show how a close reading of this archive reveals details about domestic slavery in India that have been mostly hidden from the historian's view. Such a reading also provides an opportunity to contribute to discussions of modes of slave "resistance" (especially by women) that have recently preoccupied scholars working on the history of slavery in other parts of the world. Finally, it enables me to place these issues within the context of a prevailing colonial discourse on Indian domestic slavery that represented it as a relatively benign institution—certainly by comparison with New World slavery—and therefore one not in urgent need of abolition.

Reading the Archive

It is possible to construct from the records of this case a fairly complete account of the events immediately preceding Bharati's death and an even fuller account of what transpired afterward.[15] The documents, taken together, provide a dialogue—or better, a "multilogue"—on the case, among many persons, each differently positioned in relation to it. The archive opens with a communication from the Madras superintendent of police (Major W. Ormsby) to the Government Agent, reporting that the body of a "moor" (Muslim) woman has been found buried in the sand on the ocean shore in front of Chepauk Palace, several of the nawab's guards having been observed, two nights before, in the act of carrying it to that place. This is followed by transcripts of depositions taken by the police from some female members of the begam's household and a male attendant of the nawab and the apparently verbatim testimony of these individuals and others before the Supreme Court that spring. The text of the begam's petition for royal clemency, an itemized bill from the company solicitor for services rendered on her behalf, some correspondence concerning the strategy to be followed with respect to her defense, and four letters from the nawab regent—two of them addressed to the king of England—complete the evidence.

A variety of voices speak through these texts. While Indian voices predominate, and among them "subaltern" voices are amply represented, it is the British who speak with most assurance. Not surprisingly, they have not only the first but also the last word. Furthermore, they have the advantage of owning those words in a way that none of the Indians do. They alone are allowed to speak in their own tongue, all of the Indian voices having been obscured in the process of translation and most of them further distorted by being forced into a narrative style that is formal, legalistic, and testimonial. They are heard even more darkly through the glass of the third-person form in which they are rendered. For example, the slave-girl Nekqadam's deposition begins, "This Informant being examined upon her Oath saith, that on Sunday the 20th Instant about twelve Oclock in the day by order of her Mistress . . . ," etc.[16] Even the begam's petition is couched in the third person, the Government Agent having appropriated the first-person voice for himself:

"she throws herself upon your Royal mercy and confidently trusts that you … will pronounce your petitioner's pardon."[17] Doubtless the Agent edited her original oral statement and made interpolations of his own, but the resulting text is so constructed that it is impossible to separate the two voices.

Of the four slaves whose lives were most affected by the events of that day, only two are heard to speak. One is the young Nekqadam in her initial statement to the police. The other, ironically, is Bharati herself, though at a remove, i.e., in the testimony of two other slaves, the begam's cook, Wafadar, and her seamstress, Shabrang, both of whom report hearing Bharati cry out more than once during her ordeal, "*tauba! tauba!*" ("I repent!").[18] She and the three accused, almost entirely silenced by their gender and their condition of servitude, epitomize (to paraphrase Gayatri Spivak's by now somewhat outworn phrase) the virtual inability of the subaltern woman to make herself heard in official documents of this kind.[19]

Piecing together from these documents a narrative of the events leading up to Bharati's untimely death, we learn that several months before that day two of Fakhr al-Nissa Begam's young slave-girls had disappeared from the house, Bharati herself being also nowhere to be found. Her mistress suspected that Bharati had "inveigled away and sold" the girls. Bharati was later "apprehended" (without the girls) and brought back to the Triplicane house. The begam confined her to a room and, in exercise of "her rights as a head of a family" and in accordance with her understanding of both Islamic and British law,[20] subjected her to a course of physical punishment that lasted many weeks. Wafadar testified that

> Bhurrattee some months ago enticed away two slave girls and sold them and she was brought back to the House four Months ago and Khaderbee[21] was very angry and struck the Woman and Confined her, and from that time the Woman used to be occasionally tied up and flogged by Khaderbee herself with billets of firewood, and some times she gave orders to the other slave girls to flog her.[22]

On the day before she died, Bharati made an unsuccessful second attempt to leave the begam's house. In retaliation for this, sometime before noon on the 28th of January, the begam called Bharati into the main room, the "hall," of her house and, according to Nekqadam, ordered her to be tied again, "with a rope which is used for drawing water." She took up a stick of firewood and proceeded to hit the woman with it. Then she made Nekqadam, Gulshabs, and Nargis join her in battering Bharati "on her back bottom and sides of her body … until about two hours to sun set when she was untied."[23] When they appeared in court, the two eyewitnesses confirmed the begam's assertion that their blows were "gentle": the children administered most of them, the begam herself, in the words of her petition, hitting Bharati only two or three times with "her own aged arms."[24] Shabrang, in what appears as an attempt to exonerate the begam, explains to the court that "I and the cook could have given more of a beating . . . but we were not ordered [to do so]. If the Begum had chosen she could have put the little girls aside [and asked us to take over]."[25]

But during Bharati's ordeal the two older slave-women, by their own account, tried to stay out of sight. As Shabrang explained,

> I was in another room sewing cloths and heard the cry . . . about midday. Immediately after . . . I went to a door, between two partitions. And I saw Bhurrattee in the hall . . . and the Begum and the three prisoners were beating her with firewood. I only just peeped in and came away.[26]

Later the begam ordered Bharati untied and called for Wafadar to bring water to the obviously injured woman, who was by then slumped silently on the floor. When night fell the cook was again called, this time to help the slave-girls carry Bharati into the room in which she had previously been confined. A few hours later one of them tried to rouse her and, unable to get any response, alerted her mistress. The begam, realizing that Bharati was dead, began "crying, and [was] much afraid," and asked over and over again, "Why did it happen? Why did she die?"[27]

It was now around midnight. Fakhr al-Nissa instructed Nekqadam to fetch the manservant, Shams al-Din, and have him dispose of the body. He called four other men—one of whom was later identified as Bharati's paramour—to assist him in burying her in a shallow grave on the nearby beach. One of his helpers, frightened by what he had seen, hurried to alert the nawab regent, who immediately sent one of his officers to investigate. The latter disinterred the corpse and promptly informed the town police. From that point on the investigation led swiftly to the arrest of the begam and her attendants. Shams al-Din had prudently fled the scene and, as far as we can tell, was never apprehended, though two of his companions were subpoenaed to testify for the prosecution.

In her original deposition, the begam's cook unselfconsciously used the term "slave" for herself, Bharati, Shabrang, and the three accused girls, specifically contrasting their civil status with that of another woman-worker: '[Witness deposes that] . . . herself and five other servants woman [*sic*] are the slaves of Khaderbee . . . and a free woman named Kulleemah was also in [her] Service."[28] The begam, in her petition to the king, was allowed by the Government Agent to forthrightly call a slave a slave. The nawab similarly used the term in his communications, as did the superintendent of police in writing to the chief secretary to government, Robert Clive, to report "the case of an alledged murder of a female slave, late in the Service of . . . a Nicka daughter[29] of the late Nabob Walajah."[30] Only in the English translation of their court testimony is the fact obscured that the principal players in this drama are slaves: the chief witnesses are there made to refer to themselves and the other women involved simply as "servants" or as women "in the Begam's service."[31]

In fact, slavery was very much taken for granted in Madras at this time; domestic slaves were a ubiquitous presence in aristocratic Muslim households.[32] Female and sometimes castrated male slaves served in the *zanana* or *haram,* the secluded women's quarters of a nobleman's home, where his daughters, wives, and concubines lived their lives as *pardanishin* or *goshanishin,*[33] ideally shielded completely from contact with unrelated males. The size of a man's *haram,* the variety of women it contained, the lavishness of its appointments, and the number of slaves that staffed it were all key measures of a Karnataka nobleman's honor and prestige, just as they were elsewhere in India among those of comparable wealth and status.

The Karnataka had been annexed in 1801 and the British had persuaded one of the two principal candidates for the now merely titular position of nawab to accept in exchange a one-fifth share of the annual revenue of his family's erstwhile territories. Other members of the family—of both sexes—were awarded annual stipends in amounts that varied according to their kinship to Nawab Muhammad ʿAli Walajah and their "purity" of birth (mainly gauged by whether they were [or their mothers had been] primary or secondary wives or slave-concubines). Most received sufficient income to support large numbers of dependent relatives, retainers, and slaves. In 1812, a widow of Muhammad ʿAli claimed that she supported two hundred "female relations and servants" on a stipend of Rs. 5000 per annum.[34] An elderly *nikahi* son of Muhammad ʿAli had a lower stipend and a smaller establishment of only twenty-six persons when he died in 1820. But of these, nine were female slaves and ten were slave-concubines.[35]

Slaves were obtained from a variety of sources. The international overseas slave trade, still active at this time in the Indian Ocean and Persian Gulf, brought Africans and others to be sold as slaves in India and took Indians to be sold in Arabia, Turkey, and elsewhere.[36] The nawabs of the Karnataka and others had Turkish, "Habshi," and "Circassian" slave-women from such sources.[37] However, most of their slaves were acquired through a local trade, as poverty-stricken parents sold their own children, destitute adults sold themselves, and husbands sold their wives[38] in order to avoid starvation, especially in periods of scarcity or famine.[39] There were also other suppliers of slaves, as was suggested by the superintendent of police in Madras, A. D. Campbell, in 1818:[40]

His Highness the Nabob . . . the various branches of his family, and indeed the whole of the principal Mussulmans at Madras, were in the habit of purchasing children to serve as domestic slaves in their families, and . . . to supply this demand certain native women made a trade of child stealing.[41]

But the records reveal nothing about how Bharati came to Fakhr al-Nissa Begam's establishment. The fact that she bears a name of Sanskrit derivation suggests that she was not a child when she was sold into slavery, for when a child slave entered an elite Muslim household she (or he) was normally given a new, Persianate name and raised in the Muslim faith, along with other youngsters in the family.[42] So how should we understand the initial official identification of Bharati's corpse as that of a Muslim woman? Clothing found on the body could have led the police to this conclusion. But since one of the slave-girls who participated in her ordeal describes Bharati as having had "nothing on her body only a Petticoat" at the time of her death,[43] this is doubtful. Nothing in the testimony suggests that her corpse had been prepared for a Muslim burial, and the speed with which its disposal was accomplished makes this unlikely in any case. Perhaps this preliminary identification was made simply because her body was found on the edge of a Muslim burial ground, next to the abode of a local *faqir* (a Muslim mendicant).

The documents do not provide many other details about Bharati herself. We do learn from Wafadar's testimony that she was about thirty years old "and strong" at the time of her death.[44] And the Madras police superintendent's initial report contains the intriguing piece of information that the dead woman "is stated to have been in the keeping of Hossain, a Sepoy in the service of His Highness the Prince Azim Jah."[45] But no further mention is made of this relationship and it is difficult to determine how it fits into the larger narrative of Bharati's untimely death. Few, if any, of the female slaves in the households of the Walajah nobility seem to have been married,[46] though it was not uncommon for a slave-woman to be used sexually by her master or even to bear his child.[47] Occasionally, one whom he particularly favored might attain the somewhat elevated status of *haram* ("slave-concubine")[48] or, in the very rare case, be taken in marriage.[49] But both Persian and British sources are mostly silent about the sexual lives of others.

While the work that they did allowed male slaves to move fairly freely outside the home, female slaves—like their masters' wives and daughters— were normally secluded within the *zanana*. The British perceived such seclusion as confinement. According to Campbell, female slaves,

purchased whilst infants . . . [are] employed in the seraglio or haram of the richer Muslims, to attend on their ladies; and once there enclosed, they are seldom allowed egress from it, as they are viewed as part of that establishment, which it is the chief point of honour with a Muslim to guard from the view of another.[50]

If this description is accurate, it would seem that, without the master's or mistress's knowledge and consent, it would have been both difficult and extremely risky for a slave-woman to engage in a liaison with a man living outside the household to which she was attached. If Bharati had indeed been "seldom allowed egress" from her mistress's home and Hossain (correctly, Hussain) not permitted entry to that exclusively female space, how could they have managed to cultivate and maintain an amorous relationship? Was Bharati's mistress aware of the relationship and, if so, had she sanctioned it? Was it because of Hussain that Bharati wanted to escape her mistress's home? Was he instrumental in helping her to leave? Did the begam's awareness—or recent discovery—of Bharati's love affair contribute to the excessive fury with which she punished the runaway?

In a different connection, the testimony of the begam's cook casts further doubt on Campbell's generalizations about the extent to which slave-women were invariably closely confined to the home. Wafadar clearly suggests that Fakhr al-Nissa's slaves were expected, at least on occasion, to move outside her home when she says that, from time to time, she might have "taken a message . . . [or] gone to a shop" for her mistress.[51] Was it typical practice in the households of the Walajah nobility to send female slaves on errands of this kind or did the fact that this was an all-female household, headed by a strictly *goshahnishin* woman, give her slaves more mobility than others enjoyed? Perhaps the only way to begin to answer some of these questions is to learn more about her mistress's household in its entirety.

The Mistress and Her Household

Fakhr al-Nissa Begam was the eleventh daughter of Nawab Muhammad 'Ali Walajah,[52] the eldest of four girls born to her mother, Zaib al-Nissa, a Turkish slave brought to Madras from Mecca around 1770. Zaib al-Nissa was raised and educated by a niece of the nawab and a few years later became his *nikahi* wife. In an 1810 court deposition, an elderly servant of the late nawab described this wedding as accompanied by "great Pomp and Ceremony."[53] Such a highly unusual honor given to a slave-bride, if the report is true, reflects her husband's exceptional regard for her. His relatives, however, were not so willing to overlook Zaib al-Nissa's origins. For example, the estranged husband of one of her daughters once complained to the British that the nawab had forced him and her three other sons-in-law, completely against their wills, to marry "these women born of Slaves."[54]

Fakhr al-Nissa's birthdate is not known but, as brides usually commenced childbearing almost immediately after marriage, her birth probably occurred in the mid- to late 1770s. In this case, she would have been in her forties in 1828. In her petition she refers to herself as "aged," but the meaning of that term is culturally and historically very variable. Furthermore, she describes herself in these terms in order to support her claim to be too frail to have inflicted serious injury on her slave.[55]

Fakhr al-Nissa's date of marriage is not recorded either. Her father arranged her marriage to a cousin[56] and also arranged and supervised the nuptials of her three younger sisters before his death in 1795. Since girls in aristocratic Muslim families typically married around puberty, it is probable that Fakhr al-Nissa's wedding took place in the late 1780s.[57] In any event, the couple was estranged by 1816. On the grounds that she was refusing to support him, her husband had persuaded the British to pay Rs. 100, a quarter of her pension, directly to him each month.[58] When he died in 1821 he left two other widows and eleven children, seven by these women and four by a deceased concubine. One of his daughters was already married, suggesting that one or more of these relationships had begun long before he became "self-supporting."[59]

So at the time of the event, 1828, the begam was a widow. Since 1801 she had been a woman of independent means, receiving a pension in her own name as a *nikahi* daughter of Muhammad ʿAli Walajah. Unlike most women of her class, she lived essentially on her own, with no male kinsman to manage her extra-domestic affairs, protect her modesty, or control her movements. Even her sole manservant lived elsewhere.[60] The sources make no mention of offspring. Young adult Walajah males rarely had any independent sources of income while their parents were alive and therefore had to rely on the latter for support.[61] If the begam had had a son, or even a son-in-law, he would almost certainly have lived with her or at least been drawn into her legal difficulties during the spring of 1828.[62]

Fakhr al-Nissa's household consisted, in addition to herself, of six female slaves and one free serving woman. Among the slaves there was apparently a fairly clear division of labor. The six were also differentially compensated: Wafadar received board and lodging and a rupee a month, while Bharati got only "food and cloth."[63] Two of the adult slave-women did the cooking and the sewing. Three children swept the house and massaged their mistress's limbs.[64] There is no information about Bharati's assignments or those of the free servant. As the begam's cook, Wafadar did not prepare meals for her fellow slaves. Someone else (not named) prepared their meals, a daily allotment of "rice and curry."[65] Wafadar's testimony also indicates that a slave was not expected to do tasks assigned to others. If she were so imposed upon, she says, she would pretend that she "doesn't know how," rather than risk retaliation by refusing directly.

Some months before the incident that brought her to the notice of the Supreme Court, Fakhr al-Nissa had moved, without the nawab's permission, to a rented house in nearby Triplicane. It is perhaps significant that in 1810 her own widowed mother had set a precedent for this act of female insubordination by similarly moving out of the palace compound with a number of junior members of her immediate family, including Fakhr al-Nissa Begam and her husband. That move had triggered a raid on the house by members of the Nawab 'Azim al-Daula's guard, who brought the entire group back to Chepauk, where they were confined to quarters until her sons-in-law were able to persuade the Supreme Court to intervene.[66]

On this occasion the nawab regent had not responded so decisively to his aunt's challenge. But in an 1829 communication to the king of England he did express his extreme displeasure with her. He wrote that a female family member's residence outside the walls of Chepauk Garden, where she could not be "subjected to such proper degree of restraint as by the custom of Mussulman princes is imposed on the female Members of their families,"[67] cast a serious blot upon his own honor and on that of the entire royal family. It was particularly ironic then that a slave-born mistress—the begam—who had herself fled from the "paternal" custody of her grand-nephew, would be both so watchful about retaining custody of her own slaves, and so vengeful toward the one who sought to evade it.

The Official Handling of the Case

For over seventy years the Karnataka nawabs and the British had been at odds over how much and what kind of authority they should be permitted to exercise over junior members of their "families,"[68] especially over their women and their slaves. For the nawab regent, his great-aunt's arrest and the Supreme Court's demand that it try her, rather than allow her to be privately disciplined by him or his own Islamic court of judicature (*mahkama*),[69] were clear instances of unwarranted interference in his "domestic" affairs. If she were guilty, he should be the one to inflict any punishment. He appears to have thought the begam quite capable of having killed Bharati, conceding in one of his letters that she was a woman accustomed to behaving with extreme "cruelty and profligacy." But he absolved her from any real blame by framing the problem as one of feminine excess, for which the British, having consistently undermined his "paternal authority" over her and other women of his family, were largely responsible.[70] In any event, by the time he received the news of Fakhr al-Nissa's pardon he had either accepted her claim of innocence, or decided that he had more to gain in the long term by pretending that he did.[71]

In its response to the case, British officialdom did not speak with a single voice. While the superintendent of police and the magistrate were determined to take the begam into custody and keep her there, the Government Agent, having secured the "solemn pledge" of the nawab to guard her well, managed to forestall this. The justices wanted her tried in person, but most of the others in positions of authority were persuaded that to force a woman of such elevated rank, accustomed to a life of strict seclusion, to appear in court would cause her and the entire Walajah family irredeemable disgrace. As Advocate General Compton put it, to subject "a female and a princess" to such ignominy would be utterly "revolting to the feelings of His Highness and the whole Mahomedan population."[72] On this basis he convinced the Supreme Court to dispense with the requirement that she appear personally to request bail and began strenuous efforts to develop a strategy to enable her to avoid prosecution. According such special treatment to a woman of high social status was not unprecedented. Indeed, one of the documents used to gain the Supreme Court's cooperation on the bail matter was an 1821 letter from Henry Chamier, secretary to the government of Madras, to the effect that "the appearance of females in the Court of Justice" was always to be dealt with according to "the judgement and feelings of [the local] Society." No improvement of the customs of the country could ever atone for "disturb[ing] such usages and do[ing] violence to the feelings on which they are founded."[73] A variety of documents were requisitioned from government archives to help validate the nawab's claim to "sovereign authority" over members of his own "household" and to clarify "the considered rights of authority over [slaves] amongst the highest orders of Mahomedans."[74] Ultimately Compton decided to recommend that the begam plead guilty and later apply for clemency.

British Slavery Policy in India

In 1828 slavery was alive and well in British India, despite fifty years of anti-slavery activity and the passage of legislation banning slave holding in Britain and prohibiting the buying, selling, or transporting of slaves within or among most of Britain's overseas possessions.[75] Since the turn of the century there had been growing unease about the matter of Indian slavery. A number of local regulations were passed, including several in the Madras Presidency that aimed to restrict the slave trade and limit the rights of owners over their slaves. One of these was Madras Regulation VIII of 1802, which made the intentional murder of a slave a capital offense.[76] Presumably it was initiated because of incidents that had attracted public notice. But, not surprisingly, it did not prevent the continued abuse and killing of slaves.[77] Campbell tells of "receiv[ing] some complaints" in 1816 against Nawab 'Azim al-Daula

> [that] left on my mind a strong impression of the cruelty and wanton barbarity with which ... female slaves were subject to be treated.... [T]he seclusion of female slaves ... too often precludes complaint, prevents redress, and cloaks crimes at which Europeans would shudder.[78]

He neither specifies the nature of the abuses, indicates who was responsible, nor tells how he dealt with them. But the context of his remarks, added to the fact that the incidents are not mentioned in official records of the period, suggests that the nawab was never called to account. Later, when Campbell was magistrate of Bellary, he learned that the brother of the nawab of Kurnool had been responsible for the deaths of two slave-girls but never prosecuted for the killings.[79] In frustration he complained that, although under the law it was a capital crime to kill a slave, a civil magistrate such as he did not have the power "to interfere for [her] due protection."[80]

A few colonial officials, including Campbell, had been pressing the governments of their respective presidencies to take stronger action against slavery.[81] And British and American abolitionists had begun a major effort to draw the attention of an international public to the evils of Indian slavery.[82] One indication of their success was the printing by the House of Commons, in late 1828, of a large volume of official correspondence on the subject.[83] But British Indian officialdom displayed considerable reluctance to attack slavery directly. Even those who professed to be personally appalled by slavery tended to favor a gradual approach, mainly on the ground that to take precipitous action would alienate the "native" elite, who depended so heavily on slave holding for their domestic comfort and social prestige.

In the discourse on domestic slavery in India, the notion that it was a relatively mild institution was a common theme. Indian domestic slaves were said to be treated almost as members of their owners' families. Even Campbell, who, as we have seen, was sharply critical of the treatment of domestic slaves by the Muslim nobility in Madras, elsewhere describes them as "rather ... humble members [of the family] by adoption than its servants or slaves."[84] Others emphasized that for the Indian nobleman the main value of slaves was symbolic: their possession "is a mark of affluence and station in society ... part of the pomp with which the great men of the country delight to surround themselves."[85] Not being concerned with maximum labor extraction, the argument went, slave owners had no reason not to treat their slaves kindly. Some observers acknowledged that slaves were sometimes mistreated but saw these incidents as "aberrations," not as symptoms of a systematic problem. They therefore urged that government find ways to deal with these "occasional" instances of "excessive" cruelty, not try to abolish the institution altogether.

Slavery was also believed by many to have a positive social function in a society with widespread and intractable poverty, where public institutions capable of providing adequately for the care and feeding of destitute persons were lacking. Slavery in this setting, they felt, constituted a kind of welfare measure, giving the poor and those afflicted by famine an acceptable alternative to death by starvation. Therefore, any attempts at abolition would be resisted not only by slave owners but by slaves themselves, few of whom would want to exchange their present secure situations for the uncertainty of a life of liberty. In the words of the Indian Law Commission:

> if the abuses to which Slavery gives rise in this country cannot be prevented otherwise than by its abolition, then Slavery ought to be abolished. But we think that the abuses can be otherwise prevented, with such a degree of certainty as to justify us in not advising the emancipation of the slaves . . . an unnecessary and very unpopular interference with the interest, as understood by themselves, both of masters and slaves.[86]

No doubt there was some truth to all of these arguments. In all probability the conditions under which most domestic slaves lived were tolerable, if not ideal, and since the practical alternatives were few and mostly unattractive, they were inclined to submit and make the best of their situation. But Bharati was neither the first nor the last to seek a way out.

The judicial records of all three presidencies for the early decades of the nineteenth century contain numerous cases involving slavery-related issues: disputes over the ownership of slaves or over the civil status of alleged slaves, demands for the return of runaways, and criminal prosecutions for extreme cruelty toward slaves or their killing, for their illegal transport, and for the kidnapping and sale of free persons into slavery.[87] These provide abundant evidence that not all slaves were averse to seeking improvements in their lives, even if they could not always achieve outright freedom from bondage. The number of cases is not large enough to permit definitive generalizations but the evidence suggests that physical cruelty and escape attempts were often, if not invariably, closely linked. Slaves either ran away because of mistreatment, were mistreated because they had tried to escape, or both. Runaways who came to the notice of the law were predominantly female and those responsible for the maltreatment were often female as well.

The Issue of "Slave Resistance"

In the recent literature on slavery in other parts of the world, the issue of "slave resistance" has been a central theme. Some of the earliest archival work on the subject was prompted by a desire to counter the arguments of those who, to support their claim that plantation slavery in the American South was not an extremely cruel institution, cited the apparent absence or rarity of slave revolts. These revisionist scholars also wished to discredit the notion that, whether because they had no reason or inclination to resist or because they had few opportunities and no practical means of doing so, New World slaves generally accepted their condition. They were successful in documenting the fact that armed slave rebellions had indeed occurred with some frequency during the pre–Civil War period.[88]

Once this was established, other researchers began to investigate forms of slave "resistance" short of organized insurrection,[89] including such commonplace, everyday acts as "[t]heft, foot dragging, short-term flight, and feigning illness" and other devious or subversive behaviors that one can interpret as "hidden or indirect expressions of dissent, quiet ways of reclaiming a measure of control over goods, time, or parts of one's life."[90] While not necessarily claiming that "resistance"—as defined in this broader sense—inevitably occurs wherever slavery is practiced, most scholars of the African and New World slave experience agree that in the times and places they have investigated it was at least part of the story and one that warrants further examination.

In the nineties, feminist historians began to look specifically at women's experience under slavery and to identify gender differences in the modes of "resistance" employed. It has been suggested, for example, that women were more likely to use what James Scott has famously called "weapons of the weak"[91] than to resort to confrontational or violent methods. Furthermore, women tended to act as individuals, rather than in concert with others.[92] Thus female slaves were not represented in significant numbers among those who participated in organized armed revolts. Nor did slave-women run away to find freedom in some distant place as frequently as men did.[93] When their situations became intolerable they would more often become short-term "truants," leaving to seek temporary respite, usually in the immediate vicinity, until forced by hunger or betrayal to return and face the inevitable punishment.[94] These observations have significant resonances with the case I am analyzing here.

In the third decade of the nineteenth century Indian slave owners like Fakhr al-Nissa were still in a position to exercise almost unlimited power of life and limb over their slaves. Most slaves had entered that condition as young children. Given the usual practices of female seclusion in Muslim households, girls in particular had little opportunity to become well enough acquainted with the world outside their home to seriously contemplate leaving it. Bharati may not have been as disadvantaged as most others in this respect, if I am correct in surmising that she was already grown when sold into slavery and that she even had an unusual degree of freedom of movement within captivity by virtue of her mistress's unique personal situation. But when she became emboldened to try to leave her mistress, and was apparently caught doing so, she paid with her life.

Yet what her mistress charged her with was not simply her own flight but the far graver crime of taking away and selling two child slaves belonging to her household and thus, in juristic terms, causing the begam serious economic injury. We have no independent evidence to enable us to either prove or disprove this charge against Bharati. It is conceivable that she did sell the slave-girls, perhaps in an attempt to finance her own emancipation. Such an act would not have been entirely unexpected in a region and a social context in which older female slaves as well as the slave-born were known to buy and own slaves (see Sumit Guha's essay in this volume). But we cannot rule out the possibility that the child slaves fled on their own initiative, or were kidnapped or promised succor by people outside the begam's household, and Bharati incurred the blame for their disappearance. If we believe this alternative, then it becomes even more obvious that the organization of this slave-using milieu made every slave's active resistance to servitude extremely dangerous for other slaves within the household.

The begam's power over the slaves, and her practice of pitting one slave against another, are well illustrated in the conflicting nature of the testimony given by the slaves at different times. For example, in their initial depositions both cook and seamstress described in lurid detail the begam's harsh treatment of Bharati. Thus Wafadar "has no doubt that the ill usage given by Khaderbee was the cause of the woman's death."[95] But later the same woman testifies that her mistress struck Bharati very gently and only a few times, leaving most of the beating to the little girls. And Shabrang now maintains that "I don't know the cause of [Bharati's] death . . . people said she had boils."[96] Clearly, by the time the trial started, the two had been made aware that there could be serious negative repercussions if they dared to implicate the begam too directly in Bharati's murder.

This structure of authority, upheld by fear, clearly prevented the necessary affective preconditions for cooperative action from developing among these slaves of very disparate origins who toiled side by side in the same household. Note the behavior of Bharati's peers during her final ordeal.

Rather than trying to intervene on her behalf, they were careful to stay out of sight until summoned to remove her lifeless body. In such a milieu, it is understandable that each woman should remain desperately individualist in her resistance. This is precisely the tragedy of Bharati's death. If indeed Bharati rebelled, she did so as an individual, rather than making a concerted effort, together with a cohort of women sharing common interests, to attack either the system of slavery itself or their particularly cruel mistress. The act of which Bharati was accused—stealing away and selling two young fellow-slaves for personal profit—can be seen as exemplifying the extreme individuality and self-interestedness that such a milieu engendered. Another issue that remains only dimly perceptible in the evidence presented here is the impact, on those other slaves who observed or participated in them, of such spectacles of corporal punishment as those inflicted upon Bharati by the begam. Perhaps these slave-women's inner worlds could be better studied through non-judicial records but, unfortunately, no such documents are available to us, nor are they likely to exist.

Such desperate isolation of slave-women from one another would also help to explain their apparent preference for indirect and evasive acts of resistance: recall Wafadar's telling the court how she would respond if told to do tasks that fell outside the scope of her regular duties. Female slaves in other times and places have been shown to have used such strategies when demands were placed upon them that they considered unreasonable. This cross-cultural similarity in women's responses to captivity suggests the importance, in future studies of domestic slavery in nineteenth-century India, of comparisons with other historical slaveholding societies, in terms of their prevailing household structures and patterns of same-sex interaction.

Conclusion

I have here described, and placed within its broader social and historical context, a legal case involving issues of control over domestic slaves that were central to the interplay between the British colonial power and indigenous former ruling elites in India in the early part of the nineteenth century. I have shown how, among the local Muslim nobility of Madras, the "patriarchal" authority exercised by slave owners (male and female) over their slaves was practically unlimited. Whereas in the prevailing colonial discourse Indian slavery was seen as a relatively harmless institution that even served some positive social functions, my data show that the everyday life of slaves was not always as untroubled as many colonial authorities believed. In reality, domestic slaves in India were neither universally accepting of their situation nor entirely helpless to resist their owners' impositions and abuse.

There is much evidence to show that a very few—like Fakhr al-Nissa's mother —found ways to work their way up and out of the system by making use of their sexuality and their reproductive capacities, while others tested its limits by engaging in subversive activities of various kinds or by attempting to physically remove themselves from the site of their oppression.

The coming of the British had the potential to make a difference in India. Anti-slavery sentiments had grown strong at home, the overseas slave trade was being brought to an end, and slavery itself was about to be abolished in other parts of the empire. But, for political as well as ideological reasons, many decades were to pass before the effects of these developments would be felt in India. Opportunities for domestic slaves to obtain redress for maltreatment did begin to open up somewhat with the establishment of new civil and criminal courts and the passage of laws put in place to limit the traffic in human beings and punish those who mistreated or killed their slaves. But the laws were frequently ignored or evaded in practice and the courts were not always sympathetic to those slaves who sought relief through resort to the legal system, especially if the perpetrators were people of high social standing. As I have shown, these failures were part of a broader pattern of collusion by the British establishment with males of the elite classes, particularly when the disputes in which they were involved had to do with unruly women or recalcitrant slaves and could therefore be defined as "domestic," rather than "public," in nature.

Notes

Grants from the Social Science Research Council, the Institute for the Humanities at the University of Illinois at Chicago, the British Academy, and the Institute for Commonwealth Studies made it possible for me to consult materials at the India Office Library and Records and the School of Oriental and African Studies in London. I thank Peggy Froerer and Rebecca Severson for research assistance and Karen Leonard, Indrani Chatterjee, and Richard Eaton for their helpful comments on earlier versions of the chapter.

Abbreviations for documents consulted in the India Office Library and Records:

AJMR   *Asiatic Journal and Monthly Register*

ARSC   *Appendix to the Report from the Select Committee of the House of Commons on the Affairs of the East-India Company, 16th August 1832, and Minutes of Evidence. I. Public. Appendix (K.) Slavery* (London: Printed by Order of the Honourable Court of Directors, by J. L. Cox and Son, 1833)

MGG   *Madras Government Gazette*

MPC   *Madras Political Consultations*

MPC-MB   *Madras Political Consultations Miscellany Book*

MPC-CC   *Madras Political Consultations—Country Correspondence*

Abbreviations for printed materials:

RSI   Indian Law Commission, *Report on Slavery in India* (n.p., 1841)
RSC   *Report from the Select Committee of the House of Commons on the Affairs of the East-India Company, 16th August 1832, and Minutes of Evidence* (London: Printed by Order of the Honourable Court of Directors, by J. L. Cox and Sons, 1833)

1. This was Nawab 'Azim Jah, who was the regent during the minority of his late brother's son, Nawab Ghulam Ghaus Khan.

2. The names of the Indians involved in the case are spelled in many different ways in the documents. Except when reproducing direct quotations, I transliterate them according to John T. Platts, *A Dictionary of Urdu, Classical Hindi, and English* (1884; reprint, New Delhi: Oriental Books Reprint Corporation, 1977). For helping me decipher the various names I am indebted to C. M. Naim.

3. The Supreme Court of Judicature was established in 1801. It had civil and criminal jurisdiction over all inhabitants of Madras and its environs. See John Bruce Norton, *The Administration of Justice in Southern India* (Madras: Athenaeum Press, 1853); William H. Morley, *The Administration of Justice in British India: Its Past History and Present State; Comprising an Account of the Laws Peculiar to India* (London: Williams and Norgate, 1858); Herbert Cowell, *The History and Constitution of the Courts and Legislative Authorities in India* (Calcutta: Spink and Co., 1905); and Charles Fawcett, *The First Century of British Justice in India* (Oxford: Clarendon Press, 1934).

4. Only in 1829 did Madras Regulation VII give slaves the same right as free persons to testify in a criminal court. Following Muslim legal practice, it had been "a long-standing custom that slaves could not be allowed to give evidence in cases in which they themselves were involved." D. R. Banaji, *Slavery in British India* (Bombay: D. B. Taraporevala Sons and Co., 1933), 309.

5. Juries had been employed in criminal trials in British-Indian courts since the latter part of the seventeenth century. Under the Company charters of 1726 and 1753 Indians who knew English and owned assets worth Rs. 3000 could serve on juries, though non-Christians were effectively excluded because jurors had to take their oath on the Bible. This rule was dropped for petty juries by Wynn's Jury Act, 7 Geo. IV, c. 37 of 1826 (Fawcett, *First Century*, 227).

The names of all twelve "gentlemen" on the grand jury hearing this case were English. One or more may have been Eurasian or Indian Christian, but British men clearly predominated. Several (including A. D. Campbell, one of the most vocal British critics of Muslim slaveholding practices in the Madras Presidency) were current or former East India Company officials (*Supplement* to *MGG*, April 14, 1828).

6. *MGG*, May 1, 1828.

7. *AJMR* 26 (Oct. 1828), 489.

8. *MGG*, May 1, 1828.

9. *MPC*, May 13, 1828, no. 29; *MPC*, May 29, 1829, no. 12; and *AJMR* 26 (Oct. 1828), 492.

10. The petition was dated May 9, 1828. Two male relatives of the begam "signed" as witnesses, while Fakhr al-Nissa Begam, perhaps because she was illiterate, gave "her mark." It was drawn up at a "special attendance at the House of the

said Begum" by Teed and Lushington (*MPC,* May 29, 1929, no. 12). That this audience was a major ceremonial production is indicated by the fact that the solicitor's bill came to Rs. 525, whereas for meetings with others in connection with the case he charged between Rs. 2 and Rs. 20 each. Inasmuch as no woman of rank would have appeared before, or even allowed her voice to be heard by, an unrelated man, the begam's sentiments were doubtless conveyed through intermediaries, probably the two "witnesses." A later government agent, Dr. Edward Balfour, describes this feature of the standard protocol for meetings between British officials and female members of the nawab's family in *MPC,* March 30, 1858, no. 21.

11. *MPC,* May 13, 1828, no. 29.

12. I have not been able to determine the precise date of the pardon, but in letters dated April 24, 1829, Robert Clive, then chief secretary to government, Fort St. George, notified the government agent and the advocate general that it had "just" been granted (*MPC-MB,* 1829, nos. 18 and 19).

13. Most of the secondary literature on slavery in India published from 1970 to the mid-1990s is either very general in scope or focused exclusively on systems of agricultural bondage in India, to the neglect of domestic slavery. See Lionel Caplan, "Power and Status in South Asian Slavery," in James L. Watson, ed., *Asian and African Systems of Slavery* (Berkeley: Basil Blackwell, 1980), 169–94; Dharma Kumar, "Colonialism, Bondage, and Caste in British India," in Martin A. Klein, ed., *Breaking the Chains: Slavery, Bondage, and Emancipation in Modern Africa and Asia* (Madison: University of Wisconsin Press, 1993), 112–30; and Gyan Prakash, *Bonded Histories: Genealogies of Labor Servitude in Colonial India* (Cambridge: Cambridge University Press, 1989). Others have been primarily concerned with legislative issues and with the impact on India of international slavery abolition movements. See Utsa Patnaik and Manjari Dingwaney, eds., *Chains of Servitude: Bondage and Slavery in India* (Madras: Sangam Books, 1985); Mark Naidis, "The Abolitionists and Indian Slavery," *Journal of Asian History* 15, no. 2 (1981), 146–58; and Nancy Gardner Cassels, "Social Legislation under the Company Raj: The Abolition of Slavery Act V 1843," *South Asia* 11 (1988), 59–87. More relevant to the issues I address here are the more recent works of Radhika Singha: "Making the Domestic More Domestic: Criminal Law and the 'Head of the Household,' 1772–1843," *Indian Economic and Social History Review 33,* no. 3 (July–Sept. 1996), 309–43, and *A Despotism of Law: Crime and Justice in Early Colonial India* (Delhi: Oxford University Press, 1998); and Indrani Chatterjee, *Gender, Slavery, and Law in Colonial India* (New Delhi: Oxford University Press, 1999); idem, "Colouring Subalternity: Slaves, Concubines, and Social Orphans under the East India Company," in Gautam Bhadra, Gyan Prakash, and Susie Tharu, eds., *Subaltern Studies X* (Delhi: Oxford University Press, 1999), 49–97; and idem, "A Slave's Search for Selfhood in Eighteenth-Century Hindustan," *Indian Economic and Social History Review* 37, no. 1 (Jan.–Mar. 2000), 53–86.

14. Ranajit Guha, "Chandra's Death," in Ranajit Guha, ed., *Subaltern Studies V: Writings on South Asian History and Society* (New Delhi: Oxford University Press, 1987), 135–65.

15. The chief sources are the *MPC* for the years 1828 and 1829. Reports of the trial published in the *MGG* and in the *AJMR* (26 [Oct. 1828], 489–92) include wit-

ness testimony that supplements (and in a few details conflicts with) that reproduced in the *Consultations.*

16. *MPC,* January 29, 1828, no. 16.

17. *MPC,* May 13, 1828, no. 29.

18. Ibid.

19. Gayatri Spivak, "Subaltern Studies: Deconstructing Historiography," in
Ranajit Guha, ed., *Subaltern Studies IV: Writings on South Asian History and Society*
(New Delhi: Oxford University Press, 1985), 330–63.

20. *MPC,* January 29, 1828, no. 16; May 13, 1828, no. 29.

21. "Qadir Bi" was Begam Fakhr al-Nissa's ʿurf ("alias" or "nickname"), used by
members of her household and other intimates or personal acquaintances.

22. *MPC,* January 29, 1828, no. 16.

23. Ibid.,

24. *MPC,* May 13, 1828, no. 29.

25. *MGG,* May 1, 1828.

26. *MPC,* May 13, 1828, no. 29.

27. Ibid.

28. *MPC,* January 29, 1828, no. 16.

29. The term "nicka" (Urdu *nikahi*), daughter or son, distinguished the children
of a polygynous man's secondary wives (*nikahi bibi* or *mankuha*) from those of his
first or senior (*shadi*) wife. See Sylvia Vatuk, "'The Family': A Contested Concept in
Early-Nineteenth-Century Madras," in Indrani Chatterjee, ed., *Unfamiliar Relations:
Family and History in South Asia* (New Brunswick, N.J.: Rutgers University Press,
2004), 161–91.

30. *MPC,* January 29, 1828, no. 16. The reference is to Muhammad ʿAli Walajah
(Fakhr al-Nissa Begam's father and the nawab regent's paternal great-grandfather),
who held the title of nawab of the Carnatic from 1752 to his death in 1795.

31. *MPC,* May 13, 1828, no. 29.

32. Hindus of equivalent wealth and social standing also kept domestic slaves, as
did some British colonial officials. Here, however, I confine myself to discussing
slavery among the Muslim nobility.

33. From *parda* ("curtain") and *gosha* ("corner"). In the Deccan the latter word
was used more widely.

34. *MPC,* January 21, 1812, 201.

35. *MPC-CC,* 1820, no. 50; *MPC-CC,* 1821, no. 2. The offspring of concubines,
mistresses, or slaves were often fostered by one of a man's legal wives, either because
she had no children of her own or because her children were grown and she wanted
another to occupy her time and affections.

36. See *ARSC,* 621–49; East India Company, *Slave Trade (East India): Slavery in
Ceylon* (London: House of Commons, 1838); and J. Burton-Page, "Habshi," in *Encyclopaedia of Islam,* ed. H. A. R. Gibb et al., new ed. (Leiden: E. J. Brill, 1954–2002),
3:14–16.

37. See Muhammad Karim, *Sawanihat-i-Mumtaz,* part 2, *Sources of the History
of the Nawwabs of the Carnatic IV,* trans. S. M. H. Nainar, Madras University Islamic
Series no. 7 (Madras: At the Madras Law Journal Press, 1944). This chronicle of the
Walajah dynasty, written in Persian in 1837 at the behest of the nawab regent, while
mainly devoted to documenting political and military events, provides much inci-

dental information about the nawabs' private lives. A detailed genealogical table of the Karnataka family, including slave-concubines and other women with whom the nawabs had sexual relationships and on whom they (in some cases) fathered offspring, is to be found on 190–95.

38. *RSI*, 185, 204, 252.

39. According to her cook's testimony, the begam had apparently acquired the youngest of the accused slave-girls in this way: "she came about a year and a half ago . . . it was during the famine." *AJMR* 26 (Oct. 1828): 490.

40. Campbell had a twenty-two-year official career in the Madras Presidency, retiring in 1830 as principal collector of Tanjore.

41. *RSI*, 250; see also *RSC*, 452.

42. British officials usually describe child slaves purchased by members of the local Muslim nobility as receiving "Muslim" names from their new owners. However, the Persian or Urdu names of slaves rarely have any religious significance or association and are also quite different from the Arabic names of their elite Muslim masters and mistresses. Typically the latter were named after important figures in Islamic history or had names signifying their devotion to God or to the Muslim faith or their allegiance to the Prophet. Naming practices such as these clearly distinguished the two categories of household members. Only occasionally did a slave continue to be known by her former name. For example, in a list of thirty-seven female slaves belonging to a grandson of Nawab Muhammad 'Ali, there are four names of Sanskritic derivation (*MPC-MB* 1829, no. 39). These deviations from the general rule may perhaps be explained as a consequence of the women concerned having been sold into slavery as adults.

43. *MPC*, January 29, 1828, no. 16.

44. *MPC*, May 13, 1828, no. 29.

45. *MPC*, January 29, 1828, no. 16.

46. Some male slaves were married: for example, a list of dependents of a *nikahi* widow of Nawab 'Umdat-ul 'Umra refers to sixteen "slaves having families" and twenty-five "female slaves." *MPC*, October 10, 1828, no. 1.

47. A number of such children born to slave-mothers are mentioned by Karim, *Sawanihat*, 190–95 and passim. Other plentiful examples are scattered throughout the correspondence between Walajah pensioners and successive Government Agents that is reproduced in Edward Balfour, *Carnatic Stipendiaries of 1801* (Madras: Scottish Press, 1858).

48. In Dakkhani Urdu the word *haram* (from the Arabic "forbidden" or "sacred") signified both the "women's apartments" of a nobleman's home and the "slave-concubine" who, along with other women of the master's family and retinue, occupied that designated female space.

49. This had been the good fortune of Fakhr al-Nissa's mother. See below.

50. *RSI*, 249.

51. *AJMR*, 490.

52. Karim, *Sawanihat*, 88. Nawab Muhammad 'Ali fathered children by at least sixteen different women.

53. *MPC*, June 12, 1810, 1874–75.

54. *MPC*, February 16, 1821, no. 47.

55. *MPC*, May 13, 1828, no. 2. In 1853 she was still alive, having outlived all three of her siblings and most of her half-siblings. See Balfour, *Carnatic Stipendiaries*, xi.

56. Faiz Muhammad Khan, her father's brother's son's son (*MPC,* May 25, 1810, 1772).

57. Sisters were married in strict birth order, the interval between births being rarely less than two years, for which see Sylvia Vatuk, "Older Women, Past and Present, in an Indian Muslim Family," in Sujata Patel, Jasodhara Bagchi, and Krishna Raj, eds., *Thinking Social Science in India: Essays in Honour of Alice Thorner* (New Delhi: Sage Publications, 2002), 247–63.

58. *MPC,* October 5, 1816, no. 1.

59. *MPC-CC,* 1821, no. 36.

60. *AJMR* 26 (Oct. 1828): 491.

61. There was no question of their working for a living. This was considered by the Walajahs and others of their social status to be an activity appropriate only for men of inferior rank.

62. For example, in an earlier dispute between Nawab 'Azam Jah and Zaib al-Nissa, the latter's sons-in-law took the lead in protesting to the British on her behalf. *MPC,* May 25, 1810, 1758.

63. *AJMR* 26 (Oct 1828): 490.

64. *MPC,* May 13, 1828, no. 29. "Champowing" is described in an 1832 source as one of the main duties of female slaves in elite Muslim households, for which see B. Meer Hassan Ali, *Observations on the Mussulmauns of India,* ed. William Crooke, 2nd ed. (1917; reprint, Delhi: Deep Publications, 1975), 252–53.

65. *MPC,* January 29, 1828, no. 7.

66. For further details see Vatuk, "'The Family.'"

67. *MPC,* August 29, 1829, no. 28.

68. As I have noted elsewhere, the very meaning of the term "family" and the question of who should be included in it were highly contested. Vatuk, "'The Family.'"

69. After 1801 the *mahkama,* presided over by the nawab's chief *qazi* and following Islamic law, had civil jurisdiction only in cases involving the nawab and those of his close relatives and chief officers who were exempt from the jurisdiction of British courts.

70. *MPC,* August 29, 1829, no. 28.

71. *MPC,* December 22, 1829, no. 12.

72. *MPC,* February 5, 1828, no. 1.

73. Quoted in *MPC,* May 13, 1828, no. 29. Singha notes that under Company rule generally, "[s]pecial procedures regulated the way in which women of rank gave evidence in a court of law and they could be exempted from personal appearance in a civil court." Singha, "Making the Domestic," 314n. Fakhr al-Nissa's case was, however, a criminal one.

74. *MPC,* April 11, 1828, no. 1.

75. The most important were the General Abolition Bill of 1807, the Felony Act of 1811 (51 Geo. III, C. 23), and the Abolition Act of 1833, which applied to all of the British empire except India and Ceylon. Act V of 1843 withdrew legal recognition of slavery as a civil status in British India, but the selling of persons into slavery only became a criminal offence in 1862 under the new Indian Penal Code.

76. Others included Regulation II of 1812, prohibiting the export of slaves from Malabar, and Regulation II of 1826, making explicit the applicability of the Felony

Act to cases of slave trading within or from territories within the Madras Presidency. *RSI,* 314.

77. Cf. *ARSC,* 456.

78. *RSI,* 250.

79. Not until he killed one of his wives was he briefly taken into police custody, though never tried for murder. *ARSC,* 453.

80. *ARSC,* 455.

81. In 1819, when secretary of the Madras board of revenue, Campbell had unsuccessfully proposed a law greatly limiting the rights of masters over slaves and making illegal the sale of free persons into slavery. Banaji, *Slavery,* 267–77.

82. See Naidis, "The Abolitionists."

83. *Slavery in India: Return to an Address of the Honourable House of Commons . . . all Correspondence . . . Touching the State of Slavery in the Territories under the Company's Rule . . .* (London: Ordered by the House of Commons, to be Printed, 1828).

84. *ARSC,* 453.

85. *RSI,* 317.

86. *RSI,* 335.

87. Two compilations of "precedent-setting cases" heard in courts of judicature in the Bengal Presidency between 1811 and 1829 include several disputes over slave ownership: W. H. Macnaghten, *Principles and Precedents of Moohummudan Law,* 5th ed. (Madras: Higginbotham, 1882); and *Principles and Precedents of Hindu Law,* 4th ed. (Madras: Higginbotham, 1894). Summaries of others are found in Morley, *Administration of Justice,* 589.

88. Harold Apthekar, in *American Negro Slave Revolts* (New York: Columbia University Press, 1943), provided much of the original inspiration for this work. See also John Hope Franklin, *From Slavery to Freedom: A History of American Negroes* (New York: Alfred Knopf, 1947); and Eugene D. Genovese, *From Rebellion to Revolution: Afro-American Slave Revolts in the Making of the Modern World* (Baton Rouge: Louisiana State University Press, 1979).

89. See Gary Y. Okihiro, ed., *In Resistance: Studies in African, Caribbean, and Afro-American History* (Amherst: University Of Massachusetts Press, 1986); Paul E. Lovejoy, ed., *Africans in Bondage: Studies in Slavery and the Slave Trade* (Madison: University of Wisconsin Press, 1986); and Gad Heuman, ed., *Out of the House of Bondage: Runaways, Resistance, and Marronage in Africa and the New World* (London: Frank Cass, 1986).

90. Stephanie M. H. Camp, *Closer to Freedom: Enslaved Women and Everyday Resistance in the Plantation South* (Chapel Hill: University of North Carolina Press, 2004), 2.

91. James Scott, *Weapons of the Weak: Everyday Forms of Peasant Resistance* (New Haven, Conn.: Yale University Press, 1985).

92. Elizabeth Fox-Genovese, "Strategies and Forms of Resistance: Focus on Slave Women in the United States," in Okihiro, ed., *In Resistance,* 153; also David Barry Gaspar and Darline Clark Hine, eds., *More than Chattel: Black Women and Slavery in the Americas* (Bloomington: Indiana University Press, 1996); Barbara Bush, *Slave Women in Caribbean Society, 1650–1838* (Bloomington: Indiana University Press, 1990); and Hilary McD. Beckles, *Natural Rebels: A Social History of Enslaved Black Women in Barbados* (New Brunswick, N.J.: Rutgers University Press, 1989).

93. There were, of course, good practical reasons for these differences, including the fact that women generally had more family responsibilities and attachments than men.

94. Camp, in *Closer to Freedom,* explores at length the phenomenon of female "truancy" among slaves in the American South.

95. *MPC,* January 29, 1828, no. 16.

96. *MGG,* May 1, 1828.

10

Slaves or Soldiers? African Conscripts in Portuguese India, 1857–1860

Timothy Walker

The Portuguese colonial reaction to the Indian "Mutiny" of 1857 is bound up with the question of illegal slave trafficking into Portuguese India from Africa. In Goa, the colonial government's intended use of conscripted African troops in response to the Indian uprising was hindered by existing restrictions on the slave trade in the Indian Ocean. This essay argues that older histories of military slave use by Portuguese colonial populations in the early modern world resembled, but did not replicate, contemporary Asian patterns of military slave use. This may have explained the growing divergence between Portuguese and Northern European slaveholders, differences which were to manifest themselves in dramatic ways by the mid-nineteenth century. North European abolitionist pressures could only minimally restrict the oceanic slave trade of the Portuguese colonists under the terms of the Anglo-Portuguese accord of 1842. Abolitionist pressures did not initially prohibit slave holding in the Portuguese colonies of Goa, Damao, and Diu. (See map 2.) This, in turn, allowed for the development of a contraband trade in smuggled slaves which, though opposed by the colonial governor sent out from Lisbon, continued with little discouragement from locally born officials in Portuguese India.[1]

However, the 1857 revolt of native troops in British India and the severe crisis of authority it portended compelled the serving Portuguese governor to call for a direct import of conscripts from Africa. While these conscripted Africans were supposed to be "freemen," the Portuguese governor of Mozambique refused to send them by sea to Goa, on the grounds they would appear as contraband "slaves" to British patrols. This episode offers us a glimpse of the Portuguese willingness to abrogate the terms of an abolitionist treaty and thereby reveals the fissures within abolitionist histories in general and in Lusophone histories in particular during the nineteenth century.

Military Use of Male Slaves

Potentates in the Indian subcontinent and adjacent regions had a long tradition of training foreign-born slaves for use by the state in battle, stretching back centuries before the arrival of the Portuguese. As Peter Jackson confirms in his chapter in this volume, for centuries the Delhi Sultanate used enslaved Turks in the thousands as soldiers (*ghulams*) along "Islam's Indian frontier." Indeed, Jackson asserts that, by the eleventh century, professional "Turkish slave-regiments formed the nucleus of most armies in the eastern Islamic world."

Sunil Kumar's work on the Shamsi *bandagan,* or prominent privileged slave-warriors who fought for the early Delhi Sultanate, chronicles a system in which young male slaves, typically acquired in Afghanistan or other regions of Central Asia, could be eventually assigned to positions of command over forces that included free men. Slave-commanders were empowered to restrict or forbid activities normally permitted to soldiers of free status. According to Kumar, this system flourished under the 'Abbasid caliphs of the ninth and tenth centuries, and continued under the Delhi sultans of the thirteenth century. Slaves of the sultans, because of their personal dependence on the ruler for their position and status, could be counted on to follow orders faithfully, while free commanders of independent means could not.[2]

Similarly, Richard Eaton in this volume describes the widespread martial employment of slaves in India's Deccan plateau during the early modern period. Even though the use of slaves in a military role was not a cultural norm in that area prior to the arrival of Arab Muslims from the Middle East, Deccan rulers imported a steady stream of fit Ethiopian men annually between the fifteenth and seventeenth centuries to meet that region's "insatiable demand for military labor." Such slaves, called "Habshis" in Arabic, were intended to serve exclusively as elite warriors—one Portuguese observer of the early sixteenth century referred to these specialized African soldiers as "knights" (*cavaleiros*), a term simultaneously revealing their advanced level of training and the observer's genuine respect for their martial ability.

Though historians of the Portuguese have attested to the military deployment of slaves throughout the Portuguese colonial empire from Brazil to Macau,[3] they seldom analyze the origins of such practices in comparative terms. Given the scholarly silence, we can only suggest overlaps and continuities between Mediterranean and Central Asian premodern systems of slave use. The Romans had occasionally incorporated slaves into their chronically undermanned provincial legions during the late imperial era, and their Germanic successor kingdoms in Iberia had made use of slaves as infantrymen in the fifth and sixth centuries.[4] A little later, the Portuguese became acquainted with Arab practices that commonly included martial employments for enslaved non-Muslim Slav and African captives as galley rowers or mariners among warships' crews.[5] Arab Muslims also brought mixed-race formations of slave-cavalry troops, the mamluks, to the Iberian peninsula in the ninth century; mamluk units were central to the maintenance of the Spanish caliphate's military power.[6] Portuguese and Spanish Christian warriors had again encountered mamluk slave (infantry) units during the *Reconquista*. Thus, several precedents in the Portuguese experience with military slave labor predated their arrival in the Indian Ocean. It is not entirely improbable, then, that Portuguese use of slaves in a military capacity from the outset of their colonial ventures represented an underdiscussed response to such historical precedents.

Although, upon first glance, Portuguese practices after the sixteenth century would seem to emulate those encountered among contemporary peoples of the Indian Ocean rim (in South Asia, East Africa, and the Middle East), in fact there was a crucial difference in the Portuguese conception and use of enslaved military labor, in India and elsewhere within their diverse colonial domains. The difference was that the Portuguese armed slaves only "temporarily" for a single purpose: defense against external aggression. Of course, "external" here referred to any- and everything beyond Portuguese-controlled areas as defined by the political contours of those centuries. While Muslim and non-Muslim ruling houses around the Indian Ocean region alike formed permanent standing military formations composed of professional slave-soldiers, the Portuguese did not. As Richard Eaton elucidates for seventeenth-century Indian regimes on the coast, Muslim rulers relied on their regiments of slave-troops to provide political stability within a fragile society of divided factions that vied constantly for power. Slave-soldiers in the Deccan context provided security as much or more from internal threats as from external ones. The Portuguese, on the other hand, enjoyed (for the most part) internal political order and social cohesion within their eastern colonies. Chattel slaves were therefore only pressed into Portuguese service as soldiers on a temporary basis in times of military emergency—and until 1857 they were deployed in the eastern empire almost exclusively against external enemies who sought to conquer territories of the *Estado da Índia.*

Furthermore, since the fifteenth century at least, the Portuguese in India and East Africa had also relied on convicted European criminals to swell the ranks of their colonial soldiery. Every year, hundreds of wretched young Portuguese men in Lisbon—prisoners sentenced to become military exiles—clambered aboard the ships of the India-bound fleet.[7] These Europeans were, upon their arrival in Mozambique or Goa, mustered into the permanent professional military formations of the *Estado da Índia,* where they typically had to serve punitive terms of between six and ten years of duty. But tropical diseases quickly thinned their ranks, reducing their numbers at times by half in the first year, a pattern that continued into the nineteenth century.[8]

Perhaps this may explain the preponderance of slaves mentioned in the records of military and naval conflicts between the Portuguese and other European commercial powers during the seventeenth and eighteenth centuries. In June 1622, a formidable Dutch fleet of thirteen ships and thirteen hundred men attacked Macau, at that time the only European trade port in China and a source of exceptional wealth for the Portuguese. To meet this assault, the Portuguese European population living in Macau could muster only about fifty trained musketeers and one hundred resident citizens (many of mixed European and Asian descent) capable of bearing arms; most of the town's merchants were then in Canton, buying goods at the annual trade fair. Yet this small contingent of Portuguese soldiers and townsmen, supplemented by some Jesuit artillerists and perhaps fifty or one hundred of their hastily armed slaves, dealt the Dutch a crushing defeat. In a disastrous landing operation that the Portuguese and their drink-emboldened slaves met with furious resolve, the Hollanders lost nearly three hundred men (including several top-ranking officers) and virtually all their weapons and equipment, as well as one of their main ships. Portuguese losses amounted to six killed and twenty wounded among the Euro-Asians, along with a small but unrecorded number of slaves.[9] Jan Pieterzoon Coen, the Dutch commander who had organized the expedition, complained in correspondence to the directors of the Dutch East India Company that "the slaves of the Portuguese at Macao served them so well and faithfully, that it was they who defeated and drove away our people there." On the grounds of the Macau debacle, he would later advocate the use of slaves as soldiers instead of Dutch troops, observing that "Many Portuguese slaves, Kaffirs and the like, having been made drunk, charged so fearlessly against our muskets, that it was a wondrous thing to see." "Our people saw very few

Portuguese," he concluded; "The Portuguese beat us off from Macao with their slaves."[10]

The same year as the Dutch attack on Macau, a British expedition supported by Persian allies besieged the Portuguese fortress that commanded the Straits of Ormuz (and thus controlled trade through the Persian Gulf). During the ensuing struggle, an English witness recorded that the Portuguese defense was conducted primarily by their African slaves, who threw explosive firebombs down on the enemy from the ramparts on the fortress walls with devastating effect. Courageous efforts on the part of these (mostly Angolan Bantu) slaves repulsed many Anglo-Persian assaults on the Ormuz fortifications during the spring of 1622, before the final Portuguese capitulation in May.[11]

Dutch attempts to take the fortified Portuguese slave-trading station at São Jorge de Mina on the Guinea Coast (El Mina Castle in present-day Ghana) in 1625 provided another opportunity for African slaves to fight at the behest of their Portuguese masters. The Dutch attacking forces vastly outnumbered the Portuguese defenders, but a surprise attack by a Portuguese-led force of two hundred local Africans (recruited in part from among the slaves being gathered for export) shattered the Dutch initiative. This unexpected African onslaught killed 440 Dutch soldiers, more than a third of the entire invasion force. To discourage their surviving enemies, the African warriors beheaded the slain and left them on the beach.[12]

Continued Dutch efforts to break into the lucrative trans-Atlantic sugar and slave trades also resulted in their repeated invasion and occupation of Bahia and northeastern Brazil between 1624 and 1654. At the height of this initiative, the Dutch controlled Recife, two thousand kilometers of coastline, and two-thirds of the sugar-growing region.[13] In response, the Portuguese governors of Pernambuco and Bahia maintained a guerrilla resistance with forces organized from the colonial citizenry and their numerous slaves. Among the commanders one stands out: Henrique Dias, a free black landowner who had achieved the great honor of a knighthood in the Order of Christ, was known as the "governor of the *mulattos,* the *crioulos* and all of the *pretos*"[14] (see below). The Portuguese noted that the enslaved Africans, indigenous *indios,* and mixed-race free men whom Dias formed into irregular militias in the Pernambuco bush made especially good warriors, fighting and foraging without state logistical support in the Amazonian jungles; the slaves' ferocity and valor in battle impressed their commanders, too. At the end of this long and bitter struggle, the Portuguese recognized that the expulsion of the Dutch from Brazil was achieved mainly through colonial Brazilian efforts, with little assistance from the metropole. Most of the fighting to free the colony had been done by unfree men of color, driven to perform arduous military labor (in their masters' interests) in the hope of winning their own freedom.[15]

In the army of the Portuguese *Estado da Índia* and aboard the ships of its coastal patrol squadrons during the seventeenth and eighteenth centuries, slaves commonly performed temporary military service. In 1634, one colonial administrator complained that "most of the soldiers" in the garrison defending Diu were *pretos* ("blacks").[16] When recruits had to be raised quickly for an expedition against enemy states to the north or south of Goa, slaves usually augmented the muster rolls.[17] This reflected both a shortage of European men in Goa available for service and, during the later colonial period, an unwillingness among some elites to incur risk in battle. Slaves made convenient substitute warriors for those who could afford them. Some African slave-soldiers even arrived in Goa indirectly from Brazil, having first learned their military drill and duties fighting the Dutch in South America during the seventeenth century. Small contingents of African soldiers continued to arrive in Goa from Brazil into the nineteenth century.[18] Very few chattel slaves, however, remained long in military service when they could be profitably employed elsewhere by their masters.

In September 1710, during the War of Spanish Succession, armed slave-"auxiliaries" fighting alongside hastily organized bands of citizen militia and students at the Jesuit College stubbornly fought a sizable French invasion force of professional soldiers to a standstill in the streets of Rio de Janeiro. The slaves and students particularly distinguished themselves in this combat, allowing late-arriving Portuguese regular troops time to position themselves to attack the French flank and rear, thus winning the day and effectively ending the immediate invasion threat.[19] A stronger French attempt in September of the following year was more successful, resulting in the capitulation and temporary occupation of Rio de Janeiro, even though it had been defended by "1,000 [Portuguese] regular troops, 2,000 marines, 4,000 citizens in arms and 7 or 8,000 Blacks," according to an English eyewitness.[20] The French withdrew only when a mixed-race colonial relief force some six thousand strong, recruited from among the free white, mulatto, and *mameluco* gold miners of Minas Gerais and their numerous African slaves, descended upon the city two months later.[21]

In Bahia, Brazil, in the eighteenth century, European volunteers, conscripts, and convicts, as well as free mixed-race troops of many ethnicities and hues, made up the rank and file of the two regular infantry regiments in the colonial capital's garrison. The muster roles of the four regional militia regiments, however, were segregated according to a complex semiotic of "race" described in fuller detail below: one regiment for *pretos,* one for *pardos,* one for *mestiços,* and one for *indios* (native Indians). Enlisted men in

these militia regiments (which by definition met only periodically for training and drill, and were mobilized only when needed) served under officers
of the same skin color. Although slaves could, with their master's consent,
hold a place in the regional militia, most of these part-time soldiers were
free men. (Militia units that mingled free and slave citizen-soldiers, in fact,
existed in many of colonial Brazil's municipalities.) Moreover, only free
blacks, *pardos,* or *mulatos* could serve in the colony's two most prestigious
militia regiments. These two units, one of infantry and one of artillery, were
organized exclusively by and for free men of African descent. Recognized for
their pride and spirit, the regiments were known as "Henriques," in honor of
Henrique Dias, the aristocratic *negro* captain of the African slave- and
mixed-race soldiers who had helped drive the Dutch from Brazil during the
previous century.[22]

The Portuguese practice of arming slaves in times of crisis remained
current in the nineteenth-century colonies: in 1804, during their global
struggle with Napoleonic France, British military agents contracted for
ninety-one African slaves to be sent from Goa to Ceylon, there to be trained
as soldiers in the local garrison. Four years later, the Portuguese viceroy in
Goa obtained permission from Lisbon to buy African slaves to relieve navy
crewmen who had been long at sea patrolling the Indian coast.[23]

For generations, Portuguese colonists in Brazil, India, Africa, and China
had armed their African slaves and employed them in military capacities, either as *soldados* on land or as *marinheiros* at sea. Early on in their colonial
endeavor, the exigencies of expansion had forced the chronically short-
handed Portuguese to rely on slaves as warriors from time to time.[24] The
colonial government of the *Estado da Índia* had earlier used African slaves as
soldiers, incorporating them temporarily into existing military formations.[25]
However, such recruitment was limited and indirect. The slaves that the Portuguese eastern empire employed sporadically as soldiers were levied in
small numbers from the households of Portuguese elites, and often fought
side by side with their masters. Though careful to press their slaves into military service only on a temporary basis, the Portuguese could not afford to
share the fear of reliance on armed African slaves that many of their contemporary European colonizers developed in the nineteenth century.

Among many contemporary non-European rulers and military leaders,
however, no such reluctance existed to employ slaves as regular full-time soldiers. On the contrary, arming and training slaves as elite warriors remained
common in many regions around the Indian Ocean hinterland into the
twentieth century. In his recent study of Indian Ocean slaving, for example,
Pedro Machado observed that, during the eighteenth and nineteenth centuries, "most slaves in the Persian Gulf were employed as soldiers, household

servants, sailors and dock hands, and pearl divers."[26] According to Edward Alpers's newest research, during the early nineteenth century the military bodyguard units of the ruling sherifs of Mecca, Arabia, consisted of African slave-warriors. Alpers also noted that, well into the 1930s, the sultans of the Persian Gulf Qu'ayti state relied on specialized units of enslaved African soldiers, as well.[27]

Suzanne Miers's research, too, has drawn attention to the widespread use of slave-troops in East Africa toward the end of the nineteenth century: Tippu Tip's principal warriors in what is today Tanzania were predominantly slaves, as were those of the ruler of Sudan. Miers further notes that large cohorts of slaves were recruited into the armies of Egypt and Hyderabad in the late nineteenth century. Slave-warriors in non-Muslim West Africa enjoyed a higher social status and better standard of living than did non-military slaves.[28] In Niger, Miers reports that "the armed retinues of the chiefs consisted mainly of slaves," and that "slaves of proven ability" might command armed expeditions in search of trade.[29] In the Fulani regions of the central Sudan, Miers found evidence that slave-warriors received preferential treatment when weapons were issued; they usually wielded the best and newest firearms in battle.[30]

For colonial governors throughout the Portuguese colonial system, arming slaves always involved risks and costs: the calculated risk of facilitating rebellion by slaves who had gained military experience, and the costs associated with rewarding the slaves' military service (or losing valuable slaves in battle). In most instances, though, Portuguese slaves fought in relatively small numbers in mixed military units, side by side with the free men of the colony (whether they were of European, indigenous, or mixed-race descent); this greatly minimized the risk of a general slave rebellion. By deploying them in this way, the Portuguese never gave autonomy to or relinquished control of their chattel servants. Thus, Portuguese colonial officials undertook the risk of arming slaves on a provisional basis when a dire need arose, due to shortages of manpower in the face of an external threat, but always with some inherent safeguards to maintain control over their slaves.

Such military deployment of slaves was only a small part of the social fabric. At least in the Portuguese colonies in India, enslaved Africans were used for specialized agricultural and commercial labor (as field foremen or shop and warehouse overseers), as sailors on merchant and military vessels, as concubines, and especially as prestigious liveried footmen and household servants.[31] The majority of agricultural field-laborers in Goa, however, were natives of the subcontinent. Although they were far more costly than indigenous labor, African slaves were desired mainly for their novelty and the status they imparted to their owners. So the trade in African slaves in Portuguese India was a trade in prestige-endowing luxury commodities. Such a trade did not need substantial numbers to yield high returns, since high prices ensured a substantial profit to the trader. Indo-Portuguese merchants, therefore, were to deplore the interdiction of a trade that brought them generous profits.[32]

The Social Implications of Slave Use

As the Portuguese empire had spread down the coast of Africa and into the Atlantic Ocean and beyond, Portuguese conceptions and uses of enslaved military labor began to diverge from the Northern and Western European conceptions and uses of slaves. The most obvious and dramatic differences centered on "race," which in turn generated a complex lexicon for discussions of social and legal "identity."[33] By the eighteenth and nineteenth centuries in Portuguese Goa, Damao, and Diu, slaves came from a range of "racial" backgrounds; most arrived in western India from the Portuguese East African territory on Mozambique Island. In nineteenth-century Goa, some slaves traced their origins to other territories in Mozambique, such as Inhambane, Quelimane, Ibo, Sena, or regions inhabited by the Macua people. Additionally, the presence of Indian slaves, as well as of Chinese slaves imported from Portuguese Macau, was also known; some slaves also came to Portuguese India from Malaysia.[34] Enslaved persons could be of "pure" African lineage (designated *preto*, the Portuguese word for the color black), or of mixed descent (*pardo*: Afro-European, Afro-Indian, Afro-Indo-European, or Afro-Asian).[35]

Pardo literally means "brown" or "dark." As applied to humans, it referred superficially to an individual's skin color and typically connoted someone of mixed blood—almost always African in combination with another regional or ethnic origin—without reference to his or her legal status. For example, children born to African slave-women but fathered by slave masters of European, Indian, East Asian, Native American, or Indo-European origins could be termed *pardos;* they remained slaves unless their owners chose to manumit them.[36] However, mixed-race children born of a free mother were themselves free from birth. It was the legal status of the mother that the child inherited.

The term *pardo* was a very ancient Portuguese racial designation, dating, along with *moreno* ("Moorish" or "dark"), at least to the ethnic blending consequent to the seven-hundred-year North African and Islamic occupation of Iberia and the *Reconquista*. The term was current throughout the Portuguese global empire during the early modern period, from the metropole to Brazil and Angola to Macau and East Timor. *Pardo* is a term of great imprecision, roughly synonymous with "mulatto," but the latter word, because of its New World associations, was more often encountered in continental Portugal and the Atlantic colonies than in India. Within the specialized lexicon that addressed the highly complex concept of race in the Portuguese colonial sphere (in turn the product of a deliberate Portuguese miscegenation policy), *pardo* is just one of many words denoting skin color and ethnicity. Other terms, such as *negro, preto, mulato, moreno, crioulo, mestiço, caboclo* (literally, "copper-colored," referring to an indigenous Brazilian), *mameluco* (a child of a European and a Native American), *carijó* (the progeny of an African and a Native American), *cabra* (a Brazilian term for one born of a "pure" African and a mulatto), and *descendente* (of mixed Portuguese and Indian race), distinguished "pure" continental Old Christian Europeans from their diverse imperial subject populations.

In the Portuguese world, to be of mixed race was not necessarily an impediment to great wealth or social position—free blacks and mulattos achieved high status in Brazil, Africa, and even continental Portugal as, for example, merchants, healers, landholders, and military commanders.[37] In India, mixed-race Indo-European *descendentes* (often children of well-born Portuguese *fidalgos* who had married the daughters of high-caste Indian families that had converted to Christianity) formed the core of the colonial aristocracy. However, to be sure, racial origins created barriers within the social hierarchy; to be a *pardo* (or a member of any other mixed-race group) carried the indelible stigma of having non-European ancestry, thus prohibiting access to the uppermost circles of Portuguese ruling society, whether on the European continent or in the colonies.[38]

The Vagaries of Prohibition

In the nineteenth century, British-led restrictions on Portuguese commercial interests in the Indian Ocean provided the context for the attempt to end the trade in slaves. The commercial prospects of colonial Portuguese traders, especially those doing business between Mozambique and Damao or Diu, were seriously damaged. Portuguese customs receipts in Damao from the period suggest the scale of this impact. Between 1805 and 1840, the value of legal registered commerce between Mozambique and Damao fell by more than 75 percent; in Diu the loss was even sharper.[39]

During the first four decades of the nineteenth century, opium was the subject of a bitter, protracted commercial and diplomatic struggle between the Bombay government and the Indo-Portuguese enclaves.[40] In 1838, British warships blockaded Damao, thereafter definitively halting opium shipments from Portuguese India to China. The statistics cited above reveal that opium accounted for nearly 80 percent of customs revenues at Damao that year alone. However, by 1840, Damao customs revenue had dropped by nearly two-thirds. An unabated downward spiral continued, resulting in customs revenues falling another 75 percent between 1846 and 1853.

Slaves did not constitute the majority of goods being traded with Mozambique, but were part of a larger balance of trade between various parts of the Portuguese maritime empire. For instance, in Damao for a while, traders sought to compensate for the financial losses from reduced slave trafficking by exporting more Indian *malwa* opium to Portuguese-held Macau, fifty kilometers from Hong Kong on the southwest side of the Pearl River delta. However, British competitive interests quashed this profitable trade. Damao never recovered its economic viability under the Portuguese. The Anglo-Portuguese dispute over opium thus exacerbated differences regarding slavery profits and policy in the Indian Ocean.

The Anglo-Portuguese Treaty of 1842, designed to put a definitive end to slave trafficking from Portuguese Africa to any destination within the Indian Ocean, should be seen within this larger economic context. Other equally ambitious measures had preceded it: the Anglo-Portuguese Anti-slavery Treaty of 1818 and the Portuguese Royal Edict of 1836 are the two principal examples. These initiatives had been ineffectual. Because economic inducements continued to compel merchants to ship slaves from Mozambique to lucrative markets in India and China, slave trading had remained a widely accepted commercial and domestic practice in the *Estado da Índia* (as in the Americas), long after abolition had become a celebrated cause in Europe. Portuguese elites and traders in the eastern colonies were disinclined to condemn a practice that was both profitable and consonant with their ideas of social stratification.

Furthermore, the political and administrative situation in Portuguese India during the mid-nineteenth century was such that any attempt by authorities in Lisbon to abolish slavery outright emerged as an untenable policy.[41] A lack of political will among the Portuguese governors and viceroys in India, combined with an unwillingness throughout all ranks of the Portuguese colonial military structure to compel compliance, made anti-slaveholding laws effectively unenforceable in the Portuguese Indian territories.[42] Therefore, despite intense pressure from the British government,[43] the Portuguese crown officials in Europe in 1842 consented only to interdicting the transport of human cargos on the high seas.

Articles II, III, and IV of the treaty signed at Lisbon on July 3, 1842, empowered naval officials of either nation to board and search vessels suspected of carrying enslaved Africans. The presence of leg irons, shackles, and other hardware for restraining humans was, as outlined in article IX, enough to justify the seizure of a vessel and the detention and prosecution of the crew as slave traders. However, effective enforcement fell to the British Navy in the Indian Ocean because the Portuguese maritime forces in India were weak and lacked the will.[44]

Notably, the Treaty of 1842 did not attempt to abolish slave keeping in the eastern Portuguese empire. Thus the treaty simultaneously preserved the property of Indo-Portuguese slaveholders and the authority of the colonial territorial officials by sparing them the task of enforcing an unpopular policy. The status of existing slaves (and their unborn children) as privately owned human property was not affected in the least.[45] Despite this, Portuguese colonial slaveholding was affected by the expansion of the British empire on land as well.

The Portuguese had never been able to legally pursue runaway slaves into neighboring Karnataka, Maharashtra, or Gujarat. But, beginning in the mid-sixteenth century, they had made arrangements with the Muslim and Hindu rulers of territories adjacent to the Portuguese enclaves to receive by right of treaty either the return of, or fair compensation for, slaves who escaped into other regions of India.[46] Initially, this seems to have been an issue primarily with East African Muslim slaves, who tried to flee from forced adherence to Christianity in the Portuguese enclaves. However, after the fall of the Mughals and enactment of anti-slavery laws in the British colonies, African slaves held by the Portuguese had a clear incentive for running: emancipation. By the second quarter of the nineteenth century, when all Indian territories contiguous with Goa, Damao, and Diu were subject to British anti-slavery regulations, Indo-Portuguese slave owners could not hope to recoup any losses when their forced laborers escaped over the border.[47]

While British diplomatic pressure to end the slave trade in the Indian Ocean caused intense resentment among elites in Portuguese India,[48] such resentment was exacerbated by the growing impossibility of recovery of fugitive slaves by slaveholders in Goa, Damao, and Diu. Further, British anti-slavery regulations badly damaged Portuguese trade, and substantially diminished the commercial attraction of Mozambique.[49] Given such an adverse economic context, Indo-Portuguese trading elites could hardly have been expected to acquiesce to an end to slave trafficking in the Indian Ocean. On the contrary, British measures threatened many elites' livelihoods, a circumstance that inclined Portuguese colonials involved in the slave trade to resist what they regarded as unjust encroachment. In the *Estado da Índia,* the interdiction of slaving appeared to be an abuse of Portuguese sovereignty; a British policy forced on the Portuguese colonies at the expense of imperial financial interests. These circumstances as a whole led to a clandestine trade in slaves, in defiance of both British Indian and Portuguese crown prohibitions.

If this commerce does not show up in official customs or demographic records, it is only because the trade had been proscribed and driven out of sight.[50] The scenario in Goa, Damao, and Diu most likely conformed to that envisioned by Indo-Portuguese historian Celsa Pinto in her book *Trade and Finance in Portuguese India:*

> Although British measures to suppress the slave commerce did affect the over-
> all volume of slaves being sent across the Indian Ocean . . . it helped to acceler-
> ate the illicit movement of slaves to the remote creeks and inlets, especially river
> systems with multiple mouths into the sea and then across the . . . Indian Ocean
> to western India, especially in the 1840s.[51]

The topography of Portuguese India was particularly well suited to this kind of illicit commerce. The Goan coastline is cut with numerous rivers and isolated inlets. Abundant beaches facilitate the clandestine landing of small boats and their cargos. With virtually no proper roads until the twentieth century, overland communication in Goa was exceptionally slow and difficult. Rural communities, even if situated only a handful of miles from the capital, Panjim, remained isolated from the supervision of colonial government functionaries. Damao and Diu, too, lay far from the controlling eye of the Goa-based viceroys and governors, and were known as centers of black market commerce.

Recent research has turned up compelling evidence that local officials ignored crown anti-slavery measures in the *Estado da Índia,* and that the Lisbon regime was fully aware of such irregularities.[52] For example, official local records in Goa tell of the public sale of a slave in 1847; the merchandise, a thirty-year-old African man whose name was João, had been brought to India from Mozambique. Moreover, the Portuguese home government was sufficiently suspicious of ongoing illicit slave traffic into their Indian enclaves to issue extraordinary orders to a Portuguese-born official in India, Gil José Conceição, enjoining him in 1849 to keep a vigilant eye on the Goan coastline to ensure that Portuguese policies against slave trafficking were observed.[53] That an illegal commerce in slaves continued to penetrate the permeable membrane of Goa's coastline in the 1840s and 1850s therefore seems a certainty.

Furthermore, local colonial officials in Goa and the rest of the *Estado da Índia* continued to resist regulations aimed at ending slaveholding promulgated in the European metropole. When required to conduct a census of slaves in November and December of 1855, which simultaneously compelled slave masters to register their human property, lower-echelon colonial

officials collaborated with slave owners to provide deceptive, ambiguous returns that revealed an implausibly low number of slaves in Goa, Damao, and
Diu.[54] The colonial population feared, with some justification, that the 1855
slave registry would facilitate a crown-mandated emancipation of all colonial slaves.

By early 1856, then, the colonial government in Portuguese India faced a
grave challenge to its authority. Caught between an adamant royal will to
end African slave imports and a recalcitrant pro-slavery colonial population,
the Portuguese governor was charged with upholding a policy he could not
enforce. To break this impasse, the colonial administration would require recourse to a body of law-enforcement personnel who were dependent solely
on the royal governor and could not be influenced by the populace of the *Estado da Índia.*

Reprising Fear

Given such a caustic economic context, Indo-Portuguese trading elites
could hardly have been expected to acquiesce to an end to slave trafficking in
the Indian Ocean. On the contrary, British measures threatened many elites'
livelihoods, a circumstance that inclined Portuguese colonials involved in
the slave trade to resist what they regarded as unjust encroachment. In Portuguese India (as in newly independent Brazil), abolition appeared to be an
abuse of Portuguese home-government sovereignty. Or, worse, ending the
slave trade appeared ultimately to be a British policy forced on the Portuguese and their colonies at the expense of imperial financial interests.
Moreover, while colonists in India worried about the economic impact of
abolition—estate owners feared losing their movable property held as slave-
laborers, while slave merchants saw a substantial source of income under
threat—there was a social dimension, as well: elites feared the consequences
of assimilating large numbers of former slaves into colonial society. The social repercussions of abolition on a rigidly stratified society weighed heavily
on contemporaries' minds. Even in the metropole, where abolitionist sentiment was supposedly stronger, Portuguese society did not treat manumitted
Africans kindly. Inquisition trials of a slightly earlier era reveal strident hostility toward freed blacks in continental Portugal.[55]

The Indian "Mutiny" of 1857 changed the political environment in Portuguese India regarding the overt importation of Africans for compelled
labor. Top Portuguese authorities in Goa reacted with palpable alarm when
informed of the uprising in British India. António Cesar de Vasconcelos
Correia, the governor of the *Estado da Índia* since early 1855, reported to
Lisbon that a socio-political crisis could not be kept from spreading to the

Portuguese territories if disturbances reached Bombay and Madras. He also asserted that, because of the lack of military formations composed of reliable European soldiers, the position of the Portuguese government in India could not be deemed secure. The governor's reports convey a picture of his complete helplessness, should the political situation in Goa deteriorate as a result of the Indian uprising then spreading throughout northern and central India.[56] Because of the racial and nationalist dimensions of the insurrection in British India, in which units of native sepoy soldiers turned on white officers, colonial administrators, and their dependents, European-born colonial leaders in Goa felt a sudden and acute need to take measures to ensure the availability of a corps of non-native troops on whose loyalty they could depend in a crisis.

In the *Estado da Índia* during this period, typically between a third and a half of the colonial government's effective military strength depended on units composed entirely of native infantry and sepoy militia.[57] In addition to the two regiments of regular infantry troops stationed in central Goa (each composed, theoretically, of Europeans), two strong militia battalions, called "legions" and each numbering (on paper) about seventeen hundred men, were based in the populous Salcete and Ponda provinces of Goa.[58] Membership requirements stipulated that these citizen troops be Christians of good standing in their communities; typically "legion" soldiers were drawn from the middle-caste, fully Indian Christians whose ancestors had been converted during the sixteenth century, shortly after the Portuguese conquest of Goa.[59]

In addition, the governor could call on a unit of approximately two thousand sepoy militiamen, some of whom may have been Christians but who were more likely drawn from the large Hindu population of the inland provinces incorporated into Goa during the eighteenth century (the *Novas Conquistas,* or "New Conquests").[60] Like most militia units anywhere during this period, the men of the "legions" and the sepoy formations were infrequently drilled and the weapons they were issued were substandard. Thus, their military effectiveness against a determined foe was dubious, even if their loyalty to the regime had never been seriously questioned by the colonial administration prior to the uprising in the neighboring British territories.

Of greatest concern to the Portuguese governor and his advisors, because of chronic shortages of conscripts from Europe, was the fact that even the government's formations of "regular" full-time troops included an overwhelmingly large percentage of native-born soldiers. Typically, new European conscript and convict arrivals numbered between one and three hundred annually,[61] but their ranks shrank rapidly because of tropical diseases, and levies from the metropole could never keep pace with colonial demand. Yearly mortality rates of 25 to 50 percent were common for newly disembarked European soldiers until the mid-nineteenth century.[62] Native-born troops therefore commonly outnumbered European-born soldiers in the full-time regular army units of the *Estado da Índia* four or more to one.[63]

These native-born men in the regular army units tended to be Portuguese-speaking *descendentes*. They were practicing Christians who identified culturally with their European colonizers. However, in the eyes of the recently arrived Portuguese colonial governor, news of violent native uprisings in British India had thrown the ultimate loyalty of these hybrid units into doubt. In earlier times, confidence in the native-born troops' loyalty had rested primarily on their regular practice of the Christian faith. Portuguese colonial administrators before 1857 had assumed—accurately—that their elevated status would set Indo-Portuguese Christians apart sufficiently from their Hindu neighbors, and that therefore they would feel little cultural commonality with non-Christian Indians, whether in Goa or beyond.

Population statistics for Goa, Damão, and Diu in the mid-nineteenth century give some striking insight as to why the colonial governor felt he had cause to worry about his ability to control a spreading uprising. Information remanded annually to the *Conselho Ultramarino* (the government Overseas Council in Lisbon) portrays a picture of colonial society in Portuguese India that, while heavily Christianized, typically contained a European-born contingent of about 0.5 percent. In 1851, for example, the population of all territories in Portuguese Goa was reported as 363,788 souls, well under two thousand of whom (1851, in fact) were Portuguese natives.[64]

In the absence of any hope of sufficient numbers of European troops coming rapidly from Portugal, Vasconcelos Correia turned to Portuguese Africa as the nearest source for soldiers who would not share a cultural commonality with Indian native peoples. This decision was mostly a matter of logistics, but it included a calculated manipulation of racial conceits, as well. The governor in Goa believed that he needed troops who were not ethnically Indian or of Indian descent. In an age when wind-powered transport by sea was the only option, Mozambique was the closest Portuguese-controlled region where such troops could be obtained. Portuguese colonial officials desired the presence of a battalion of African soldiers who, because they were culturally alien in Portuguese India, could meet a perceived internal threat from potentially mutinous Indo-Portuguese troops.

Soon after news of the native troops' uprising in British India reached Goa in summer 1857, *Estado da Índia* governor Vasconcelos Correia wrote to his subordinate, the governor-general of Mozambique, Lieutenant Colonel João Tavares de Almeida, with an urgent request for military reinforcements. Specifically, Vasconcelos Correia wanted the government authorities in Mozambique to dispatch two hundred Africans (*negros*) as quickly as possible to Goa—raw recruits "to serve in the army of this state [Portuguese India]."[65] Vasconcelos Correia wanted these recruits to create a distinct elite African battalion for use as a countervailing force to his Indian-born regulars and sepoy soldiers, whose character and loyalty suddenly seemed unreliable.

On May 10, 1858, with the following monsoon mails, Governor Tavares de Almeida in Mozambique replied that sending *negro* recruits was not immediately possible, "not only because of a lack of men and means," but because of the existing interdiction on procuring the desired Africans from the traditional East African slave ports—Kilwa, Zanzibar, Quelimane, and Inhambane.[66] With these comments, the colonial administrator in Mozambique revealed that the Africans he had been asked to procure for ostensibly legitimate military purposes would have come from illicit sources. Most likely, African recruits secured by compulsion along the East African coast in the years following a widely publicized slave ban would have had to be restrained while traveling. Governor Tavares de Almeida was clearly worried, therefore, that any sizable body of recruits he might dispatch aboard a ship bound for India would appear to be contraband, subject to interception and confiscation by the British Navy patrols then frequenting the waters of the Mozambique channel.[67]

Tavares de Almeida had good reason for concern; of this he was reminded daily. At the very moment when Vasconcelos Correia was writing from India to request conscript troops, the government in Mozambique was embroiled in a major international incident involving the attempted illegal embarkation of slaves from Portuguese East Africa. In December 1857, the French bark *Charles et Georges,* Captain Maturin François Rousel commanding, had been detained in Conducia, a small Mozambique port, under suspicion of trafficking in slaves. This resulted in the seizure (and thorough inventory) of the vessel and the arrest of the captain; both were eventually sent to Lisbon for prosecution by a special Admiralty high court tribunal.[68] The Portuguese, in short, made an example out of the *Charles et Georges* case to demonstrate for the British their anti-slavery resolve. In a political environment such as this, Tavares de Almeida was not about to jeopardize his position to send a few hundred African conscripts to Goa.

The practical difference in appearance between a vessel carrying a cargo of imprisoned African army "recruits" (even if they had been legally compelled to serve through official military "conscription") and one laden with African slaves was simply too small to risk shipping such a valuable bulk consignment, regardless of their legal status. The potential political costs were high, too; neither colonial governor would have wanted to be implicated in the international incident that would have resulted had they been caught in contravention of the Anglo-Portuguese Treaty of 1842.

Indeed, the Portuguese would have found it very difficult to circumvent the legal issues of transporting their African "conscripts" to India. In a substantive sense they were, despite having been legally conscripted, slaves, forcibly taken from their homeland and compelled to perform military service in India. However, given the gravity of the crisis in India and the clear exigencies involved in controlling this uprising, Vasconcelos Correia may have hoped that the British Navy would elect to turn a blind eye toward the legally questionable transport of African conscript soldiers to Goa.

In fact, the colonial government in Mozambique had already tested the attitude of the Portuguese home government regarding the legal principle in question. Four years earlier, Vasco Guedes de Carvalho e Meneses, then the governor-general in Lourenço Marques, had written to the Overseas Council in Lisbon, seeking permission to allow the shipment of "a certain number of free contract laborers" recruited in Inhambane to the French colony on Reunion Island.[69] A Gujarati merchant and a French plantation owner had approached the Portuguese colonial officials in Mozambique with this scheme in 1854, but the Overseas Council in the metropole refused to approve the plan, citing explicitly the interdiction of such human traffic under the terms of the 1842 Anglo-Portuguese treaty. In its directive on the matter, dated February 27, 1855, the Overseas Council stated that any such contracts for exporting "free laborers" would "be an incentive to expand the scale of the traffic of slaves in all the forests of that coast [Mozambique]," which in turn would cause the Portuguese government "many difficulties" with the British government, precisely because such labor contracts would contravene the 1842 treaty.[70]

This exchange of colonial administrative correspondence helps to explain the reluctance of the Mozambique governor to meet demands for African conscript recruits from his superior counterpart in India. Whether Governor Vasconcelos Correia in Goa knew of this Overseas Council ruling at the time of his request for African soldiers is unclear but, from his point of view, the changed circumstances occasioned by the Indian uprising obviously justified bending the treaty rules to obtain the military means necessary to safeguard the Portuguese enclaves.

In contrast, João Tavares de Almeida clearly felt that the 1842 treaty tied his hands. In a letter to the king and the Overseas Council dated February 26, 1858, the Mozambique governor-general justified his not complying with Vasconcelos Correia's orders from Goa, arguing that "all of the Africans resident in the Portuguese territories are either slaves or free . . . slaves may not enlist, and the free Africans [*negros livres*] will not volunteer for military service abroad." Tavares de Almeida complained that he was unable to fill the many vacancies in his own colonial armed forces, let alone find enough willing free Africans to fill an entire battalion for service in India. Conscription was not an option, he asserted, because the eligible free blacks would, upon hearing that forced military conscription was underway in the colony, flee to the forests of the interior, beyond the reach of Portuguese press gangs.[71]

As the capstone to his argument, the governor-general of Mozambique cited the standing crown interdiction on the export of forced African laborers, based on the 1842 Anglo-Portuguese treaty: "For here you see a difficulty of no small size, . . . to avoid this very powerful inconvenience, I am asked to raise my hand . . . [and employ] the expedient that ordinarily has been adopted in this province to obtain soldiers. But can this be the intention of the [home] government? It would appear not, because of the express prohibition on the exit of *negros* under the title of free colonists" in then-current anti-slave-trafficking regulations. Tavares de Almeida then suggested that the only way to get free Africans to willingly volunteer for military service abroad would be to offer them "a bounty of five or six *patacas*." The governor vowed to "study that objective" and "employ all of [his] strengths" to fill the ranks of the battalion Vasconcelos Correia had requisitioned.[72]

By February of 1859, the Goan colonial governor's continued wariness of his native soldiers was sufficient for him to order a shift in troop deployments within the *Estado da Índia*. Vasconcelos Correia moved a battalion of his best soldiers, elite *caçadores* (literally "hunters"—a specially trained light infantry regiment composed principally of Europeans) to guard the governor's palace in Panjim, thus relieving them of their usual duty of guarding Goa's borders. In place of the *caçadores,* he sent one of his much larger (and largely native-born) battalions of *infantaria* into the frontier provinces, hoping to minimize their potential for mutiny by dispersing them around Goa's 150-mile perimeter. This decision made logistical sense: during the period of crisis in British India, the more numerous regular infantry, broken into smaller units and under the close supervision of their European officers, could better control access to Goa, denying admission to outside agitators and censoring printed materials that crossed the frontier. At the same time, dividing this mixed-race battalion among Goa's numerous border posts and ordering them to conduct regular small-unit patrols greatly reduced the likelihood that the native troops would conspire to unite in rebellion.[73]

On February 18, 1859, Vasconcelos Correia wrote to Mozambique again to press the governor there to fulfill the request for troops made the previous year. Vasconcelos Correia wanted the two hundred *negros* to be sent with the coming monsoon, and promised to reciprocate with an equal number of "recruits" from India. An exchange of soldiers "would be very advantageous for Goa and Mozambique," Vasconcelos Correia wrote, "because the recruits native to this state [India] will serve well there [in Mozambique], and not have the horrible mortality that we unhappy Europeans have had." The governor asserted that he would "send the recruits from India with the next monsoon [that is, at the end of February 1859], so that the same ships can return from Mozambique at the end of winter with the requested two hundred *negros.*"[74]

To convince his reluctant subordinate, Vasconcelos Correia claimed that he had obtained permission from the home government to exchange recruits (a highly unlikely assertion, given the time required for the necessary correspondence to have reached Lisbon and a response returned). African troops were desirable in India, he continued knowingly, because they "provide good service, without being despoiled by the climate, as happens in general to Europeans."[75] (The practice of using non-native troops to control indigenous populations did in fact develop during a later period and worked both ways: Indian soldiers were also sent to Mozambique in the nineteenth and twentieth centuries to police the cities. Police in Maputo are, to this day, known colloquially as *cipaios*, or "sepoys" in Portuguese.[76])

Vasconcelos Correia knew as well as the governor of Mozambique that the line separating the practical circumstances of the life of an African military conscript from those of a slave was virtually non-existent—particularly for untrained recruits being conveyed unwillingly across the Indian Ocean. In experiential terms, the difference between these two statuses was mostly a matter of semantics, the thin veil of a legal definition. However, in the charged political climate following the Indian Mutiny of 1857, the governor in Goa recognized that this key legal distinction could be used to admit illicit, captive Africans into Portuguese India and mask the underlying nature of their forced military labor. Moreover, given the contemporary social climate among elites of the *Estado da Índia,* who had demonstrated through their deliberate non-compliance with the slave registry of 1855 that they resented crown policies designed to curtail slavery, Vasconcelos Correia could expect little criticism from local colonists for his action.

The decision of the *Estado da Índia*'s governor to order forced conscriptions of African recruits from Mozambique in 1858 reflects an acute official fear of the potential power of the indigenous population living in Portuguese Indian territories. The decision reveals a deep-seated dread of imminent rebellion, or at least of serious trouble stirred up by agitators from across the border spilling into the Portuguese enclaves.

However, when considering the expedience and propriety of employing Africans as soldiers (whether as slaves or conscripts), and when taking a decision about this matter in 1857, the precedent the Portuguese governor of the *Estado da Índia* considered was not regional practice but age-old global Portuguese experience. Pressing African conscripts into military service in 1858–59 was a pragmatic act of desperation and necessity, but a long-used one, not a course based on the venerable martial traditions of neighboring Muslim and Hindu potentates.

That is, the Portuguese approach to and use of enslaved military labor was qualitatively different from that found in the other Indian Ocean societies discussed in this volume. African slaves in Portuguese colonies (be they Indian, South American, African, or Asian) became soldiers only on a temporary basis in response to an impending military threat, after which they were returned, usually well rewarded,[77] to their accustomed labors.

Portuguese colonial officials throughout their empire assiduously avoided setting any precedent that would have predicated their rule on the existence of standing units of slave-soldiers. Only extremely late in their colonial experience, and when faced with the extraordinary threat of an Indian native uprising, did the Portuguese colonial officials in Goa opt for the creation of a standing unit of "homogenous" African soldiers to reinforce their authority over native subject peoples. And even then, the men destined for service in that unit were meant to be legal conscripts levied from a "free" native population in Mozambique, not slaves.

In the event, Portuguese fears in India were unfounded; in the wake of the "mutiny" in British India, the Portuguese colonial areas remained calm. Colonial military unit cohesion held firm, and native-born soldiers serving under the Portuguese flag never threatened an uprising against their colonial rulers.[78] After all, for most Indo-Portuguese troops, their European officers and colonial governors were also their co-religionists. Christianity was (and remains) central to Indo-Portuguese identity in Goa, Damao, and Diu, providing a source of status and distinction from their Hindu and Muslim neighbors. If the Indian rebellion was a test of the deliberate Portuguese policy of using religious conversion to create a loyal colonial populace, then one could point to the political stability in Goa during the crisis of 1857–59 as vindication of that policy.

However, this episode also provides an insight into contemporary Portuguese attitudes toward the continued use of African forced labor in their overseas colonies. Top officials in the *Estado da Índia* demonstrated their easy willingness to circumvent existing international anti-slavery regulations to meet what they perceived as overriding imperial demands.

To compare the Portuguese situation in India with that of the British: the ability of the British to maintain the loyalty of their own English and, more importantly, very large numbers of Scottish troops in India was never in doubt (even during the Jacobite uprisings of 1745). Further, the British were able to maintain sufficient numbers of European regiments, with their superior training and weapons, to administer the Indian colonies and coordinate military operations with native troop formations. The comparatively strong British presence in India was, until 1857, able to effectively exploit religious differences between Hindus and Muslims, as well as rivalries between regional native rulers, to achieve military and political dominance. Hence, the British did not find it necessary to import African soldiers to India to create a countervailing force—the British learned to manipulate indigenous countervailing forces already present in India.

In the exploitation of African labor for military ends, the Portuguese colonial enterprise transcended Indian Ocean regional patterns and forms, though Portuguese methods certainly appeared on the surface to resemble some of the practices found in that region from the fifteenth to the twentieth centuries. One key difference is that neither in India nor anywhere else did the Portuguese as a rule maintain standing regular units of enslaved soldiers. African slaves were known by experience to fight exceptionally well for their European masters but, across the empire, in Macau, Malacca, Goa, El Mina, and Brazil, slaves were pressed into service only on an ad hoc basis. Most frequently, African slaves fought as temporary levies in mixed militia units or ships' crews, alongside European volunteers or convicts—technically the slaves' social superiors, but equals in martial terms under conditions of battle.

After a military crisis had passed, Portuguese officials were quick to reward loyal slaves for their martial exploits (with money, goods, privileges, or even manumission), but equally quick to disband or stand down the ad hoc militia units in which slaves had fought. Consequently, in the Portuguese sphere, slave military formations did not develop the status or *esprit de corps* that, in the other societies considered for this volume, was so fundamental to maintaining the loyalty, reliability, and efficacy of the wholly enslaved standing military formations on which state political stability depended.

During the early modern period (before the nineteenth century), only in Brazil did the Portuguese allow the formation of militia units homogeneously composed of "black," "*pardo*," or "mulatto" soldiers (divided deliberately by racial characteristic), whose prestige and *esprit de corps* rested substantially on the skin color identification of the men in the respective units. But the crucial difference is that these soldiers were not slaves but free men of color who volunteered for military service expressly to partake of the esteem imparted by soldiering in a regiment whose very identity was defined by the racial characteristics of the men who formed its rank and file.[79]

Conclusion

The Portuguese enclaves in India continued to illegally absorb and exploit African slave-laborers long after the Anglo-Portuguese treaty of 1842. A significant number of Indo-Portuguese slaveholders did not willingly give up their slaves after 1842, and purposefully conspired to underreport their actual ownership of slaves when required to do so in 1855. Some colonial officials, sympathetic to this cause, were complicit in the popular resistance to their sovereign's anti-slavery policies. Regional administrators filed misleading documentation and concealed the true extent of slave holdings in Portuguese India. Thereafter, top-rank officials in the *Estado da Índia* found quasi-legal means to circumvent both the spirit and the letter of the 1842 treaty. No less a figure than the royal governor of Portuguese India arranged for the illicit, clandestine transport of Africans into Goa for the purpose of performing forced labor, even if it was military service in a time of imperial crisis.

What was the ultimate fate of this Mozambique contingent of conscript soldiers in 1858–59? The historical record is not clear. There is no British Navy record of a Portuguese vessel carrying African troops being made to submit to a search while crossing the Indian Ocean in the late 1850s. If this battalion of raw East African troops did arrive in Goa in late 1859 or 1860, they would have found the uprising in British India effectively over. The perceived dire need for their presence as a countervailing force had thus passed, so it is unlikely that they were ever trained for or saw military service. Given the impecunious state of the Portuguese colonies in India at that time, it is probable that any conscripted African recruits arriving in Goa after 1860 would have been contracted out as civilian laborers, in order to allow the government of the *Estado da Índia* to recoup some of its expenditure for their procurement and transport. However, for the Africans being compelled to work in a foreign land they could not escape, the practical difference between their legal conscript labor and the illegal toil of slaves would have been essentially meaningless.

This brief consideration of the Portuguese response to the 1857 revolt in British India offers scholars of Lusophone studies a valuable caveat about accepting too benign a view of events in the history of slavery in Portugal's eastern colonies—a view that posits a period of sustained regulation and eventual abolition, thus facilitating a relatively painless transition from a slaveholding culture to a society with a healthy disdain for slavery. Such a view glosses over a strong legacy of racism in Portuguese colonial society, as well as the documented continued exploitation of forced laborers in East and West Africa, even into the twentieth century, under conditions that differed from slavery only in name.[80]

Notes

Abbreviations:

AHU	Arquivo Histórico Ultramarino (Portuguese Overseas Historical Archive), Lisbon, Portugal
HAG	Historical Archive of Goa, India
MR	Livros do Monções do Reino (annual volumes of official state correspondence to the *Estado da Índia*).
cap.	*capilha* (folder)
cx.	*caixa* (box)
doc.	*documento* (document)
fol.	*folho* (folio)

Parts of this article were first presented at the conference "Slavery, Unfree Labor, and Revolt in the Indian Ocean Region," organized by Professor Gwyn Campbell at the University of Avignon, France (Oct. 4–6, 2001). I wish to thank the American Institute of Indian Studies and the National Endowment of the Humanities of the United States for providing the grant that made this research possible. In addition, for logistical support in Goa, India, I am grateful to the Xavier Centre for Historical Research and the Portuguese Fundação Oriente.

1. Celsa Pinto, *Trade and Finance in Portuguese India: A Study of the Portuguese Country Trade, 1770–1840*, Xavier Centre for Historical Research Series no. 5 (New Delhi: Concept Publishing Company, 1994), 170–71.

2. Sunil Kumar, "When Slaves Were Nobles: The Shamsi Bandagan in the Early Delhi Sultanate," *Studies in History* 10, no. 1 (Jan.–June 1994), 23–25, 52.

3. Charles R. Boxer, *The Golden Age of Brazil: Growing Pains of a Colonial Society, 1695–1750* (Manchester, U.K.: Carcanet Press, 1995), 88–89, 142–43; idem, *Fidalgos of the Far East, 1550–1770* (Oxford: Oxford University Press, 1968), 76–87.

4. William D. Phillips, *Slavery from Roman Times to the Early Trans-Atlantic Trade* (Minneapolis: University of Minnesota Press, 1985), 78.

5. Ibid., 78.

6. Ibid., 77–78, 86–87.

7. Timothy J. Coates, introduction to *Convicts and Orphans: Forced and State-Sponsored Colonization in the Portuguese Empire, 1550–1755* (Stanford, Calif.: Stanford University Press, 2002).

8. For mortality and disease attrition rates of newly arrived European convict soldiers in the nineteenth century, see HAG MR, nos. 180B (1800), fol. 442; 181A (1801), fol. 201; 182 (1802), fol. 278; 196B (1818–19), fol. 810; and 212A (1838), fol. 199.

9. Boxer, *Fidalgos of the Far East*, 76–87.

10. Correspondence of Jan Pieterzoon Coen quoted in ibid., 85.

11. Journal of Edward Monnox, the English factor at Ormuz, cited in ibid., 85–86.

12. Ibid., 86.

13. See Frédéric Mauro, ed., *O Império Luso-Brasileiro, 1620–1750*, vol. 7 of Joel Serrão and A. H. de Oliveira Marques, eds., *Nova História da Expansão Portuguesa* (Lisbon: Editorial Estampa, 1991), 25.

14. Joaquim Romero Magalhães, "A Construção do Espaço Brasileiro," in Francisco Bethencourt and Kirti Chaudhuri, eds., *História da Expansão Portuguesa*, 5 vols. (Lisbon: Circulo de Leitores, 1998–2001), 2:55.

15. Mauro, ed., *O Império Luso-Brasileiro*, 32–37.

16. Quoted in Michael N. Pearson, *The Portuguese in India*, New Cambridge History of India 1, (Cambridge: Cambridge University Press, 1990), 95.

17. P. P. Shirodkar, "Slavery in Coastal India," in *Purabhilekh-Puratatva* (Panaji, Goa: Journal of the Directorate of Archives, Archaeology, and Museum) 3, no. 1 (Jan.–June 1985), 32.

18. Archana Kakodkar, "Source Material for Latin America in Goa (with Special Reference to Brazil)," in Teotónio R. de Souza, ed., *Essays in Goan History* (New Delhi: Concept Publishing Company, 1989), 211.

19. Boxer, *Golden Age of Brazil*, 87–90.

20. Quoted in ibid., 96.

21. Ibid., 101–102.

22. Ibid., 142; and A. J. R. Russell-Wood, "Comunidades Étnicas," in Bethencourt and Chaudhuri, eds., *História da Expansão Portuguesa*, 3:220–21.

23. Shirodkar, "Slavery in Coastal India," 36–37.

24. To cite one example, in a letter dated July 23, 1726, Bernardo de Sousa Estrela, the administrator of the royal treasury in Bahia, Brazil, wrote to the king in Lisbon, Dom João V, about the lack of money to pay soldiers, and asking permission to augment the garrison regiments with levies of slaves. Arquivo Histórico Ultramarino-Baia, cx. 23, doc. 82 (AHU Administração Central; Conselho Ultramarino; Series 005 [Bahia], cx. 27 doc. 2469). See also Rene J. Barendse, *The Arabian Seas: The Indian Ocean World of the Seventeenth Century* (Armonk, N.Y.: M. E. Sharpe, 2002), 341.

25. Barendse, *Arabian Seas*, 111.

26. Pedro Machado, "A Forgotten Corner of the Indian Ocean: Gujarati Merchants, Portuguese India, and the Mozambique Slave Trade, c. 1730–1830," in Gwyn Campbell, ed., *The Structure of Slavery in Indian Ocean Africa and Asia* (London: Frank Cass, 2004), 19.

27. Edward Alpers, "Flight to Freedom: Escape from Slavery among Bonded Africans in the Indian Ocean World, c. 1750–1962," in Campbell, ed., *Structure of Slavery*, 57.

28. Suzanne Miers, *Britain and the Ending of the Slave Trade* (New York: Africana Publishing Company, 1975), 58, 76, 127–29.

29. Suzanne Miers and Igor Kopytoff, eds., *Slavery in Africa: Historical and Anthropological Perspectives* (Madison: University of Wisconsin Press, 1977), 142.

30. Ibid., 170.

31. Barendse, *Arabian Seas*, 357.

32. Jeanette Pinto, *Slavery in Portuguese India, 1510–1842* (Bombay: Himalaya Publishing House, 1992), 24–33.

33. See A. C. De C. M. Saunders, *A Social History of Black Slaves and Freedmen in Portugal, 1441–1555* (Cambridge: Cambridge University Press, 1982).

34. HAG 2976, fols. 2v–6r.

35. Pinto, *Trade and Finance,* 164–68; see also HAG no. 2976, fols. 2v-6r. Finally, see Rudy Bauss, "A Demographic Study of Portuguese India and Macau as Well as Comments on Mozambique and East Timor, 1750–1850," *Indian Economic and Social History Review* 24, no. 2 (Apr.–June 1997), 199–216.

36. For a discussion of this point, see Bauss, "Demographic Study," 209. Bauss's analysis is flawed in two respects. First, he reported that, in the population records of Portuguese India, anyone termed a *negro* was a slave, while anyone referred to as a *pardo* was a free person of color. These assertions are incorrect. Bauss's semantic misunderstanding of these Portuguese terms in turn distorts his demographic representation of slavery in Portuguese India, causing him to underestimate the total number of slaves in the nineteenth century.

37. See Mauro, ed., *O Império Luso-Brasileiro,* 32–34; and Magalhães, "A Construção," 55–57.

38. See Russell-Wood, "Comunidades Étnicas," 211–22.

39. Carlos Xavier, "Daman Port and Shipyards," in *Purabhilekh-Puratatva* 3, no. 1 (Jan.–June 1985), 10–12. Annual customs receipts at Damão port fell from 64,501 *xerafin*s in 1838 to 26,626 *xerafin*s in 1840, and from 21,662 *xerafin*s in 1846 to 7,529 *xerafin*s in 1853.

40. Ibid., 131–59.

41. Pearson, *Portuguese in India,* 151; Pinto, *Trade and Finance,* 169–71.

42. Pinto, *Trade and Finance,* 170.

43. Miers, *Britain and the Ending of the Slave Trade,* 23–28.

44. Ibid., 368–74.

45. Captain Kol, "Statistical Report on the Portuguese Settlements in India," in *Selections from the Records of the Bombay Government (No. 10, New Series): Memoir on the Sawunt Waree State . . .* (London, 1855; reprint, New Delhi: Asian Educational Services, 1995), 368–69.

46. Shirodkar, "Slavery in Coastal India," 30–31. When slaves had converted to Islam and been resold to Muslim masters, their money value was remitted to Goa; runaway slaves who refused to renounce the Christian beliefs they followed while working under Portuguese rule were to be returned to their masters in Goa.

47. Pinto, *Trade and Finance,* 169–71; and Shirodkar, "Slavery in Coastal India," 37–39. These circumstances also helped give rise to Siddi communities of fugitive Afro-Indians living in British India. See Pinto, *Slavery in Portuguese India,* 137–38; and R. R. S. Chauhan, *Africans in India: From Slavery to Royalty* (New Delhi: Asian Publication Services, 1995), chapter 2.

48. Miers, *Britain and the Ending of the Slave Trade,* 24.

49. Pinto, *Trade and Finance,* 168–69; and Shirodkar, "Slavery in Coastal India," 38.

50. To this observation should be added the caveat that the English traveler Richard F. Burton, who spent several months in Goa in 1850, did not think the slave population there substantial enough to merit mentioning, except vaguely in passing, in his account of Portuguese-held Goa written at mid-century. See Richard F. Burton, *Goa and the Blue Mountains; or, Six Months of Sick Leave* (London, 1851; reprint, New Delhi: Asia Educational Services, 1998), chapter 2.

51. Pinto, *Trade and Finance*, 170–71.

52. Timothy Walker, "Abolishing the Slave Trade in Portuguese India: Documentary Evidence of Popular and Official Resistance to Crown Policy, 1842–1860," in Ned Alpers, Gwyn Campbell, and Michael Salman, eds., *Slavery and Resistance in Africa and Asia* (New York: Routledge, 2005), 82–98.

53. Pinto, *Trade and Finance*, 170–71.

54. Walker, "Abolishing the Slave Trade," 87–89.

55. Timothy Walker, "Slaves, Free Blacks, and the Inquisition in Early Modern Portugal: Race as a Factor in Magical Crimes Trials," in *Bulletin of the Society for Spanish and Portuguese Historical Studies* 25, no. 2 (autumn 2000), 10–14.

56. P. P. Shirodkar, "Insurgency, 1857 Mutiny in Western India and the Portuguese," in *Researches in Indo-Portuguese History* (Jaipur: Publication Scheme, 1998), 2:181–82.

57. HAG MR no. 212A, fols. 198–205; and HAG MR no. 196B, fols. 808–12.

58. HAG MR no. 173, fol. 228 r/v; HAG MR no. 176A, fol. 263 r/v; and HAG MR no. 181A, fol. 64 r/v.

59. See Padre M. J. Gabriel de Saldanha, *História de Goa (Politica e Arquelógica)* (Goa, 1925; reprint, New Delhi: Asia Educational Services, 1990), 284–85n1.

60. Ibid. "Sepoys" was written as *sepoias* in eighteenth-century Portuguese documents.

61. See HAG MR no. 181A, fols. 9–45; and HAG MR no. 181B, fols. 370–98.

62. See HAG MR no. 181A, fols. 65, 194–201; and HAG MR no. 212A, fol. 200v.

63. HAG MR no. 212A, fols. 198–205; and HAG MR no. 196B, fols. 808–12.

64. HAG MR, cited in José Nicolau da Fonseca, *An Historical and Archaeological Sketch of the City of Goa* (New Delhi: Asia Educational Services, 1994), 8.

65. HAG no. 1449, fols. 81v–82r.

66. Ibid.

67. As the sole authority responsible for approving the export of Africans from Mozambique, the governor would have incurred a great deal of professional risk by sending African conscripts to Goa. See Barendse, *Arabian Seas*, 357.

68. AHU-ACL-SEMU-DGU (Moçambique), cx. 1301, pasta 19, caps. 1-1 to 1-2, December 1857–December 1858 (Direcção Geral do Ultramar-Moçambique).

69. AHU-ACL-SEMU-DGU (Moçambique), cx. 1298, pasta 16, cap. 5, doc. 186, dated February 27, 1855 (Direcção Geral do Ultramar-Moçambique).

70. Ibid. The governor-general, for his part, disagreed with the Overseas Council's finding. In his response, dated December 12, 1855 (included in the same AHU document), Carvalho e Meneses sought to demonstrate that, "contrary to the conclusions of the Overseas Council, . . . it is of greater convenience to the province [of Mozambique] to send workers to Mauritius for determined times"; he therefore requested that the home government authorize him to "permit their exit through the medium of contracts conveniently legalized" for this purpose.

71. AHU-ACL-SEMU-DGU (Moçambique), cx. 1302, pasta 20, cap. 1, doc. 57, dated February 26, 1858 (Direcção Geral do Ultramar-Moçambique).

72. Ibid.

73. HAG no. 1449, fols. 81r–81v.

74. Ibid., fols. 81v–82r.

75. Ibid.

76. I am grateful to Dr. Sérgio Mascarenhas, director of the Fundação Oriente in Goa, for this reference, and for his critical reading of this chapter.

77. Immediately following their victorious defense of Macau, slaves were manumitted on the field of battle and provided with gifts of food. See Boxer, *Fidalgos of the Far East*, 85.

78. Shirodkar, "Insurgency, 1857 Mutiny," 183–84.

79. Boxer, *Golden Age of Brazil*, 142–43; and Russell-Wood, "Comunidades Étnicas," 220–21.

80. See Pearson, *Portuguese in India*, 150–52; and Miers, *Britain and the Ending of the Slave Trade*, 27–28.

11

Indian Muslim Modernists and the Issue of Slavery in Islam

Avril A. Powell

> Three radical evils flow from the faith, in all ages and in every country, and must continue to flow *so long as the Coran is the standard of belief.* FIRST: Polygamy, Divorce, and Slavery, are maintained and perpetuated; —striking as they do at the root of public morals, poisoning domestic life, and disorganizing society.
>
> William Muir, *Life of Mahomet,* 1861[1]

> The main intention behind everything that the Prophet of God did, and all the orders that the Prophet issued, was to liberate slaves and to annihilate slavery.
>
> Saiyid Ahmad Khan, "Ibtal-i ghulami," 1871[2]

By the end of the nineteenth century some Indian Muslim men, broadly categorized as "modernist," rejected, *inter alia,* the legitimacy of slavery in Islam; these had begun to influence thinking "far beyond the boundaries of Indian Islam."[3] Slavery was one of a cluster of issues with which any scholar concerned to present an agenda for social change would be obliged to deal, since Western abolitionist ideologies had reinforced an ongoing criticism of Islamic societies. The charge by William Muir, a strongly evangelical civilian administrator in north India, was typical of many put forward in works on Islam published by Europeans after the rebellion of 1857–58. Yet the responses by educated Indian Muslims, notably by Sir Saiyid Ahmad Khan, scarcely touched the Indian practices of slavery in early or later centuries. The practice of military slavery, a characteristic institution of medieval polities in northern India, was never referred to in these discussions. Even domestic forms of slavery, the focus of the European critiques, were referred to in the early stages of the controversy either euphemistically, or only in reference to other regions of the Muslim world. Instead, their responses took the form of exegesis on the bases for slavery in the Qur'an and *hadith* (reports of the sayings and actions of the Prophet and his companions); offering favorable comparisons to non-Muslim social systems and practices in Europe and America, they read as apologia for Islamic social organization. So, if slavery in its historical and contemporary forms in the Indian environment was not at the heart of the matter, why was it among Indian Muslims more than other Muslim communities that a legalistic and largely rhetorical response was first articulated in the 1870s?

This essay argues that the debate over slavery among Indian Muslims was originally a narrowly focused and peculiarly north Indian phenomenon, reflecting irritants particular to the immediate post-Rebellion environment in colonial northwest India. Two of the three key Indian Muslims whose responses to the colonial British critique this essay analyzes were to have important political roles later and were to enjoy a wide readership in late nineteenth-century India. One was Sir Saiyid Ahmad Khan, formerly *sadr amin* in the British civil courts, and later founder of the Anglo-Muhammadan College at Aligarh (see map 2). The other was Justice Saiyid Ameer Ali (Amir 'Ali), chief justice of the Calcutta high court in the 1890s. The third, Cheragh Ali (Chiragh 'Ali), was a close associate of Saiyid Ahmad and an administrator in the princely state of Hyderabad.[4] All three served long periods in British employment, mainly in legal capacities. Curiously, this brought them into social intercourse with, even proximity to, the colonial authors whose views they challenged. Their initial target readers and lecture audiences were the British reading public, as well as English-knowing Indian Muslim students. Both Amir 'Ali and Saiyid Ahmad, while resident in London, published in English first. Clearly, their primary common purpose was to provide a well-founded response to "popular" critiques of Islam in the language of its critics. Subsequent publications in Urdu, it will be shown, were speedily redirected to a new and broader Indian Muslim readership, but with some crucial changes in emphasis.

The significance of their initial responses, in the early 1870s, has not been adequately recognized. This is largely because their writings on slavery and other social questions in the early period went into many editions, especially in the 1890s, when the issues were attracting wider attention outside India. Later editions, in which the authors too had introduced changes, were more readily cited. The result was an anachronistic assessment of the value of Saiyid Ahmad's "Ibtal-i ghulami" (Refutation of Slavery) and Amir 'Ali's

Spirit of Islam for the history of Islamic modernism. The reformist writing on slavery and related social issues belonged to the genesis of Indian Muslim rethinking in the specific colonial context of the 1860s and 1870s, not the 1890s. Misperceptions of the chronology have, in turn, led to a generalized oversight of the causal relationship between these first London-published English texts and the spate of similar, but differently nuanced, essays and articles on slavery that appeared in northwest India in Urdu within a few months of the first English publications in the early 1870s. This essay draws attention to some hitherto unnoticed publications of this kind, notably by Saiyid Ahmad. These were historically significant because, when redirected to a north Indian Muslim readership, they prompted a response from some conservative *ulama* circles. This happened twenty years before their translations into Arabic began to feed into deliberations on slavery within the vast domains of the Ottoman Empire in the 1890s. For this reason, too, we need to understand how a local Indian Muslim debate over slavery became part of a global debate on Islam and history.

Both nineteenth-century colonial servants and Muslim religious scholars had reason to be ambivalent about the existence of various categories of slavery and servitude in Indian Muslim communities. Legislation was supposed to have ended slavery as well as slave trading in 1843, but the British East India Company's employees proved half-hearted in implementing the law. A recent study has shown that the courts "continued to adjudicate in matters concerning claims in slaves, and vitiated administrative practice into the 1870s."[5] Some high-minded efforts by local magistrates to investigate both law and practice proved ineffective. Many officials continued to look the other way when faced with evidence of domestic slavery, their erasures and denials morally justified by prevailing notions that Indian forms of domestic slavery were uniquely benign.[6] In this environment Muslim spokesmen were only rarely called on to give advice.

Yet it is significant that when they were so asked, their condemnations of the institution were fairly comprehensive. For instance, a leading mufti in British service in Delhi condemned slavery in the mid-1820s in tones of moral and humanitarian fervor very similar to those some modernists would employ nearly fifty years later.[7] On the other hand, *fatwa*s (decisions on points of Islamic jurisprudence) supporting the Qur'anic basis of slavery, such as one issued in Saharanpur, do not seem to have circulated widely at the time. In spite of some intermittent and half-hearted attention, slavery in Islam remained non-contentious until some local colonial officials began in the 1860s to make slave institutions a significant part of their broader condemnations of Islamic societies as inherently incapable of initiating progressive measures.

The European critics of Islam most resented by Indian Muslim scholars were those scholar-administrators long employed in the colonial service of the North-Western Provinces. Sir William Muir, the British official whose critique heads this chapter, was one of the most regularly cited in Muslim modernist rejoinders in the period between 1870 and 1890s. By the time the first "modernist" replies to him were published, Muir held the influential position of lieutenant-governor of the North-Western Provinces. Muir and Saiyid Ahmad had been young colleagues, even "friends," in the provincial administrative service in the 1840s, when Muir began the collection of Arabic manuscripts on which his *Life of Mahomet* would later be based. This biography commenced as an ostensibly sympathetic and scholarly study but evolved into a damning critique of Islamic social institutions; in it slavery, legitimated by and underscored in the Qur'an, was identified as one of the "radical evils" (together with polygamy and divorce) making change impossible in Muslim societies. Muir's evangelical perspective and immense influence as a colonial administrator added greater weight to his frequently publicized conviction that Islamic societies were inherently incapable of adaptation.

Relentless though this flood of Western criticism seemed, some earlier British apologists for Islam, such as Charles Forster, Godfrey Higgins, and Thomas Carlyle, had found various positive qualities in it. In the 1860s, they were joined by an assortment of London-based clerics, literary figures, teachers, and journalists who chose, both for sincere and for somewhat perverse reasons, to abet the Indian modernists in their apologetic efforts on behalf of Islam.[8] So to London in the late 1860s discussion now turns.

The London Context for Discussion of Slavery in Islam

Unexpectedly, London provided an opportunity for both Saiyid Ahmad and Amir 'Ali to publicize in English their responses to the criticisms of Muir and others on slavery and other issues. One of Saiyid Ahmad's motives in taking leave from the British judicial service in 1869 to accompany his student sons to London and Cambridge was to collect data from libraries and archives to answer the "injustice and bigotry" of Muir's biography of the Prophet: it "has cut my heart to pieces," he said.[9] His original plan was probably to publish a reply in Urdu after his return to India. Immediate events and encounters precipitated instead a series of twelve quickly written essays, ostensibly on the life of the Prophet, but several of which concerned social aspects of both pre- and post-Islamic societies. The collection was rapidly published in London in English before his return to India in 1871.[10]

In contrast, Amir ʿAli, still a student, had arrived with no plans for the lectures and publications that quickly materialized from his own encounters with abolitionists and other British and American social reformers, and from his reading of the same provocative European works as were agitating Saiyid Ahmad. During their residences in London both of these lawyers had numerous opportunities to observe English social life, thanks to invitations from "returned" Raj officials. Though they occasionally met to discuss politics, they tended to move in separate social circles and, as far as their memoirs reveal, did not discuss the social questions they were both investigating.[11]

Of the two it was the much younger Amir ʿAli, ostensibly studying for bar exams and still completely untried in the literary and political world of Calcutta, who threw himself more enthusiastically into liberal and reformist discussion circles in London. These included Hyde Park rallies with members of the embryonic women's property and suffrage societies, accompanied sometimes by the campaigners Millicent and Henry Fawcett, who had befriended him on his first arrival. Another early friend was Mary Carpenter, who invited him into her recently founded National Indian Association, where he was soon invited to join the council. Acutely conscious of the personal advantages he might gain from these friendships, he seized every opportunity to debate and compare the social systems of Europe, America, Arabia, and India in salons, learned societies, and open-air meetings. Within a year of his arrival, while he was still only twenty-one, he had delivered a lecture to the National Indian Association titled "The Mahommedans of India" that was rapidly published as a pamphlet.[12] Although he did not broach the topic of slavery in this first lecture, its success encouraged his first full-fledged monograph in English on Islamic history. This was published in London in 1873 as *A Critical Examination of the Life of Muhammad*. It included a short chapter on slavery, and another on the position of women in Islam.

Saiyid Ahmad, already much better known in British Indian official circles than Amir ʿAli, had access to a more upper-class social circle than his younger colleague. During visits to a number of public and learned institutions, he gave talks in Urdu, which were translated into English. Although both were very aware of the previous decades' abolitionist fervor over slavery (which Saiyid Ahmad later reviewed in one of his Urdu articles), it was Amir ʿAli who chose to engage in face-to-face informal discussion of slavery with such figures as William Henry Channing, member of a leading American abolitionist family, now living in London. To Channing he later attributed the stimulus to write his first book on the Prophet's teachings. As Clare

Midgley and others have shown, many abolitionists were by then diverting their energies from Atlantic slavery into new liberal and progressive campaigns, notably on women's issues, in which Amir ʿAli too, early in his London visit, began to show an interest.[13]

Neither Saiyid Ahmad nor Amir ʿAli mentioned India in their early works on slavery: their reference points were rather the slave systems of the ancient world, of pre-Islamic Arabia and the transatlantic plantations. Their own stances remained essentially apologetic at this stage. In addition to directly confronting the Qurʾanic exegesis of Muir and other critics, they cited some of those Western authors, already mentioned, who had chosen to be helpfully apologetic concerning Islam. Godfrey Higgins's *Apology* for the "celebrated" and "illustrious" prophet, published forty years earlier, was especially favored by Saiyid Ahmad. Higgins had criticized the Christian hypocrisy he felt was implicit in the transatlantic slave trade, comparing its deleterious effects to the advantage of forms of household slavery practiced under Islam.[14] Saiyid Ahmad also received on-the-spot assistance from one John Davenport, an obscure litterateur and linguist, who assisted him with his plans for responding to William Muir. Reciprocally, Saiyid Ahmad then arranged for Davenport's own *An Apology for the Koran* to be published in Urdu in Delhi within a year.[15]

The results of these collaborations were first seen in an essay by Saiyid Ahmad, published in English as "Whether Islam Has Been Beneficial or Injurious to Human Society in General, and to the Mosaic and Christian Dispensations."[16] At this stage, and for this particular readership, he stopped short of asserting that slavery had been completely prohibited in Islam. However, he informed his British readers that, while slavery had evolved and flourished in all early sedentary societies, including pre-Islamic Arabia, it was the Prophet Muhammad who had made the first efforts to proscribe it—unlike the Mosaic leaders and Jesus Christ. Appreciative though he was of Godfrey Higgins's view that domestic slavery as practiced by Muslims was as nothing "compared to the cruelty and horrors of the African slave trade, and the plantations of the West Indies," Saiyid Ahmad considered Higgins's *Apology* to be misleading in underestimating just how close the Prophet had come to the complete abolition of slavery. Thus he commented, "To the remark of Mr. Higgins that 'it is unfortunate for the cause of humanity that neither Jesus nor Mohammed should have thought it right to abolish slavery,' we wish to add that Mohammed *did* almost entirely abolish slavery."[17] The proof he adduced at this stage was from the *hadith,* showing that the Prophet, his daughter, and the early caliphs treated their domestics as equals: "If this be the slavery which Sir Wm. Muir represents as 'disorganizing society,' we cannot conceive what equality of rights would be. Such a slavery, indeed—if slavery it can be called at all—would highly organize society and improve public morals."[18]

For the moment Saiyid Ahmad passed quickly over the crucial Qur'anic verses that would later underpin his view that the Prophet did indeed prohibit even paternalistic forms of household slavery, merely hinting here at divisions among Indian Muslim lawyers on the issue of war captives and slavery. He thought that, for an English readership, it was enough to establish that the justification for taking war captives at all was the beneficent one of "saving their lives," while he personally inclined to an unconditional "free dismission" after capture rather than entry into domestic slavery. Saiyid Ahmad admitted the "wretched character of the domestic slavery" still practiced in "Mohammedan States" as well as "some Christian countries," but made no explicit references. His readers were reminded that it was the wretched treatment of slaves, rather than the mere fact of slavery itself, which made slave owners into "guilty sinners" for "evidently acting in opposition to the principle of their religion."[19] His purpose in London was limited to undermining Muir's contentions concerning the endemic "evils" of Islamic societies.

Amir 'Ali had the benefit of reading both Saiyid Ahmad's English essays and his first Urdu articles just before finalizing his own text in 1873. He placed an even stronger emphasis on the argument that, though reprehensible in all circumstances, slavery as it existed in Islamic societies was an advance on the practices of all other societies both before and after the preaching of Islam. If the Jews, Greeks, Romans, and ancient Germans were all at fault, he was particularly concerned to show, like Saiyid Ahmad, that the Christian record Muir passed over was marred by the failure to denounce slavery. "The Church itself held slaves, and recognised in explicit terms, the lawfulness of this baneful institution."[20] The establishment of such culpability was important to Amir 'Ali's goal—to demonstrate the ameliorative measures that Islam had introduced into existing slave systems. Like Saiyid Ahmad, he then stressed the various ways the Prophet had facilitated manumission, the Qur'anic injunctions to treat slaves equably, the uniqueness of Islamic law in not separating family members, and the prohibitions on both slave lifting and slave trading, and on making Muslims into slaves. The only legitimate reason for taking slaves was as a result of "*bona fide* legal warfare," in self-defense against unbelieving aggressors.[21] "The gradual emancipation of slaves" was nevertheless the long-term intention of the Prophet, a "legislator" who "himself looked upon the custom as temporary in its nature, and held that its extinction was sure to be achieved by the progress of ideas and change of circumstances," in fulfillment of the true "spirit of the Teacher's precepts."[22]

Both Saiyid Ahmad and Amir ʿAli had been concerned first and foremost with challenging their European critics' portrayals of the harsh and ineradicable nature of Islamic forms of slavery. Since they wished to be seen as representing a consensus, their responses did not emphasize the existence of differing schools of Qurʾanic exegesis. Saiyid Ahmad merely hinted at such when he said, "Our lawyers are divided in their opinions as to the circumstances under which free dismission is to be granted to war captives."[23] Amir ʿAli, too, while admitting the existence of "two points of view" in India ("the one showing that Islam completely abolished the system; the other, that . . . Mohammed's religion provided for its gradual but absolute extinction"), proceeded no further down these paths.[24]

Nor did either of them relish any close engagement, in English, with the specific question of female slavery and its concomitant in all European discussion of Islamic societies, concubinage. Thus, in spite of the prominence of references to "female slavery and concubinage" in the European works, modernist replies in English were made in ungendered language wherever possible. Saiyid Ahmad referred only to an idyllic scene in which the Prophet's "young maids" ground wheat with their mistress, signifying domestic harmony between owners and slaves. Amir ʿAli also avoided gendered language, usually using the neutral term "slavery." On the few occasions he admitted a gender perspective, he balanced "bondsmen" with "bondswomen" and "male slaves" with "female slaves," with no particular emphasis on the latter.[25] The thrust of Muir's own focus on the concomitance of female slavery with concubinage was scarcely admitted at all in these early responses in English.

The North Indian Context in the 1870s: Legal Wrangles among the *ʿUlama*

Any British reader who knew the north Indian scholarly religious scenario would have been aware that the artificial consensus of theological views implied in the London apologia was then at its most challenged. In the aftermath of the rebellion of 1857, when Muslims were stigmatized by the British as conspirators, various Sunni *ʿulama* gradually concluded that it was necessary to reassess, on the grounds mainly of the Qurʾan and the *hadith,* what was actually required of Muslims living under non-Muslim rule. If the modernist reevaluation of Islamic sources favored by Saiyid Ahmad was one answer, others disagreed. The disagreements surfaced publicly in the 1870s in an outpouring of tracts, *fatwa*s, and newspaper statements on points of theological and social teaching and practice. Among Saiyid Ahmad's many opponents were the *ʿulama* associated with a new *madrasa* at Deoband, who considered themselves specialists in Qurʾanic and *hadith* studies. They took particular issue with him on many issues, one of which was slavery.

Amir ʿAli faced no such challenge in Calcutta. For the next fifty years he continued to republish his views on slavery and on other issues without substantial change and without arousing any apparent backlash. As a self-described Shiʿi Muʿtazalite (Rationalist), and a professional jurist in the British courts, he was well equipped to synthesize differences between the theological schools, both Sunni and Shiʿi, in order to present a common, homogenized "spirit of Islam." He later became well known in Calcutta for his attempts to encourage incremental change in Muslim practice in accord with such a "spirit," for instance on matters concerning women's status. He managed to hold this line consistently because he was not a *madrasa ʿalim* and was never required to represent himself as anything other than an apologist for Islam vis-à-vis the West. Bengali *ʿulama* were in any case less eager to engage in the kind of public disputation that was to occur in post-1870s northwest India. The contestation with mosque and *madrasa ʿulama* that brought Saiyid Ahmad's controversial views on slavery into the public sphere very quickly in the northwest did not occur in eastern India. Some ambivalence on slavery in some of his much consulted legal texts, in which he at first retained the "slavery clauses" and only later justified their reduction to a minimum on the ground of redundancy, appears to have passed without comment.[26]

Saiyid Ahmad, in contrast, chose to enter the fray almost immediately on his return to northwest India in 1871, publishing later that year a series of articles entitled "Ibtal-i ghulami" (Refutation of Slavery) in his own newly founded Urdu journal, the *Tahzib al-akhlaq*.[27] Printed at his private press in Urdu, and subtitled in English *The Mohammedan Social Reformer,* this journal was to become the mouthpiece for the theologically and socially "modernist" views espoused by Saiyid Ahmad and his subsequent followers in the "Aligarh Movement," and thus drew to its authors the anger of many *ʿulama* of the other schools. Among the regular contributors to the *Tahzib* was Saiyid Ahmad's acolyte Maulawi Chiragh ʿAli, whose views on Western and Islamic slavery, published in both Urdu and English, eventually linked north Indian modernist discussions with ongoing debate among scholars outside India.[28]

Saiyid Ahmad told his co-religionists that slavery had been completely prohibited rather than merely ameliorated in the Qurʾan. He first stated this in a brief reference to the "wickedness" of the practice and its contradiction of Islam in an article defining "civilization."[29] As an introduction to a full exploration of the issue, to be later republished separately as "Ghulami fitrat-i insani ke barkhilaf hai" (Slavery Is Contrary to Human Nature), it was followed with a categorical statement that slavery contradicts both "nature" and "God's will." He included an overview of the history of slavery from ancient times (in Vedic as well as Greek and Roman civilizations) until the nineteenth century, covering recent reform in Egypt as well as the transatlantic slave trade and the European abolition movements. Gone now was the pointed criticism of Christendom and the later European powers for perpetuating slavery in contradiction of the Gospel so strongly emphasized in his English essays. He emphasized "well wishers of humanity" and "good hearted persons" rather than the evangelicals, and the "English" now drew his praise for their initiation of the anti-slavery movement. For his Indian Muslim readers, Saiyid Ahmad now condemned all slavery, including that practiced by Muslims, as unnatural, inhumane, barbaric, and un-Islamic.[30]

In ensuing articles in the *Tahzib,* and on the basis of a detailed examination of the relevant Qur'anic *ayat*s (verses), he declared that even temporary enslavement of war captives was un-Islamic: "There is no order in the Qur'an or the authentic traditions making captives of *jihad* into slave-girls [*laundi*s] and slaves [*ghulam*s]."[31] Saiyid Ahmad's emphasis here and subsequently on *sura* 47:4–5, which he now termed the *ayat-i hurriyat* ("freedom verses"), differed significantly from his earlier very brief reference in English, in which captivity during legitimate warfare had remained a *raison d'être* for future slavery.[32] Now he asserted that only two options are available for those prisoners, including women and children, who survived the actual battle: either a free release or ransom. The temporary enslavement acknowledged in the earlier English essay received no mention here. Consequently and logically, nor did the masters' maintaining of captured slaves "in the same style of living as they do themselves," which he had required of them in his earlier English essay.[33]

Was Saiyid Ahmad aware that, like Ram Mohan Roy fifty years earlier, he was "engaged in an intellectual conflict on two fronts" which would necessarily involve some contradictions?[34] If so, had he modified his stance in order to prepare in the future an even more categorical refutation of Western criticism? Or, and as seems the more likely, did the change reflect a growing debate with some north Indian ʿulama who objected to Saiyid Ahmad's criticism both of ongoing domestic slavery within India and of slave trading and holding in some other parts of the contemporary Muslim world? There is some evidence of the latter. For he refuted a *fatwa* bearing the seals of a number of influential north Indian Sunni ʿulama, led by one Maulawi Wajih al-din Saharanpuri. These scholars had ruled that legitimate war against non-Muslims justified enslaving even those who sought refuge after the bat-tle was ended. Saiyid Ahmad discussed this ruling in chapter 3 of the *Ibtal*, subtitled "Why the Islamic *ulama* have understood possession as slavery."[35]

A closer look at the signatories reveals a broad regrouping after the tur-moil of 1857–58. For instance, among the signatories was Maulana Saiyid Nazir Hussain, an *alim* who had been prominent in Tariqa-i Muhammadiyya ("Wahhabi") circles in Delhi since the mid-1820s. In the 1870s Nazir Hus-sain provided leadership to the regrouped Ahl-i Hadith movement in its conflicts with the modernists and other new religious movements, one ele-ment of which concerned the Qur'anic legitimation of slavery.[36] Some other signatories to this *fatwa* had earlier put their seals on two other *fatwa*s issued during the mid-1850s. The first of these had condemned Christianity, and the second had supported a *jihad* against the British during the rebellion of 1857. Several of these signatories were members of a group of Sunni *ulama* concentrated in the *doab* region north of Delhi, specifically the districts of Muzaffarnagar and Saharanpur. Their standing is exemplified by Shah Ah-mad Sa'id, a leading Naqshbandi Sufi in the tradition of the Delhi *pir* Shah Ghulam 'Ali. It is well recognized that whether or not they actually "re-belled" in 1857, many *ulama* of these upper *doab qasbah*s were strongly op-posed to all influences associated with the British presence.[37] This was the core catchment area for the new *madrasa* founded at Deoband in 1868. The Deobandi *ulama* were as critical of the modernists' interpretation of Islam as they were of Christian missionary theology. Near to Deoband was Saha-ranpur, with a Deobandi-style school of its own, which became the strongest center of Deobandi views.[38] Not surprisingly, some of Saiyid Ahmad's other theological opinions expressed in the 1870s triggered open hostility among the Deobandi and Saharanpuri *ulama*.[39] By this time too there were many other *ulama* elsewhere, of various affiliations, but notably the Ahl-i Hadith, who were alarmed by the increasingly controversial views Saiyid Ahmad ex-pressed in newspapers, lectures, tracts, and commentaries during the quar-ter century before his death in 1898.

For instance, from 1871 onward, Saiyid Ahmad maintained a strongly expressed, and severely contested, opinion that the Qur'an does not support enslavement even in a legitimate war. This is proved by the reprinting of his "Ibtal-i ghulami" newspaper articles as a separate pamphlet in 1893, just five years before his death, with scarcely any changes.[40] Saiyid Ahmad's Urdu publications thus indicate, in strong contrast to his initial forays in English, a radical and complete repudiation of the legitimacy of slavery in any form. He based this repudiation squarely on Qur'anic authority, and he even tra-duced the evidence being drawn on by his opponents among the Indian *ulama* as "inauthentic."

Not surprisingly, all this created an intellectual uproar within the Muslim intelligentsia. One of the responses to Saiyid Ahmad's articles illustrates the extent of the provocation on both sides. His *Ibtal* was taken up by one Saiyid Muhammad ʿAbd Allah, whose *Haqiqat al-Islam,* published in 1874, criticized Saiyid Ahmad's *Tahzib* articles and reaffirmed the Qurʾanic basis for the taking of slaves during "legitimate" warfare.[41] Saiyid Muhammad scathingly denied that the Qurʾan requires the "freedom" for captives on which Saiyid Ahmad had recently built his own interpretation.[42] Chiragh ʿAli then came to Saiyid Ahmad's defense with an article of his own in the *Tahzib* journal; he amplified this for a wider debate in Hyderabad some ten years later.

Such debates were not merely intramural and parochial little spats. Saiyid Ahmad's debates with the north Indian ʿulama over slavery spread rapidly from northwest India into Western Asia. That his views were well known, even at this early date, in parts of the wider Muslim world is made clear by the inclusion of slavery in a list of Saiyid Ahmad's theological errors that Maulawi ʿAli Bakhsh Khan of nearby Badayun, a fellow British government servant, took to Mecca in 1873 in the hope that prominent ʿulama in the Hijaz would condemn them.[43] The Meccan ʿulama issued a *fatwa* of *kufr* (infidelity) against Saiyid Ahmad.[44] Undeterred, Saiyid Ahmad then tried to forge alliances with emerging modernist opinion within the Ottoman Empire by writing to the editor of a radical Arabic newspaper, *Al-jawaʾib,* published in Istanbul. This paper had published in 1875 the correspondence between Hussain Pasha, a minister in the Tunisian government, and the American ambassador to Tunis who, during the American Civil War, had questioned the steps being taken toward the prohibition of slavery in Tunis.[45] Significantly, the pasha's reply had not engaged at all with the Qurʾanic *ayat*s on slavery specified by Saiyid Ahmad as crucial. He had argued, instead, that as the Qurʾan's prescription of humanitarian treatment for slaves was no longer being honored in the contemporary world, the emancipation of slaves that the Qurʾan also encouraged was now the appropriate path for present-day Tunis.

Such pragmatic rationalization, closer to Saiyid Amir ʿAli's stance in his *Critical Examination* than to Saiyid Ahmad's in the *Ibtal,* completely missed the central point of Saiyid Ahmad's fully evolved abolitionism. Saiyid Ahmad's letter in Arabic to *Al-jawaʾib*'s editor avoided the pasha's argument altogether. Instead, it reiterated forcefully his own assertion in "Ibtal-i ghulami" that there was no Qurʾanic basis for slavery of any kind: the *ayat-i hurriyat* (freedom verses) categorically promulgated the "freedom" of all who might ever in the future be captured in battle. The letter ended with a request to the ʿulama of Istanbul, Tunis, and Egypt to point out to him any Qurʾanic *ayat* that gave a clear command instituting slavery. Characteristically, Saiyid Ah-mad then proceeded to publish the whole correspondence in his own journal in 1877.[46] His anxiety to advertise his own participation in this Tunis-Istanbul phase of interchange, and to make his Indian readers aware of the radical steps being taken in Tunis, even if he disagreed with the rationale being given for them, is palpable. It provides some firm evidence of his awareness by the mid-1870s of a new "Islamic world" context of ongoing debates on the legitimacy of institutions such as slavery even if, as far as is known, the *ulama* of the Ottoman Empire did not take up his invitation to respond.

Otherwise, the "slavery in Islam" controversy in 1870s India seems to have formed merely one strand in a complex rhetorical contest for the minds of those north Indian Muslims who were increasingly divided by pulls either to defend "traditional" interpretations of religious injunctions, as the Deobandis were doing, or to accept the modernist emphasis on the need for some adaptation to the colonial situation. Slavery was frequently included in a long list of theological and social issues that were common themes of lectures and journal articles in the 1870s. Thus Maulawi Saiyid Mahdi 'Ali, one of Saiyid Ahmad's closest associates, gave it a brief treatment in a lecture on *tahzib* (civilization) at a small, newly founded upcountry literary institute in the North-Western Provinces in 1873. He discussed slavery between, on the one hand, his thoughts on subjects such as the status of women, divorce, and purdah, and on the other, the caliphate, kingship, and tyranny.[47] If such literary gatherings were a sign of the times, some of the issues so endlessly debated among the *ulama* in a period of intense theological debate and the formation of new socio-religious movements now appear highly scholastic and pedantic.[48] Their arguments over the Qur'anic basis of slavery probably seemed particularly recondite to many readers even at the time. Only over the issue of female slavery and concubinage, sidestepped in the London phase but implicitly if not openly at the heart of Saiyid Ahmad's current dispute with the *ulama*, did the rhetoric of exquisite legalism meet the reality of ongoing Indian practices.

Domestic Slavery and Concubinage in the Princely States

This one important exception reflected a new sensitivity among the modernists to the continuance of domestic slavery, particularly in the princely states. The preference of many British officers to "look the other way" where household slavery was concerned continued, in spite of "delegalization," into the 1870s and 1880s. Even William Muir, who as a young evangelical officer in the 1840s had spoken out on such domestic issues, took care, after promotion to a provincial governorship, to avoid implicating any particular Indian court or household in his condemnations of "female slavery and concubinage." The examples he gave were drawn from early Arab, not from Indian, history. All his contemporary references were to reports of slaving raids beyond the borders controlled by the British government of India—in contemporary Kafiristan or slave markets in Mecca. In the second edition of his *Life of Mahomet,* published in 1877, Muir's comment in the earlier edition that female slavery "will never be put down willingly" by Muslims was now supported by a description of the buying and selling of "male and female slaves of all races" in the Meccan slave market by one he described as "a shrewd observer." This was Sikandar Begam, the ruler of Bhopal.[49] But neither the begam herself nor Muir mentioned that she then brought some Meccan slaves back to Bhopal as domestic servants.

Saiyid Ahmad shared Muir's reluctance to detail domestic slavery in India, which, like many colonial officers, he had represented briefly in his English essays as a benign form of household servitude. But the writing of the "Ibtal" brought out a deep sense of anger, expressed as "shame," that he felt at the knowledge of female slaves being sold "like cows" in the bazaars of Arabia.[50] He was now prepared to deprecate not only that slaves were sold in the Indian princely states, but that in British territories, too, nautch girls and catamites were in demand with poets and princes alike. Both women and men were still being traded in India, the responsibility for which he laid firmly at the door of the government: further legislation was clearly required.[51] Several chapters of the "Ibtal" refuted the widespread notion that the Qur'anic references to the permissibility of sexual relations with those "thy right hand possesses" had legitimated concubinage. On another occasion, Saiyid Ahmad publicly listed the illegality of taking girls into slavery as one of eleven doctrines on which he was in full agreement with his friend Saiyid Mahdi 'Ali Khan.[52] He had his own reasons, like Muir, for not addressing this sensitive question any more specifically, and he held back from naming names, remaining reluctant, as recent work on Muslim women's education has shown, to be drawn into any more positive agendas on female issues.[53]

A few others were, however, prepared to be rather more outspoken. In Lower Bengal, one Dilawar Husain Ahmad castigated the nexus between polygamy, concubinage, and slavery as a cause of "Muslim decline."[54] Among the Aligarh-influenced networks of Upper Bengal and the Deccan, meanwhile, Saiyid Ahmad's younger colleague, Maulawi Chiragh 'Ali, already more radical and outspoken in his opinions on other theological issues than his mentor, linked female slavery more explicitly with concubinage in a critique firmly grounded in the Qur'an and the *hadith.*

Very little has been published in English concerning Chiragh ʿAli since Aziz Ahmad's important study *Islamic Modernism* in the late 1960s. Urdu studies of modernist thought largely ignore him because of his literary style: a critic describes it as "the heaviest and most wooden" of the Aligarh school.[55] Nevertheless, his intellectual contributions were significant. He was "one of Saiyid Ahmad's strongest supporters on religious questions" and his influence on his mentor appears to have been just as significant as his mentor's had earlier been on him. A letter from Saiyid Ahmad suggests that a theological work Chiragh ʿAli was preparing would upset conservative opinion in both Aligarh and Hyderabad. It suggests both the younger man's radicalism and a symbiotic relationship between the two scholars.[56] His contribution to the debate on slavery, particularly the discussion of concubinage, shows Chiragh ʿAli as an important link between Aligarh-initiated reformism and contemporary social and political practices rooted in elite household and courtly cultures.

Even though they were written while Chiragh ʿAli served in the petty colonial government, his Urdu articles in the *Tahzib al-akhlaq* supported Saiyid Ahmad's reform agenda. Among these was an important article, "Islam ki dunyevi barakatin" (Islam's Worldly Blessings), which was published in 1875. In it he reiterated, in a list of more than thirty "blessings," his mentor's interpretation of *sura* 47:4–5, namely that the Prophet intended that there should be no new slavery. Though Chiragh ʿAli argued that the treatment of slaves among Muslims was "more liberal than in other nations," he insisted that the "freedom verses" created a "law of universal obligation" to abolish all future slavery and concubinage "by ordering the captives of war to be either dismissed freely or ransomed."[57] His posting to the Nizam's service in Hyderabad in the late 1870s, on Saiyid Ahmad's recommendation, led to some more assertive statements in English based on his own observation of the domestic life of the court he served, and the misconstructions of Muslim practices that such courts were affording to European commentators.

But his reasons for publishing two significant tracts on slavery during the 1880s—in quick succession—were complex. His *Proposed Political, Legal, and Social Reforms in the Ottoman Empire and Other Mohammedan States* was published in Bombay in 1883. It was quickly followed by his "Slavery and Concubine-Slaves as Concomitant Evils of War," published in the form of an appendix to his *A Critical Exposition of the Popular "Jihad"* in 1885, in which he reiterated Saiyid Ahmad's view "that slavery is not sanctioned by the Prophet of Islam."[58] Since both were published in English, their arguments were clearly intended to refute a particularly virulent outpouring of European criticism in the late nineteenth century. In addition to William

Muir's revised works were a recently published *Dictionary of Islam,* by a Peshawar-based missionary, Thomas Hughes, and an especially Islamophobic article in the *Contemporary Review,* "Are Reforms Possible under Mussulman Rule?" Written by Malcolm MacColl, the article repeated, in ill-informed and lurid prose, Muir's indictment of Islamic societies as being inherently incapable of reform. Slavery, along with the poor treatment of women, was for MacColl one of the "incurable vices" which "bar for ever all possibility of reform" in Muslim societies.[59] Chiragh ʿAli's "chief object," as he clarified in his prefaces, was to eradicate such erroneous impressions of Islam "from the minds of European and Christian writers" who "suffer under a delusion that Islam is incapable of any political, legal or social reforms."[60]

Yet his dedication of the *Proposed Political, Legal, and Social Reforms* to the Ottoman sultan, ʿAbd al-Hamid II, suggests that Chiragh ʿAli also intended to follow up Saiyid Ahmad's so far unsuccessful efforts to place Indian reformist thinking within a much wider Muslim arena. Such unsolicited advice to the sultan received no response. This was hardly surprising, considering Chiragh ʿAli's reminder on the first page that "the British empire is the greatest Mohammadan Power in the world." In fact, he was probably merely using the Ottoman name to legitimate and give prestige to a radical exposition of slavery and concubinage actually intended for the rulers of the "other Mohammedan states" of the book's title, including the Hyderabad of his current employment, as much as for Islam's Western critics. Much of his own prestige in Hyderabad, where he was honored with the title of Nawab Aʿzam Yar Jang, was based on a series of publications drawing attention to the illustrious history of the state under the Asaf Jahi dynasty and his praise of the administrative reforms currently taking place. Any critique of matters such as women's status in Islam, marriage laws, and concubinage, and any insinuations of untoward happenings in the court of Hyderabad in particular, could be undertaken only obliquely. That British officials in Hyderabad did believe that slavery was still widespread was clear from a report that "every Arab who comes to Hyderabad . . . brings with him one or two Habshi slaves."[61] Sexual insinuations often followed, as in a report on another province that "Destitute Mahomedan girls can frequently obtain a livelihood as unpaid maid servants in the houses of wealthy Mahomedan gentlemen, where they doubtless lead a life of concubinage."[62]

Mindful of such insinuations, Chiragh ʿAli, in the final section of his *Proposed Political, Legal, and Social Reforms,* firmly denied that "concubinage" is sanctioned in the Qurʾan, a position he reiterated two years later in writing of "slavery and concubines as concomitant evils of war."[63] In a detailed refutation of William Muir's statement, republished in the 1877 edition of his *Life of Mahomet,* that "Female slavery, being a condition necessary to the legality of this coveted indulgence [concubinage], will never be put down, with a willing or hearty co-operation by any Mussulman community," Chiragh ʿAli countered that "Mohammad never sanctioned concubinage, but on the contrary he prohibited it to Arab society."[64] Even during the pre–*ayat-i hurriyat* phase, owners of female war captives had been urged to marry them; afterward the question no longer arose during either Muhammad's lifetime or the early caliphate. Like Saiyid Ahmad and Amir ʿAli, Chiragh ʿAli blamed subsequent Muslim rulers, who ignored the Qurʾanic prohibitions, for the reemergence of both slavery in general and concubinage in particular, at various Muslim courts and more widely in other social strata. He was particularly critical of what he termed "devices" employed historically by Muslim exegetists to "legitimise," on the basis of "unreliable" authorities (mainly *hadith*), the practice of concubinage with captured females.[65] He implied that such devices continued to work in the same way in the present.

Even though he addressed the issue of concubinage much more directly than any of his predecessors, Chiragh ʿAli too avoided explicit references both to the current practices in India hinted at by Saiyid Ahmad and to those ʿ*ulama* who still claimed Qurʾanic justification for its continuance. Prepared to admit some truth in Muir's comment that no Muslim community would willingly put down female slavery, he strove to make a firm distinction between female domestic slavery as admittedly still practiced in the Islamic world, including India, and concubinage, for "it is also right to say that the Mohammedan jurists who legalize slavery do not allow concubinary practice with the slave girls now imported from Georgia, Africa, and Central Asia." But neither the jurists who had so ruled, nor the locations or occasions of such transactions as he admitted to be still occurring, were specified. The closest he came to a precise case of ongoing child traffic, and one he deprecated strongly, involved the importation of "Moslem children kidnapped by the Gellabs or slave-lifters from various Mohammedan ports." These, he insisted, "can in no way be considered legal slaves, or a lawfully acquired property."[66] Deliberately vague as to whether such practices were still to be found only within the Ottoman Empire, in unadministered frontier regions in Central Asia, within India's semi-autonomous princely states, or within British India, he remained equally circumspect about his Muslim addressees, other than the Ottoman sultan. Clearly he intended his words for a group of statesmen, since he identified them in general terms as "other Mohammedan states." It seems that in spite of a discreet vagueness, and a rhetorical flourish in the direction of the caliph, his real object was to ensure that the condemnations of slavery in general and particularly of its female forms, including concubinage, were now heard at those Indian Muslim courts where the delicacy of the subject, and his own position at the Hyderabad court, still necessitated very careful wording.

A recent legal case concerning Bhopal, which was widely publicized in the press, may have suggested the need for some statement on these issues.[67] A charge of importing slave-girls from Mecca to Bhopal implicated both the ruler of the state, Shah Jahan Begam, and her consort, Sidiq Hasan Khan, a leading member of the Ahl-i Hadith, whose publications were currently supporting the Qur'anic basis of slavery in opposition to Saiyid Ahmad's interpretation. The begam, whose mother, Sikandar, had certainly imported slaves from Mecca twenty years earlier without apparently exciting any adverse comment, as mentioned above, tried to justify her own involvement through her *vakil* in an order read to the court reminding her accusers that "It is a very pious act among the Mahommedans generally to buy these people and give them their liberty. Many noblemen do so."[68] Lepel Griffin, the Central Indian agent to the viceroy, seemed to admit in his commentary on the case that government officials still tended to "look the other way" from the "institution of domestic slavery which prevails in most Native States," and the fact that "every petty Rajput gentleman has some."[69] Yet he criticized the illegal importation of slaves from abroad to supply such courts' domestic needs, whether or not they were manumitted, as the begam contended, either before or after their arrival in India. Although concubinage had not been mentioned directly, it was in just such a context of unwelcome attention being drawn to the domestic arrangements of mainly Muslim courts that Chiragh ʿAli hoped that his reminders that slavery and concubinage were not sanctioned by the Qur'an and *hadith* would have some resonance.

Conclusion

It is the argument of this chapter that slavery loomed as large as it did in late nineteenth-century Indian modernist thinking because Western critics, several of them employed as civil servants in northwest India, packaged it with other social institutions they deemed to be obstacles to "change" in Islamic societies. These alleged obstacles, notably polygamy and divorce, mainly affected the status of women. Concerns about slavery also slid immediately into the issue of concubinage and drew it into the wider "woman question." By the late nineteenth century, the Raj was obsessed with the "woman question." Nothing that belonged to this could be separately considered.

In any case, the image of slavery as separate from other political and social issues of the day was impossible to maintain in the face of the repetitious charges that a retired William Muir continued to make. In these reiterations, he avoided any engagement with the responses of the modernist Indian Muslims studied here. When other European intellectuals took up Muir's refrain, the effect of a one-sided dialogue was completed. Though, within the Indian empire, colonial officials continued to overlook such evidence of domestic slavery as did exist, by the early twentieth century there was comparatively little slave holding except in the erstwhile princely states. Amir ʿAli's faith in its gradual withering away in accord with the changing "spirit of the times" seems, in this sphere at least, to have been well grounded. In any event, such a concentration on both attacking and defending slavery as occurred in northwest India in the last quarter of the nineteenth century has never been repeated in South Asia.

Some reflections on the longer and wider significance of this episode are thus worth airing. The narrowly "textual" basis of the discourse, confined to the Qurʾan and the *hadith,* made this an affair exclusively of the ʿulama and those lay scholars who, like Saiyid Ahmad and Amir ʿAli, could claim equal interpretative authority, albeit strongly contested, with the *madrasa ʿulama.* The result, however, was circular and repetitive. After the initial shock of Saiyid Ahmad's exegesis, particularly on *sura* 47:4–5, there was little new thinking. Amir ʿAli's longevity (he died in 1928) gave continuity to a body of modernist thought which had emerged as early as 1870, but to which little of originality was added in the interim. Among the defenders of the Qurʾanic basis of slavery, novelty of course is not to be countenanced: hence there is an unsurprising continuity in the "chain of authorities" from the Saharanpuri ʿulama of the 1830s and the Ahl-i Hadith ʿulama of the 1870s to latter-day "Wahhabi" and Jamaʿat-i Islami renditions of the Qurʾanic basis of slavery in various parts of the Muslim world. Worth noting, too, is the use of the Qurʾan by both sets of protagonists in ways resonant of the use of the Bible in late eighteenth-century Western discourse, both pro- and anti-slavery, in the early stages of the transatlantic abolitionist campaign. Such textual dependency reinforces the narrowly theological and "revelatory" framing of an issue which was largely rhetorical in India, yet had extensive social and legal implications in other parts of the Muslim world.[70]

The findings indeed point to the significant conclusion that the Indian modernists were ultimately much more significant in debates outside India and in states where slavery still remained, as Aziz Ahmad termed it, a "burning political issue."[71] Gervase Clarence-Smith's comprehensive work on the abolition of slavery in an "Islamic world" context places considerable emphasis on the effects of the transmission of the Indian modernists' rationales for the prohibition of slavery on Muslim scholarly thinking in areas as diverse as the Crimea and Java, as well as some of the central Arab lands and

North Africa.[72] It was, however, a one-way traffic of ideas. A short book by one Ahmad Shafiq, first published in Cairo in French in 1891, and soon afterward in Arabic, challenged a recent campaign by a French cardinal against slavery as still practiced among Muslims in Africa. The tenor of this response to renewed European criticism, *L'esclavage au point de vue musulman*, like Saiyid Ahmad's first response to William Muir twenty years earlier, was apologetic. The dissemination of further translations of the book, including into Turkish, generated wide discussion. Yet in India, where an Urdu translation of *L'esclavage* was published from the Arabic in 1907, it was largely ignored.[73] After the 1870s the interest generated by slavery issues was never revived with the same intensity.

Even when contestation over slavery has intermittently reemerged in South Asia, the political circumstances have been so different from the late nineteenth-century colonial context that a direct succession of thinking within South Asia itself should not be too readily assumed. It is nevertheless probably correct to conclude that, on the one hand, the general tenor of the initial modernist thinking on slavery has been assimilated, though seldom with any direct attribution, into the common assumptions shared by most of South Asia's markedly heterogenous and diverse Muslim populations. On the other hand, when reassertion of the Qur'anic justification for slavery has occurred as part of campaigns for a fuller emphasis on the role of the *shariʿat* in the state, then, most notably, the Jamaʿat-i Islami's sources for "right interpretation" of slavery in 1970s Pakistan were the same Qur'anic texts as the Ahl-i Hadith and other opponents of the modernists had put forward in the 1870s.[74] To say as much, and yet as little, is merely to reinforce the rhetorical and essentially legalistic parameters of a contestation in which social and humanitarian considerations must always be argued from the single standpoint of revealed religion.

Notes

1. Sir William Muir, *The Life of Mahomet and History of Islam to the Era of the Hegira,* 4 vols. (London: Smith, Elder and Co., 1858–61), 4:321. The italics are Muir's own.

2. Saiyid Ahmad Khan, "Ibtal-i ghulami" [Refutation of Slavery], in *Tahzib al-akhlaq: Mohammedan Social Reformer* (Aligarh Institute Press; hereafter *TA*) 2, no. 16 (Ramzan 15, 1288/Nov. 28, 1871), 151.

3. H. A. R. Gibb, *Mohammedanism: An Historical Survey,* rev. ed. (London: Oxford University Press, 1969), 124.

4. Among the vast literature on Saiyid Ahmad Khan both in Urdu and English, the studies most relevant here are J. M. S. Baljon, *The Reforms and Religious Ideas of Sir Saiyid Ahmad Khan* (Leiden: E. J. Brill, 1949); Christian W. Troll, *Sayyid Ahmad*

Khan: A Reinterpretation of Muslim Theology (New Delhi: Vikas Publishing House, 1978); and Hafeez Malik, *Sir Sayyid Ahmad Khan and Muslim Modernization in India and Pakistan* (New York: Columbia University Press, 1980). Apart from specific Urdu publications detailed in the text, much use has been made of Muhammad Ismaʿil Panipati's edition of Saiyid Ahmad's collected works, *Maqalat-i Sir Saiyid*, 16 vols. (Lahore: Majlis-i Taraqqi-yi Adab, 1962–65). For appreciative studies of Saiyid Amir ʿAli, see K. K. Aziz, *Ameer Ali: His Life and Work* (Lahore: Publishers United, 1968); and Syed Razi Wasti, ed., *Memoirs and Other Writings of Syed Ameer Ali: Syed Ameer Ali on Islamic History and Culture,* 2 vols. (Lahore: People's Publishing House, 1968); for a recent critical account, Martin Forward, *The Failure of Islamic Modernism? Syed Ameer Ali's Interpretation of Islam* (Bern: Peter Lang, 1999).

5. Indrani Chatterjee, *Gender, Slavery, and Law in Colonial India* (New Delhi: Oxford University Press, 1999), 223–24. See also idem, "Abolition by Denial: The South Asian Example," in Gwyn Campbell, ed. *Abolition and Its Aftermath in the Indian Ocean, Africa, and Asia* (London: Routledge, 2005), 150–68; and Radhika Singha, *A Despotism of Law: Crime and Justice in Early Colonial India* (Delhi: Oxford University Press, 1998), chapter 4.

6. See Vatuk, this volume, for similar responses to slavery among British officers in the Madras Presidency.

7. ʿAbdal Qadir, *ʿIlm wa ʿamal (Waqaʿ-i Abdal Qadir Khani),* ed. Muhammad Ayub Qadri, trans. into Urdu from Persian by Muʿin al Din Afzalgarhi, 2 vols. (Karachi: Academy of Educational Research, All Pakistan Educational Conference, 1961), 2:184–85.

8. Rev. Charles Forster, *Mahometanism Unveiled* (London: J. Duncan and J. Cochran, 1829); Godfrey Higgins, *An Apology for the Life and Character of the Celebrated Prophet of Arabia, called Mohamed, or the Illustrious* (London: Roland Hunter, 1829); and Thomas Carlyle, *On Heroes, Hero Worship, and the Heroic in History* (London: Chapman and Hall, 1840), which was republished many times, including in 1870, coinciding with the arrivals of Saiyid Ahmad and Amir ʿAli in London). A significant new contribution came from John Davenport, *An Apology for Mohammed and the Koran* (London: Printed for the author, 1869).

9. Saiyid Ahmad Khan to Mahdi ʿAli Khan, August 20, 1869, in Muhammad Ismaʿil Panipati, ed., *Maktubat-i Sir Saiyid* [Letters of Sir Saiyid], 2 vols. (1976; reprint, Lahore: Majlis-i Taraqqi-yi Adab, 1985), 1:430–31.

10. Saiyid Ahmad Khan, *A Series of Essays on the Life of Mohammed, and Subjects Subsidiary Thereto* (London: Trübner and Co., 1870). He directed his reassessments, he affirmed in his preface, mainly to the attention of those English-knowing Indian Muslim college students whose confidence in Islam he feared might be undermined not only by their secular education in government institutions, but specifically by those Arabists, William Muir prominent among them, who while engaged as administrators and educationists in north India had openly criticized Muslim society.

11. Saiyid Ahmad Khan to secretary, Aligarh Scientific Society, October 15, 1869, quoted in G. F. I. Graham, *The Life and Work of Sir Syed Ahmed Khan* (Edinburgh: William Blackwood and Sons, 1885; new edition, London: Hodder and Stoughton, 1909), 127–28. Amir ʿAli's memoirs, of which the second installment is concerned with his first visit to London, were published posthumously as "Memoirs of the Late Hon'ble Syed Ameer Ali," in *Islamic Culture* 5, no. 4 (Oct. 1931), 509–42; 6 (Jan.–Oct. 1932), 1–18, 163–82, 333–62, 503–25.

12. Saiyid Amir ʿAli, *The Mahommedans of India: A Lecture Delivered to the "London Association in Aid of Social Progress in India,"* lecture delivered November 16, 1871 (London: National Indian Association, 1872), 18.

13. Clare Midgley, *Women against Slavery: The British Campaigns, 1780–1890* (London: Routledge, 1992).

14. Higgins, *Apology*, 47–49.

15. John Davenport, *Muʿaiyid al-Islam* [In Confirmation of Islam], trans. Muhammad ʿInayat al-Rahman (Delhi: Khwaja Qamr al-Din Khan, 1870). Saiyid Ahmad often refers to his communications with Davenport in his letters to Mahdi ʿAli.

16. Saiyid Ahmad Khan, "Whether Islam Has Been Beneficial . . . ," essay 4 in *A Series of Essays*, 40. Slavery is discussed on pp. 20–25.

17. Ibid., 24, Saiyid Ahmad's italics.

18. Ibid., 23–24.

19. Ibid., 25.

20. Saiyid Amir ʿAli, *A Critical Examination of the Life of Muhammad* (London, 1873), 254.

21. Ibid., 258–60.

22. Ibid., 256–59.

23: Saiyid Ahmad Khan, "Whether Islam," 25.

24. Ibid., 255.

25. Ibid., 251, 257. A brief reference to *jarya*s (Arabic, "female slaves") in a footnote in the 1873 edition was brought into the main text in the 1891 edition to be discussed in the context of Western criticism of concubinage, a term not used in the earlier edition. Cf. ibid., 242–43; and Syed Ameer Ali, *The Life and Teachings of Mohammed, or, The Spirit of Islam* (London: W. H. Allen, 1891), 349–51.

26. For example, Amir ʿAli's Tagore Law Lectures, published in 1885 on the Muslim laws of inheritance, discussed slaves' legal capacities to be *mutawali*s, trustees, testators, and executors, and the bequeathing of slaves, with only a sentence to the effect that "the emancipation of slaves is highly commendable under the Mahommedan Law and religion" but "the subject is, however, of no practical importance, and therefore it is unnecessary to dwell upon it." Syed Ameer Ali, *The Law Relating to Gifts, Trusts, and Testamentary Disposition among the Mahommedans* (Calcutta: Thacker, Spink and Co., 1885), 247, 442, 481, 548, 590. Forty years later he stated more firmly, "As the status of slavery does not exist in India, this rule of Mahommedan Law has only an antiquarian interest." Idem, *Student's Handbook of Mahommedan Law,* 7th ed. (Calcutta: Thacker, Spink and Co., 1925), 68.

27. Saiyid Ahmad [Khan], "Ibtal-i ghulami" [Refutation of Slavery], *TA* 2, nos. 12–17 (Rajab 15–Shawwal 1, 1288/Sept. 30–Dec. 14, 1871), 115–62. Thanks to S. J. Qadri for assistance in translating these and other articles.

28. Maulawi Chiragh ʿAli (1844–95) was employed during the 1870s in various subordinate administrative posts in government service in northwest India. See Francis Robinson, *Separatism among Indian Muslims: The Politics of the United Provinces' Muslims, 1860–1923* (Cambridge: Cambridge University Press, 1974), 124.

29. Saiyid Ahmad [Khan], "Kin kin chizon men tahzib chahiye?" *TA* 1, no. 6 (Zuʾl-hijja 1, 1287/Feb. 22, 1871), 58–60.

30. Saiyid Ahmad [Khan], "Ghulami," *TA* 2, no. 8 (Jumada al-avval 15, 1288/Aug. 2, 1871), 81–86, reprinted as "Ghulami fitrat-i insani ke barkhilaf hai," prefixed to *Ibtal-i ghulami* (Agra: Matbaʿ Mufid Inam, 1893), 1–17.

31. Saiyid Ahmad, *Ibtal*, 129.

32. "When ye encounter the unbelievers, strike off their heads, until ye have made a great slaughter among them; and bind them in bonds: and either give them a free dismission afterwards, or exact a ransom; until the war shall have laid down its arms." *Sura* 47:4–5, in *The Koran*, trans. George Sale, new ed., 2 vols. (London: J. Johnson, Vernor and Hood, 1801), 2:376. See also Aziz Ahmad, *Islamic Modernism in India and Pakistan, 1857–1964* (London: Oxford University Press, 1967), 51–52.

33. Saiyid Ahmad, *Ibtal*, 116.

34. David Kopf, *British Orientalism and the Bengal Renaissance: The Dynamics of Indian Modernization, 1773–1835* (Berkeley: University of California Press, 1969), 196–208.

35. Saiyid Ahmad, *Ibtal*, 126–29.

36. Saiyid Ahmad was vague about the date of the *fatwa* (*ek muddat hu'i*, "a long time ago") but it was probably issued during the 1830s. Many of the *'ulama* listed, all of whom were prominent in Sunni circles, had scholarly links with Shah 'Abdal Aziz and the pre-1857 circle of scholars at the Madrasa-i Rahimiyya in Delhi. On Saiyid Nazir Hussain, one of the signatories who wrote extensively on theological matters, see Barbara Daly Metcalf, *Islamic Revival in British India: Deoband, 1860–1900* (Princeton, N.J.: Princeton University Press, 1982), 290–91.

37. For signatories to these *fatwas* see Avril A. Powell, *Muslims and Missionaries in Pre-mutiny India* (Richmond, Surrey: Curzon, 1993), 258.

38. On the Saharanpur Deobandi school see Metcalf, *Islamic Revival*, 128–31.

39. See "Fifteen Principles Submitted by Sayyid Ahmad Khan to the Ulama of Saharanpur, 1873 or 1874," in Troll, *Sayyid Ahmad Khan*, 276–78. Muhammad Qasim Nanautawi, founder of the Deoband *madrasa*, later made a detailed reply, *Tasifyat al-'aqa'id* (Delhi, 1890), trans. Peter Hardy as "Assessment of Religious Tenets," in Aziz Ahmad and G. E. von Grunebaum, eds., *Muslim Self-Statement in India and Pakistan, 1857–1968* (Wiesbaden: Otto Harrassowitz, 1970), 60–76.

40. See note 30.

41. Saiyid Muhammad 'Abd Allah, *Haqiqat al-Islam* (Cawnpore: Matba' Nizami, 1874). 'Abd Allah was probably the same Sayyid Muhammad 'Askari whom Aziz Ahmad identified as the author of this work. See Aziz Ahmad, *Islamic Modernism*, 63. Among a number of refutations of Saiyid Ahmad's views published from the same press in Cawnpore was Muhammad 'Ali, *Radd al-shiqaq* [Refutation of the Opponent's Arguments against Slavery] (Cawnpore: Matba' Nizami, n.d. [1874?]), 312.

42. 'Abd Allah, *Haqiqat*, 5–39, 67.

43. Baljon, *Reforms and Religious Ideas*, 108–109. On Maulavi 'Ali Bakhsh Khan Badayuni, see Maulavi Rahman 'Ali, *Tazkirah-i 'ulama-i Hind* (Karachi: Pakistan Historical Society, 1961), 344. Appointed *sadar al-sadur* by the British, who also praised his work for English education, he wrote refutations of some Shi'i publications as well as of Saiyid Ahmad's.

44. Metcalf, *Islamic Revival*, 325.

45. For the three-stage process by which slavery was abolished in Tunis between 1846 and 1891, see R. Brunschvig, "'Abd," in *Encyclopaedia of Islam*, ed. H. A. R. Gibb et al., new ed. (Leiden: E. J. Brill, 1954–2002), 1:37. For the short history of the *Al-jawa'ib* (1860–83), see Albert Hourani, *Arabic Thought in the Liberal Age, 1798–1939* (London: Oxford University Press, 1970), 98.

46. *TA* 7, no. 7 (Rabiʿ al-akhir 1, 1294/Apr. 15, 1877), reprinted in Panipati, *Ma-qalat-i Sir Saiyid,* 4:378–89. The article in *Al-jawaʾib* was titled "Eʿtaq al-raqiq" (Emancipation of Slaves), 378–86; Saiyid Ahmad's reply, 386–89.

47. Mirzapur, October 22, 1873, reported in *TA* 4, no. 14 (Shawwal 1, 1290/Nov. 22, 1873), 138–51.

48. On the proliferation of new movements among Sunnis in north India in the 1870s–80s, see Kenneth W. Jones, *Socio-religious Movements in British India* (Cambridge: Cambridge University Press, 1989); and Metcalf, *Islamic Revival.*

49. Sir William Muir, *The Life of Mahomet and History of Islam, to the Era of the Hegira,* 2nd ed., abridged (London: Smith, Elder and Co., 1877), 3:347, quoting Mrs. Willoughby-Osborne, trans. and ed., *A Pilgrimage to Mecca by the Nawab Sikandar Begum of Bhopal, G.C.S.I.* (London: W. H. Allen, 1870), 87–89.

50. Saiyid Ahmad, "Ghulami fitrat-i insani," 15–16.

51. Ibid., 14–15. Although he placed the onus on the Raj government, he admitted elsewhere that it was only in Islamic states that the "darkness" of slavery still persisted, all other powers having by then seen the "light."

52. See "Beliefs Agreed Upon with Mahdi ʿAli," *TA* 1 (Oct. 23, 1873), cited here from Troll, *Sayyid Ahmad Khan,* 274–75.

53. On Saiyid Ahmad's conservative stance on female education and women's rights in Islam, see Gail Minault, *Secluded Scholars: Women's Education and Muslim Social Reform in Colonial India* (Delhi: Oxford University Press, 1998), 17–19, 72–73.

54. Dilawar Husain Ahmad Mirza, "The Causes of the Decline of Mohammadan Civilization," written between 1869 and 1879; republished in Sultan Jahan Salik, ed., *Muslim Modernism in Bengal: Selected Writings of Delawarr Hosaen Ahamed Meerza (1840–1913)* (Dacca: Centre for Social Studies, Dacca University, 1980), 59, 65.

55. Muhammad Sadiq, *A History of Urdu Literature* (London: Oxford University Press, 1964), 285. Ram Babu Saksena, *A History of Urdu Literature* (Allahabad: Ram Narain Lal, 1927), 302–303, lists his Urdu publications.

56. Saiyid Ahmad Khan to Chiragh ʿAli, n.d. (c. 1882), in Panipati, ed., *Maktubat-i Sir Saiyid,* 1:189–90.

57. *TA* 5, no. 2 (Safar 1, 1291/Mar. 20, 1874), 14–40; no. 3 (Rabiʿ al-awwal 1, 1291/Apr. 18, 1874), 42–56.

58. Moulavi Cheragh ʿAli, *The Proposed Political, Legal, and Social Reforms in the Ottoman Empire and Other Mohammadan States* (Bombay: Education Society, Byculla, 1883). Slavery is discussed on pp. 143–73. Idem, *A Critical Exposition of the Popular "Jihad"* (Calcutta: Thacker, Spink and Co., 1885), appendix B, 193–223.

59. Malcolm MacColl, "Are Reforms Possible under Mussulman rule?" *Contemporary Review,* August 1881, pp. 274–81. Such attack on, and, exceptionally, defense of Islamic societies was a mainstay of the correspondence columns of the leading British quarterlies and dailies in the 1880s. For a new European apologist for Islam, see the letters of Dr. G. W. Leitner, an Arabist and Punjab educationist, to the *Times,* the *Daily Telegraph,* and the *Asiatic Quarterly Review* between 1883 and 1888, published in appendices to his *Muhammadanism* (Woking: Oriental Nobility Institute, 1889).

60. Chiragh ʿAli, *Critical Exposition,* i; and idem, *Proposed Political, Legal, and Social Reforms,* i.

61. Resident at Hyderabad to foreign secretary to government of India, November 30, 1870, quoted in Chatterjee, "Abolition by Denial," 167.

62. Deputy commissioner of police, October 17, 1872, quoted in Sumanta Banerjee, *Under the Raj: Prostitution in Colonial Bengal* (New York: Monthly Review Press, 1998), 88.

63. *Proposed Political, Legal, and Social Reforms*, 173–83; Chiragh ʿAli, "Slavery and Concubine-Slaves as Concomitant Evils of War," appendix B to *Critical Exposition*, 193–223.

64. *Proposed Political, Legal, and Social Reforms*, 176–77, quoting Muir, *Life of Mahomet*, 2nd ed. (1877), 3:347.

65. *Proposed Political, Legal, and Social Reforms*, 178–82.

66. Ibid., 177–78.

67. "Bhopal slave dealing case: trial of Abdul Qayyum at Bombay," 1882, Bhopal Residency records, India Office Records, Oriental and India Office Collections of the British Library, R/2/423/27. Thanks to Siobhan Lambert-Hurley for drawing my attention to this case.

68. Translation of the begam's order, dated April 5, 1882, on a petition from Abdul Futtah, superintendent of gardens, Bhopal, dated Jamadi al-avval 15, 1299/April 4, 1882, concerning the arrest in Bombay of his brother, Hafiz Abdul Qayyum, for bringing in Siddee girls from Mecca for the Bhopal state. Bhopal Residency records, R/2/423/27.

69. Lepel Griffin to foreign secretary, Simla, November 8, 1882, secret (copy), on "Bhopal slave dealing case," Bhopal Residency records, R/2/423/27.

70. David Brion Davis, *The Problem of Slavery in the Age of Revolution, 1770–1823* (Ithaca: Cornell University Press, 1975), especially chapter 11, "The Good Book," 523–56.

71. Aziz Ahmad, *Islamic Modernism*, 52.

72. William Gervase Clarence-Smith, *Islam and the Abolition of Slavery* (London: C. Hurst, 2005), an expanded version of his inaugural lecture to the School of Oriental and African Studies, University of London, January 16, 2002.

73. Ahmed Chafik Bey [Ahmad Shafiq], *L'esclavage au point de vue musulman* (1891; 2nd ed., Cairo: Imprimerie Misr, 1938); Arabic translation, *Al-riqq fi al-Islam* (Cairo: al-Matbaʿah al-Ahliyah al-amiriyah bi-Bulaq, 1892); Urdu translation by Tajammal Khan, *Islami ghulami* (Junagarh: Sada-I Hind Press, 1907).

74. Among many statements by Maulana Abul Aʾla Maududi on slavery, see comments on slave-girls in his *Purdah and the Status of Woman in Islam*, originally published c. 1935, trans. and ed. Al-Ashʿari, 6th ed. (Delhi: Markazi Maktabi Islami, 1995); and idem, "The Position of Slavery in Islam," discussed by Maududi in a talk given in Urdu in Lahore on November 16, 1975, translated and published as *Human Rights in Islam* (Lahore: Islamic Publications Ltd., 1976). For an example of Muslim criticism of Maududi's views on slavery, showing the continued reliance by both sides on Qurʾanic texts, see Hafiz Muhammad Sarwar Qureshi, *The Qurʾan and Slavery, a Critique of Maudoodi's Commentary on Sura Ahzab* (London: H. M. Sarwar, 1983).

12

Slavery, Semantics, and the Sound of Silence

Indrani Chatterjee

Despite the considerable advances in conceptualizing slavery in global histories, studies of the same phenomenon in South Asian pasts cause profound unease among modern scholars. Avril Powell suggests a history of this sensibility. This essay provides another history for contemporary ambivalence by analyzing imperial censorship of local terms for "slavery."

The indigenous terms that invited imperial censure were initially registered as gendered nouns by a polyglot assistant surgeon—as *bay-pa* and *bay-nu* for the slave-boy and slave-girl respectively.[1] During 1894–97, the first Christian missionaries to the Indo-Burmese borderlands of the Lushai Hills (see map 4) wrote the word down as *boih* or *boi*, so that the gendered noun was either *boih-pa* or *boih-nu*.[2] The missionaries used the Roman script for writing down the sounds they heard. Since Tibeto-Burman language groups relied on tonality to distinguish different meanings for identical arrangements of consonants and vowels,[3] the choice of script then resulted in a distinct new orthography. The Roman script could not incorporate tonality except by drawing out, adding, or shortening vowels. British military and colonial officers thus transcribed the sound 'o' as "aw," so that the word previously written *boih* became *bawi* in the early twentieth century.[4] Pronounced with a broad vowel, the word becomes indistinguishable from the English euphemism for a male slave, and in the later nineteenth century for an apprentice—"boy." Yet British officers and missionaries used the word to refer to individuals of both sexes as well as to their condition. *Boi* or *bawi* came to mean both "slave" and "slavery." English speakers failed to specify the gender of the slave. They also failed to identify the owner or master of the slave in describing the condition of *bawi*-hood. Such innovations must have struck local audiences whose grammar included prefixes indicative of the age and gender of slaves.[5]

This essay analyzes the ways in which colonized populations manipulated such new vocabularies against their dispossessors. In their attempt to reclaim meaning for themselves, local people too engaged in cultural translations and symbolic reappropriations. In doing so, they foregrounded a particular experience of the past as the basis of an alternative authority to the one forwarded by colonial administrators. The latter's response was complex: a round of semantic manipulations aimed at silencing the very human beings engaged in the struggle to name themselves, followed by other kinds of repressions. Yet these strategies were not unfamiliar to local populations either. Indeed, it was the familiarity of these semantic feints that led some among them to recognize the intent embodied therein. However, their ultimate failures left the bodies of women and young children vulnerable to multiple projects of control and "invisibilization," while simultaneously leaving the meanings of many words unsettled.

War, Labor, and Local Societies

The people among whom the Duhlien languages were spoken lived across the contemporary borderlands of western Myanmar (Burma), eastern Chittagong (Bangladesh), and southern Manipur (India) (see map 4). One of the commonest features of this region between the late seventeenth and early nineteenth centuries was warfare. Histories of Manipur, Tripura, Cachar, and Assam suggest a decentralization of military power in these centuries and its mustering under specific conditions by "royal" order.[6] This decentralization of soldiering brought local households and peripheral regions into regular relationships with the kings and courts, and shaped the nature of social structures. Labor was wealth to be accumulated in warfare between the Burman, Arakanese, Ahom, Manipuri, Tripuri, and Tai-Shan polities between the fourteenth and nineteenth centuries.[7] Captives counted.[8] In the seventeenth century, a Manipuri ruler who had captured a thousand "Kachari" soldiers "appointed them to work as bugler, drummer, dhobi, mahout of elephant, syces for horses and other works according to their respective qualities."[9] A neighboring ruler of Tripura resettled captives from the coastal Arakanese (Magh) populations in the highlands, where they were to clear forests for cultivation.[10] This acquisition of labor power through warfare continued in the nineteenth century.[11]

Chronicles also outlined the exchange values of such war booty. The Tripura *Rajamala* records that the wages of sixteenth-century military levies were based on monetized values of plunder. Verses give four *anna*s as the value of each cow, two *anna*s for each goat, and sixteen *anna*s (or a full rupee of silver) as the value of each human captured. Military levies from Sylhet were paid in human captives as a result (*looter monushyo nite nripe aadeshilo*).[12] Captives could be transferred in different ways within and between different social groups as "tribute," "rewards," or "fines." Chronicles of Manipur record that a seventeenth-century scarcity drove the poor of a village to kill a royal elephant for food, but the offenders compensated the king with "twenty-two slaves, cows, and horses." Another group of tributaries to the court of Manipur (named "Thongjai" in the Manipuri literature, and "Kuki" in the Bengali) paid their "tribute" in human wealth (along with guns, gongs, and animal wealth), which was then redistributed further. By the eighteenth century, food shortages had driven the value of each captive to a critical point: "nineteen *maund*s of grain."[13] Under such conditions, we can only guess at the worth of the reward that kings gave to polo players or the carpenters of royal apartments when they gave them "a slave."[14] We can also guess at the value of royal "offerings" of slave-couples to the idol of the Vaishnava Hindu deity Govindaji, in the Manipur palace temple, at the same time.

In northeastern India, as in medieval Chola contexts (see chapter 2 of this volume), the dyadic relationships implied in the term "slave" could be located both in the warrior-prince's household and entourage and in the service of the temples and monasteries. The differences of location became important only under specific conditions. During times of peace, skilled and trained captives might have preferred to be attached to princely and royal households and workshops. But during war, those attached to individual or royal households might have preferred enslavement to religious institutions, especially since offerings made to the gods were guaranteed exemption from impressments of labor and taxes. Slaves who wished to escape labor services for which they might be "volunteered" by their elite masters and mistresses might have preferred to escape to religious establishments in the vicinity during war. That such escapes happened, and annoyed the secular holders, is suggested by early nineteenth-century Burmese royal decrees which categorically exempted male captives attached to individual ministers, members of the royal family, and monasteries from military conscription during war.[15] Some have claimed that such exemptions were post facto legitimations of a fiscal and secular process already underway, as the Burmese military *ahmud-an* escaped from court control into the entourages of local wealthy figures who offered "protection" through relationships based on debt.[16] This was the background of the groups that the East India Company encountered from the mid-nineteenth century, as tea cultivation spread southward from the Assam Hills.

Though Company officers were all too willing to describe these labor groups as "little republics" or as "ethnicities" tied together by blood and marriage, and to use names like "Lushei" Chin and Kuki for them, the populations which supplied military levies to all the political centers were not homogenous. Older histories of war, relocation, and payment of labor obligations created patterns of mobility and heterogeneity. So among soldiers banded under one of the contenders for the Manipur throne in early 1860 were male cultivators identified as "Looshai, some Munipuri, and a few Hindustani, the latter most likely old mutiny sepoys."[17]

"Settlement" under Colonial Rule

In addition to the relocations of captives referred to above, warfare also caused repeated subsistence crises. Local populations fled ravaged fields or military conscription or both. Late in the twentieth century, an ethnographer was told by his Mizo informants of old Mizo songs with refrains that translated as "we ran out of Siam" and "we left Shan state because of great famine."[18] The significance of such statements was that such groups laid no claim to "ancestral possession" of the lands they cultivated, pastured cattle in, or inhabited. Instead, they claimed mobility, and migration for subsistence.

The colonial Indian administration that grew over the contiguous Burmese, Ahom, Manipuri, and Cachari political entities between 1826 and 1885 opposed such mobility.[19] It preferred permanent landlords and monetized taxes payable on fixed dates. The new dispensation pressed hard on hitherto mobile populations, who practiced dry rice cultivation and were used to making annual payments in kind—of livestock, elephant tusks, local precious metals like gold, homespun cloth, raw cotton. A compromise was eventually reached by mid-century. Many of the swidden cultivators paid a house-tax (*gharchukti kar*), but it was levied at different rates—some groups paid Rs. 2, while others paid between Rs. 4 and 8 (Chittagong Hill tracts), and some even paid Rs. 10 (Riang households in Tripura). These taxes were realized in varying mixes of cash and kind, and collected by clan and village headmen (called *ghalim, gabur, sardar samanta* [in Tripura], and *lal* [in the Lushai Hills]) who served as intermediaries. In some instances, these agents further subcontracted this collection as "rights" in property developed further in the region.

Tax payments in cash rested on an ongoing commercialization of tea, cotton, bamboo, rubber, and timber production in the region, the proliferation of markets and entrepôts, and the enhanced monetization of local economies. These brought increasing numbers of small traders from the Bengal plains to sell salt, iron, brass, and copper utensils in exchange for rubber and ivory from the hills. At the same time, these traders also became moneylenders. The conditions of the loans varied according to district and time. Thomas Herbert Lewin, a British military officer administering the hills of Chittagong district in the 1860s, observed two distinct processes. In one, the children of debtors were pledged against loans given by the chiefs. "If a man wished to borrow money he deposited as security a son or daughter, whose services were taken as payment of interest for the debt, and the release of whom was dependent on the repayment of the original loan."[20] A second process, involving colonial judicial structures, led to the permanent bondage of adult males. This latter process began with the levying of high rates of interest on small loans of money, followed by the moneylender's manipulation of colonial judicial structures, and eventual enslavement of the debtor to the *mahajan*.[21] If the revenue collector was himself the moneylender, then the defaulting hillman became "the chattel of some petty subfarmer of revenue, and was bound to pay him head-money and do him service, on pain of being sold up or otherwise punished by order of the courts."[22]

The asymmetric relationships between debtors and moneylenders became particularly strained during drought and other calamitous events. To judge from the secondary accounts, such scarcities were a regular feature of the local economies. In 1832–33, there was severe famine in Cachar and Sylhet. An infestation of rats ate up the rice crops in 1868–69 in the same region. In the 1880s, the indigenous rubber trade was destroyed by overtapping at the same time that an entire rice crop was destroyed by rats, and a ten-month-long famine broke out in this region. Rats appeared again in 1901, and yet another severe famine broke out in 1911. Such famines devastated local economies and societies in multiple ways, but were especially destructive to the local webs of exchange relationships that revolved around women's labor.

Gendered Labor and Plunder

Women's labor was central to all "economic" activities of the region— growing and preparing food, harvesting cotton and weaving it into cloth, fetching water, keeping poultry and livestock, and transporting and selling. It was remarked on by every observer of the region's societies. Passing through Manipur territory in 1831, Francis Jenkins noted the exclusively female shopkeepers at one bazaar, and added that everywhere else, women remained "eternally busy picking cotton, weaving cloth, husking rice."[23] When he walked up to a "Kuki" hamlet and found the exhausted men resting after having brought in grain and cotton from the hills, he again commented on the women "husking rice and weaving . . . [who] appeared to be overworked—for they carry just equal burdens with their lords." In the Lushai Hills, too, the earliest published reports by Bengali-speaking plainsmen, commenting on seven different cycles of rice-growing in the swiddens, had described the centrality of women's labor during the sowing and harvesting seasons, and the constant weeding necessary to keep the crop from being choked off.[24] A little later, another colonial officer wrote that the women were the "hardest workers, the chief toilers."[25]

Acquiring female labor through circuits of marriage and birth depended upon the ability to negotiate, and pay, bride-wealth in most such populations. Sometimes such payments were made in kind, in the form of labor by a potential groom on the fields of a potential bride's father for two years. More often than not, however, they were made through transfers of cattle, heavy metal gongs, jewelry, beads, and woven cloth. But war and famine periodically destabilized such payments. As a result, plunder from neighboring localities or hostile groups remained a viable option.

Violence and commercialization thus occurred together. Commercialization enhanced the value of labor at the same time that it eased access to European firearms. Though official bodies of the time did not gather numerical data on either, it is possible to discern that the monetary value of human "booty" and "securities" for loans was both gendered and rising. A young male captive, who could be trained as an assistant to a headman or chief, brought only three head of cattle (*mithun*) if sold, whereas a single female captive could bring five. Officer after colonial officer admitted that "raids" produced mostly female captives, who were deemed to be the personal property of their captors. "As a rule only children and marriageable women were taken captive, and the latter were disposed in marriage, the lucky captor acting in loco parentis and taking the marriage price. The children grew up in the captor's house as his children."[26]

Other records from populations that lost such female labor appear to corroborate this.[27] The geographical and social distances traversed by female captives were evoked in songs of contiguous regions, for instance one in which a Mizo "princess" is described as having been taken "from a far-away village" to be "like a slave" to her husband.[28] Emotional, social, and geographical distances are also recorded in anecdotal accounts of "a woman in a village in the Rangamati area [in Tripura], who had been taken captive by another group of raiders (Howlongs) and been sold by them to Sydoha [Burma]."[29] Women and children captured by the Pui Shendu were "sold to the Sailoos for two old tower muskets, and the Sailoos carried them off to the village of their chief, Johwata, beyond the Kainsa Thoung or Blue Mountains" in Burma in 1878.[30] Such anecdotal evidence highlights the wide network of exchanges that local war-machines fed. Such distances urge us to treat the group of polities as a clustered whole. But they also defeat attempts at discovering the "original" identities of captives as they traveled through space and time. In addition, feminization and infantilization were associated with captives, which created problems of self-perception for warrior males taken prisoner.

Colonial Frames

The British annexation of Upper Burma in 1886 was resisted fiercely by the polyglot and heterodox groups living in the Chin and Lushai hills. Their resistance lasted till 1892, when it was finally crushed by British arms. Fiscal needs of the imperial regime directed that "indirect rule" be established here, with "chiefs" to keep order on the ground. From 1894, education was handed over to the Church. The Baptist missionaries Frederick W. Savidge and J. Herbert Lorrain, sponsored by the Arthington Trust at Leeds, were asked to tend to these newly vanquished peoples.[31] Two others from the Welsh Presbyterian Church, Edwin Rowlands and David Evan Jones, arrived in the region in 1897–98.

But missionaries and local chiefs were equally answerable to the colonial military superintendents. The model for all later chiefs of executive was John Shakespear, who had acted as an intelligence officer (or spy) during the Chin-Lushai expedition in 1889–90, after which he became superintendent of the Lushai Hills (1898–1905). The authoritarianism of this regime was evident from the start of the military occupation, which caused many servants in chiefly households to flee old masters. Shakespear's "tour diaries" referred to these servants as having been in the old master's house

> ever since they were children and had been fed at his expense till they were able to contribute towards the labor of the household, and Saipuia [the chief] had given the man his wife. This form of parental slavery is a Lushai custom that I see no reason to interfere with. *They are not captives,* but merely people who from one cause or another have sought the shelter of the Chief's house; and in return for their keep work in the Chief's jhooms &c.[32]

Yet his later entries proved that there was no distinction between "captive" and "slave": runaway servants turned out to be captives taken in long-ago raids.[33] Even when such long-domiciled captives were allowed to depart, their erstwhile masters demanded compensation from the new masters, or those the fugitives sheltered with, in a pattern reminiscent of that in early modern western India.[34] (See chapter 7 of this volume.) Unlike the peshva's officials, who caught slave-fugitives in order to enhance treasury holdings, British officials like Shakespear left the matter "between the chief and the slave" to resolve.[35] Yet such collaboration with "chiefs" was intended to have the same result as it did in the Maratha state. It made locally dominant households responsible for imperial tax-collection, and it maintained the lines of command within every tax-paying unit—that is, every household.

Earlier Burmese and Assamese taxation systems grouped commoners into those who owed labor service (or could commute it to cash) to the state and those who did not. But with British "pacification" came a regime of forced labor for all households that was neither optional nor commutable. The superintendent and his assistants were authorized to collect taxes at specified annual rates: Rs. 2 in cash, or 20 *seers* of cleaned rice or 1 *maund* of unhusked rice per house, in addition to each house supplying the services of one porter (*coolie*) for carriage and transportation or road construction for ten days each year.[36] This additional taxation in labor service destroyed older grids of social respectability. All labor services, especially in sections of *jhum* (swidden) cultivation, were limited to activities that were considered especially hard, such as weeding. They were not ones which an unbonded subject—who paid fixed amounts of grain to his chief—performed,[37] but were left to bondsmen and bondswomen, and to captives. By demanding that every household supply both cash or grain and labor service, colonial rule appeared to assimilate the non-slave but newly subjected commoner and the slave. Having collapsed and erased the distinction between subjection, coerced provision of labor, and the particular clanlessness marking slave lives, British military officers then misattributed the reasons for the widespread resistance that they encountered from all the hillsides to their demands for such corvée.[38]

Inversion and Invention

Colonial erasures of difference between slave and non-slave commoner in each village and between all dependents within chiefly households rested upon a novel equation. Colonial authorities considered the physical proximity of members of a household to its head, and his provision of food and raiment to them, as the substance of a seamless intimacy. Shakespear wrote that

> Widows, orphans, and others who are unable to support themselves and have no relatives willing to do so, form the bulk of this class of *boi*. . . . [They] are looked on as part of the chief's household, and *do all the chief's work in return for their food and shelter.* The young men cut and cultivate the chief's jhum and attend his fish traps. The women and girls fetch up wood and water, clean the daily supply of rice, make cloths, and weed the jhum, and look after the chief's children. . . . he can only purchase freedom by paying one mithan or its equivalent in cash or goods.[39]

The *boi* or *bawi* who lived in physical proximity to the chief (*inpuichhung*), such officials inferred, was better off than one who lived in a separate house (*inhrang*).

In establishing equivalences between food-sharing and freedom, physical proximity and intimacy, officials inverted local equations of the provision of food and shelter with the creation of binding obligations.[40] Relations of indebtedness and reparation were initiated when food and drink was offered to corporeal "guests" and invisible "spirits" alike.[41] Codes of aggressive hospitality were important in setting chief apart from commoner, and the honorable from the dishonored: the most honorable of men was the *thangchhuah,* one who had fed the spirits of ancestors with sacrificed men and animals, and had given numerous feasts to the villagers on these occasions.

Missionaries, however, pointed to the distinctions between recipients of hospitality when they named various clan-groups (Hualhang, Hualngo, Hmar, Vaisal, and Khiangte) which had been prisoners of war, and whose descendants were the *boi*s in many chiefs' houses in 1909–12.[42] Missionaries, who were familiar with local lifestyles, described how families of reputed worth would be supplied with rice by the chief, who would then claim the family as his *boi*s. Nor was this mode of recruiting versatile labor limited to these borderlands alone. In the northernmost parts of Burma, for instance, 60 percent of the three-thousand-odd bondsmen of Assamese provenance told colonial officials in 1925 that when their ancestors two centuries ago had taken "refuge with the Jhingpaws [latter-day Kachins] in the Hukawng Valley who gave them shelter and food . . . the Jhingpaws refused to release them declaring that they have become their slaves."[43]

Official readiness to assimilate dependence and intimacy rested on a whole range of ideological and political factors. Biblical theology itself elevated the acts of feeding and sheltering of the poor and needy as charitable actions deserving of rewards in the afterlife. This theology, and the circumstances of being "little kings" in the domains they were sent to govern, predisposed individual British superintendents to characterize their own deployment of such young boys and girls in domestic service as examples of Christian charity. As the memoirs of James Johnstone, the Political Resident in Manipur, reveal, the ideology of paternalist benevolence rested, in turn, upon mischaracterizing ransom payments as payment of "debt."[44] The same creative spirit enabled British administrators of the Lushai Hills to extend the mantle of saviorhood to the chiefs they nominated as governors of newly sedentarized settlements. Aggression was thus readily represented as charity. The conscription of able-bodied kinless people (orphans, debtors, and destitutes alike) was recast as a customary form of benevolence.[45] Instead of perceiving the extraction consequent upon the feeding as unjust, both chiefs and officials represented this co-constituted masculinist paternalism as a symmetric exchange: "If the Chief's house was to be made a poor-house and an asylum, it was only equitable that he should be given some hold over the inmates."[46]

Such formulations overlooked contrary evidence: the boys, girls, and women who tried to avoid entering the chief's house themselves, and tried to ensure that their relatives stayed out as well. Only other poor men—albeit "white" and Christian—noticed their efforts. Edwin Rowlands, a missionary, described a twelve-year-old, already "for long a little slave girl, afflicted with facial paralysis," who was sent by her mother to the missionaries during the famine of 1901. Another three-year-old was brought by villagers the morning after her ailing grandmother died, for they had been told of her fear that "the little child would be taken and brought up a little slave girl."[47] In his earliest reports to his directors at home, Rowland named three female "slaves in the chief's household," Hnunziki, Pawngi, and Chal-lian Kuki, the first of whom had even been ransomed by locals at his urging.[48] The second girl then ran away to the mission; Rowlands later said that she "came to us some years ago, a little run-away slave-girl."[49] Another eighteen-year-old boy recounted that in 1908, when his father fell short of food and "entered the chief's house," he had tried to evade the same fate for himself by eating at his relatives' houses. But his father's "patron" threatened to fine anyone who took him in. Eventually, the boy gave up.[50]

Many descendants of erstwhile captives as well as first-generation victims of famine recorded the ignominy and the loss of reciprocity that followed from such feeding. Khawtawpa, who identified himself as a *vanlung-bawi* (glossed by the missionaries as the "slave living in the outer room of the chief's house"), said,

> Even though we raise much rice, we cannot spend any as we like, it belongs to the chief. The chief has spent very little on us excepting the rice which we have eaten when we were young. . . . when the rice is scarce the chief does not like to buy from other villages, we sometimes fast, even when we live in the chief's house, but the chief has food for himself.[51]

Instead of showing the master as a benefactor of the famine-struck, Khawtawpa's words reveal that famines worsened the vulnerability of such "indwelling" *bois*.

For the indwelling *boi* not only accumulated the debt of her or his own food and shelter, but also embodied the debt of a parent, and in turn, bequeathed such debt to children, whether they were born before *boi*-hood or during it. In that sense, physical proximity to the chief only increased "debt" and thus the payments required for redemption. When former masters attempted to renegotiate and maximize returns from such dependents, those who had thought they had paid adequate ransoms found out otherwise. Thus, writing after the onset of famine in November 1911, a missionary doctor recorded having to medicate a slave who had been severely beaten with a cane by his chief "because the ransom he had paid was not considered sufficient by the chief even though the slave showed him a government order stating that the amount of the ransom paid had freed him."[52] Mary Fraser reported at the peak of the famine that Pawngi, a former slave whose child with a male slave remained in the chief's possession, was "breaking her heart for her child. She walked into my bedroom the other day and wept, with her head on my breast . . . a broken hearted mother who has paid the ransom years ago and cannot get her very own child."[53]

Dispossession as Undignified Afterlife

As the story of Pawngi and the child she could not "mother" reveals, even repaying a "debt" did not ensure the resumption of kin relationships. It did not reverse the natal alienation that resulted from the provision of food and "protection" by a chief or headman. Indeed, the dispossession of parenthood, the symbol of dignity and personhood in many societies in this period and region, occurred precisely as a result of becoming a "debtor." Adult *bois*, along with their sons and daughters, lost all claims to belong to ritual and social networks outside of the chief's household. For instance, a *boi*-parent had to hand over her or his share of bride-wealth payments (*manpui*) for her or his own daughters to the chief whose food he ate. Marriage payments, like rituals of sacrifice, marked the boundaries of "belonging" within the clan as a whole. The giving up of *manpui* by adult *bois* amounted to a renunciation of both clan status and material prosperity. Both condemned descendants to further indignities. Material impoverishment reinforced their inability to pay "debts" and "ransoms," and ritual exile from sacrifices spelt out their exclusion from networks of kinship between the living and the dead. While non-*boi* locals valued clan names (*phun*), such dispossessions made the descendants of captives and debtors clanless and nameless— "anonymous ones."[54] This was what all *bois* had in common: the gradual stripping away of personhood during life, and the completion of non-being by death, when their irrevocable exile from the group of ancestors was rendered visible by the absence of death-dignifying ceremonies for the *boi*.

Anonymity was hateful because it was reiterated during the rituals of "sacrifice," elaborate funerals, and feasts of others. Only those who belonged to clans and lineages partook of the sacrifices made to the spirit protector of the clan (*sakhua*) at these performances. Estrangement from clanship and kinship led to an undignified funeral, when those without socially recognized descendants received no animal or bird sacrifices to accompany their souls on the journey to *Pialral* (the paradise reserved for great hunters and feast-givers) or *Mithikhua* (the abode of the dead). Hence dispossession of kin led to an undignified afterlife as well. Having received no food from mortals, in turn, these dispossessed and indebted souls were believed to remain "hungry" as spirits, desirous of "eating up" the wealth—animals and children—of the living.

Hindu-Buddhist notions of transmigration embedded in karma coexisted with the veneration of supernatural beings across Southeast and South Asia.[55] Some scholars have remarked on this, calling it contradictory.[56] But as Aung-Thwin points out, the two coexisted precisely because there were always some "green" or violent deaths, which had not been "fed" the appropriate libations by living kinsmen and hence troubled the living.[57] Only patient folklorists could disentangle the congealed memories of these undignified deaths from the stories told in the late twentieth century—stories which entwined captivity, food production, and freedom into a single narrative. In one of these, a mother spirit (*phungpuinu*) whose spirit children were killed and who was herself captured by men had to buy her freedom by conjuring up implements that produced plentiful food for her captors.[58] That is how local legend explains the origin of the magic horn (*sekibuhchhuak*) that produced delicious food and boiled meat without any human effort.[59]

Bois and God's Word

Faced with the terrors of a perpetual anonymity, *bois* began to seek out aspects of Christian eschatology and a ritual world in which every death was mourned and the possibility of paradise was assured to each believer. Though memoirs authored by such men in later life said little about native concerns about an afterlife, missionary records suggest that the theme of "resurrection" held the key to the *bois*' flight from local sacrificial practices to the Christian church.

In becoming interested in "God's word," *bois* also continued older practices of seeking betterment of their state. Faced with intensified labor regimes under military occupation, many earlier slaves had sought sanctuary at sacred sites and with sacred figures. They may have done the same in the late nineteenth century, if the contempt of the officials can be historicized appropriately. Shakespear recalled that in 1899 he dismissed a group of missionaries who had appealed to him on behalf of Christian porters to end "Sunday Labour," exulting that he had "defeated them by saying that . . . the Sabbath was made for man and not man for the Sabbath."[60] Two decades later, another officer refused to give any credence to the Christian *bois'* attempts to stop work on Sundays. He justified this denial of rest on the grounds that it would have constituted a "special consideration" to one religion. Missionaries who converted slaves to Christianity, he argued, should be fully apprised of the impossibility of giving any religion preferential treatment as a special "favor."[61]

But it was not missionaries who were the agents here. To many local *bois*, becoming Christian meant rest in the afterworld. An elderly Mizo pastor recalled years later that he had first heard of the Gospel as a "serf" in a chief's house, and that when he read the five widely circulated books of the New Testament (Luke, John, and Matthew in 1906, I and II Corinthians by 1907), he wanted to become a Christian; as he said, he wanted to "believe" God's word, not men's.[62] Such stories were repeatedly offered in the testimony of former *bois*. So the young man called Kapchhunga, whose ancestor had been captured in war, said that the goad to his flight was I Corinthians 23: "Ye were bought with a price, become not bond-servants of men." Other missionaries noted similar verses that had great effect on their audience.[63]

As more *bois* began to interest themselves in "God's word," the trickle of individual fugitives from the chiefly households to the mission compound began to swell. By the time Peter Fraser and his wife arrived in 1908, entire "families" of *bois* were running away to the mission.[64] Most of these had "inherited" their *boi* status from their parents. For instance, three brothers and a sister left their master's house and settlement for the mission without having paid their commutation-dues or ransom.[65] At one point, Fraser counted forty-nine Christian *bois* who had fled to the mission to enroll as "schoolboys" so that they could learn God's word (*Pathian thu*). But his resources allowed him only to commence building a small schoolhouse to house twelve of these boys, "who are, or have been, slaves."[66]

Such flights were inevitably followed by demands from the former patrons that the fugitives or the persons now giving them refuge pay compensation. The former creditors would call this "repayment of debt," and the new patrons would resent their demands for "ransom." Few missionaries before Peter Fraser had had the resources to pay out such sums of money. But Fraser was different. As a man who had had a lay medical career in Edinburgh for fifteen years before he came out as a missionary, he had access to more funds than his fellow missionaries. He was also willing to spend it in redemption payments. And it was only when Fraser paid out the requested sums from his and his wife's private funds that the colonial administration responded quickly and adversely.

Conjuring with Words

From November 1909, imperial officers revealed their hostility to Fraser's goal of redeeming the fugitive bondsmen. It was in that month that Cole, the new superintendent of the Lushai Hills, announced that

> What they call *bawi* (slavery) in the Lushai Hills is not "bound" slavery. By paying ransom money they can be free according to their pleasure; they can go wherever they like; for that reason it does not appear that they are real slaves. So because they can do as they desire, it is only "Membership of the Household." Henceforth without calling it "Slave Price" (*Bawi man*) it is called "Payment for board of household members" (*Chhungte Chawm man*). So whoever wants to ransom himself if he gives to the chief payment for board of household members (*chungte chawm man*)—forty rupees or a *gayal* [cow], one family will be allowed to ransom themselves.[67]

Within five years, these semantic strategies solidified. Imperial fiat ensured that the "use of the word 'bawi' should as far as possible be discontinued."[68]

The conjuring with words can perhaps be seen as another chapter in the long history of not calling a slave a slave—a policy enshrined as law in Act V of 1843. It also continued the imperial regimes of extraction of labor and capital in the region. For some superintendents, the latter constituted a stronger incentive than other factors. For instance, Cole, a "terrible hand at juggling with funds,"[69] hoped to avoided paying compensation to chiefs for their runaways, which he might have had to do if he had counted them as "slave" property. Cole's fiscal zealousness spurred him to unprecedented levels of taxation, even though his tenure also coincided with famine. In 1908–1909, just as the flowering bamboo that warned of a ruined rice crop began to appear, Cole demanded Rs. 32,371 in taxes. Every household had to raise the house tax in cash: exemptions were only allowed to males who served in the Lushai Labor Corps, the Army Bearer Corps, or the Burma Rifles.[70] Elevated levels of assessment acted as a pincer, driving the more vulnerable local hillmen into imperial militias or into "closer ties" with local chiefs. Both administrator and chief actively discouraged the remaining option—migration to uncultivated land on neighboring hillsides. As villages became stationary, and the proliferation of chiefs outpaced the availability of cultivable lands,[71] all villages became ever more dependent on the work provided by female and male *bois* for the chief's *jhum* cultivation. Famine gave some chiefs greater incentive to maintain the numbers of households within each village from which they could collect *fathang* (a basket of rice given to the chief as dues).

There were political factors also in Cole's conjuring. Not only did the doctor's willingness to pay release money to the chiefs indicate a certain independence of income, unusual for a missionary, but these payments threatened to destabilize political hierarchies established by force since the 1890s. The danger was that the liquidity of cash could enable lesser chiefs to attract subject-cultivators who were bonded to the greater chiefs. This in turn might turn the ire of the greater men against the colonial regime. Such a danger seemed especially imminent in 1908–1909, when the anti-imperialist struggles against the partition of Bengal took an "extremist" turn. The skill and determination with which Fraser, the educated missionary, joined a transatlantic anti-slavery network of communications on behalf of the *bois* only heightened official fears of Bolshevist internationalism. Thus the superintendent hinted darkly at "outside influences at work" in the flouting of his orders, and warned of "unfortunate political results" of such missionary disobedience.

In order to prevent any further resistance, the superintendent adroitly combined a policy of intimidating Christian *bois* and chiefs along with an attempt to isolate their ally, the doctor, from his fellow missionaries by characterizing him as "independent" and of "unsound" mind. He impugned Fraser's local knowledge as superficial, and denied his right to intervene in "political" matters. Most of these ends could be pursued by casting aspersions on Fraser's understanding and use of the word *boi* or *bawi*. Hence Fraser, in his conflict with the superintendent, was impelled to record the testimony of those who came to him asking for release and redemption money.

Taking Back the Word

If the conditions of its production caution us about the "scriptedness" of such testimony, there is equal need to steer clear of charging these words with being the effects of missionary ventriloquism alone. Doing so erases the resilience of local cultures and semiotics. Local speech regimes had long histories of deceiving "hungry spirits" through lexical feints. Men walking in forests would say *tho-hna-pa* ("medicine") rather than *mi* ("goat") because trees were believed to house predatory spirits.[72] Observers of other preliterate upland populations had also recorded that, if a man escaped a tiger attack, he "changes his name so that the animal may not know him again. If he is killed all his relatives change their names to escape the same disagreeable recognition."[73] We must grant people who lived in such speech cultures the wit—and the autonomy—to recognize linguistic manipulation when it was practiced against them in turn. Hence it might be useful to consider in its entirety the protest of an old male former *boi* against the substitution of terms decreed by Cole. Told by the officers that *bawi*s or *boi*s were "miscalled slaves," this old man objected,

> *Bawi*s are really slaves. Why should they not be considered slaves? How many times will the slaves have to pay "Chawmman" and suffer? How many times have each of the slaves paid? I am an old slave. All we, the Hualngo and Hualhang are old slaves. When we fought with the Sailo clan (i.e. when they were becoming rulers of the country) we lost, and they made us captives. A few Hualhang and Hualngo ran away to the Pawi country, some to the Sailo (villages) we all who were with the Sailo chiefs became slaves.
>
> . . . In the year 1893 I became a Headman, and I often spoke (had dealings with) to the Government for the chief who made me a slave. . . . I noticed some things done when I assisted the chief for about seven years.
>
> If a man (father) who has not many relations died, and if we found out that he had no good relations to help him how did we consider about him? Who knows? *I* know. If one can make these orphans to be slaves to the chief, it will be popularity for the headman with the chief. Therefore we have to try our best (to make them slaves) if they only had no relations to help them. Are there many whom the chiefs rescued from sorrow and trouble? Not many.
>
> Therefore are the slaves living without doing anything for the chiefs? Some have suffered for three or four generations. Those who became like cattle—good cows—for the chiefs for many years, those captive slaves, who became slaves because of losing in battle, what length of suffering will be enough for them to be free from "Chawmman."
>
> For what period of "chawmman" is this "chawmman" which is to be. If slavery is not right what does the greater service, the chief making slaves or the slaves who have been as good cattle for many generations or many years working for the chiefs?
>
> Did the chief have much trouble when he made slaves? Many became slaves only because of the headman's cunning. I also was a headman for a chief for about 7 years. I know about it during that period.[74]

An eloquent—if hard to parse—testimony about the transformation of defeated prisoners of war and locally born orphans into *boi*s, this also shows how a headman who was himself a former slave reproduced the system. It was a shrewd protest against the paying of compulsory ransom by those slaves who viewed their labor itself as having repaid the "debt" of food to the chiefs. In sum, it exemplifies the resistance of precisely those people whom officials would consider "hereditary" bondsmen, the outdwelling or *inhrang boi*s.

With the phrase "Who knows? *I* know," Vanchhunga attempted to claim authority as both an erstwhile *boi* and as a procurer of *boi*s for his chief. In doing so, he contradicted every aspect of imperial proclamation and policy on the matter. For instance, against the official axiom that the *inhrang boi*s who lived separately were non-slaves, Vanchhunga asserted that the children of such *inhrang boi*s remained vulnerable to repossession by the chief. That he was being truthful is suggested by the testimony of others. Two boys whose father had been an *inhrang boi* had had to reenter the chief's house in 1910, together with their sisters, when their father died without having paid off his own ransom. When he was fifteen years old, one of these boys recorded that the transformation from *inhrang* to indwelling or *inchhang* status meant relocation within a hard labor regime for the boys and their three sisters equally. Apparently gesturing at the erasure of boundaries that had earlier distinguished males' labor from females' and the labor of free people from that of slaves, the boys spoke of their six years as *inchhang boi*s in terms of the equality of indignity. The younger boy served as a personal attendant to members of the household, and the older boy cultivated rice and did other work on the *jhum*s. Though the boys eventually fled to the mission compound ninety miles away, and Fraser even raised the requisite ransom money for them, their former owner brought a claim for these runaways to Superintendent Cole. By October 1910 Cole had returned the ransom money to Fraser, and returned the boys to their former owner. Cole decided that the elder boy would work for the Public Works Department for one month every year, performing the dreaded porterage and road-building tasks, till he could pay three installments of thirteen rupees, five *anna*s, and four *ganda*s toward his ransom.[75] The records say nothing of his sisters.

The *boi*s who attempted to speak with, and through, Fraser were a minority of the most resistant or energetic or curious. Many more never sought anything from the missionaries. Yet, curiously enough, no other officials ever produced a narrative from a "compliant" *boi* in their own records, not even to counter the testimony supplied by Fraser. This lends the voices recorded by Fraser greater resonance, especially as their words demolished much of the official colonial fabrication of "household intimacy."

Furthermore, while official correspondence never produced a single narrative by a female *boi*, Fraser's records reveal a large number of young girl-slaves. Only Fraser recorded how a sixteen-year-old girl became a *boi* after her father died, leaving an ill wife and hungry children: "My mother knew that if we entered the chief's house, as long as we were alive, until the ransom money is paid, we are bound to be slaves. But I did not know that we would be slaves like that. I thought that we should be able to go away from the chief's house just as we could go away from the houses of ordinary people when they dislike us. We were slaves for about four years." Ultimately, she explained, she ran away because her chief (master) tried to persuade her to "lie with him," and even after she ran away to the mission compound in Aijal the chief's headmen were sent to persuade her to go back.[76]

Translating Culture and Power

Despite the detailed evidence Fraser produced, he could not convince his fellow Protestant missionaries. The most painful conflicts over interpretation occurred within the group of Methodist missionaries. The Methodist Church itself was never a monolithic institution, either in the British Isles of the eighteenth century or in antebellum America.[77] These disunities and denominational differences cropped up again in the British Indian empire in 1909–11. Though Peter Fraser had written to the other missionaries in the region, who were largely British and American Baptist, in 1909–10, exhorting them "to set at liberty them that are bruised," even calling for a collective petition to the government of India and the people of England,[78] he failed to rally most of them.

There were many reasons for the overwhelming rejection of the doctor's urgings. Fraser's nonconformism was obvious: he had come out as a "layman" to a place where only the ordained had dared to go. His submission to the hierarchies and doctrines that guided both Anglican and Baptist ecclesiastical and British imperial military administration was less than total. The Welsh Calvinist Methodist Mission as a whole had been co-opted by the government into its educational administration in 1854, with a small grant of money to the mission in the Khasi Hills for the printing and use of missionary tracts in the schools the government assisted.[79] The mission's educational program depended on bureaucratic goodwill. No missionary (save Fraser) was willing to endanger that. Perhaps equally significantly, there were missionaries who genuinely believed in the doctrine of separation of church and state,[80] and preferred to characterize slavery as a secular matter, best left to the secular authorities to resolve. Moreover, the directors of the mission in Liverpool referred to "the present state of feeling in India" and to the special character of the British Empire in India in directing their missionaries to adopt a "patient and hearty co-operation with the authorities whom God has, in His wise providence, placed in India." Ironically, such a secular directive was also glossed biblically; the directors referred to the Apostle Paul, arguing that "the principles of his teaching struck at the root of all forms of slavery but he did not interfere directly with the evil as it existed within the Roman Empire."[81]

By 1912, the executive committee of the Welsh Calvinist Mission, under some degree of imperial pressure as conveyed through Cole's letters, had asked Fraser to work in the Khasi Hills as a medical missionary.[82] Fraser refused and left for Wales, an ill and tormented man.[83] Opinion within the metropolitan anti-slavery groups was badly divided on this. When the Anti-Slavery and Aborigines Protection Society asked Henry Lytton, a former viceroy of India, for information on the matter, he advised the group to desist from "agitating" against Major Cole, whom he declared a man of great experience and no prejudice.[84] Despite such pressures, the Anti-Slavery and Aborigines Protection Society did write to Secretary of State Montague in 1913 to appeal that the *bois* be immediately liberated and their holders compensated.[85] But the outbreak of the First World War distracted attention from all such demands, as many of the male *bois* were seconded by their chiefs to imperial battalions overseas.

Perhaps the absence of such male *bois* explains the skewed gender distribution when the first (and last, and pitifully flawed) unofficial census of "indwelling" *bois* was taken in 1914. In the thirty-four villages and the sixty-eight separate families counted, a disproportionate number of *bois* turned out to be women and children. For instance, among the limited number of villages that were surveyed, census-takers found 119 indwelling *bois*, of whom 96 were women and children while only 23 were males between the ages of 16 and 60. Extrapolating from the overall census figures for the hills (which gave a total population of 91,204), administrators then estimated that the total number of the indwelling *bois* in the district was approximately 550, of whom 110 would have been males, and 440 women and children.[86] Not a word had been uttered about the redemptions, ransom, or *chawmman* of the women and children.

Conclusion: The Return of the Repressed

Fraser died in Wales in 1919.[87] However, two significant episodes marked the afterlife of the conflict. First, populations identified as Thado Kukis and Chins revolted against their recruitment and transportation to European battlefields across the region between 1917 and 1919.[88] Second, the Convention of Saint Germain-en-Laye of 1919 affirmed an international desire to secure a complete suppression of slavery in all its forms and of the slave trade by land and by sea. When the sixth assembly of the League of Nations drafted a convention to implement these ends, the British member committed the government of India to the same agenda.[89] An aggrieved official of the latter responded that the government was committed to a program of abolition without having assented to a novel definition which put "captured" people under the category of "slave" for the first time.[90] Official unwillingness notwithstanding, metropolitan and transatlantic bodies such as the Anti-Slavery Society again prodded local imperial administrations about the *boi*s.[91] Unsurprisingly, the only response they received was a reminder that the terms *bawi* and *bawiman* were no longer used.[92]

Such semantic tactics affected everyone, albeit in unequal measure. Dispossessed ancestor-mothers like Pawngi and their descendants went literally unnamed in colonial legal dispensations, as well as in postcolonial histories of the region. Missionaries and administrators alike were compelled to reattach meanings that had been dislodged from words. In the 1920s, a young missionary described the experience of teaching students chapters 5–8 of the Epistle to the Romans, which referred to Christians as "bondservants to righteousness." The missionary acknowledged that the word for bondservant was *bhoi* (adding the unnecessary aspirate after the consonant), but he greatly approved of the social system which replaced "workhouses" with chiefly care. His approval thus extended to imagining a model of Christian discipleship in which his students could identify themselves as "God's *bhoi*s" (which would have been consonant with the *bhakti* and Sufi sense of being "slaves of the lord," as well as with the Buddhist sense of being the "servant of religion"). Yet, when asked, several of his students protested, claiming instead (apparently without irony) that they were "God's Sons" (i.e., Jesus!). At the close of the school day, he asked the same question of his students, in front of a visiting chief. The chief responded that *boi* and "son" meant the same thing, to the great merriment of the students.[93] If this unsettled state of meaning appeared to distinguish generations and statuses within the same society in the 1920s, another scene of unsettled meaning appeared in the word that had replaced the old one.

Superintendents were hard pressed to clarify *chawmman* (payment for board, or price of food) after the First World War, which had taken members of the Lushai Labour Corps to France and brought them back after demobilization with small savings of cash. One official, Nevill Parry, described the members of this corps as "*orphans* [who] prior to going to France had been living in the houses of *people who were no relations of theirs* and on their return went back to their former homes.'" Facing the possibility of continuing resistance by the hill populations, and looking to ensure that a fresh infusion of cash did not reinforce these struggles, Parry had to address the payment of ransoms by such returned orphan-soldiers. Specifying that a "man who has gone on a military expedition outside the district" had undertaken extraordinary hardship and risk, he ruled that the person who had supported such an orphan-soldier could claim *chawmman* in the ordinary way, but could not annex the money earned by the orphan-soldier while on expedition.[94]

In an ethnographic account of the same region published four years later, Parry, now retired, returned to his repressed knowledge of the real status of the "orphans" in his jurisdiction. Though he began with the tired and perfunctory ritual of disavowing the word "slavery" (a "complete misnomer today"), he then proceeded to show exactly how sanctuary and nurture had created recognizable "slaves." "If a chief or noble brought up an *orphan belonging to another clan* from childhood, the orphan became the *slave* of the man who brought him up. It was not possible for a man to enslave an orphan belonging to his own clan in this way, as fellow-clansmen were regarded as having duties to each other." Once articulated, the memories proved too powerful to contain. Complete with descriptions of rituals that had transformed captives into the living dead and the preponderance of females among the slaves, Parry's ethnographic account echoed with other sounds—such as that of a slave named Dawma who had been "buried alive with a certain amount of food and drink and a gong, and was told to beat on the gong as long as he was alive. Dawma's relations ran a bamboo down into the grave, and could hear the slave beating on the gong for nine days, after which there was silence."[95]

In the postwar forties, another colonial administrator, Anthony McCall, referred to the "elaborate system of paying for hospitality" that existed under the name of *chawmman*,[96] but felt compelled to vilify a certain "Doctor A" for having misunderstood the *bawi* system.[97] Fraser, long since dead, had survived in the memories of young and old alike in these hillsides.[98] It might even be possible to reimagine Fraser as the ultimate "hungry spirit" in the hills who consumed Superintendent McCall's reputation or "good name." McCall ended his career with a reprimand from his superiors for having used forced labor.[99]

Let us close then with the "unsettlement" of language. Language was, and had remained, an important historical factor in the politics of dispossession and power. Yet the original analytic remains not language per se, but the politics that simultaneously weighted languages down and vaporized them. Erasing certain words and replacing them with others has particular freight when the word being banished is "slavery." Postcolonial scholars must be particularly aware of this, given the more refined silencing techniques now available to those who were deaf to the sounds of the dispossessed to begin with. To refuse "slavery" is to repeat the acts of dispossession all over again.

Notes

Abbreviations:

CMA   Church Missionary Archives
Commr.   Commissioner
NAI   National Archives of India, Delhi
NLW   National Library of Wales, Aberstywyth
Offg.   Officiating
OIOC   Oriental and India Office Collections, British Library, London

I thank Suzanne Miers for sharing her files of evidence with me and for her encouragement. I also thank the American Council of Learned Societies for the Frederick Burkhardt Fellowship for 2004–2005, which allowed me to visit the Welsh missionary archives housed in the National Library of Wales, Aberstywyth, and to write up this material. The writing could not have been begun without the input of colleagues at Rutgers, namely Temma Kaplan, Nancy Hewitt, Sue Cobble, and Barry Qualls. It would not have been completed without the assistance of the librarians at the Institute for Advanced Study, Princeton; of Firestone Library, Princeton University; and of my colleagues in the Thanatology Seminar at the School of Historical Studies. I am especially grateful to Caroline Bynum, Susan Morrissey, Susan Einbeinder, and Karl Morrison for their contributions to developing the arguments here, to Thomas Keirstead and Julia Thomas for invaluable advice on writing, and to my co-contributors to this volume—Richard Eaton, Michael Fisher, Sumit Guha, Ramya Sreenivasan, and Sylvia Vatuk—for their detailed suggestions for revisions of an earlier draft.

1. Brojo Nath Saha, *Grammar of the Lushai Language, to Which Are Appended a Few Illustrations of the Zau or Lushai Popular Songs and Translations from Aesop's Fables* (Calcutta: Bengal Secretariat Press, 1884), 6. Saha's linguistic skills and medical knowledge impressed another visitor, for which see Emil Riebeck, *The Chittagong Hill-Tribes: Results of a Journey Made in the Year 1882,* trans. A. Keane (London: Asher and Co., 1885), 3.

2. J. Herbert Lorrain and Fred W. Savidge, *A Grammar and Dictionary of the Lushai Language (Dulien Dialect)* (1898; reprint, Firma KLM Private Limited, Calcutta, 1976), 3, 63. The word already reveals the extra aspirate sound that missionaries were warned against adding by their Lushai teachers, for which see E. Lewis Mendus, *The Diary of a Jungle Missionary* (Liverpool: Foreign Mission Office, 1956), 22 (entry for 1922).

3. See Eugenie J. A. Henderson, "Notes on the Syllable Structure of Lushai," *Bulletin of the School of Oriental and African Studies* 12, nos. 3–4 (1948), 713–25.

4. This is suggested by a passage arguing the need for a single sound to transcribe short and long vowels in J. H. Lorrain, *Dictionary of the Lushai Language* (Calcutta: Asiatic Society, 1940), vii–viii. For the continuing relevance of the debate regarding orthography, transcription, and pronunciation, see No Than Kap, "The Written Word of Chin," http://www.ycld.org/literature/THEWRITTENWORDOFCHIN.html (accessed March 18, 2005).

5. Vrajagopal Simha, *Manipuri o kukibhasha shikkhar sahaja upai* (Koilashahar, Independent Tripura: published by the author, 1326/1916), 3, 28n128. The Bengali

words *dasa* ("male slave") and *dasi* ("female slave") are translated into Manipuri as *naai* ("adult male slave") and *naainupi* ("adult female slave"), and *chhelpa* ("young male slave") and *chhelnu* ("young female slave").

6. *Tripurar rupakatha* (Agartala: Upojati O Topshili Kalyana Bibhaga, 1980), 123–29.

7. See among others, Michael Walter Charney, "A Reinvestigation of Konbaung Era Burman Historiography on the Beginnings of the Relationship between Arakan and Ava (Upper Burma)," *Journal of Asian History* 34, no. 1 (2000), 53–68; idem, "Crisis and Reformation in a Maritime Kingdom of Southeast Asia: Forces of Instability and Political Disintegration in Western Burma (Arakan), 1603–1701," *Journal of the Economic and Social History of the Orient* 41, no. 2 (June 1998), 185–219; Jacques Leider, "On Arakanese Territorial Expansion: Origins, Context, Means and Practice," and Stephan von Galen, "Arakan at the Turn of the First Millennium of the Arakanese Era," both in Jos Gommans and Jacques Leider, eds., *The Maritime Frontier of Burma: Exploring Political, Cultural, and Commercial Interaction in the Indian Ocean World, 1200–1800* (Leiden: KITLV Press, 2002), 127–49 and 151–62; Sanjay Subrahmanyam, "Slaves and Tyrants: Dutch Tribulations in Seventeenth-Century Mrauk-U," *Journal of Early Modern History* 1, no. 3 (Aug. 1997), 201–53; Amalendu Guha, *Medieval and Early Colonial Assam: Society, Polity, Economy* (Calcutta: Published for the Centre for Studies in Social Sciences by K. P. Bagchi, 1991); and idem, "Ahom Political System: An Enquiry into State Formation in Medieval Assam, 1228–1800," in Surajit Sinha, ed., *Tribal Polities and State Systems in Pre-colonial Eastern and North Eastern India* (Calcutta: Published for the Centre for Studies in Social Sciences by K. P. Bagchi, 1987), 143–76.

8. For the sixteenth century, see Jon Fernquist, "The Flight of Lao War Captives from Burma Back to Laos in 1596: A Comparison of Historical Sources," *SOAS Bulletin of Burma Research* 3, no. 1 (spring 2005), 41–68; and Volker Grabowsky, "Forced Resettlement Campaigns in Northern Thailand during the Early Bangkok Period," *Journal of the Siam Society* 87, nos. 1–2 (1999): 45–86. For reports of late eighteenth-century captives of warfare between Burmese forces and the Arakanese, as well as for Manipuri raids into Upper Burma, see D. G. E. Hall, ed., *Michael Symes, Journal of His Second Embassy to the Court of Ava in 1802* (London: George Allen and Unwin, 1955), introduction.

9. "Diary of Manipur: Typewritten at the State Office by Nithor Nath Banerjee, 1904," Mss. Eur. D 485, OIOC, fol. 10. According to a letter of T. C. Hodson dated October 28, 1946, this is the Meithei historical chronicle titled *Meithei Ningthanrol.* Yet another chronicle, identified as the *Cheitharol Kumbaba* or the Manipur Chronicle (From 33 A.D. to 1897 A.D.), is L. Joychandra Singh, comp. and ed., *The Lost Kingdom: Royal Chronicle of Manipur* (Imphal: Prajatantra Publishing House, 1995). According to Singh, the British government had commissioned Bama Charan Mukherjee in 1891 to collect all recensions of the *Cheitharol Kumbaba* and to translate it into English; this had been done with the help of fourteen local "pandits" and was completed in 1897. The same phrase regarding the resettlement of captives can be found on p. 6 of Singh's work. For a larger discussion of these histories, see S. N. Pandey, ed., *Sources of the History of Manipur and the Adjoining Areas* (New Delhi: National Publishing House, 1985), 79–121. For criticism of all of the above, see Saroj Nalini Arambam Parratt, *The Court Chronicle of the Kings of Manipur: The Cheitharon Kumpapa; Original Text, Translation, and Notes,* vol. 1, 33–1763 CE

(London: Routledge, 2005), 1–17. The latter translation nevertheless reveals the same emphasis on captures of people through the seventeenth and eighteenth centuries.

10. S. K. Bhuyan, ed., *Tripura Buranji, or A Chronicle of Tipperah, Written in 1724 by Ratna Kandali Sarma and Arjun Das Bairagi* (Gauhati: Government of Assam, 1938), 30.

11. For the Burmese conscription of labor from Arakan in the 1790s, see Hall, ed. *Michael Symes,* xxviii; and G. E. Harvey, *History of Burma from the Earliest Times to 10 March 1824* (London: Longmans, Green and Co., 1925), 280–83. For reports of Burmese captives taken by Manipuri armies from Upper Burma, see ibid., 208. For the Burmese occupation of Manipur and Assam, and conscription of laborers by all the armies, see H. K. Barpujari, *Problem of the Hill Tribes: North-East Frontier, 1822–42,* 2 vols. (Gauhati: Lawyers' Book Stall, 1970), 1:26–27; and S. L. Baruah, *Last Days of Ahom Monarchy: A History of Assam from 1769 to 1826* (New Delhi: Munshiram Manoharlal, 1993), 219–28.

12. K. P. Sen, ed., *Sri Rajamala,* 3 vols. (Agartala, Independent Tripura: The Palace, 1927–31), 3:13.

13. "Diary of Manipur," fol. 43; and Singh, ed., *Lost Kingdom,* 27.

14. "Diary of Manipur," fols. 24, 34, 38; and Singh, ed., *Lost Kingdom,* 15, 21–22, 24.

15. Than Tun, comp., ed., and trans., *The Royal Orders of Burma, A.D. 1598–1885,* vol. 6, *1807–1810* (Kyoto: Center for Southeast Asian Studies, Kyoto University, 1987), 143–53, orders of Oct. 19–25, 1808.

16. Victor Lieberman, *Burmese Administrative Cycles: Anarchy and Conquest c. 1580–1760* (Princeton, N.J.: Princeton University Press, 1984); also more recently summed up again in Tony Day, *Fluid Iron: State Formation in Southeast Asia* (Honolulu: University of Hawai'i Press, 2002), 231–33.

17. Private letter from earl of Mayo to duke of Argyll, January 18, 1869, Mss. Eur. B 380/1, OIOC, fols. 28–29.

18. B. B. Goswami, "The Mizos in the Context of State Formation," in Sinha, ed., *Tribal Polities and State Systems,* 310.

19. See Ni Ni Myint, *Burma's Struggle against Imperialism, 1885–1895* (Rangoon: Universities Press, 1983), esp. 123–37 for the Kachin Hills, 138–54 for the Chin Hills till 1894; and Michael Adas, *The Burma Delta: Economic Development and Social Change on an Asian Rice Frontier, 1852–1941* (Madison: University of Wisconsin Press, 1982). For the ethics informing resistance, see Mikael Gravers, *Nationalism as Political Paranoia in Burma: An Essay on the Historical Practice of Power* (Richmond, U.K.: Curzon, 1999), 10–30; Parimal Ghosh, *Brave Men of the Hills: Resistance and Rebellion in Burma, 1825–1932* (London: Hurst and Co, 2000), 83–101; Mary Callahan, *Making Enemies: War and State Building in Burma* (Ithaca: Cornell University Press, 2003), 26–27; and Thant Myint-U, *The Making of Modern Burma* (Cambridge: Cambridge University Press, 2002), 198–254.

20. T. H. Lewin, *A Fly on the Wheel, or How I Helped to Govern India* (London, 1912; reprint, Calcutta: Firma KLM, 1977), 204.

21. Ibid., 225–26.

22. Ibid., 207.

23. Private journal of Francis W. Jenkins on his trip from Calcutta to Chundrapoor in Cachar in 1831, entry for December 8, 1831, MSS. Eur F 257/2, OIOC.

24. "Shubhokori," *Dacca Prokash,* Bhadra 3, 1271 B.E./August 18, 1864.

25. T. H. Lewin, *The Hill Tracts of Chittagong and the Dwellers Therein, with Comparative Vocabularies of the Hill Dialects* (Calcutta: Bengal Priting, 1869), 36.

26. John Shakespear, *The Lushei Kuki Clans* (London: Macmillan, 1912), 50.

27. Kailashchandra Singha, *Rajamala ba Tripurar Itibritta* (Calcutta, 1896), 360–62. This raid is attested to by Lewin, *Hill Tracts of Chittagong*, 107.

28. T. Liankhohau, *Social, Cultural, Economic, and Religious Life of a Transformed Community: A Study of the Paite Tribe* (New Delhi: Mittal Publications, 1994), 34–35.

29. Diary of civil officer, Right Column, Lushai Field Force, entry for November 23, 1871, NAI, Foreign Political A, August 1872, no. 37.

30. John Beames, *Memoirs of a Bengal Civilian,* written in 1896 (London: Chatte and Windus, 1961), 286.

31. For a background of the Quaker response to another Bengal missionary, St. John Dalmas, see A. M. Chirgwin, *Arthington's Million: The Romance of the Arthington Trust* (London: Livingstone Press, 1935).

32. Official tour diary of John Shakespear, entry for week ending June 20, 1891, in memo of offg. commr., Chittagong, June 29, 1891, Mss. Eur/Photo Eur/89/1, OIOC, fol. 89.

33. Tour diary of John Shakespear, entry for August 22–31, 1891, in memo of offg. commr., September 9, 1891, ibid, fol. 106.

34. One master's son demanded eighteen rupees and a pig as the price for a male adult runaway in 1891. See demi-official note from R. S. Hutchinson, asst. district superintendent, to superintendent of South Lushai Hills, November 15, 1891, Mss. Eur/Photo Eur/89/1, OIOC, fol. 127. Official discussions two decades later suggest that ransom had been stabilized at forty rupees both for single individuals and for an entire family.

35. Tour diary of John Shakespear, entry for week ending July 4, 1891, in memo of offg. commr., July 19, 1891, and entry for week ending August 22, 1891, in memo of offg. commr. August 31, 1891, Mss. Eur/Photo Eur/89/1, OIOC, fols. 92, 104.

36. Assam regulation of Oct. 1, 1897, quoted in Lalrimawia, *Mizoram: History and Cultural Identity, 1890–1947* (Guwahati: Spectrum Publications, 1995), 91–92.

37. A. W. Davis, *Gazetteer of the North Lushai Hills, Compiled under Orders of Chief Commissioner of Assam* (Shillong: Assam Secretariat Printing Office, 1894), 8–12.

38. Stuart Blackburn, "Colonial Contact in the 'Hidden' Land: Oral History among the Apatanis of Arunachal Pradesh," *Indian Economic and Social History Review* 40, no. 3 (2003), 335–66.

39. Shakespear, *Lushei Kuki Clans,* 46–47, emphasis added.

40. Hayami Yoko, *Between Hills and Plains: Power and Practice in Socio-Religious Dynamics among Karen* (Kyoto: Kyoto University Press; Melbourne: TransPacific Press, 2004), 103.

41. F. K. Lehman, "Can God Be Coerced? Structural Correlates of Merit and Blessing in Some Southeast Asian Religions," in Cornelia Ann Kammerer and Nicola Tannenbaum, eds., *Merit and Blessing in Mainland Southeast Asia in Comparative Perspective* (New Haven, Conn.: Yale University Southeast Asia Studies, 1996), 20–51; and Penny Van Esterik, "Nurturance and Reciprocity in Thai Studies," in E. Paul Durrenberger, ed., *State Power and Culture in Thailand* (New Haven, Conn.: Yale University Southeast Asia Studies, 1996), 22–46.

42. David E. Jones's response to Cole, undated, in CMA 5, no. 27, 318, NLW, fols. 14–17.

43. "Report of a Tour Made by Mr. J. T. O. Barnard, Deputy Commissioner, Burma Frontier Service, in Hukawng Valley from 9 March to 9 April 1925," chapter 4 of *Memorandum Regarding Slavery in the Hukawng Valley in Upper Burma* (Geneva: League of Nations, 1925). I am grateful to the librarian and the interlibrary loan services of Rockefeller Library, Brown University, for providing me with a photocopy of this document.

44. James Johnstone, *Manipur and the Naga Hills* (reprint, New Delhi: Gyan Publishing, 2002), 112–13.

45. *Military Report on the Lushai Hills Compiled in the Intelligence Branch, Division of the Chief of Staff, India,* written by Captain L. H. Baldwin in 1902 and brought up to date by Lt. Col. W. Malleson (Simla: Government of India, 1906), 9.

46. B. C. Allen, chief secretary to the chief commr. of Assam, to secretary to government of India, June 23, 1915, Foreign and Political, June 23, 1915, L/PS/11/95, OIOC.

47. Edwin Rowlands to Reverend Williams, December 10, 1907, NLW, CMA 5, file no. 27, 314.

48. Edwin Rowlands, in Report of the Foreign Missions of the Welsh Calvinist Methodists for the Year ending December 1901, Presented by the Executive Committee to the General Assembly held at Liverpool, 1902, NLW, CMA, GZ/84–88, 56.

49. Edwin Rowlands to Reverend Williams, December 10, 1907, NLW, CMA 5, file no. 27, 314.

50. Statement dated December 11, 1909, in P. Fraser, *Slavery on British Territory: Assam and Burma* (Carnarvon, Australia: W. Gwenlyn Evans and Son, 1913), 55–56.

51. Statement dated October 8, 1910, in ibid., 55.

52. Peter Fraser to Dr. Williams, November 3, 1911, NLW, CMA 5, no. 27, 318, fol. 326.

53. Mary C. Fraser to Mr. Williams, June 21, 1912, NLW, CMA 5, no. 27, 318, fol. 192. This part of the letter is crossed out in the original, as though the letter-writer did not intend to convey this "sad news" to her director of missions.

54. Lian H. Sakhong, *Religion and Politics among the Chin People in Burma (1896–1949)* (Uppsala, Sweden: Uppsala University, 2000), 112.

55. For the period between the eleventh and seventeenth centuries, see Victor Lieberman, *Strange Parallels: Southeast Asia in Global Context, c. 800–1830,* vol. 1, *Integration on the Mainland* (Cambridge: Cambridge University Press, 2003), 115–18, 136–38; for the eighteenth and nineteenth centuries, see Than Tun, "The Influence of Occultism in Burmese History with Special Reference to Bodawpaya's Reign, 1782–1819," in his *Essays on the History and Buddhism of Burma,* ed. Paul Strachan (Whiting Bay, Isle of Arran, Scotland: Kiscadale Publications, 1988), 133–49.

56. See Shigeharu Tanabe and Charles F. Keyes's introduction to their edited volume *Cultural Crisis and Social Memory: Modernity and Identity in Thailand and Laos* (Honolulu: University of Hawai'i Press, 2002), 1–42.

57. Michael Aung-Thwin, "Divinity, Spirit, and Human: Conception of Classical Burmese Kingship," in Lorraine Gesick, ed., *Centers, Symbols, and Hierarchies: Essays on the Classical States of Southeast Asia* (New Haven, Conn.: Yale University Southeast Asia Studies, 1983), 45–85.

58. Laltluangliana Khiangte, *Folktales of Mizoram* (Aizawl, India: LTL Publications and Art and Culture Department of Mizoram, 1997), 16–18.

59. Lalrunga, "Hero of Mizo Folktales," in Soumen Sen, ed., *Folklore in North-East India* (New Delhi: Omsons Publications, 1985), 191–94.

60. John Shakespeare to A. G. McCall, June 25, 1934, Mss. Eur E 361/5, OIOC, fol. 5a.

61. Note by R. W. von Morde, assistant superintendent of the Lushai Hills, December 23, 1909, on case no. 4, Lalbuta chief against Tekawla and others, NLW, CMA 5, no. 27, 318, unpaginated.

62. J. Meirion Lloyd, *History of the Church in Mizoram: Harvest in the Hills* (Aizawl, Mizoram, India: Synod Publication Board, 1991), 103. Lloyd, a missionary of the Welsh Presbyterian Church, arrived in 1944, and knew most of the Mizo leaders of the early years.

63. John Vanlal Hluna, *Church and Political Upheaval in Mizoram* (Aizawl, Mizoram, India: Mizo Historical Association, 1985), 31–32.

64. Peter Fraser to Rev. Williams, November 13, 1908, NLW, CMA 5, no. 27, 315, fol. 247.

65. Miscellaneous case no. 4 of 1909 of the court of the assistant superintendent, Lushai Hills, NLW, CMA 5, no. 27, 318.

66. Fraser to Williams, October 29, 1909, NLW, CMA 5, no. 27, 315.

67. Copy of government order, November 1909, in *Chanchinhu Newspaper,* November 1909, fol. 213 in Collections of the Anti-Slavery Society, Rhodes House, Oxford.

68. Chief secretary to chief commr. of Assam to secretary to the government of India, Foreign and Political Department, February 2, 1914, Assam Administration, Political Dept, Political Branch, P/1097/1914, OIOC.

69. John Shakespear to A. G. McCall, March 29, 1934, Mss. Eur E 361/5, OIOC, fol. 3a.

70. Lalrimawia, *Mizoram,* 93.

71. A. G. McCall, *Lushai Chrysalis* (London: Luzac and Co., 1949), 245–46.

72. Reginald A. Lorrain, *Five Years in Unknown Jungles for God and Empire* (1912; reprint, Guwahati: Spectrum, 1988), 121.

73. Rev. William Carey, *A Garo Jungle Book, or the Mission to the Garos of Assam* (Philadelphia: Judson Press, 1919), 24.

74. Statement signed by Vanchhunga Evangelist, November 4, 1910, in Fraser, *Slavery on British Territory,* 32.

75. When Fraser appealed Cole's order, the commissioner of the Surma Valley and Hill districts, Silchar, rejected the appeal on grounds of misrepresentation, by orders of February 7, 1911, for which see correspondence in Governor's Secretariat Confidential Proceedings, Political B, June 1912, nos. 3–18 (Dispur, Guwahati, Assam).

76. Statement of July 8, 1910, in Fraser, *Slavery on British Territory,* 48.

77. For recent studies of Welsh Methodism in the eighteenth century, see David Ceri Jones, *"A Glorious Work in the World": Welsh Methodism and the International Evangelical Revival, 1735–1750* (Cardiff: University of Wales Press, 2004); for denominational divisions in antebellum America, see particularly Christopher H. Owen, "'To Keep the Way Open for Methodism': Georgia Wesleyan Neutrality toward Slavery, 1844–1861," and John R. McKivigan, "The Sectional Division

of the Methodist and Baptist Denominations as Measures of Northern Antislavery Sentiment," both in John R. McKivigan and Mitchell Snay, eds., *Religion and the Antebellum Debate over Slavery* (Athens: University of Georgia Press, 1998), 109–133, 343–64.

78. Peter Fraser to "Brothers in the Master's Service," December 17, 1909, in Fraser, *Slavery on British Territory,* 8.

79. Stephen Neill, *A History of Christianity in India, 1707–1858* (Cambridge: Cambridge University Press, 1985), 352–54.

80. Letter from D. E. Jones to Major Cole, Mission House, Aijal, September 23, 1910, NLW, CMA 5 27, 315, not paginated.

81. R. J. Williams to Revs. D. E. Jones and Dr. Fraser, March 18, 1910, in *Adroddiad ir Cyfarwyddwyr Cyffredinol or Drafdaeth Ynglyn A'r Parch. Peter Fraser* (Manchester, U.K.: J. Roberts and Sons, n.d.), 17; copy in NLW, CMA 5, 27, 318. I thank Linda Healy for translating it for me.

82. Rev. R. J. Williams to Dr. Fraser, February 3, 1911, NLW, CMA 5, no. 27318.

83. E. Williams to Rev. Williams, October 29, 1912, no. 27314.

84. Henry Lytton to Travers Buxton, April 11, 1911, Mss. Brit. Emp. S 22, G352, Papers of the Anti-Slavery Society, Rhodes House, Oxford.

85. See Appeal for Action, dated July 13, 1913, cited in McCall, *Lushai Chrysalis,* 123–24.

86. B. C. Allen, chief secretary to chief commissioner of Assam, to the secretary to the government of India, Foreign and Political, June 23, 1915, L/PS/11/95, P 2973/15, OIOC.

87. Last Will and Testament of Peter Fraser, probated on April 9, 1920, in St. Asaph's Diocese, NLW, *Wills of 1920,* 132.

88. Gautam Bhadra, "The Kuki Uprising (1917–1919): Its Causes and Nature," *Man in India* 55, no. 1 (March 1975), 10–56; and Asok Kumar Ray, *Authority and Legitimacy: A Study of the Thadou-Kukis in Manipur* (Delhi: Renaissance Publishing, 1990), 63–85.

89. Viscount Cecil to Austen Chamberlain, September 28, 1925, Annexure A, NAI, Foreign and Political, GOI, 359-x of 1926, serial nos. 1–76.

90. Note by Denys Bray, February 14, 1925, Printed Notes on Serial no. 1, ibid, p. 2. For a précis of the status of slavery up to this period, see also notes by J. P. Thompson, December 21, 1925, and by R. R. Maconachie, March 26, 1926, in the same file, on pp. 3–4 and 10 respectively.

91. Secretary of the Anti-Slavery Society to Earl Birkenhead, secretary of state for India, February 18, 1927, Mss. Brit. Emp. S 22, G448, file no. 5, Papers of the Anti-Slavery Society, Rhodes House, Oxford.

92. Unsigned letter from the India Office, dated March 8, 1927, in Mss. Brit. Emp. S 22, G352, ibid.

93. Journal of E. Lewis Mendus to his parents, entry for April 5, 1923, NLW, HZ1/3/38, no. 1.

94. N. E. Parry, *Lushai Custom: A Monograph on Customs and Ceremonies* (Shillong, India: Assam Secretariat, 1928), 61–62.

95. N. E. Parry, *The Lakhers* (London: Macmillan, 1932), 223–24, 226.

96. McCall, *Lushai Chrysalis,* 117. According to the preface, he began the book in 1939 and had to "accommodate the limitations imposed by rules and custom upon

any writings by serving officers." This censorship, too, apparently failed to drive out the word "slave" from the text entirely.

97. Ibid., chapter 5, 121–31.

98. Mary C. Fraser to Mr. Williams, February 17, 1925, NLW, CMA 5, no. 27314. As a widow, she spent her days teaching music in the mission school in Shillong, where she wrote her last extant letter, dated August 1931. In the letter cited above, she reported on various groups who "tell me they can never forget him [my husband] and his tender prayers." Oral traditions I collected during 2005 confirm the vitality of the local memories of Fraser.

99. A. G. McCall to governor of Assam, March 8, 1942, Mss. Eur E 361/45, OIOC, fols. 1–4.

CONTRIBUTORS

Daud Ali is Lecturer in History, School of Oriental and African Studies, University of London. He is author of *Courtly Culture and Political Life in Early Medieval India;* editor of *Invoking the Past: The Uses of History in South Asia;* and co-editor of *Querying the Medieval: Texts and the History of Practices in South Asia.*

Indrani Chatterjee is Associate Professor of History, Rutgers University. She is author of *Gender, Slavery, and Law in Colonial India* and editor of *Unfamiliar Relations: Family and History in South Asia.*

Richard M. Eaton is Professor of History, University of Arizona. His books include *Sufis of Bijapur, 1300–1700; The Rise of Islam and the Bengal Frontier, 1204–1760; A Social History of the Deccan, 1300–1761: Eight Indian Lives;* and *Essays on Islam and Indian History.* He is editor of *India's Islamic Traditions, 711–1750.*

Michael H. Fisher is Danforth Professor of History, Oberlin College. He is author of *A Clash of Cultures: Awadh, the British, and the Mughals; Indirect Rule in India: Residents and the Residency System, 1764–1858; The First Indian Author in English: Dean Mahomed (1769–1851) in India, Ireland, and England;* and *Counterflows to Colonialism: Indian Travellers and Settlers in Britain, 1600–1857.*

Sumit Guha is Professor of History, Rutgers University. He is author of *The Agrarian Economy of the Bombay Deccan, 1818–1941; Environment and Ethnicity in India c. 1200–1991;* and *Health and Population in South Asia: From Earliest Times to the Present;* and editor of *Growth, Stagnation, or Decline? Agricultural Production in British India.*

Peter Jackson is Professor in Medieval History, Keele University. He is author of *The Delhi Sultanate: A Political and Military History* and *The Mongols and the West, 1221–1410;* and co-editor of *The Timurid and Safavid Periods,* volume 6 of *The Cambridge History of Iran.*

Sunil Kumar is Reader in the History Department, Delhi University, and editor of *The Indian Economic and Social History Review,* Delhi. He is author of *The Present in Delhi's Pasts* and *The Emergence of the Delhi Sultanate, 1192–1286.*

Avril A. Powell is Senior Lecturer in the History of South Asia, School of Oriental and African Studies, University of London, and author of *Muslims and Missionaries in Pre-mutiny India*. She is also co-editor, with Siobhan Lambert-Hurley, of *Rhetoric and Reality: Gender and the Colonial Experience in South Asia.*

Ramya Sreenivasan is Assistant Professor of History, State University of New York at Buffalo. She is author of articles and a forthcoming volume on the historical narrations of the Padmini legend between the fifteenth and the nineteenth centuries.

Sylvia Vatuk is Professor Emerita of Anthropology at the University of Illinois at Chicago. She is author of *Kinship and Urbanization: White Collar Migrants in North India* and editor of *American Studies in the Anthropology of India,* and has written extensively on issues related to the Indian family and the history of Muslim families in south India.

Timothy Walker is Assistant Professor of History, University of Massachusetts at Dartmouth. He is author of *Doctors, Folk Medicine, and the Inquisition: The Repression of Magical Healing in Portugal during the Enlightenment* and articles on maritime histories in the early modern world.

INDEX

Italicized page numbers refer to maps and data tables.

ʿAbbasid caliphs, 63, 65, 71, 235
ʿAbd al-Rashid, 71, 93
Abhyankar, Tryambak, 171
Abkhazians, 23
abolition (of slavery), 197, 245, 264,
    305–306; Britain's claims about, in its
    empire, 32–33, 274–75; France's, 15n8;
    as not inevitable, 2; legal cases brought
    by masters against slaves after, 35, 264;
    movement for, 221, 226, 234–35, 262,
    266–67, 280, 301; as not an urgent
    matter, 212; of slave transporting in
    Indian Ocean, 9–10, 234, 244–45, 250,
    305
Abu'l-Hasan (Mughal artist), 133n37
Abyssinians. *See* Ethiopia; "Habshis"
Act V of 1843, 32, 300
ʿAdil Shahis (Bijapur), 116
Aditya I (king), 53
Aditya II (king), 55
affirmative action (U.S.), xi
Afghanistan, 113n74; military slaves in
    India from, 101–102, 106, 108, 235;
    Mongols' conquest of, 87; Rajput slaves
    from, 6, 7, 15n4, 142–43, 152; slaves
    traded for horses from, 11, 12
Afrasiyabi lineage, 99
Africa (Ifriqiya): Europeans' conquering
    of, in name of freedom, 2; free military
    men from, in Brazil, 240; free persons
    from, in Portugal, 247; influence of, on
    the Deccan, 126–27; military slaves
    from, 1, 4, 6–10, 20, 72, 115–21,
    234–57; other slaves from, 35, 168, 170,
    172, 197, 215, 278; people from, in
    Britain, 33, 189; slave trade in, 13, 15n8,
    117–21, 189, 190; slaves from, as lend-
    ing status to their owners, 189, 205,
    241–42. *See also* plantation slavery;
    transatlantic slavery; *specific countries*
Ahavamalla (Chalukya king), 51
Ahl-i-Hadith movement, 272, 279,
    280–81
Ahmad, Aziz, 276, 280, 284n41

Ahmad, Dilawar Husain, 275
Ahmad, Nizam al-Din, 92, 94–95
Ahmad Bahmani II (sultan), 121
Ahmadnagar, 116, 117, 122, 123–27, 129,
    130
Ahmadnagar sultanate, 4, 6, 8, 123, 128,
    129
Ahom, 28, 288, 290
Aijal, 304
Aitamar, 88
Ajmer, 138, 141, 147
Akbar, Jalal al-Din Muhammad (Mughal
    emperor), 11, 16n17, 123–25, 127, 152
ʿAlai lineage, *84*
Alam, Muzaffar, 30
ʿAlam, Rukn-i, 95
Alaol, 30–31
al-Daula, ʿAzim, 219, 221
al-Din, Malik Nasir (Iltutmish's son), 97
al-Din, Shaikh Najib, 88, 89
al-Din Malik Saif, 87
al-Hamid, ʿAbd, II, 277
ʿAli, Amir (Saiyid Ameer Ali), 10, 263–64,
    266–70, 273, 278, 280, 283n26
ʿAli, Chiragh. *See* ʿAli, Maulawi Chiragh
Ali, Daud, 3, 4, 18, 20, 26, 31, 44–62
ʿAli, Maulawi Chiragh (Cheragh Ali), 9,
    263, 270, 273, 275–79
ʿAli, Maulawi Saiyid Mahdi, 274
ʿAli, Saiyid Ameer. *See* ʿAli, Amir
ʿAli, Shah Ghulam, 272
alienation, 18–19, 23; of low-born,
    98–104, 108. *See also* ethnicity; natal
    alienation; slaves: cultural "insiders" vs.
    cultural "outsiders" among
Aligarh, 263, 270, 275–76
al-Jahiz, Abu Uthman Amr Ibn Bahr al-
    Kinani, 70
Al-jawaʾib (Arabic newspaper), 273
Allah, Saiyid Muhammad ʿAbd, 273
Allepee (Travancore, India), 193
al-Mulk, Nizam, 70, 91, 115, 120
al-Nissa, Zaib (Fakhr al-Nissa Begam's
    mother), 217, 219, 226

Qizlbash, 31
quantification (in South Asian slavery
  study), 20–21, 45, 65, 116, 119, 173
Qu'ayti state (modern Kuwait), 241
Qubacha (slave), 92
Quelimane (Mozambique territory),
  242, 250
Querabeg, Malik, 103
Quman tribe. See Cumans (Qipchaq)
Qur'an, 69; "freedom verses" in, 271,
  273–74, 276, 280; slavery as underlying
  discussions about principles of, 32,
  262–86. See also Muhammad (prophet)
Qutbi lineage, 84

race: caste linked to, xi, xii, 33; colonial
  emphasis on, 32, 206; as factor in
  Indian Mutiny (1857), 247–48; Persian
  (Mughal) emphasis on, 122, 123–24,
  127–28, 130, 137–38; Portuguese em-
  phasis on, 239–40, 242–43, 255–57; as
  source of conflict among multiple
  wives, 125–26. See also class; ethnicity;
  hierarchies; "miscegenation"; "purity"
  of lineage
Raghunath, Sahni, 144
Raj, 9
Rajadhiraja, 61n36
Rajamala chronicle, 288–89
Rajapur, 179
Rajaraja I (Chola king), 48, 52, 54
Rajasthan, 4, 7, 27, 68, 136, 138, 159n5
Rajataringini verse, 27
Rajavyavaharkosa, 164
rajbeti, 167
Rajendra I (Chola king), 52, 53
"Rajput" (as a term), 24
Rajput elite, 136–61; British as overlords
  over, 147, 148–49, 155–56, 158; chroniclers of, 9, 19, 34, 138–61; concubines
  vs. wives among, 7, 136, 144, 152, 154;
  exchange of slaves among, 4, 5, 9, 15n4,
  140–43, 152–53, 157–58; female slave-
  performers for, 1, 140–43, 145–46,
  152–53, 158; origins of slaves recruited
  by, 6, 138–40; queens of, 142–45, 147,
  148–49, 150–51, 151, 154, 156; slavery
  under, 22; and slaves' children, 8, 143;
  uses of female slaves by, 4, 12, 139–46
Ram, Jhootha, 148
Ramabai, Pandita, 35
Ramadevi, Catton, 53

Rangamati area, 292
Rangopa (female slave-performer), 142
Rangray (patar), 141, 142
ransoming (of captives), 9, 17–18, 22,
  166, 271, 276, 296, 297, 299–303,
  306–307
Rao, Mansa, 139
Rao, Velcheru Narayana, 47
Raskapur (concubine), 147
Rathor Rajputs, 137, 139, 147
Ratnagiri district, 166
Ratnavali (Dutt), 34
Rawal Ranaji ri bat, 154
Raziyya (Delhi sultana), 71, 72, 84,
  112nn49,50, 113n75
rebels, 11, 12, 23, 126. See also resistance
  (to slavery and servitude)
Recife, 238
reciprocity (in master-slave relations),
  2–3, 46, 120–21, 152, 295–96
Reconquista, 236, 242
Red Sea, 116, 117
"redemptions," 165. See also ransoming
  (of captives)
Register of Jodhpur State, 142–45, 149,
  151, 153
religions: Asian slave voices articulated
  through, 29–31; as contingent category,
  24–25; eviction of, from European
  public sphere, 29. See also paganism;
  specific religions
resistance (to slavery and servitude): fear
  of, by colonial governments, 240, 241,
  252, 253, 306; historical obfuscations
  of, 27–28; in Indo-Burma borderlands,
  294, 301–304, 306; as not inevitable, 2;
  question of, 211–12, 223–25; theft and
  arson as examples of, 192–94, 223; by
  Turkish military slaves, 71–73, 85; in
  the United States, 223; ways of avoid-
  ing, 26; by William Hickey's servants,
  201–202. See also abolition: movement
  for; Indian Mutiny (1857); rebels; runaway slaves
resurrection, 298
Return (ship), 190
Reunion (Indian Ocean island), 15n8,
  251
revenue. See taxes
rhetoric: of freedom, 14n1, 33–34; about
  Islamic slavery in 1870s and 1880s,
  262–81; of servitude by non-slaves,